The European Community and the Crises of the 1960s

This book is a detailed study of the European Community's development between 1963 and 1969. The leitmotiv of the period was the struggle between France and its EC partners over the purpose, structure and membership of the emerging European Community. On all three, French President Charles de Gaulle held divergent views from those of his fellow leaders.

The six years in question were hence marked by a succession of confrontations over what the Community did, the way in which it functioned, and the question of whether new members (notably Britain) should be allowed to enter. Despite these multiple crises, however, the six founding members continued to press on with their joint experiment, demonstrating a surprisingly firm commitment to cooperation with each other.

The period thus highlights both the strengths and the weaknesses of the early Community, and the origins of many of the structures and procedures that have survived until the current day.

N. Piers Ludlow is a Senior Lecturer at the Department of International History at the LSE. His research is primarily focused on the early development of the European Community. He is the author of *Dealing With Britain: the Six and the First UK Application to the EEC* (Cambridge University Press, 1997).

Cass series: cold war history

Series Editors: Odd Arne Westad and Michael Cox

ISSN: 1471-3829

In the new history of the cold war that has been forming since 1989, many of the established truths about the international conflict that shaped the latter half of the twentieth century have come up for revision. The present series is an attempt to make available interpretations and materials that will help further the development of this new history, and it will concentrate in particular on publishing expositions of key historical issues and critical surveys of newly available sources.

1 **Reviewing the Cold War**
   Approaches, interpretations, and theory
   Edited by Odd Arne Westad

2 **Rethinking Theory and History in the Cold War**
   Richard Saull

3 **British and American Anticommunism before the Cold War**
   Marrku Ruotsila

4 **Europe, Cold War and Co-existence, 1953–1965**
   Edited by Wilfred Loth

5 **The Last Decade of the Cold War**
   From conflict escalation to conflict transformation
   Edited by Olav Njølstad

6 **Reinterpreting the End of the Cold War**
   Issues, interpretations, periodizations
   Edited by Silvo Pons and Federico Romero

7 **Across the Blocs**
   Cold War cultural and social history
   Edited by Rana Mitter and Patrick Major

The European Community and the Crises of the 1960s

Negotiating the Gaullist challenge

N. Piers Ludlow

Routledge
Taylor & Francis Group

LONDON AND NEW YORK

First published 2006
by Routledge
2 Park Square, Milton Park, Abingdon, Oxon OX14 4RN

Simultaneously published in the USA and Canada
by Routledge
270 Madison Ave, New York, NY 10016

Routledge is an imprint of the Taylor & Francis Group

© 2006 N. Piers Ludlow

Typeset in Times by Wearset Ltd, Boldon, Tyne and Wear
Printed and bound in Great Britain by Antony Rowe Ltd,
Chippenham, Wiltshire

British Library Cataloguing in Publication Data
A catalogue record for this book is available from the British Library

Library of Congress Cataloging in Publication Data
A catalog record for this book has been requested

ISBN 0–415–37594–0

To Wenna

Contents

Tables

Acknowledgements

Most of the funding necessary for the completion of this book has come from the British Academy and the Arts and Humanities Research Board (AHRB). The former supported me as a Postdoctoral Research Fellow at Balliol College, Oxford, when the groundwork for this research project was largely completed. They were also extremely generous with their travel grants, allowing me to spend a number of summers visiting archives in locations so pleasant that few of my colleagues could believe that I had gone there for legitimate research reasons. The latter took over when my three years as a Postdoctural Research Fellow came to end. They too paid for a number of follow-up visits to archives in Brussels, Paris, Koblenz, The Hague and Florence, and in 2003 they funded a three month research leave, allowing me to double the length of my LSE sabbatical and complete the manuscript. I hope that they both feel that this book is worth its lengthy gestation. I should also thank the Department of International History at the LSE, whose staff research fund has financed a number of shorter research trips. The Department has been a highly congenial base for an international research project, with the commitment and example of both staff and students providing a constant reassurance that, however unfashionable, research into the history of European integration was a respectable and important endeavour.

Equally important was the help that I received from archivists and colleagues across Europe. Any researcher rash enough to try and write about the history of six different countries at once needs all the international support available. Part of this has come from the staff of the archives that I have visited. I would therefore like to thank M. Palayret of the Historical Archives of the European Community in Florence, Madame Collonval in the Commission archives in Brussels, M. Stols in the Council of Ministers archives, as well as several very patient reading room assistants in the Bundesarchiv, the Auswärtiges Amt, the Quai d'Orsay, the Archives Nationales in both central Paris and Fontainebleau, the Dutch Foreign Ministry and the Public Record Office. All have provided valuable advice and shown themselves to be extremely tolerant of my varying degrees of linguistic competence.

Still greater is the assistance that I have been given by fellow researchers. The list of those with whom I have discussed my research and compared notes over the last nine years is almost too long to recall. But particular thanks is due to Nigel Ashton, Laurence Badel, Gérard Bossuat, Jan-Willem Brouwer, Elena Calandri, Anne de Castelnau, Lucia Coppolaro, Barbara Curli, Anne Deighton, Véronique Dimier, James Ellison, Ken Endo, Maurice Fitzgerald, Robert Frank, Eleonora Guasconi, Max Guderzo, Fernando Guirao, Anjo Harryvan, Jan van der Harst, Claudia Hiepel, Wolfram Kaiser, Hussein Kassim, Christina Knudsen, Giuliana Laschi, Johnny Laursen, Wilfried Loth, Ivo Maes, Andy Moravcsik, Leopoldo Nuti, Torsten Oppelland, Helen Parr, Craig Parsons, Régine Perron, Melissa Pine, Morten Rasmussen, Martin Schaad, Georges-Henri Soutou, David Stevenson, Guido Thiemayer, Jeffrey Vanke, Antonio Varsori, Odd Arne Westad, Andreas Wilkens, Pascaline Winand and John Young. Several of them have also read and commented on parts of the manuscript, with Drs Brouwer, Calandri, Ellison, Knudsen and Rasmussen, plus two anonymous readers, providing invaluable comments on the whole thing. Their vigilance has rooted out many of the errors that lurked there, although I of course bear sole responsibility for any that remain.

Finally I must also thank my family. My parents have remained as supportive as ever, providing accommodation whenever I was in Brussels, mobilising their network of friends for hospitality elsewhere, and providing endless encouragement. To my father in particular I owe much of my insight about how the EU works today and therefore, to an extent, what trends and directions to investigate in its past. My daughters Lydia and Eva meanwhile have provided the best sort of distraction from my computer, books and files. And most of all I must thank my wife, Morwenna, who has lived through all nine years of this book's emergence, has shared some of the travel involved, has survived repeated exposure to my prose, and has proved my most constant source of strength. To her this book is dedicated – it is the very least that she deserves.

Oxford,
6 January 2005

Abbreviations

AAA	Political Archives of the Auswärtiges Amt (German Foreign Ministry)
AAPD	Akten zur Auswärtigen Politik der Bundesrepublik Deutschland
ACS	Archivio Centrale dello Stato, Rome
AN	Archives Nationales, Paris
ANF	Archives Nationales, Fontainebleau
BAK	Bundesarchiv, Koblenz
BDI	Bundesverband der Deutschen Industrie
BDT	Bande de Transmission
BKA	Bundeskanzleramt (Federal Chancellery)
CAP	Common Agricultural Policy
CDM	Maurice Couve de Murville papers, Paris
CDU	Christlich-Demokratische Union
CET	Common External Tariff
CMA	Council of Ministers Archives, Brussels
COREPER	Committee of Permanent Representatives
CSU	Christlich-Soziale Union
DDF	Documents Diplomatiques Français
DE-CE	Service de Coopération Economique, Quai d'Orsay, Paris
DM	Deutschemark
ECHA	European Commission Historical Archives, Brussels
ECJ	European Court of Justice
ECSC	European Coal and Steel Community
EDC	European Defence Community
EEC	European Economic Community
EFTA	European Free Trade Association
ENP	Emile Noël papers, Florence
EUI	European University Institute, Florence
FCO	Foreign and Commonwealth Office, London
FDP	Freie Demokratische Partei
FEOGA	Fonds Européen d'Orientation et de Garantie Agricole
FO	Foreign Office, London

FRUS	Foreign Relations of the United States
GATT	General Agreement on Tariffs and Trade
HAEC	Historical Archives of the European Communities, Florence
IMF	International Monetary Fund
MAE	Ministère des Affaires Etrangères (Quai d'Orsay), Paris
MBPE	Ministero del Bilancio e della Programmazione Economica, Rome
MBZ	Ministerie Van Buitenlandse Zaken (Foreign Ministry), The Hague
MEP	Member of the European Parliament
NATO	North Atlantic Treaty Organisation
NLFM	Netherlands' Foreign Ministry, The Hague
OECD	Organisation for Economic Cooperation and Development
OEEC	Organisation for European Economic Cooperation
PREM	Prime Minister's Files
PRO	Public Record Office (now National Archives), London
SGCI	Service Générale de Coordination Interministérielle
SPD	Sozialdemokratische Partei Deutschlands
UC	Unité de compte
UNR	Union pour la Nouvelle République
WEU	Western European Union

Introduction

Writing a supranational history of the EEC

The first four years of the European Community's existence were conspicuously successful. Between 1958 and 1962, the six founding member states demonstrated an ability to implement and even go beyond their original treaty bargain which surprised and delighted those who negotiated the Treaty of Rome.[1] The new institutions appeared to function. By 1962 the European Commission had seemingly overcome its teething problems and had shown itself to be a fertile source of policy proposals and a skilful advocate of Community advance.[2] The early track record of the Council of Ministers, meanwhile, had underlined that even without the generalised use of majority voting that was due to begin in 1966, wide-ranging consensus could be effectively and rapidly built between six governmental representatives. The European Court of Justice seemed intent on continuing that process of forming a far-reaching body of European jurisprudence that had been the hallmark of its operation within the European Coal and Steel Community (ECSC).[3] And even the European Parliamentary Assembly – the Cinderella institution in terms of power and influence under the original treaty-rules – had shown an energy and a commitment to both its own development and the wider advance of European integration that made it unlikely that its comparative powerlessness would continue indefinitely. Its 1962 decision to call itself the 'European Parliament' rather than its treaty-given name – and the way in which this altered title was generally accepted by all but the French – said much about both its ambition and the chances of some of its aspirations being realised.[4]

The emergence of common policies was also further advanced than many had expected. The clearest example of initial expectations being exceeded was the 1960 decision taken by the Six to 'accelerate' the timetable for creating a customs union set out in the Treaty of Rome.[5] This meant that both the establishment of tariff-free trade amongst the Six and the creation of a uniform tariff towards the outside world were likely to be completed substantially before the 1 January, 1970 deadline originally agreed. Similar encouragement could be drawn from the way in which the Six had by 1961 managed to agree on all of those problematical tariff positions left undefined in the original Treaty – the so-called 'List G'.[6] But perhaps still more striking for those observing the EEC's early steps was the way in which a European agricultural policy did appear likely to emerge. The 1950s discussions about agricultural cooperation on a European scale had seemingly shown that the evident desire of several European countries to promote European agricultural integration co-existed with a formidable and possibly insurmountable range of obstacles.[7] There had thus been many who had believed that those articles of the Treaty of Rome stipulating that the new body should have a European agricultural policy would remain as purely paper pledges. However, the landmark decisions of January 1962, defining the basic shape and manner of operation of the common agricultural policy (CAP), indicated that within the EEC, progress towards a 'green Europe' might be smoother and quicker than the 1950s precedent had appeared to suggest.[8] In particular, the way in which an effective pro-CAP alliance between the French, the Dutch and the European Commission had been able to overcome the hesitations of the West Germans and Italians, established a pattern of advance that if repeated might see a working agricultural policy established simultaneously with the planned customs union. Little wonder then, that when looking back at this initial surge of institutional and policy success, the European Commissioner Robert Marjolin should describe the 1958–62 period as 'the honeymoon years'.[9]

International reactions to the early integration process had also been highly encouraging. That the United States government had been supportive should perhaps not have come as a total surprise. Ever since 1947 Washington had championed the idea of European unity, primarily for cold war reasons.[10] Nevertheless, the closeness and warmth of the rapport built up between Walter Hallstein's European Commission and the Eisenhower and Kennedy Administrations was both remarkable and, in the context of a superpower-dominated world, extremely valuable.[11] The wave of US academics who descended upon the Brussels of the late 1950s and early 1960s to describe in immensely (and excessively) favourable terms the process of transformation underway was also indicative of positive US sentiments towards the early EEC,[12] and US goodwill was more than matched by the almost unseemly rush amongst other Western-leaning countries to establish ties with the nascent Community. Within two years of the EEC's establishment, Greece, Turkey, Israel and Lebanon had all begun negotiations with the Community with a view to establishing some type of privileged relationship, while countless other countries had set up representative offices and missions in Brussels so as to be able better to observe and influence the process underway amongst the Six. In 1961, outside attention had become even more flattering, if potentially disruptive, with requests for membership submitted by Britain, Ireland, Denmark and Norway.[13] Not all of those involved with the Brussels experiment were entirely pleased that such applications had arrived at so early a stage of the Community's development, but it was undeniable that, as

Sicco Mansholt, another of the first Commissioners, put it, 'we can view the British, Danish and Irish membership applications as proof of the success of our Community'.[14]

Such success was all the more notable, and welcome, for coming at a time when other political developments seemed only to confirm Europe's reduced status in global affairs. For the French, the 1958 to 1962 period was dominated by the latter stages of the Algerian trauma: the collapse of the IV Republic in 1958, precipitated primarily by events in North Africa, was followed by the fraught attempts to extricate France from the bloody colonial war and by the wave of bitterness and internal strife that this 'retreat' provoked – bitterness encapsulated most prominently by the multiple attempts to assassinate General de Gaulle.[15] For Germany, meanwhile, the repeated crises over Berlin in 1958–59 and then again in 1961 only served to underline its vulnerability as a front-line state in the cold war, its dependency on the goodwill of its alliance partners, and its fear of being the victim of a settlement struck behind its back by the US and the Soviet Union.[16] The building of the Wall in 1961 did bring a stability of sorts, but only by quite literally setting in stone the postwar division of the country. And, for all of Europe, the Cuban Missile Crisis of 1962 seemed to epitomise the continent's relative powerlessness. During the confrontation all of the Six had risked annihilation and yet none had had either privileged information about or any influence over the course of American policy. Instead, they had been mere spectators as the US President determined the Western response to the most dangerous crisis of the cold war.[17] For countries that had grown accustomed to considering themselves as at the centre of world affairs, this was a difficult state of affairs to accept. Against such a gloomy backdrop, European integration was not merely a welcome success story, but also a process which might, in the medium term at least, begin to redress the imbalance of power that had existed since 1945.

Despite four years of successful operation, however, the Community of 1962 had not yet advanced far towards answering the two crucial questions, implicit in, but unanswered by, the Treaty of Rome. The first of these was that of 'what the Community should do': in other words, which policy areas of the integration process should the Six initially concentrate on. The second was that of 'how the Community should operate'. This centred on the institutional make-up of the EEC. On neither did the Treaty of Rome provide a complete answer. In terms of the EEC's policy agenda, the Rome Treaty was very much a 'traité cadre' – a framework document that provided the mechanisms for cooperation but left up to later decision-makers the choice of what policies should flank the basic customs union. Agriculture, transport and social policy were all referred to briefly as possible areas of common activity, but for none were the details or the timetable of progress spelt out. And on institutional matters the Treaty text was equally open. Some of its provisions and some of its vocabulary seemed to suggest a direct line of descent from the avowedly federal Schuman Plan of 1950. There was thus plenty of scope for those eager to see the rapid establishment of a fully united Europe to press ahead with their ambitions. But other aspects of the Treaty seemed, by contrast, to show the extent to which Europe's leaders had retreated from the federalist mechanisms of the early 1950s. In both powers and name, the European Commission was hence very different from the High Authority of the ECSC. Likewise, the EEC Council of Ministers had a centrality within the institutional make-up which underlined how far it had come since being a belated Benelux addition to French ideas in 1950.

To these two initial unanswered questions a third had then been added by the approach of the British, Irish, Danes and Norwegians in 1961, namely that of 'who should participate in the Community'. Here too the EEC's founding charter offered little precise guidance. There was a treaty article – number 237 – which set out the mechanism by which a membership application might be received. The treaty preamble furthermore spoke of the Community being open to all European states. But no details were given as to when these applications might occur, what criteria, if any, should be used to decide which applications were acceptable, and how the EEC might avoid its internal progress being seriously disrupted by the eagerness of new states to join the process. The 'what', 'how' and 'whom' of early integration were all equally undefined.

At the very beginning of the integration process this degree of ambiguity had been a positive asset. The openness with regard to the Community's agenda had allowed each member state to hope that its preferred areas of joint activity would flourish, whereas those cooperative ideas with which it had little sympathy would remain on the drawing board. The Italians had thus envisaged a Community with a much greater 'social policy' dimension than the Germans; the French and the Dutch had thought in terms of a much more extensive (and expensive) agricultural policy than had the Germans or the Italians. In similar fashion, the multiple institutional aspirations compatible with the basic treaty text had allowed the widest possible range of pro-Europeans to support the setting up of the EEC. Within the broad coalition that had rallied behind the Treaty of Rome were committed federalists, certain that only a truly united Europe would suffice and confident that this would be the eventual outcome of the integration process, and partisans of a much more cautious intergovernmental approach. Many of the latter had just as much faith that the institutional balance created by the Treaty of Rome would evolve in 'their' direction as had the federalists. And even the uncertainty over the exact membership of the EEC had allowed the co-existence within the early Community of many of those who had been most enthusiastic about the British-led plans for an 18-member European free trade area alongside partisans of a smaller, tighter and exclusively continental grouping.[18] The ability of so many different strands of opinion to cohere together behind the institutions of the Community was one of the key reasons that the Six had all been able to attain the necessary parliamentary backing to ratify the Treaty of Rome.

As the Community developed, however, it was inevitable that some of those who held these divergent beliefs would begin to realise that their hopes were likely to be frustrated. A Community that existed could not hope to be all things to all people in quite the same way as one that had yet to emerge. And, as this happened, the latent disagreements about the policy agenda, the institutional balance and the membership of the EEC were bound to come out into the open. After May 1958 this was all the more likely to happen because of General de Gaulle's return to power in France. On all three of the crucial questions, the new French leader was suspected of having radically different views from the majority of his European counterparts. He was also known to aspire to a world role for Europe which differed markedly from that of the prevailing Atlanticist consensus.[19] His re-emergence as Prime Minister and then President of France – the country that had hitherto exercised the greatest influence, both positive and negative, over the integration process – was therefore a source of significant concern across Europe.[20]

For his first four years in power, de Gaulle had, however, confounded those who had predicted an immediate clash. Rather than rejecting his pre-decessors' European commitments, he had instead reformed the French economy, thereby allowing the country to honour its Treaty commitments much more completely than the leaders of IV Republic France themselves had expected to do.[21] And far from casting off all supranational shackles and proclaiming France's total freedom from external constraints, he had actually pushed energetically for a common agricultural policy that was as binding on Community member states as was possible and which gave considerable powers of initiative and oversight to the European Commission.[22] Gaullist France seemed as committed to the Community game as any of its partners.

There were, admittedly, periodic rhetorical outbursts that gave rise to some concern. The most celebrated of these – that of 15 May, 1962 – prompted several ministers to resign from the French government.[23] And there were those who believed that the French President's ambition to create a political Europe to place alongside the economic Europe being con-structed in Brussels was no more than a Machiavellian ploy to subvert the integration process.[24] But even on this issue, the fact that de Gaulle allowed the Fouchet Plan to be blocked by two states as small as Holland and Belgium could have been construed as a sign of playing by the European rules rather than trying to tear them up.[25] Whether through the weakness that arose from leading a coalition government, a total concentration on Algeria, or a disinclination to upset a process from which his country drew tangible benefits, the General seemed unwilling to turn his verbal sallies into an assault on the realities of integration as practised in Brussels. The Gaullist challenge appeared to be no more than a paper tiger.

All of this changed dramatically in January 1963. The French veto of British membership – announced in the famous press conference of January 14 – marked the moment when de Gaulle's divergences of view from his Community partners ceased simply being theoretical and became an immediate danger. At the same time, the veto also marked the transition from Marjolin's 'honeymoon years' to the 'time of crises'.[26] And it is on these crises – and the Community's painful recovery from each of them – that this book is intended to focus. It is hence a study of the most traumatic period in the EEC's early development rather than its most successful.

In part this focus reflects a belief that it is at moments of crisis that the nature of a political system like the early EEC can best be perceived. During the 1958–62 period, the Community's forward momentum was so irresistible that even many of those who harboured doubts about the integration process chose to remain silent. Similarly, with success following on from success, the effort that had gone into each was at times all but concealed. In the later period, by contrast, not only did the divisions that the pursuit of greater integration caused emerge more clearly, but the efforts needed to push that process forward became that much more evident and hence easier to analyse. Both the dynamics driving supranational Europe onwards and the forces holding it back are as a result easier to dissect at a time when they were closely balanced than during one where only the pressures for integration were clearly apparent.

The concentration on the years of crisis is also, however, a result of the fact that the clash between de Gaulle and his partners over the nature of the Community is frequently referred to by EC/EU experts, but seldom understood. Several of the episodes which this book will assess in detail – like the empty chair crisis or the Luxembourg compromise of January 1966 – have assumed near mythical importance in the version of history most often referred to in Community circles and amongst those academics who work on the current EU.[27] They have become seen as the key moments when the Community dream went awry, a process of downfall that only the equally mythological rebirth of the 1980s was able to undo. And yet such assertions are nearly always made without the benefit of any detailed study of the later 1960s themselves. The myth has thus long-since ceased to bear much resemblance to historical reality.

Thanks to the fact that most western European archives exercise a 30 year rule and hence release hitherto secret papers after three decades have elapsed, the myth is now ripe for correction. Rather than relying on the well-rehearsed account which describes the way in which de Gaulle was able to strip the Community of virtually all of its dynamism, thereby condemning it, from the mid-1960s until the mid-1980s, to nearly two decades of frustration, this study will use archival documents to demonstrate that the reality of the Community's development during the 1963–69 period is both more complicated and more important than the standard history would suggest. For not only did de Gaulle *not* 'win', but the period in question also witnessed the emergence and consolidation of an institutional system that would function throughout the next decades. Indeed, significant features of it are still with us today. Revealing what happened to the EEC in the course of the 1960s is thus more than a matter of simple historical interest. Instead it is a vital part of understanding how the Community system was created and, therefore, why crucial parts of it function as they do at present. Such comprehension is necessary for anyone seeking to analyse the current system, let alone those who seek to reform its future operation. A better understanding of how the EC/EU emerged may, in other words, make at least a small contribution to the debate currently underway about where it should go.

The task of demythologising the recent past by means of newly released archival documents is of course a familiar one to any contemporary historian. Where this book will diverge from the norm, however, is in its attempt at the archival reconstruction of a supranational system. Most contemporary history remains resolutely national in its approach. Multiple archives are often employed, but they tend to be those of different government ministries, different private interest groups, or different individuals, all acting within the same national sphere. And this has remained true of the majority of efforts so far devoted to the origins and early development of European integration. A range of books and articles thus explore German industry and the integration process, Italy and early European agricultural integration, or France and the plans for European political union.[28] Similarly, the rich profusion of edited volumes devoted to the postwar emergence of European unity tend to be organised around chapters on the Netherlands, Italy, France, Britain, Denmark, and so on.[29]

There have admittedly been some historians who have attempted to transcend the purely national framework. Alan Milward's important studies on the pre-1958 development of European integration did deploy a wide range of different countries' records, albeit grouped most often in national case-studies rather than combined together to form a single, continuous strand of pan-European analysis.[30] Likewise, a number of American scholars have sought to take a multi-country approach to recent European history.[31] In this fashion they have been following the example set by those like Marc Trachtenberg who have tried to trace the evolution of the cold war in Europe using archives in a variety of European countries.[32] And there have been a series of Italian historians who have turned the inadequacies of their own national archives into a spur for writing truly multinational history.[33] There has also been a sizeable sub-genre dedicated to bilateral relationships in post-war western Europe. That between France and Germany has understandably been the most comprehensively studied, but there have been attempts to apply the same technique to Anglo-German, Anglo-French, Franco-Italian and even Dutch-German relations.[34]

Few of these studies, however, have really come to terms with the fact that, from 1958 onwards, national actors within a European context shared some of their power with supranational institutions and exercised their influence collectively as well as singly. This means that the development of the EEC cannot be understood purely by lining up in parallel revelations from the study of France, Germany, and every other EEC member state. Instead the interplay between each national policy as well as the extra input of the Community institutions themselves need to be added to the historical analysis.

This is not, of course, the same as asserting that national actions or national interest ceased to be relevant in Community Europe and that all could be understood merely by scrutinising the policy and motives of the European Commission. To do this would be to repeat the mistakes of a generation of over-enthusiastic US political scientists whose better judgement was swept away in their excitement at, and fascination in, the operation of early supranational Europe – and who then had time to repent at their leisure once the experiment seemingly diverged from their expectations from the late 1960s onwards.[35] For this reason, the gradual emergence of a serious historical literature on the early European institutions, while very useful and overdue, cannot of itself plug the gap.[36] Nor can the fascinating official history of the ECSC suffice, given the way in which that body ceased to be the principal locus of the integration process from 1958 onwards.[37]

Rather it is to argue that the European Community of the 1960s – much as the European Union of today – was a hybrid system in which national interest was very much alive but was worked out in a setting where compromise with other competing national interests was essential and where the views and influence of supranational actors like the European Commission or the European Court of Justice were also of importance in determining the eventual outcome. As a result, the historian seeking to understand the way in which the system functioned must be prepared to work in as multinational and supranational a setting as the politicians and civil servants who populated Community Brussels of the 1960s.

In practice this means using the historical archives of both the European institutions themselves and those of the individual member states. The methodology used in this book is therefore to start with scrutiny of the supranational records (especially the detailed records of Council discussions held in the Council of Ministers archive in Brussels) in order to establish how collective European decisions were taken, before then going back to the principal member states so as to determine why each national delegation acted as they did. The various national archives themselves also of course contain much information about what happened in Brussels. Each delegation, after all, tended to report back to their national capital, setting out what had happened and making their predictions about where discussions *à Six* were likely to go next. These national accounts thus form a useful complement to the official Council minutes and the Commission records of debates amongst the permanent representatives. But in most cases they lack either the level of detail or the neutrality of the Council records in particular. Where the national records come into their own, by contrast, is in their coverage of internal policy debate within each member state and of the bilateral diplomacy away from Brussels that happened in parallel to the multilateral discussions within the EEC institutions. Since both of these often mattered greatly, the national collections of the French, the Germans, the Italians and the Dutch are crucial archival components of the research that has gone into this book.

In an ideal world, all of the supranational and national collections in the early Community would have been used to write the history of the early EEC. Sadly, however, the records of Belgium proved inaccessible, whereas the Italian papers seen were obtained only through the generosity of a friend and fellow-researcher. This book hence draws primarily on the archives of the European Council of Ministers (held in Brussels), those of the European Commission, (also in Brussels although duplicated in part in Florence) the papers of the Quai d'Orsay, the Service Général de Coordination Interministérielle (SGCI) and President Pompidou in France, those of the Dutch Ministry of Foreign Affairs, and the Auswärtiges Amt and the Bundeskanzleramt in West Germany. In addition a small number of private collections have been used, notably the papers of Emile Noël, the long-standing Executive Secretary (later Secretary General) of the European Commission, which are preserved in Florence, and those of Maurice Couve de Murville, the French foreign minister for most of the period studied, held at Sciences Po in Paris. Also vital have been the published collections of French and still more German foreign policy documents. And, to provide a useful outside viewpoint, a number of British and American documents have also been employed. The British were not only directly interested in Community membership for much of the period surveyed, but were also by far the best collectors and recorders of diplomatic gossip in Europe. The files of the Public Record Office in London thus abound in stories told in confidence to British representatives by countless politicians and officials from amongst the Six. Similarly, the published collection of American documents on western Europe demonstrate the way in which some Europeans, notably from Germany and from the Commission, were often more candid in setting out their hopes, fears and motivations to their transatlantic allies than they were to their European partners.

Naturally any study put together using so wide a variety of national and supranational sources will lack some of the detail achievable in more narrowly-targeted research projects. Those wanting an in-depth explanation of how the European policy of Kurt Georg Kiesinger differed from that of Ludwig Erhard, or a lengthy analysis of the influence of internal strife within the *Democrazia cristiana* on the Italian approach to de Gaulle, will have to look elsewhere. Likewise the decision to study all of the key controversies within the EEC between 1963 and 1969 rather than concentrating just on the evolution of the CAP or on the Community's approach to the Kennedy Round of GATT negotiations means that a certain amount of precise information has had to be left out.[38] But the comprehensive approach does begin to capture the way in which policy was actually made in the EEC of the 1960s, with multiple national and supranational pre-occupations colliding on a panoply of different issues, in such a fashion that a Belgian gain at Germany's expense in one field was more often than not matched by a Belgian concession or 'side-payment' to Germany else-where. Only a broad approach can therefore hope to describe and under-stand the full range of interplay between the multiple actors within the Community system.

Furthermore, a comprehensive approach also proves to be the most revealing way of analysing the institutional evolution of the EEC in particular. Many of those writing about the way in which the Community's structures have developed over time seem to imply that institutional con-troversies have been the leitmotiv of the EEC. It sounds at times, indeed, as if the recent Convention on the future development of the EU had been sitting in permanent session ever since January 1958. In fact, however, institutional issues have tended to be approached in a much more prag-matic fashion by most of those involved in the Community process. What individual states and individual statesmen have been primarily concerned about, more often than not, has been the way in which a particular policy might work and hence affect the national interests tied up in the Commun-ity's operation. As a result, the exact power of the Commission, or the relationship between the permanent representatives and some of the ad hoc committees that proliferated around the Council structure, mattered much less than the ability of the institutions to carry out the tasks that the member states wanted them to do. The study of the way in which the EEC *worked* has thus never been possible to separate entirely from the study of what the EEC was intended to do. On the contrary, the interweaving of the controversies about the agenda and the institutional balance of the Community will be one of the recurrent themes of the pages that follow.

Over all then this book is intended as an experiment in the writing of supranational history.[39] Many of the ideas contained within it and some of the overall judgements made will doubtless be challenged over time. And it is certainly not intended to displace entirely the national and traditional international histories that currently predominate, any more than the existence of a European level of governance has replaced either national politics or traditional international diplomacy. But it does reflect a belief that, just as the circumstances of the post-1945 world obliged the ruling elites of western Europe to devise radically new forms of cooperation in order to prosper, so too the existence of those new cooperative structures forces some at least of the historians of western Europe to adapt in their turn. The building of supranational Europe deserves a supranational history rather than the simple multiplication of national histories.

1 Back from the brink

January–December, 1963

On the night of 29 January, 1963, six senior governmental delegations gathered for a meeting in Brussels. This was not a normal Community occasion, however. For a start, the mood of the participants was more angry than at even the most tense of EEC Council meetings. Second, the venue was not Rue Ravenstein where the Council habitually met, but instead the offices of Paul-Henri Spaak, the Belgian foreign minister. And third, and most significantly, the countries represented were not the six states which had founded the European Community five years earlier. France, in many ways the most influential of the founding members, was not present, its place taken instead by the United Kingdom, a country whose path into the EEC had just been barred by General de Gaulle's veto. The 'new Six' – a term widely used at the meeting and in subsequent days – had come together immediately after the enlargement negotiations had been suspended to vent their irritation and distress at this development and to debate how best to ensure that the French President's intervention neither drove Britain and the Community apart, nor pushed the development of the EEC in directions alien to most of its founder members.[1]

This extraordinary encounter was to prove unique. The British and the five member states which had supported enlargement would not gather again in such open defiance of the French – or at least not until much later in the decade.[2] And the heights of anti-Gaullist rhetoric employed by Spaak and his fellow ministers that night were seldom to be matched again.[3] But in the wider context of the European Community's early development, there are two reasons why the 29 January meeting deserves to be remembered.

The first is the way in which the rebelliousness of late January 1963 underlines the depth of anger, confusion and near despair created by de Gaulle's veto. Not only had it brought to naught the 18 months of complex negotiations which had been held between the Six and the British, the Danes, the Norwegians and the Irish.[4] The successful French effort to abort the British membership negotiations had also postponed indefinitely an enlargement of the Community's membership which had been ardently desired by many within the early EEC.[5] Worst of all, the manner of de Gaulle's veto had broken all the unwritten rules of cooperation and trust upon which the Community's member states had come to rely. The French decision had been taken unilaterally, without any form of consultation, and had been announced in a peremptory fashion which left France's supposed partners to learn of the General's new stance from radio reports. The angry denunciation of so flagrant a violation of Community norms by Rolf Lahr, one of the principal German negotiators, would have been endorsed by virtually all of those involved with the British membership negotiations:

> The Community rules on negotiating together – a set of rules which France's partners had scrupulously observed, despite it being contrary to their viewpoints and interests to do so – have been seriously wounded by France. Her partners have been given the impression that, on all decisive questions, France recognised only her own interests and coldly disregarded those of her partners and of the Community. France's insincerity and lust for power have been exposed: after 15 months of long negotiation during which her partners as much as the English have been held back by means of almost intolerable insistence upon individual articles of the Treaty of Rome and the agricultural regulations, the French have acted outside of the Treaty rather than through it, and revealed an aspiration to a leadership role which they were not prepared to share with Great Britain. Were France to maintain this attitude, the willingness of her partners to make sacrifices in the interests of the Community will ebb away and, given that such sacrifices are necessary for the integration process, the process itself will be seriously hindered.[6]

The patience of German, Italian, Benelux and Commission representatives, already sorely taxed by the various delaying tactics which France had employed prior to the veto, was close to breaking point.[7] And that basic level of mutual trust upon which the Community depended for effective operation had been seriously undermined.[8]

The level of anger and mistrust felt was aggravated by the identity of the statesman who had barred Britain's path and by the timing and context of the announcement. As explained in the introduction, many in the Community had long harboured suspicions about the depth of General de Gaulle's European commitment and the likelihood of Gaullist France playing a constructive role in the building of an integrated Europe. Until January 1963, however, such fears, while kept alive by the French President's periodic verbal sallies against supranationalism and the institutions of the EEC, had always been tempered by the recognition that France was acting legitimately and reasonably in Brussels. De Gaulle's deeds had therefore appeared to belie his words.

The veto of British membership, however, seemed to signal that the period of Gaullist restraint was over. Furthermore, few participants in the Brussels negotiations could view the blocking of British membership as an entirely isolated event. Instead most viewed it in parallel to de Gaulle's simultaneous rejection of President Kennedy's Multilateral Force (MLF) proposal, a scheme which would have replaced the putative national nuclear deterrents in western Europe with a multinational, NATO-centred strike force. Also added to the equation was the French President's signature, a week later, of the bilateral Elysée treaty instituting a privileged relationship between France and West Germany. Taken together the three Gaullist moves appeared to constitute a determined attack on the nascent Atlantic 'partnership' between the United States and the EEC, and an alarming attempt to replace integration and cooperation, with nationalism and old-fashioned power politics.[9] Lying behind the heated rhetoric of the January meeting, there was thus a widespread fear that the French leader intended to impose his vision and his priorities on the European Community and on Europe's relations with the United States.[10] Latent fears about France's overall intentions blended potently with anger at its immediate actions.

Paradoxically, however, the second reason for recalling the meeting of the 'new Six' on 29 January was precisely that the very real anger and concern described above did not lead to the type of dramatic break which a gathering of the Five plus the British and without the French appeared to presage. Even in the course of the 29 January meeting, the underlying caution of several of the more senior Community ministers had become apparent. While the Dutch foreign minister, Joseph Luns, blustered furiously about 'an agonising reappraisal' of The Netherlands' foreign policy in the wake of the veto, Gerhard Schröder and Attilio Piccioni, his German and Italian counterparts, counselled against over-hasty action and spoke of the need to meet again, with the French, before taking any concrete step towards linking Britain with the EEC. Spaak too resisted British suggestions that the 'new Six' should issue a statement to the press, observing that 'the fact that the Five should be meeting alone with Britain was already sensational enough'.[11] It was therefore predictable that over subsequent weeks there would be repeated declarations that the Community experiment had to go on, that it was not in Britain's interests to see the EEC stagnate and even that the best way to overturn de Gaulle's decision would be to push forward cooperation amongst the Six to the point where majority voting rather than unanimity became the basic rule for Community decision-making.[12] The late night discussions between the British and their Community counterparts were thus as significant for what they did not do, as for the fact that they had happened at all. As another German participant recalled, not without a tinge of regret, 'when we departed from our hotels the next day, nothing remained of the "new Six" of this emotional night'.[13]

This strong vein of caution was in one sense a natural result of the degree of European conviction felt by western Europe's political leadership during the early 1960s. The continuation of the EEC was deemed vital for the health of the continent's economy, was popular with the general public and still more so with parliamentarians in most of the member states, and constituted a central pillar of the foreign policy alignment of Germany, Italy, and the three Benelux states. Many of those shaping the foreign policies of the Six had at some stage over the previous five years, moreover, participated directly in one of the multiple negotiations held in the EEC Council of Ministers, thereby gaining a personal stake in the EEC's success. But even where doubts remained, the nature of the Gaullist challenge ensured that loyalty to the Community structures was the obvious response. The French President after all was believed to be attacking the concept of integration, seeking to break the bonds that tied Europe to the United States, and attempting to return to an era where the larger European powers could once again afford to disregard the interests of the small. In such circumstances it made very little sense to endanger a Community which was the principle vehicle for European integration, which had been strongly backed since its inception by the United States, and which was seen by the smaller European powers as the best means of preventing the tyranny of the strong.[14] Rather than something which could be readily sacrificed to appease the French leader, the EEC was thus widely seen as a crucial element in the battle to contain his challenge.

This combination of on the one hand anger and alarm at how Europe had been affected by de Gaulle's actions, and on the other a profound sense that the Community had to pick itself up quickly and regain its forward momentum, constitutes the starting point of any analysis of how the Community recovered from the crisis of January 1963. Nowhere was the gravity of the immediate situation denied. Only a tiny minority, however, doubted that the best response to the Gaullist challenge was to press ahead with European integration, if possible in a coordinated fashion with those states, led by Britain, to whom immediate membership had been denied. The challenge over the early months of 1963 was therefore to strike a balance between three conflicting priorities. The first was that of marking the Five's dissent from the French position and possibly retaliating with a blow against French interests. The second was that of securing as close a bond as possible with the British so as to ensure that a disillusioned London did not drift away from the EEC. And the third was that of reviving the Community and reminding France of the way in which it too needed a functioning Europe. The principal focus of this chapter will be on the failure of the Five to reconcile these three priorities, and on the way in which the last emerged as the dominant concern.

A gradual resumption

Predictably perhaps it was in Brussels that the desire to resume constructive Community cooperation was most immediately apparent. Only hours after the end of the British negotiations, a meeting of the Commission underlined its condemnation of de Gaulle's action and its ongoing support for enlargement, but noted: 'The Community must go on. Its raison d'être and its long term objectives are in no way compromised by the set-back it has just experienced. They should not be compromised by the political consequences of one government's policies, however serious these last are at present'.[15] The priority of the Community institutions should therefore be to 're-establish a climate of confidence and conciliation between the member states'.[16] It was in order to pursue this last aim that Walter Hallstein, the Commission President, undertook to visit all of the six Community capitals in the course of February.[17] In each, his message was that retaliatory measures should be discontinued, that Community cooperation should resume as soon as possible, and that links with Britain could best be ensured by the building of a partnership between the Community, the United States, Britain and the Commonwealth.[18]

The Committee of Permanent Representatives (COREPER), the weekly gathering of member state ambassadors to the Community which already in 1963 had become a crucial nerve centre of the EEC, also returned quickly to its normal patterns of operation. It was admittedly true that some of the Permanent Representatives were deeply hurt by the collapse of the membership negotiations, and bitterly angry towards the French. Günther Harkort, the German Permanent Representative, for instance sent a long despatch to Bonn in early February decrying the Commission's call for 'business as usual' and arguing that the Community should devote most of its immediate attention to the task of devising new links with the British and the other applicants.[19] It was also the case that the first COREPER session after the breakdown of the negotiations achieved little, with the behaviour of Albert Borschette, the Luxembourg chairman who sought hard to push the meeting in a constructive direction, being denounced to the British as 'deplorable'.[20] But only a week later, the Permanent Representatives seemed to have rediscovered their usual pattern of work, throwing themselves with some enthusiasm into a debate about the respective roles of the Commission and the member states in the forthcoming trade negotiation with Iran. As Emile Noël, the Executive Secretary of the Commission who attended the meeting noted wryly, once procedural questions of this sort were raised, 'the Committee then rediscovered its former unanimity so as vigorously to oppose the Commission's hopes of being placed in charge of these negotiations. All of the participants exchanged friendly admonishments and appeals that the Commission have the sense not to re-open institutional quarrels.... The Community goes on'.[21] Amongst diplomats who met weekly in order to deal with

Community affairs and whose whole raison d'être was cooperation, the instincts and patterns of behaviour developed over the preceding five years thus quickly reasserted themselves over the confusion and mutual recrimination caused by the January crisis.[22]

Away from Brussels such a process took rather longer. Not only were the habits of cooperative action less deeply ingrained at a member state level, but the political need to demonstrate anger towards the French was also felt more acutely. This was especially true in Germany and Italy, where some domestic politicians were known to harbour views similar to those of de Gaulle. In Bonn, the prime suspect was Chancellor Konrad Adenauer himself who had been bitterly criticised for placing his desire to cement Franco-German relations above the need to rescue the British membership application. As a result, all of those jockeying for position in the forthcoming battle to succeed Adenauer were determined to establish their own anti-Gaullist credentials as securely as possible.[23] Too hasty a political reconciliation with France was thus inadvisable. Likewise in Italy, the government of Amintore Fanfani recognised that an anti-Gaullist crusade would serve to unite the Socialist and centrist Christian Democrat members of the ruling coalition against the right of the Christian Democratic party which was not only hostile to Italy's ongoing centre-left experiment but was also known to be close to de Gaulle in foreign policy terms. With elections fast approaching, such a rallying point was of considerable value.[24] Italian diplomats, moreover, felt that to seek a compromise with France too quickly would be to fail to demonstrate sufficiently how isolated de Gaulle had become.[25] It was equally hard for the Dutch immediately to disregard the past. Just as Britain's application to the EEC had been particularly enthusiastically welcomed in The Hague, so its indefinite postponement was most sorely felt. Furthermore, the Dutch political leadership which had long held an extremely jaundiced view of de Gaulle, reacted with great anger as their suspicions were apparently confirmed.[26] The opportunity strongly to protest, especially at a time when other member states appeared to share Dutch concerns, was too good to be missed.

The Dutch and the Italians did therefore seriously contemplate retaliatory measures; both adopted a hard line against too rapid a resumption of normal ministerial meetings in Brussels.[27] Both countries also raised objections so as to slow down the signature of the Association Convention which had been concluded between the EEC and its African partners, most of whom were former French colonies, and which was hence seen as an agreement primarily of interest to France.[28] Fanfani also reacted very angrily to Hallstein's appeal for a rapid resumption of normal Community work, complaining that the Commission President's suggestions 'amounted to saying that they [the Five] must resign themselves to accepting what the French had done and seeking to make the amputation less painful for all of the Six. This was not acceptable'.[29] Revealingly, however, the difficulties of reconciling such a stance with the *communautaire* patterns of behaviour which had previously characterised both member states soon began to tell. Even at the very first post-crisis meeting of COREPER, the Italian representative had been somewhat reluctant to admit that it had been at his country's suggestion that the committee was considering the postponement of the planned 11 February Council meeting.[30] A week later, moreover, Attilio Cattani, the Secretary General of the Italian Foreign Ministry, was urging his colleagues to find means of frustrating the French without sabotaging the Community in the process,[31] and by March, Germany, which had previously been supportive of Italian and Dutch protests, had joined the French and the Commission in calling for a rapid signature of the Association Convention. Spaak too attacked a move which would punish impoverished African countries for a disagreement which had arisen amongst the wealthy Community member states.[32]

Under such pressure, both the Netherlands and Italy sought to present their hesitations as something other than a protest against de Gaulle. For the Dutch, the need for various technical amendments to the convention was pointed to as the cause of delay.[33] The Italian minister, meanwhile, attributed his country's inability to sign to the imminent general elections and the consequent early dissolution of the Italian parliament.[34] It thus came as no surprise that both countries would soon quietly jettison their go-slow policies. The association convention was belatedly signed in July 1963.

Schröder to the rescue?

It was in Germany, however, that the tension between registering dissent from France and allowing the Community to resume normal operation was most decisively settled in favour of the latter. The Federal Republic indeed would emerge as the key player in putting forward the package of coordinated proposals, collectively known as Schröder's Action Plan, which would enable the Community not merely to begin low-level work once more, but actually to re-discover that pattern of significant forward progress which had characterised its first five years of existence.[35] Given the depth of anger which the French veto had caused in Bonn, and the ferocious internal debate which Adenauer's seeming acquiescence had provoked, it is important to establish why, only a couple of months later, the Germans were to emerge as the engineers-in-chief of the Community's relaunch.

At a fundamental level, of course, Bonn's activism in putting the Community back on track reflected the degree to which the Federal Republic was politically committed to European integration. Ever since 1949, close cooperation with its western European allies had been, alongside commitment to the Atlantic Alliance, one of the twin pillars upon which Adenauer's foreign policy rested.[36] European integration had served to bind Germany firmly to the West, had allowed its economy to thrive in a fashion which did not alarm its neighbours unduly, had acted as a vehicle through which the Chancellor's dream of Franco-German reconciliation could be realised, and had underlined the total discontinuity between the foreign policy of the Federal Republic and that of its Imperial and National Socialist predecessors. Such political motivations had in due course been buttressed by the economic advantages which membership of the EEC appeared to bring.[37] But Germany's involvement remained essentially a political choice, based on an assessment of the country's position in Europe and the world which the events, however serious, of January 1963 had done nothing fundamentally to alter.

The circumstances of early 1963 had in fact only added to Germany's political need for a working European Community. For a start it was necessary both to rescue and to justify the Franco-German treaty around which so much controversy had raged. To let the EEC stagnate and to allow the newly-devised mechanisms for dialogue with the French to remain unused would be a certain way of ensuring that the international criticism to which Bonn had been subjected for going ahead with the signature of the Elysée treaty on 22 January had been pointlessly endured.[38] It might also embitter relations between France and Germany for years. Instead it made much more sense to use whatever extra leverage in Paris had been obtained to work for a resolution of the crisis and to press France to behave in a more cooperative manner in the future. Were this to be achieved it would both further rapprochement between Bonn and Paris (a project which while closely associated with Adenauer was always much more than the Chancellor's personal crusade) and vindicate Germany's initial defence of the treaty against its international critics.[39]

Second, Germany needed to act decisively at a European level in order to demonstrate to those who had attacked the Franco-German treaty that its new commitment had not superseded its old loyalties. The bilateralism of the Elysée treaty in other words would look much less suspicious and threatening in the eyes of Washington, Rome, or The Hague, if Bonn simultaneously acted in a fashion which underlined its ongoing commitment to multilateral cooperation. In the defence sphere this had already been achieved to some extent by Adenauer's acceptance, in mid-January, of the American MLF project. This underlined the Federal Republic's ongoing commitment to NATO and to American leadership of the West. But both the US and Germany's European partners would be still further reassured were Bonn to provide tangible proof that it remained firmly attached to European integration. The Italians, for instance, had set to one side their earlier disquiet at Franco-German cooperation and were prepared to admit that 'Germany is clearly the key to any relaunch programme that can constructively counter de Gaulle'.[40] And in order to provide this at a time of minimal activity within the Community, Bonn would need to display an unprecedented willingness to take the initiative in Brussels. That activism at a Community level which the Germans had always previously eschewed for fear of awaking their partners' latent anxieties about German hegemony was now necessary so as to demonstrate that Bonn had not changed and did not want to dominate, either alone or in tandem with Gaullist France.

At the same time, a German initiative in Brussels would also provide Bonn with an opportunity to address some of its underlying concerns about the way in which the Community had been developing. These centred primarily on the policy agenda of the EEC. Foremost in importance for Germany were two questions of balance. The first of these was that needing to be struck between the Community's twin objectives of internal industrial free trade and the establishment of a common market for agricultural produce. The second was the equilibrium necessary between the EEC's internal liberalisation and its development of a coherent policy towards the outside world. In Bonn's eyes both were in severe danger of going awry. In the first case, France's relentless drive (aided and abetted by the Dutch and the European Commission) for the establishment of the CAP seemed, to the Germans at least, in danger of outstripping the Community's advance towards other aspects of a full internal market. In the second, the Community's internal trade development seemed to be moving much faster than the emergence of a common commercial stance towards the outside world. Where the Community was developing an outside profile, moreover, particularly over agriculture, it appeared to be doing so in a way almost guaranteed to alienate many of its main trading partners. This might prompt retaliation. As a result, there appeared to be a serious danger that the Community would be punished internationally for its protectionist aspects in a manner which hit hardest those member states, like Germany, which depended on a flourishing export trade beyond as well as with its five EEC partners.

January 1963 had of course only made matters worse. At the most obvious level this reflected the way in which General de Gaulle's intervention had not only postponed British membership, but had also blocked any chance of resolving the wider division of western Europe into two competing trade blocs, the EEC and the European Free Trade Association (EFTA) – the seven nation body comprising Britain, Sweden, Norway, Denmark, Austria, Switzerland and Portugal. As a major exporter to the EFTA markets, and as a long-standing advocate of an agreement between the two organisations, Germany could not but be adversely affected by this setback.[41]

The premature ending of the enlargement negotiations also cast a degree of doubt over the likely evolution of global commercial liberalisation, something of even greater importance to the Germans. Kennedy's drive for a new and far-reaching round of negotiations under the General Agreement on Tariffs and Trade (GATT) had, after all, been closely tied up with the enlargement of the European Community. The President had urged Congress to grant him the necessary powers to negotiate a far-reaching international trade deal so as to match the liberalising dynamism of the expanding EEC. The American Trade Expansion Act of 1962 had been drafted, moreover, in a way which made the furthest reaching of its provisions conditional on EEC enlargement going ahead. The so-called dominant supplier clause which foresaw the total elimination of tariff barriers on those goods where the US and the EEC together accounted for more than 80 per cent of global production would only be triggered were Britain and some of its EFTA partners to join the EEC.[42] The failure of the Community's attempt to widen its membership would thus at very least negate the most radical parts of the planned commercial negotiations, and at worst might cause the whole initiative to unravel. This too was an alarming prospect for Bonn.

Almost worse than either was the way in which France's brutally unilateral conduct in January 1963, if repeated more generally, could seriously undermine Bonn's economic interests inside the Community. Would a France that could sabotage the enlargement process after 18 months of detailed negotiations, hesitate to break up the Kennedy Round of GATT negotiations should it be in its interest to do so? And could a France which as Lahr had pointed out so flagrantly violated the rules of Community diplomacy over the question of British membership, be expected to allow German and other member state interests to shape the future internal evolution of the EEC? Bonn's recurrent nightmare of being trapped in a protectionist Community and forced to watch powerless as its overseas exports withered away had never been more potent, and awful, than in the immediate aftermath of January 1963. Witness for example Harkort's agonised warning: 'no doubt can now remain that the grouping of the Six to which the French aspire will be French-led, anti-American in orientation, and inward-looking – in other words totally other than that which the remaining Five and the Federal Republic in particular have wanted since the foundation of the Community, continue to want, and must go on wanting in the future'.[43]

The best possible means of countering all of these concerns would be to seize the initiative in Brussels. Doing so would of course be facilitated by the fact that the member state which had in the past tended to be the most dynamic source of ideas and proposals, France, was temporarily so unpopular as to be unable to act. But more importantly a German move would enable Bonn to place its priorities and interests firmly at the top of the Community's agenda. It would also allow the Germans to devise a deal which contained enough of interest to Paris to lure the French back to the Community negotiating table, but at the same time made the realisation of French EEC ambitions conditional on the simultaneous achievement of German Community priorities. These last could include some type of arrangement to preserve harmonious relations with Britain and to ensure that the receding prospect of actual UK membership did not lead the

British to rethink their whole European alignment. Economic considerations thus dovetailed neatly with the political motivations analysed above to convince the German leadership that early 1963 was an ideal opportunity for a determined move in Brussels. Despite all of its previous hesitancy about acting too decisively at a European level, and regardless of the potential for provoking internal disagreement which European political questions still possessed in Bonn, the incentives for Germany to seize the European initiative in 1963 were so strong as to be impossible to ignore. Erhard, ever more clearly the Chancellor-in-waiting now that Adenauer was vilified for siding with de Gaulle, summed up the situation clearly in a letter to Heinrich von Brentano, a former German foreign minister: 'Either we go onwards, heeding only the unilateral and subjective interests and ideas pursued with such forcefulness by the French President and thus running the danger of course that the internal resistance to this on the part of our public could kindle a new, pernicious nationalism, or we plead with equal forcefulness for our German vital interests, but on a European and Atlantic basis'.[44]

German action began as soon as the meetings in Brussels ended. On his return to Bonn, Schröder wrote three important, yet subtly different letters. The first was an extremely warm note to Edward Heath, the principal British negotiator during the unsuccessful membership negotiations. This assured Heath of Germany's regret at the outcome in Brussels, predicted that enlargement would still come about in the long run, promised that Germany would do all that it could to stop Britain and the EEC diverging politically or economically, and ended with a generous tribute to Heath's own conduct in the course of the negotiations.[45] A day later this was followed by letters to Maurice Couve de Murville, the French Foreign Minister, and Dean Rusk, the US Secretary of State. To the former, Schröder underlined the vital need to do something about the relationship with Britain. Such action must take precedence over anything else. But he also stressed Bonn's commitment to the Franco-German treaty and its desire to consult with France about the future of the EEC.[46] The prospect of progress at a Community level was thus implicitly dangled in front of the French so as to tempt them into discussing interim arrangements with the UK. Likewise Schröder's letter to Rusk, while firm in its condemnation of de Gaulle's actions and sincere in its promise to work for a solution to the rift between the UK and the EEC, also noted that the Federal Republic would have to go on working with France so as to further develop the Community.[47] As early as 1 February, 1963, the Germans had thus recognised that efforts to reach a modus vivendi with the British would have to go hand in hand with an attempt to restart the EEC. This last, moreover, would have to be worked out in close consultation with Paris.

Over the ensuing months this twin track approach would continue, but the relative priorities of crafting a stop-gap solution with the British and developing a plan to revitalise the European Community gradually shifted in favour of the latter. This reflected a growing awareness in Bonn that satisfactory arrangements with the UK would be very hard to devise, not least because of London's own ambivalence, while advance within the EEC was both more attainable and more alluring than initially assumed. How this developed can be traced by looking first at Germany's dialogue with the British, then at the consultations held with the French and finally by examining the evolution of Bonn's own internal assessment of its European policies and goals.

Anglo-German talks during the first months of 1963 were very amicable in tone, but frustratingly vague. Typical, for instance, was the 8 February visit to Bonn of Sir Eric Roll, the deputy leader of the British negotiating team. Roll met Lahr at length but despite the friendly atmosphere and the ease with which both men agreed when condemning the French, advance proved much more difficult when discussion turned to the mechanisms which might serve to keep Britain and the EEC on parallel courses. Association was seen as problematic and hard for Britain's Commonwealth partners to accept, a new free trade area plan was likely to be opposed by the French, and a British policy of simply adapting its agricultural policies towards those of the Community was unacceptable in the absence of a powerful British voice in Brussels.[48] Similarly, the meeting of the Anglo-German economic committee in early March made clear what was not possible – the Germans firmly ruled out any multilateral contacts between the British and the Five – but saw no real consensus on what steps might actually be feasible.[49] The British also showed little enthusiasm for German suggestions that the two countries underpin their current closeness with a joint political declaration.[50] By April there was thus remarkably little to show from three months of dialogue.[51]

The talks between France and Germany, by contrast, recovered from a rocky start and began to open up real prospects of advance. The first official encounter, the 9 March talks between Lahr, Alfred Müller-Armack, his opposite number from the German Economics Ministry, and Olivier Wormser, a senior official at the Quai d'Orsay was, by Lahr's own admission, 'negative'. Wormser was strongly critical of all the possible arrangements which might be devised between Britain and the Six, and reiterated a series of hard-line French demands about the direction in which the EEC should evolve. Only his indication that France would be prepared to participate constructively in the planned GATT negotiations could be taken as an encouraging sign.[52] But less than a month later in another encounter between Lahr and Wormser, the French showed themselves to be much more flexible. This time Wormser indicated that France was keen to see relations normalised within the Community and progress resumed, and would welcome any German proposals designed to achieve this. Furthermore, the French were prepared to signal their goodwill by going ahead with the tariff cuts and external tariff alignments planned for 1 July, 1963, to talk about renewing a variety of commercial offers to India, Pakistan and Ceylon which had been made in the context of the enlargement negotiations, to consider Austria's request for association, and to approach the forthcoming Kennedy Round of GATT negotiations in a positive spirit. If further proof of this last were required, Wormser also suggested that the French were likely to allow the temporary 20 per cent cut of the Common External Tariff (CET), which had been agreed as part of the previous Dillon Round negotiations, to be made permanent.[53] That this new French line which constituted a deliberate attempt to appease the Five was retrospectively acknowledged by Jean-Marc Boegner, the French permanent representative to the EEC.[54] The effect, however, was to help convince Bonn that important progress could be made at a Community level, provided the Germans themselves were prepared to show some flexibility on the issue of consultations with Britain.

While talking to the British and the French, the Germans had also been conducting their own internal review of European policy.[55] Led by Schröder and Erhard – the Chancellor himself had been marginalised in the wake of the January crisis and had to content himself with a few critical broadsides from Cadenabbia, his holiday home on the shores of lake Garda – this only served to emphasise how much it was in Germany's interest to seize the initiative in Brussels.[56] In particular, Germany could press for a balanced development of policies within the Community and a systematic attempt to project a liberal image to the outside world.[57] In the light of the encouraging signals from Paris, these ambitions might prove possible to achieve. The German cabinet, sitting in the Chancellor's absence, thus decided to use the 2 April Council meeting, designed to allow a discussion of the general political situation of the Community, to launch a package of proposals intended to restore political momentum to the EEC.[58] The need to improve relations with Britain would certainly be stressed in the German proposal, but it would be but one of a series of issues which Schröder would urge the Community to discuss. What in January had been seen as the central concern of German European policy, had by April become merely one of several priorities.

The idea at the heart of Schröder's 2 April speech to the Council of Ministers was 'synchronisation'. In the past, he argued, the Community had placed too much emphasis on some aspects of its development at the expense of others. This had led to a situation in which the distribution of the benefits and costs of European integration had been unfair. If the Community was to escape from its current crisis – a crisis he noted which had seen national interests being pursued at the expense of Community interests – it was necessary for a more equitable system of advance to be devised. This could be done, he suggested, not by linking together individual policy decisions in order to obtain a 'price' for each concession – the system of 'préalables' which was widely seen as a symptom of the January crisis – but instead by putting together a much broader work programme which if implemented in its entirety would ensure that the development of the European Community would once again rediscover the equilibrium of interest set out by the treaty framers.[59]

In practice this meant that in the course of 1963, the Council should try to devise its opening stance for the Kennedy Round negotiations; construct a consultation mechanism which would allow a high-level of dialogue to be maintained with Britain and the other applicants; begin association negotiations with Austria; complete the association negotiations underway with Turkey; and sign the Association Convention. Alongside this engagement with the outside world, the Community should also reform its institutions. It should hence proceed towards the fusion or merger of the EEC and Euratom Commissions and the High Authority of the European Coal and Steel Community (ECSC) and grant more powers to the European Parliament. Finally it should press ahead with the planned set of tariff reductions, take a number of steps towards full economic union, and continue with the establishment of the CAP. In this last case, however, Schröder claimed that it would be necessary to review a number of the decisions already taken, since some of them had been shown to work less well than intended, particularly in their impact on countries outside the Community. COREPER should therefore immediately be asked to draw up a detailed work programme which could then be discussed by ministers at the next Council meeting.[60]

Rescuing Schröder

The ministerial speeches made in response to Schröder's statement were largely positive. All of the ministers present in Brussels recognised the importance of the German move; none could dissent from the notion of 'balanced progress' and 'synchronisation'. Emilio Colombo, the Italian minister of industry, Couve de Murville, Spaak, Luns and Eugene Schaus, the Luxembourg foreign minister, all took advantage of the general debate to air their own views about the Community's priorities. And there were a few veiled hints that some aspects of the German programme would not be easy for all member states to accept. But 2 April was a day on which such hesitations and divisions were played down by all of those present, and where the emphasis was on the shared need to advance.[61] As Spaak put it: 'Schröder's intervention can be summarised as saying that the Community had been subjected first to a shock, then to a crisis, and now to a desire to overcome this crisis through a relaunch. The number of ministers around this table is an encouraging sign and shows that everyone has become conscious of the importance of the issues that now confront us'.[62]

The mood was very different, however, when the text of the German work programme, despatched to the Secretary General of the Council of Ministers on 19 April, came to be discussed amongst the Permanent Representatives a few days later.[63] As the COREPER meeting soon made clear, most of Germany's partners, while accepting the basic political need for a synchronised action plan, objected strongly to many of the details of what Bonn had proposed. The first problem, identified most vehemently by the Dutch and the Belgians, was that the seven page German proposal simply listed too many questions which would have to be addressed.[64] It would have been much better, according to Dirk Spierenburg, the Dutch permanent representative, had the Germans sought to differentiate between important issues and secondary ones, and included only the former in the work programme. Also criticised, this time primarily by the Italians and French, was the suggestion of dividing the work programme into three different stages. Indeed Boegner, the French representative, felt that the way in which the Germans had suggested dealing with the CAP only in phases two and three was entirely contrary to the notion of synchronisation which ostensibly underpinned the plan. Furthermore, the German three stage approach was in clear breach of the CAP timetable as set down by the agreements of 14 January, 1962. If synchronisation was to mean anything at all, it was thus important that existing commitments be honoured and that progress towards agricultural integration ran parallel to the various types of industrial and commercial liberalisation suggested by Bonn. And finally, all of Germany's partners were sceptical about the balance which the German proposal struck between the internal development of the Community and the evolution of the EEC's external relationships. To place as much importance on the latter as the Germans had done, was to make the Community's recovery unduly dependent on factors such as progress in the GATT negotiations, which would be determined as much by the actions of third parties as by the steps taken by the EEC and its member states.[65]

Germany's action plan, designed to rescue the Community from the after-effects of the January crisis, thus had in its turn to be rescued. Schröder's unlikely saviour was Borschette, acting for the rotating EEC Presidency. The Luxembourg Permanent Representative preserved the basic idea of a synchronised work programme, but recast the contents entirely: in place of a seven page document, divided into multiple stages, the Borschette Plan amounted to little more than a single page of text. It foresaw a simultaneous effort to achieve progress in three distinct fields: external relations, where the only priorities mentioned were the establishment of a Community negotiating position for the Kennedy Round and the start of regular contacts between COREPER and the British head of mission to the EEC; the CAP, where the next tranche of regulations were to be agreed before the year's end; and the institutional reinforcement of the EEC, notably fusion and greater powers for the European Parliament.[66] Of the lengthy German list of external negotiations upon which the Community should embark, or the detailed measures designed to push forward the move to full economic union, there was no sign. It was thus on the basis of a highly abbreviated, but much more politically realistic text, that the EEC began to negotiate. Germany had correctly identified the need for an initiative, but the actual manner in which it had made its move rather betrayed its inexperience as a progenitor of Community proposals. It was only when the German scheme was reworked by the experienced Luxembourg representative, that a viable basis for future advance was actually devised.

Even Borschette's plan represented only a starting point. The danger of immediate paralysis had been averted by the Presidency's compromise text, but it would still take until September before a full agreement on the Community's future timetable could be reached. It is therefore necessary to examine briefly the three main issues at dispute and the attitudes adopted by the principal delegations. Appropriately enough the three topics upon which argument was most heated amongst the Six during the spring and summer of 1963 almost exactly mirrored the three fundamental questions about the Community's evolution, outlined in the introduction.

The central controversies

The first controversy centred on the internal deadlines which the Community should set itself for the next batch of CAP regulations. These were to include the regulations for beef, dairy products and rice, and movement towards, if not the final fixing of, the common price level for cereals. Behind these seemingly arid and technical subjects lurked two major controversies. The first was a primarily Franco-German dispute over whether the CAP was being built too quickly or, on the contrary, not nearly fast enough. And the second, even more fundamental question, was whether or not the progress towards a European agricultural policy made to date was deeply flawed and liable to do irreparable harm to the Community's global commercial image. Here too, the principal axis of confrontation was between Paris and Bonn.

In the event, the actual discussion was over very quickly. By 9 May, the French had been forced to concede that their initial insistence that the Community honour the 14 January, 1962 timetable and conclude the three new regulations by 1 July, 1963 was unrealistic. Their legalistic line failed to attract support even from the Commission and the Dutch, so often their allies when CAP matters were discussed. The preferred German deadline of 31 December, 1963 – a much more realistic target given the circumstances – was accepted instead. But looked at more carefully, this seeming German victory was less complete than might at first have appeared. For Schröder, who had represented the Federal Republic, had won little backing for his critique of the CAP's hurried and flawed construction. On the contrary, it was the French line, that the CAP was a central aspect of the Community, a source of Community pride and a matter of great economic and political importance, which had largely carried the day. Furthermore, Couve de Murville had strongly repulsed any suggestion that CAP advance be made strictly conditional on parallel advance in the

GATT negotiations.[67] The French admission that the date they had initially proposed for the new regulations was not feasible, was thus a token concession which concealed the fact that they had largely won the intellectual battle at the Council meeting.[68] Germany would be made painfully aware of this fact later in the year.

The second dispute, that over the arrangements to be devised for maintaining contact with the British, took rather longer to resolve. Here too it had initially seemed likely that the French would be forced to retreat in the face of a clear five-against-one split.[69] But as the French continued to argue strongly against any COREPER-based arrangement – maintaining that to allow regular meetings between the British head of mission and the permanent representatives would be to invite the British to exploit differences of opinion amongst the Six – the solidity of the Five began to crumble.[70]

For a start, the Commission made clear that it shared the French anxiety about a non-member state like Britain gaining a multilateral forum with which to negotiate *within* the Community machine.[71] Hallstein and his colleagues were keen instead to increase their own role in liasing with the British, arguing that the Commission should handle much of the dialogue with London. To this end they suggested an expansion of the size and duties of the ECSC High Authority's London representative office.[72] But it also soon became clear that while all of the Five member states were in favour of some type of mechanism for talking to the British, several were prepared to be flexible about exactly what type of arrangement they could accept. They were hence extremely susceptible to the French tactic of suggesting other, less *communautaire* methods of dialogue between the UK and the Six – for instance the establishment of an EEC/EFTA liaison office in Geneva.[73] And there was further uncertainty amongst the Five about whether or not the arrangements to be devised were to apply exclusively to Britain or were also to be extended to the other countries which had applied to join the EEC. The Germans had always felt strongly that the Danes, Norwegians and Irish should benefit from similar links; the Belgians by contrast insisted that anything done for the British should not set a precedent for other would-be member states.[74]

By early July it was also apparent that most of the member states were keen to settle a dispute which otherwise threatened to disrupt the Community's return to good health. Colombo, for instance, noted that a failure quickly to agree on the details of a work programme announced back in April would soon be interpreted as a significant setback.[75] The German ministers, moreover, arrived in Brussels fresh from a bilateral summit with the French which had confirmed that Paris was extremely unlikely to agree to a Brussels-centred solution to this problem.[76] As a result, the Dutch grew increasingly isolated in their continuing advocacy of a COREPER-based solution, with all of the other delegations ever more convinced that the only viable solution would be one centred upon an existing seven-nation body entirely distinct from the Community institutions, namely the Western European Union (WEU). Britain and all of the Six were founding members of this organisation and it thus seemed well suited for a liaison role. It was hence on a solution of this type that mediation efforts during the Council meeting, led by Colombo and Spaak, focused. And it was an arrangement of this sort which was eventually agreed on 11 July: British ministers would meet with their counterparts amongst the Six once every three months at the WEU in order to discuss 'the European economic situation'.[77] At such exchanges the European Commission would be invited to be present.[78]

The deal done contained enough to please all of the Six. Those member states, like Germany, which had been keen to see as close as possible a forum for contact with Britain established, could point to the regularity of the discussions, their freedom from any constraints as far as subject matter was concerned, and the presence at the debates of the Commission. The British would therefore be able to voice any concerns they felt about Community developments at a gathering where all of those involved in shaping the EEC's evolution were present. It was also the case that the WEU arrangement constituted just part of the overall solution; Britain would be able to talk directly to the European Commission and to make its views known to individual permanent representatives. And it could further be argued that the use of the WEU for these purposes was faithful to the remit of an organisation which since its creation had served as a link between Britain and the Six.[79] But it was equally possible for the French to feel that they had removed from the deal most of those elements about which they had been most anxious. In particular, they had succeeded in ensuring that any multilateral talks with the British took place outside of the Community framework and away from Brussels.[80] As a result, the prospect of a non-member state being able to exercise a strong influence over the evolution of EEC discussions about future policy was decisively reduced.[81] And for all of the Six, including even the Dutch, it was a relief to have brought a successful end to an increasingly sterile and ill-tempered debate, thereby clearing the way for the remaining portions of the work programme to be discussed.[82]

The final controversy of mid-1963 was institutional in nature. At first sight, the inclusion of two institutional matters – the fusion of the EEC, ECSC, and Euratom 'executives', and an increase in the powers of the European Parliament – in not only the German action programme but also the slimmed down Borschette Plan might appear surprising. Why, after all, raise such sensitive points at a time when the first task was to get the Community going again? This seemed especially true since institutional matters had always been prone to precisely that type of split between France and its five partners that it was in everybody's interest to avoid in 1963. But such an assessment would be to ignore both the great symbolic importance which most of the Five attached to institutional advance, and the willingness of the French to purchase greater room for manoeuvre on the more substantive issues by showing a degree of flexibility on institutional matters.

For some amongst the Five, the two institutional changes under discussion mattered greatly. Fusion would end many of the anomalies inherent in having three separate Communities and allow the formation of a more effective, and therefore in theory more powerful, single European 'executive', while an increase in the powers accorded to the European Parliament was seen as an important first step away from a technocratic construction to one which was more democratically accountable. The Dutch were particularly strong adherents of both these views, but these ideas also attracted strong backing, especially at Parliamentary level, in Italy, Germany and Belgium. They were, moreover, strongly championed by the European Commission (which expected to be the greatest single beneficiary of fusion) and by members of the European Parliament. But as important to many politicians as the specific changes under discussion was the simple fact that institutional evolution was occurring at all. This reflected the nature of the Treaty of Rome. The Community's founding document did not set out a precise road map leading to a united Europe; on the contrary, one of the reasons it had been able to attract so broad a coalition of support was precisely that it left open both the nature of Europe's eventual destination and the means by which this goal would be attained. The hopes of those who sought rapid progress towards a much more united Europe therefore centred on the belief that the type of economic change triggered by the Treaty would inevitably (and quickly) spill over into other fields of activity and would equally inevitably and rapidly give rise to a series of institutional changes, culminating, most hoped, in a fully federal structure. By 1963 – after five years of successful implementation of the Treaty of Rome – there was a widespread sense that the first signs of this process were overdue. Virtually any institutional alteration – provided it could be portrayed as a step towards a more federal arrangement – would thus be highly welcome to pro-European opinion and would relieve some of the parliamentary pressure being exerted on the Dutch, German and Italian governments.

This desire for change was made even more acute by the clash with de Gaulle. The General's opposition to federalism was well known. He was widely believed to harbour a desire to wrench back from the Community institutions some of the powers and the duties which they had gained through the Treaty of Rome, and he was certainly held to be contrary to any further steps taken in the direction of a stronger and more federal Europe.[83] For the Community to accomplish any institutional change in these circumstances would thus constitute a major victory against Gaullism and would send a clear signal, to European opinion and, almost as important, to Transatlantic observers, that the Five had not merely contained the Gaullist challenge launched on 14 January but were actually turning it back. The symbolic importance of fusion and a slight increase in the powers of the European Parliament was thus far greater than the actual intrinsic difference which the institutional changes might make. Any comprehensive action plan for an EEC *relance*, had to include an institutional dimension.

Fortunately for the Five this determination to advance in institutional terms did not encounter the type of total French opposition which might have been expected. It was true that the French government was deeply against any significant change in the powers or status of the European Parliament (or European Parliamentary Assembly, as the French alone went on calling it). Quai d'Orsay documents reveal that the French case against an increase in Strasbourg's power, while not yet as sophisticated as it would become by 1965, was already a powerful one, grounded in the belief that the current institutional balance should not be decisively altered and that it would be anomalous and irresponsible to attribute budgetary control of Community expenditure to an Assembly which was in no way accountable for the amount of money raised.[84] But the French representatives in Brussels were sufficiently confident of the strength of their case (and dismissive of the actual commitment of their partners) to be prepared to allow discussions of this topic to begin, certain that they could be prevented from producing any concrete results.[85] As far as fusion was concerned, meanwhile, Paris was prepared to be much more accommodating. There were two reasons for this. First was the realisation that flexibility on an issue of this type would allow France rapidly to regain the moral high ground in Brussels and therefore lessen the pressure it would come under to make more expensive and painful concessions in other areas of Community business.[86] Token gestures on how the Community operated would, in other words, reduce France's need to be flexible on what the Community did. And second, the French were also aware that the type of change which fusion would bring about would not necessarily be contrary to its interests. A merger between the Commissions of the EEC and Euratom and the High Authority of the ECSC might permit a degree of administrative rationalisation and hence reduced expenditure – a prospect which was bound to please some in Paris. But it might also be the case that the fusion of the three institutions would pave the way for an outright fusion of the three communities and the consequent redrafting of their treaties, a step which could involve the pegging back of the high degree of supranational power granted to the ECSC institutions by the 1952 Treaty of Paris, to the rather more moderate level associated with the 1957 Treaties of Rome. Fusion could hence be seen as a step *away* from supranationalism and federalism as well as a step towards these goals.

The institutional discussions of July and September 1963 were therefore not nearly as bitter and hard-fought as might have been expected. Indeed the principal objections to progress, on fusion at least, came not from the French but from Luxembourg. Although presented as doubts about the principle of fusion, these Luxembourg protests actually reflected the tiny member state's apprehension that any administrative merger of the three 'executives' would lead logically to their concentration in Brussels. This would deprive Luxembourg of the prestige and revenue which it had gained since 1952 by playing host to the High Authority of the ECSC. Schaus would thus only allow the 24 September agreement to study the issue of fusion after having made a unilateral declaration, duly recorded in the Council minutes, which noted that this decision in no way constituted an acceptance by Luxembourg of the principle of a merger.[87] The fight on this issue was merely postponed.

The atmosphere and tone of debates about all three controversies had benefited, moreover, from the simultaneous progress which the Community was making, almost without dispute, on other issues. By far the most important of these was the effort to establish a Community negotiating position in advance of the Kennedy Round in GATT. Rather contrary to expectations, the discussion about this did not produce the type of ill-tempered clash between reputedly protectionist France and some of the more liberal member states. The French in fact seemed quite willing to envisage a constructive EEC approach to the world trade talks, and they were able quickly to rebuild a consensus view amongst their partners, which had first appeared during the 1960–61 Dillon Round of negotiations, that a straightforward linear cut of tariffs – the formula which the Americans were suggesting be used in the tariff negotiations – would leave many US tariffs much higher than those of the Six. The reason for this was that whereas one fifth of US tariff positions were currently of 30 per cent or more, only 1 per cent of EEC tariffs were this high. A linear cut would therefore mean that several sectors of the US economy would continue to enjoy significant levels of protection even after all tariffs were halved, while in Europe the CET would almost uniformly be under 10 per cent.[88]

In order to avoid such an inequitable outcome, the Community member states rapidly agreed that supplementary steps would need to be taken against those US products which were particularly heavily protected. This line of argument, soon dubbed in the jargon of the GATT round, the 'disparities' case, was not however a cunning French imposition on an otherwise sceptical group of member states – it was instead something which reflected a view shared remarkably widely amongst the EEC member states.[89] Symptomatically it was a German representative, Müller-Armack, who first suggested that the EEC ask for a special GATT working group to be set up to study this issue.[90] The initial stages of the preparatory work for the Kennedy Round thus helped rather than hindered the Community in its rebuilding of mutual trust.[91] It should therefore be considered alongside the signature on 20 July of the Association Convention in Yaoundé and that on 13 September of an association agreement with Turkey as an important psychological milestone in the Community's gradual recovery from the crisis and near despair which had marked the beginning of 1963.

In essence, however, the work programme was no more than a timetable setting out future needs, rather than a substantive end in itself. Only the deal about contacts with Britain could immediately be put into action; the other outcomes were simply agreements about the timing of future negotiations. To fully recover from the January crisis, the EEC therefore needed to implement the work programme and meet the ambitious negotiating targets it had set itself. In the first instance this meant finalising the next batch of CAP regulations before the year's end, and establishing the Commission's negotiating mandate for the Kennedy Round negotiations by the same date. Any remaining doubt about how much was still at stake moreover was dispelled by the press conference given by de Gaulle on 29 July which while relatively serene in tone and devoid of any needless attacks on the re-emerging European consensus, nevertheless stated clearly that should the agreements of 14 January, 1962 not be honoured and the CAP regulations concluded by the end of December, 'the development of the whole entity would be stopped'.[92] A failure to meet its own self-imposed target might, in other words, mark a return to the impasse of January.

Towards the December accords

Orderly progress towards the December deadline for agricultural agreement was, however, rudely interrupted by a German *coup de théâtre*. On 15 October, Lahr and the state-secretary at the German ministry of agriculture, Rudolf Hüttebräuker, launched a joint attack on the CAP. Pointing to a sharp drop in Germany's food imports from outside the Community, and the harm this was doing to European neighbours like Denmark, close allies such as the US and third world countries seeking to sell rice or other commodities to Europe, both ministers suggested that the EEC needed fully to absorb the lessons provided by the first, flawed, set of regulations before proceeding to finalise the next batch. Hüttebräuker, furthermore, identified a series of fairly important modifications which needed to be made both to the mechanisms of CAP and to the procedure employed by the Community for day-to-day agricultural decision-making. Prominent amongst his first type of proposal was the idea of granting third-world countries reduced-levy or levy-free quotas, while his most radical procedural suggestion was that the use of management committees chaired by the Commission should be scaled back in favour of more Council-based decisions.[93]

Although both ministers were at pains to deny that their speeches constituted a frontal assault on the CAP – both on the contrary claimed that they remained committed to the policy's rapid advance, with Hüttebräuker requesting that his suggestions be considered 'improvements' rather than 'revisions' of the existing policies – the degree of German dissatisfaction with the way in which the CAP had been developing was painfully clear. Bonn had never been particularly comfortable with the idea of an ambitious common agricultural policy, and had grudgingly agreed to each previous advance in EEC farm policy, primarily out of an awareness that not to do so would be to invite serious political consequences both at a Community level and in its bilateral relationship with the French. Acceptance of the CAP had thus been made for political reasons and rather against Germany's immediate economic interests. But throughout 1963 the wisdom of this choice had been increasingly questioned.

First of all, as argued above, the January crisis had fanned smouldering German anxieties about the Community's drift into agricultural protectionism.[94] Secondly, the imminence of the Kennedy Round made Bonn extremely alive to the need for the Community to project as liberal as possible a commercial image abroad. And thirdly, the 'chicken war' of mid-1963 in the course of which Washington had threatened multiple commercial reprisals against the Community were steps not taken to redress the dramatic fall in US poultry exports to the EEC in general and Germany in particular, had provided all too graphic a demonstration of what might happen on a much larger scale should the CAP not be reined back substantially.[95] In the event, a compromise solution had quickly been negotiated by the US and the Commission. But this speedy resolution had not prevented the Germans from regarding the dispute as an alarming harbinger of likely troubles ahead. That dissatisfaction with the CAP which had been a sub-text of Schröder's comments in April and May, was thus set out once more, this time with little or no disguise, in mid-October.[96]

This passionate appeal had remarkably little impact. On 15 October itself, the two German speeches were greeted with near silence, no national minister choosing to reply. And by mid-November, when ministers of agriculture returned to Brussels, the Commission had undermined many of the German claims by publishing its own assessment of the CAP's first year of operation. This report, in addition to making the pragmatic observation that it was unwise to radically rethink a policy as complex as the CAP on the basis of the figures from a single year, also demonstrated that virtually all the problems of which Lahr and Hüttebräuker had complained were specific to Germany. Thus for example the slide in German imports of pork and bacon, primarily from Denmark, had been more than compensated for by the rise in Italian imports. Furthermore, Sicco Mansholt, the Commissioner responsible for agricultural matters, was able to provide an array of figures to show that the fall in German imports was no greater in 1962–63 than it had been in the previous two years, and that it was therefore much more convincing to attribute it to the sharp rise in German domestic agricultural production than it was to blame the newly-formed CAP.[97] The intellectual foundations of the German case were thus seriously undermined.

The timing of Lahr and Hüttebräuker's move was also suspect. Even had Bonn's complaints been fully justified – and the subsequent evolution of the CAP would make some of their alarmist predictions look uncannily accurate – there were few elsewhere in the Community who were pre-pared to start a root and branch reform of the CAP just two and a half months before a crucial deadline, a deadline moreover of Germany's own choosing. The Council debate which followed Mansholt's exposition was thus notable primarily for the reluctance of those present to get involved in a complex controversy. Virtually all of those who spoke merely reiter-ated their country's general approach to the CAP rather than trying to respond specifically to either Germany's complaints or its suggested remedies.[98]

At a deeper level, however, the October–November failure of the German reform drive also reveals the way in which Bonn was still too iso-lated in 1963 to mount a serious challenge to the CAP. Of the French commitment to seeing an effective agricultural policy rapidly established, little more needs to be said here.[99] Likewise the European Commission was determined to push forward its flagship policy, not least because of its awareness that a successful CAP was the single greatest guarantee it could acquire that Gaullist France would not carry out its threatened assault on the Community institutions.[100] But the Germans were scarcely more suc-cessful in attracting support from the Dutch or the Italians. The former, although sharing Bonn's desire for a commercially liberal Community, were major agriculture exporters and as such had a strong economic incen-tive to see an effective CAP set up as early as possible. The Dutch solu-tion, moreover, to the problem of how to reconcile the building of a CAP with the maintenance of a healthy level of imports from outside the Community – namely a desire to see an agricultural policy which would allow Europe's efficient farmers to thrive while driving its marginal and inefficient producers out of business – was politically unacceptable to Germany's much less efficient farmers and to those CDU politicians who depended on the farm vote. A Bonn–The Hague alliance on farm matters in the Community was thus very hard to sustain. Nor was there yet much scope for the Germans to align themselves with the Italians, who in 1963 were still extremely hopeful that they would in the future benefit substan-tially from European agricultural support.[101] The gap between Rome and Bonn was particularly deep on the issue of CAP finance, where Italy was pressing for a generously-funded policy in the belief that a great deal of money would flow in its direction in the form of 'guidance' grants designed to improve the structure of Italian agriculture, and the Germans were seeking all means of containing the costs, including preventing the emer-gence of a sizeable guidance fund. With Belgium and Luxembourg only marginal players in the CAP talks, both more interested in crafting com-promise which might bring the negotiations to a speedy and successful conclusion, the Germans had no real backing in their desire radically to alter either the first or second tranche of agricultural regulations.

In late 1963, Germany's own stomach for a major fight on this was also questionable, for at least two reasons. The first of these was Germany's own desire to see a successful outcome of the negotiations. Like all of its partners, Germany was keen to see parallel agreements reached. To fail to meet the CAP deadline would certainly, under the very synchronisation principle which Bonn had invented, jeopardise the Community's ability to provide the Commission with an agreed mandate for the Kennedy Round talks in the New Year.[102] It might also, if the multiple French threats were to be believed, lead to renewal of the crisis with which 1963 had begun. A successful outcome, by contrast, would signal the definite end to the post-veto tension and vindicate Germany's efforts to reduce this tension. Second, the focus of German agricultural anxieties was dramatically altered in early November 1963 by the Commission's publication of the Mansholt Plan, a proposal to introduce common cereal prices by July 1964.[103] Both the importance of this issue and the difficulties that it posed for Bonn in particular will be extensively explored in the next chapter. At this juncture it is enough to point out, however, that with the appearance of this major new threat, the Germans must have recognised that they could not afford to alienate their partners with a general assault on the CAP when they needed as much backing as they could muster in the Council in order to postpone the Commission's cereal price plans. The Commissioner for Agriculture's 4 November proposal thus began the rout of Lahr and Hütterbräuker, that Mansholt's own counter-arguments completed a week later. By early December at the latest, Germany had thus realised that it should temporarily abandon all thoughts of wider-scale CAP reform and concentrate on protecting its national interests as best it could in the discussions of the milk, beef and oil regulations and in the debate about CAP finance and the timetable for a common cereals price. With its partners similarly inclined, the negotiation became much more similar to earlier Community marathons: hard-fought, but with all players committed to ultimate success.

In the event it took until 23 December to reach agreement. By the final stages some were predicting failure, with all that such an outcome might entail. Sir Pierson Dixon, the British Ambassador to Paris for instance, wrote a despatch to London outlining the renewed crisis in the Community and suggesting, on the basis of a conversation with an unnamed official close to Couve de Murville, that the impasse reflected the way in which de Gaulle's view of the EEC had been soured by the row over British membership.[104] Sir Con O'Neill, Britain's new Head of Mission in Brussels was, however, swift to contradict his colleague: 'I think I should record that the atmosphere here in Community circles is not (repeat not) one of crisis'; instead most of those involved in the negotiations conveyed a 'general impression of comparative relaxation' in which French threats were dismissed as tactical atmospherics.[105] The latter's assessment proved the more reliable. Thanks in no small part to a skilful last minute package deal, unveiled on the night of 22 December by the Commission, an agreement on both the agricultural regulations and the GATT mandate was reached. The key sections of the action plan had been completed.

A major success?

Reactions were predictably euphoric. In Germany, the unanswered state of many of the country's anxieties about the CAP was temporarily eclipsed by a sense of relief that a deal had been concluded.[106] The successful outcome of the negotiations also signalled a further important step forward towards the construction of an economic community at least. As one Bundeskanzleramt report put it: 'The agreement in principle over the four new agricultural regulations and over the guidance and guarantee funds has brought the EEC closer to the point of "no return"'.[107] The Germans had managed in the course of the negotiations to obtain some of the targets they had set themselves. They had thus successfully postponed the moment at which the Community decided upon a common cereal price and obtained a stay of execution before a margarine tax needed to be introduced. They had also received EEC sanction for the maintenance of domestic milk subsidies for the duration of the transitional period, inserted a number of references to the importance of external trade in the text of the agricultural regulations, and above all, seen the Commission given a negotiating mandate which would allow the Kennedy Round talks to start in May with full EEC participation.[108] More significant still, the Community had signalled an ability to return to normality, with negotiations being conducted in a civilised and balanced manner very different from the unilateralism of January. It was this that Auswärtiges Amt's assessment chose to emphasise:

> The agreement reached was only possible because all states were willing to make concessions in the interest of the Community and its standing in the world. The decisions offer a successful balance of advantages and disadvantages to each member state. One cannot therefore speak of winners and losers amongst the member states – the winners should simply be identified as the Community and the free world: the danger that the difficulties of the year's beginning would lead to a stagnation of the EEC's progress has been overcome and further progress of integration in the agricultural field is to be expected.[109]

The French seemed equally pleased. Boegner's retrospective analysis, referred to before, makes little attempt to conceal the satisfaction that he felt with the deal which France had been able to secure. Not only had the CAP advanced, but it had done so without France having to make many telling concessions en route – indeed Boegner identified the permission given to the Germans to retain their milk subsidies as the sole meaningful step backwards that French negotiators were obliged to make. But like German analyses cited above, the French Permanent Representative was keen to stress the political significance of the outcome:

> If the December 23 agreement is a significant event because of the measures it includes, it is also in its implications, direct and indirect, and in its likely consequences. Without wanting to dwell on the simplistic theme of re-found confidence, one can nevertheless claim that the December 23 deal has erased the immediate consequences of the crisis caused by the breaking off of negotiations with England. It is quite striking to note that, in the course of the negotiations that led to the accord, no one asked whether any particular measure might further complicate Great Britain's eventual membership. In this respect, the British roadblock has been partially removed.[110]

Rather more succinctly, but equally revealingly, de Gaulle wrote a Christmas greeting to Adenauer, now in partial retirement, in which he spoke approvingly of 'the success of our Europe in Brussels'.[111]

While understandable, such positive assessments partially concealed the extent to which the December accords had only become possible because many of the most problematic decisions had been postponed to a later date. This was true even at the level of what the Community did – the question upon which the German action plan had invited the Community to focus, partly out of the belief that it was the easiest of the three controversies on which to find an answer acceptable both to France and its five partners. As far as the CAP was concerned, both the struggle to set a single cereal price and the equally sensitive choice of how the policy should be funded remained to be taken. Likewise, even some of the more difficult aspects of the new regulations remained to be settled definitively; Germany and the Netherlands would thus have to resume at some future date their campaign to avoid the imposition of a tax on margarine, designed to subsidise the production of olive oil. More fundamentally, the deep level of German anxiety about the CAP which had been so vividly brought to the surface in October, had not really been addressed, and might return at any future point.

Similarly, the setting of a mandate for the Kennedy Round, while an important first step, constituted no guarantee that much more serious internal tension might not result once concrete negotiations began in Geneva. The Community's internal deliberations had after all confirmed that there was some degree of division in the priority given to the GATT talks between countries like The Netherlands and Germany on the one hand, and France, Italy and Belgium on the other. Although the fracture between 'liberals' and 'protectionists' was much less clear-cut than some observers had expected, there was enough difference of opinion for future rows to be likely.[112] Furthermore, the coordination of future advances between the CAP and the GATT talks was likely to grow more difficult once the timetable ceased to be a purely internal Community affair, but instead became dependent on the manner in which other countries approached the Geneva talks. The December 1963 agreements did not therefore settle the major controversies about the Community's agenda one way or another. 'Synchronisation' had worked once but it would need to go on working for several more years were future disputes about the EEC's economic priorities to be averted.[113]

The Community's response to the other two questions was even more open. Institutionally, 1963 could be regarded as a positive year. The institutions of the Community had weathered the January storm intact, and the habits of cooperation built up amongst the Six had proved sufficiently ingrained to have rapidly reasserted themselves in the first months of the year. Indeed, by December the events of early 1963 had proved distant enough for the alliance between the French and the European Commission which had been so crucial to the EEC's early success to re-emerge and to play a major role in the successful outcome of the talks.[114] The WEU solution to the British problem, moreover, had temporarily solved this controversy in a manner which was unlikely to obstruct the smooth operation of the Community machine.[115] And there had even been some advance in the discussions about future evolution. Although the institutional chapter of Germany's work programme remained incomplete, COREPER had successfully completed a preliminary report on fusion and its implications on 18 December.[116] The ground had thus been prepared for ministers to resume their discussions of institutional matters early in the New Year.

Amongst this encouragement, however, there were also signs of future difficulty. At their most trivial, these included the obstinacy Luxembourg had displayed over fusion; appeasing the smallest member state's anxieties on this issue looked destined to form a major part of any future institutional talks. Similarly, 1963 had also demonstrated that the French would remain as hard as ever to convince that the European Parliament deserved greater powers. Less immediately noticeable, but in the long-run potentially rather more serious, was the growing gap between the Commission's own vision of its institutional role and that of even the more *communautaire* of member states. This had been perhaps most obvious during the debate about how best to maintain an active dialogue with the British when Hallstein had suggested arrangements which would have left almost all the responsibility for this task to the European Commission, implying that as long as the British were making their views known to the self-styled executive, their needs would be catered for. None of the Five had shared this assessment, arguing instead for an increased dialogue between Britain and the member states, and more particularly between the British head of mission in Brussels and the national permanent representatives. And the French, in so energetically opposing this last type of arrangement, also showed that they shared the view that Council (and its subordinate committees like COREPER) rather than the Commission was consolidating its position as the central institution of the EEC. But even more significant, arguably, in demonstrating the Community's gradual divergence from the type of proto-federal institutional vision harboured by Hallstein and many others, was the way in which Germany, by putting forward an action plan for 1963, had usurped that agenda-setting role which had previously been assumed to belong solely to the European Commission. The German plan indeed had almost entirely marginalised an earlier action plan for 1963 which the Commission had put forward in October 1962.[117] Although softened at the time by the Commission's own recognition of the need for some action to resolve the immediate crisis, the most telling blow to the Commission's sense that it was pre-ordained to develop into a future European government, had been delivered not by de Gaulle but instead by an 'ally' in the form of Bonn.

Finally, it also remained questionable how far 'the British roadblock' had been lifted by the Community's actions or Britain's own temporary loss of interest in the EEC. Just as that first flurry of activity amongst the 'friendly Five' and Britain had largely reflected London's desire to salvage something from the wreckage of its first membership bid, so too the sidelining of the issue in mid to late 1963 was significantly influenced by a reduction in British activity in Brussels. A higher powered representative had admittedly been appointed and the status of the British mission to the EEC had been upgraded. And UK ministers did make use of the regular WEU consultations to make their views known. But with Harold Macmillan having resigned through ill-health and replaced with an Alec Douglas-Home government more concerned with the general election expected for 1964 than with anything else, the prospects of a major British push in Brussels were slight. In such circumstances it was understandable that the polarisation within the EEC which the prospect of enlargement had produced should fade; whether it would reappear should Britain approach the EEC once more, remained, however, a very open question.

The seasonally apt peace and goodwill which reigned in Brussels over Christmas 1963 was not, therefore, built upon totally solid foundations. The immediate crisis of January 1963 had been overcome, but many of the underlying uncertainties and divisions of opinion continued to lurk just below the surface. Whether the Community's recovery could be prolonged into 1964, and could cope with the new surge of optimism which the successes of December were likely to provoke, would thus depend on whether the German activism, French restraint, and determination of all of the Six to succeed, which had been such vital ingredients in rescuing the Community from its first major experience of division, could be repeated in the New Year.

2 From the cereals agreement to Council breakdown

January 1964–June 1965

At first sight it would appear that the Community-level progress which had characterised the latter half of 1963, continued throughout 1964 and the first half of 1965 before coming to an abrupt halt in June 1965. That mixture of German activism, French restraint and the collective determination of the Six to press ahead with the integration process which had seemingly rescued the Community from the crisis of January 1963, persisted into the 18-month period following the December 1963 accords. Furthermore, the election in October 1964 of a Labour government in Britain seemed to confirm that *le problème anglais* – the dispute between France and its partners that had lain at the heart of the 1963 breakdown – was temporarily at least much less pressing and divisive. As a result, the months between the January of 1964 and April of 1965 were characterised by a number of significant EEC successes – most spectacularly that of December 1964 when a further agricultural marathon culminated in the setting of a uniform price for cereals, a central component in the whole CAP system. Charting and analysing this tale of Community advance will thus constitute the first task of this chapter.

The empty chair crisis which began at the end of June 1965 was not, however, purely the outcome of the Commission's over-ambitious financial and institutional proposals of March 1965 – a needless dispute interrupting the advance of an otherwise healthy Community. Instead, it was a confrontation which was primarily caused by growing levels of unease and mistrust between the principal members of the EEC. As the second half of the chapter will seek to explain, the visible successes of the 1964–65 period coexisted with a number of underlying divisions and tensions. Indeed, the very achievements of the Community during the preceding year and a half contributed significantly to the build-up of mutual suspicion and mistrust that was to flare so dramatically in the summer of 1965. The apparent contrast between the advances of 1964 and early 1965 and the disaster of mid-1965 will thus be shown to conceal a much greater degree of continuity in the ongoing dispute separating the Five from Gaullist France.

Cereal success

The most eye-catching of Community accomplishments in 1964 was the agreement reached on 15 December establishing the uniform level of cereal prices which were to apply throughout the Community from July 1967.[1] The significance of this sprang from the importance of cereal prices in the overall CAP system, from the degree of member state division and dispute that the issue had caused, and from the prospects of future progress that were opened up by the resolution of the cereal price row. The setting of uniform prices for wheat and other cereals was an absolutely crucial milestone in the advance of the CAP.

As envisaged by the European Commission, and by Sicco Mansholt, the Commissioner responsible for agriculture in particular, the EEC's agricultural policy was to be based for most commodities upon a managed internal market.[2] Prices for each agricultural product would be sustained at the same level in each of the six countries, with agricultural produce circulating freely between member states. Non-Community produce meanwhile would be subject to a variable levy designed to ensure that all imported foodstuffs entered the EEC at a price above that set for commodities grown within the Community. As a result, Community producers would be guaranteed to undercut external competitors, irrespective of the level of the world market price. Should they need to export – in cases for instance where Community supply outstripped Community demand – they would be enabled to do so by EEC subsidies designed to make up the difference between the low world price and the artificially-supported internal Community price. Community farmers would thus enjoy price stability within the EEC and free access to each other's markets, while being protected from outside competition and allowed to compete internationally thanks to Community financial support.

In order to construct such a system, however, the Community needed to take four vital sets of decisions. The first of these, the decision on the principles of the protective levy, had been taken in December 1960.[3] The second tranche, namely the establishment of detailed rules for each individual commodity, had been spread over the hard-fought agricultural negotiations of December 1961 to January 1962 and the agreements of December 1963.[4] The third, the level of internal EEC prices – and especially those of cereals which were expected to act as the guide for all subsequent price level decisions – had been on the Community negotiating table ever since November 1963 when the Commission had submitted the so-called Mansholt Plan. Of the fourth – the financial regulation stipulating how this potentially highly expensive system was to be paid for – much more will be said below. The importance of the third step was beyond dispute, however, since without the ending of the substantial variations in agricultural prices between different member states, nothing like the system described above could be introduced. As one Commission official reportedly put it in a meeting with German farmers' leaders, 'No price alignment – no agricultural policy – no European unity'.[5] The 15 December, 1964 settlement, pricing grain at 425 DM per tonne, was thus a huge step towards Mansholt's overall design.

Furthermore, it was a decision that did much to determine both the level of European agricultural production and the degree to which the Community became agriculturally protectionist. It had been widely recognised that were Community prices to be set at a high level, most European farmers would flourish, pushing up production levels by maximising the amount of land under cultivation. The space left within the Community market for imported produce would be correspondingly reduced and the prospects of the EEC disrupting world markets by exporting its own subsidised surpluses would become much greater.[6] A low price, by contrast, would drive marginal producers out of business and limit internal European production to levels where substantial imports from outside of the EEC were likely to remain necessary and where the need to export beyond Europe was correspondingly small. The level of the cereal price would therefore go a long way towards pushing the CAP in a liberal or protectionist direction. The 1964 decision to adopt a price at which all but the most inefficient European farmers could go on producing thus set the CAP on a path towards rising European production, shrinking imports and ever greater quantities of EEC farm exports.[7] In the immediate aftermath of the agreement, however, the long term dangers of this policy decision were largely masked by the euphoria at having taken so vital a step towards a fully-functioning CAP.[8]

The degree of relief felt in December 1964 reflected the deep divisions that the issue had caused. Most prominent of these was the disagreement aroused between France and Germany.[9] Ever since the issue of cereal prices had first been discussed at Community level in 1962, there had been awareness of the difficulties that would have to be faced in overcoming the gap between the high German producer price and the much lower French figure.[10] Too sudden a movement from either extreme, could cause severe hardship for German farmers or encourage massive overproduction by the French. Furthermore, there was a deep conflict of interests within Germany between those sensitive to industry's need for a liberal European Community willing to import foodstuffs as a counterpart to its manufactured exports, and those who attached greater importance to the potential problems of German farmers. The former ought to have wanted low, French-level prices, since these would pushed the CAP in a much less protectionist direction.[11] It revealed much about the bizarre nature of German electoral politics, and the relative organisational strengths of German industry and German agriculture, that it was the latter group who had prevailed, however. Both Adenauer and Erhard's governments had therefore shunned the opportunity gradually to reduce German food prices and had instead tried to postpone the implementation of cereal prices at a European level to the very end of the transition period in 1970 at the earliest. The rapid timetable for the introduction of cereal prices envisaged by the Mansholt plan, which foresaw the setting of a common price by 1966, was consequently greeted with some horror by the German government.[12]

As Chapter 1 explained, Bonn had been initially successful in its quest to push back the Mansholt timetable. Indeed, one of the main causes of German pleasure at the December 1963 accords was precisely that they did not include a decision on cereal prices. But such was the importance of the issue to all of those keen to see the CAP established – the European Commission of course, but also the French and Dutch governments in particular – that it was never likely that this German victory would last long. By the spring of 1964, therefore, the Commission and its backers amongst the member states had returned to the offensive, pressing again for an immediate decision. This time the Germans had been even more outspoken in their defiance. Aware perhaps of their growing isolation on the issue, Werner Schwarz and Rudolf Hüttebraüker, the German Minister of Agriculture and his State Secretary, rejected the Commission's call for common prices in so sweeping a fashion that they appeared to cast doubt on their very commitment to the whole CAP.[13] They were even prepared to call for the majority voting provisions of the Treaty of Rome, due to enter into force from January 1966, to be suspended for agricultural price decisions, so as to ensure that the Germans could not have low prices forced upon them after this date.[14] And throughout four successive Council meetings in April, May and June they showed themselves ready to ignore not only their fellow negotiators' mixture of admonition and supplication, but also a substantial revision by the Commission of its original proposals specifically designed to accommodate German concerns (and indeed held by some – notably the French and Dutch – to go much too far in the direction of appeasing Bonn).[15]

In the autumn the confrontation resumed, this time given additional urgency by the need to establish a Community opening stance in the Kennedy Round discussions of agricultural trade which the Americans were pressing Europe to begin. According to the Commission at least this was something that could not be done without the likely level of future cereal prices being known. The Commission had hence set 15 December as the absolute deadline for a cereal price decision. To underline the importance of the issue further, the French had also reverted to the tactics they had employed the previous year and threatened to reconsider their whole European commitment were cereal prices not agreed. As Alain Peyrefitte, the French government spokesman, announced in October, 'France will stop participating in the European Economic Community if the agricultural Common Market is not organised in the way that was agreed.'[16] Even the Americans got involved, refusing to permit further progress in the GATT negotiations until the Community stance on agriculture was known – and therefore by implication until the cereal price level was fixed.[17] It was in other words being made very clear to Bonn that it could either face down its domestic farmers and their CDU and FDP backers, or see the Kennedy Round and possibly even the EEC itself placed in jeopardy. Nevertheless it still took until 1 December, before Kurt Schmücker, the German minister of economics, was able to announce in Brussels that his country was prepared to accept the principle of cereal price cuts, and a further fortnight of intensive negotiations before final agreement was reached on the price level, the timing of its introduction and the level of compensatory subsidies German, Italian and Luxembourg farmers would receive.[18] The hyperbole that greeted the eventual deal was thus in part at least a function of how fraught the preceding negotiations had been.[19]

Finally, the significance of the cereal price deal lay in the widespread sense that it had constituted one of the last great obstacles between the Community and rapid further advance. To a certain extent this was an inevitable consequence of the centrality of cereal prices to the CAP. Given that the agricultural policy itself was very much at the heart of the 1960s Community's business, any substantial CAP advance was bound almost automatically to raise morale and create expectations of further progress in Brussels. But it also reflected the perception that a common price level for major agricultural commodities would forge almost indissoluble bonds between the economies of the member states, thereby obliging the Six to coordinate much more tightly their economic policies, their exchange rates and their whole economic development.[20] It was no coincidence that just days after the agreement Robert Marjolin, the Commissioner responsible for economic policy coordination amongst the Six could write: 'monetary union has ceased to be a dream or even a project of uncertain realisation. It has become an imperative necessity.'[21] Not all Community observers would have gone quite so far. Even amongst somewhat cooler heads, however, there was a strong sense that having fought their way to this most difficult and painful of decisions, the Six were now likely to move forward quickly towards the commercial liberalisation envisaged in the Treaty of Rome.[22]

The sense that forward movement was possible – even inevitable – was accentuated by the fact that other aspects of the Community's economic programme were also progressing. Most important in this respect was probably the Council's 16 November, 1964 finalisation of the exception list for the Kennedy Round of GATT negotiations. Predictably, this proved contentious, with several member states, notably France, adding substantially to the number of tariff positions originally included on the Commission's list, and several others, including Germany, objecting that too many exceptions would undermine the whole impact of the Kennedy Round.[23] Equally predictably, some observers, both internal and external, interpreted the inevitable compromise as a sign that the Community was being dominated by the protectionist French.[24] In reality, however, the

Community's ability to decide on this potentially hugely divisive matter said much more about the member states' willingness to take seriously the demands of negotiating jointly than it did about any incipient protectionist trend. Indeed, those most inclined to view the French attitude towards trade liberalisation with a jaundiced eye rather overlooked the remarkable fact that Paris's representatives did not make their agreement to the exception list conditional on a cereal price deal, despite the fact that the Council meeting devoted to the GATT talks preceded Bonn's concessions on the cost of grain. This was just one of several hints that the real French attitude towards the industrial aspect of the trade talks was distinctly less negative than de Gaulle's bluster implied and that critics of the French, whether within the Community or outside, normally assumed.[25]

Fusion – the first step towards treaty reform

These forward steps on the Community's agenda – the question of what the Community should do, examined in the introduction – were flanked by smaller, and yet still significant, advances on the issue of how the EEC should be run. At this level, the most important development occurred with the signature in April 1965 of the fusion treaty bringing about the merger of the EEC and Euratom Commissions with the High Authority of the ECSC – the first alteration to the Treaty of Rome since 1957. Here too, agreement had long proved elusive.[26] Throughout much of 1964 and during the early months of 1965, Luxembourg's representatives, especially Pierre Werner, the Foreign Minister, had fought a determined campaign to extricate the maximum possible compensation for the losses that the Community's smallest member state would incur from the departure of High Authority. This included a wide variety of suggestions of what portions of EEC activity should be transferred to Luxembourg by way of recompense.[27] In the end a formula had been devised which moved a number of Commission functions to Luxembourg and pledged that certain Commission and Council meetings would be staged there each year. The degree of sensitivity over the whole issue of where the Communities should have their seat – and whether indeed they should have one seat or many – had only been confirmed. Another disappointment for some was the way in which the hoped-for breakthrough on the powers of the European Parliament had not occurred. This had been discussed at length as part of the discussion of fusion but the French had proved obdurate in their refusal to grant either budgetary or any other substantive powers to an Assembly that continued to be made up of national parliamentarians rather than directly-elected MEPs.[28] So much importance was attached to the issue by several of France's partners, not to mention by the Community institutions themselves, that it was all but inevitable that the question – and hence the deep division between French and the Dutch in particular – would soon recur.

It would be misleading, however, to allow these last controversies totally to obscure the importance of the fusion treaty. For a start, the merger of the three self-styled executives was an important administrative rationalisation, which while more disruptive in the short- and medium-term than many had anticipated, would have had to be confronted at some point in the Community's development. The EEC Commission's de facto takeover of the moribund ECSC and Euratom entities tidied up some of the bureaucratic jumble caused by the existence of three separate European Communities and confirmed the dominance of the Economic Community over its two counterparts. It also demonstrated, moreover, that some institutional advance was possible while de Gaulle remained in the Elysée. And above all it suggested that, the rows over the European Parliament notwithstanding, there was a surprising degree of consensus amongst most of the member states (if not yet shared by either the Dutch or the Commission) about the institutional direction in which the Community was evolving.

This was clearly apparent in the March 1964 Council debate over the fusion treaty, when the Germans broke with the traditional federalist vision of the Community's organisation to speak of the Council of Ministers constituting 'an important part of the Executive, particularly as it could be more accurately compared to a national Government than could the European Commission'.[29] This observation produced no immediate protests from any of Bonn's partners. And the Germans then reinforced the point by suggesting that members of the Council should periodically consent to appear before the Strasbourg Assembly. This procedure too would imply that the Council at least as much as the Commission was the 'governmental' body that the Parliamentarians needed to scrutinise. Significantly, the French were willing to accept steps in this direction.[30]

Much the same trend was evident in June 1964 when the Dutch and the Commission were powerless to prevent a text formalising the position of COREPER – a committee whose remarkable gains in importance had belied the fleeting and tangential mention it earned in the Treaty of Rome – from being added to the draft treaty. Once more the German representative who spoke openly of giving COREPER's role 'an unassailable legal base' appeared much closer to the French stance than to the Dutch or Commission viewpoint.[31] The fusion negotiations thus provided a salutary reminder that institutional matters did not throw up the crude five-to-one split between France and its partners that is often suggested, and that the French were not alone in feeling that the manner in which the Community was actually developing had diverged significantly from the federalist path to which some still clung dogmatically. If any member state government was significantly out of line on these issues, it was The Hague and not Paris.

The drift away from federalism was also detectable in the other institutional development of 1964, namely the torrent of national proposals designed to revitalise the stalled political union process. This was the effort, dormant since 1962, to devise European institutions capable of coordinating the Six in the foreign policy sphere.[32] Erhard, the driving force behind arguably the most important of these member state initiatives – the German proposals of 4 November, 1964 – quite explicitly justified his desire to flank the existing Community with new structures within which the Six could discuss East–West relations and other issues outside of the normal EEC remit, with the observation that economic integration alone could not bring about full European unity. In January 1964, for instance, the Chancellor contrasted Commission views with his own:

> The European Commission tends to claim jurisdiction even where this is not formally foreseen by the Treaty... In the Commission's view, the relinquishing of national powers and the gradual takeover of sovereignty leads towards a politically united Europe.
>
> As against this, one should not forget that resistance [to this process] grows the more sovereignty that the Commission takes over. When from January 1966 onwards decisions by majority voting become possible in the Council of Ministers and this encroaches on the interests of a country, especially perhaps a big country, this must lead to considerable opposition. It is already difficult to tolerate that when we hand over power to another, it is not to a politically controlled institution but rather to the Brussels bureaucracy. With every new widening of Commission competence it becomes ever harder for the Council of Ministers, on technical grounds, to uphold the established relationship between the Commission and the member state governments. This well-established Commission practice will not lead to its goal: 'if we want a politically united Europe, then we must try to reach it through the main entrance and not the back door.'[33]

Such views did not of course imply a German rejection of the economic route to integration so far taken – although the warning shot about majority voting fired almost two years to the day *before* the Luxembourg compromise was of some importance – but it did imply a strong sense that the fate of the European experiment was not something which could be entrusted entirely (or even primarily) to the European Commission. In Erhard's view, the member states needed to remain firmly in charge of the process, whether in the existing economic domain or, still more, in any future forays into the fields of foreign policy coordination. That the German November proposals called for political union initially to take a highly decentralised form, was thus not just an attempt to rally French support; instead it was a feature that acknowledged a growing orthodoxy amongst German leaders also.[34] The near simultaneous Italian proposals, not to mention Spaak's more cautious attempt in late September, were also primarily member state centred – although the Italian scheme, like the German, did envisage an increased role for the European Parliament.[35]

The timing of the Belgian, German and Italian proposals was also connected to the final development which needs to be reviewed in this section,
namely the Labour Party's narrow victory in the 1964 General Election
and the consequent diminution in the level of British interest in European
developments.[36] It is of course true that official Labour policy was careful
to avoid ruling out EEC membership. But the difference in emphasis and
tone between the two main British parties was certainly not lost on continental observers.[37] It was also the case that many pro-Europeans viewed
Britain's apparent turn away from the continent as a cause for concern
rather than celebration. Nevertheless, Labour's victory did make it easier
to plan both further Community level advance and, still more, new forays
into the field of political union where one of the key obstacles had hitherto
been the Belgian, Dutch and sometimes Italian insistence that the British
participate fully. With Britain slipping ever further into self-imposed exile,
it was much less difficult for the Six to concentrate on the first and second
of their crucial choices – what to do and how to do it – without concerning
themselves unduly about the still unresolved issue of the Community's
long-term membership. To the extent that the Six would have to discuss
their links with the outside world in the future, they seemed likely to be
able to concentrate on the much less acrimonious – although not entirely
trouble-free – topic of association agreements and limited commercial
treaties, rather than contemplate full-scale membership applications.

The grounds for optimism about the EEC's future development did
therefore seem very real. The substantive agreements reached on cereal
prices and the Kennedy Round exception list appeared to confirm that the
Six had fully regained their ability to thrash out agreement, however far
apart their individual national starting points had been. The advance
moreover of both the CAP and the Community's international commercial profile only increased the manner in which the EEC became central to
the economic strategies of each participating nation and vital for important constituencies – farmers and industrialists – within each. The costs
associated with any slowdown, let alone reversal, of the integration
process became correspondingly higher. The renewed talk of political
union and the successful negotiation of the fusion treaty meanwhile suggested that progress – however painstaking – was also possible on the institutional level. And the membership controversy had calmed significantly,
with the ambivalent attitudes towards Europe displayed by Wilson's new
government, permitting the Six the space and the time to consolidate their
internal developments before having to discuss the prospect of enlargement. Little wonder then that the British annual review of EEC progress
stated boldly that '1964 was a good year for the EEC' and went on to
suggest '[t]he EEC's prospects for 1965 are good, and it has probably now
passed "the point of no return" '.[38]

The problems of success

The sense of optimism around Brussels in early 1965 was genuine, justifiable, and not confined to the somewhat anxiously watching British. Alongside the hopes for the future, there were however, a large number of misgivings, both about what had already been done and what might lie just around the corner. The very rapidity of previous advance indeed led to a strong sense of uncertainty; if the successes of the past meant that a total collapse of the EEC was unlikely, there was little sense that any of the individual policies were yet set in stone or that the hoped-for gains were entirely secure. The EEC could still evolve in directions contrary to some of the national hopes vested within it. The prospective returns on member state investment in the Community might fail to materialise. Furthermore, as the EEC began to move from glittering prospect to functioning reality, the question of how the rewards and costs of integration were distributed became that much more real. At the outset, all had been able to dream. By the mid-1960s some of the actual outcomes were beginning to become apparent and not all member states were entirely content with what they saw. The second half of this chapter must therefore review some of the evolving national attitudes towards the EEC and its advance, and explain how the combination of mounting levels of frustration and conflicting ambitions contributed to the outbreak of Community crisis in June–July 1965. Before looking at the individual national perspectives, however, it is important to begin by identifying three broader trends that also fed into the build-up of tension in early 1965 and played their part in the development of a fully-fledged Community crisis.

The first contextual development to which reference must be made is the evolving nature of international politics, both within the western bloc and between the West and its Communist rival. European integration, and the more general relationships between countries in western Europe, had never been completely insulated from the manner in which the cold war evolved.[39] The spread of détente in the mid-1960s therefore inevitably had its impact. First of all, it meant that Europe's centrality to international politics seemed further reduced. The comparatively fixed nature of the European settlement, in contrast to the still fluid cold war borders in the Third World, accentuated that relative marginalisation of Europe in world affairs which had earlier been apparent with the rise of the superpowers and disintegration of the major European empires.[40] Global attention was more often focused on the superpowers themselves or on their new loci of confrontation within the developing world, than it was on the earlier flash points of Berlin, Trieste, or Greece. While this was of course a largely positive development – from a western European point of view at least   it did lessen the ability of individual European states to play a major part in determining the course of international relations. As a result, it became ever more clear that if European countries were to regain that international prominence that they had once taken for granted, they would have to act collectively rather than individually. The political incentive not merely for economic integration, but also for the spread of cooperation into the foreign policy field, had never been greater.[41]

However, the lessening of cold war tensions with Europe also made that very process of foreign policy coordination harder by increasing the range of policy choices open to western powers contemplating their approach to international politics. At the height of the cold war, the gravity of the situation had forced a degree of foreign policy cohesion on the countries of western Europe which had at the very least made the process of integration easier and had in certain instances actively encouraged European cooperation. With East–West confrontation less acute, however, that cohesion had vanished, with different Europeans analysing the evolving cold war in divergent fashion, and devising ever more contrasting policy responses. This was as true within individual countries as it was between them. Inside Germany for instance, the early- to mid-1960s was to witness the intensification of an impassioned and painful debate about the best way of addressing the divided nature of the country – a debate which was of course to culminate in the *Ostpolitik* of Willy Brandt's government.[42] Between France and its partners, there was to erupt an ever more radical divide over the organisation of western defence and the place of the United States within the Atlantic Alliance.[43] The Gaullist challenge, however, was never solely a debate between one member of NATO and the others; it was also a dispute which had echoes within the foreign policy discussions of most western European countries. The inevitable friction between and within European governments that these differences of opinion produced could rarely be kept entirely separate from the pursuit of economic cooperation between those same governments. This was all the more true given the way that certain issues that had to be addressed as part of the integration process – ranging from detailed questions of whether there should be a Community policy on the credits available for trade with the Eastern bloc, to the much wider issue of how the EEC interacted, in GATT and elsewhere, with the United States – were inevitably intertwined with the broader questions of cold war policy and inter-alliance relationships. Disruption and dispute at the one level tended to filter through into unease at very least at the other.

The second broad trend which would prove significant at the Community level, was the gradual swing of western European politics away from the previously dominant parties of the centre-Right and towards the centre-Left. A full discussion of why this happened lies far beyond the scope of this chapter. Possible explanations extend from the gradual replacement of the postwar problems of want with those of managing affluence, to the reduction of cold war tension referred to above. The full process, moreover, would last from the early 1960s and the beginning of Italy's *apertura a sinistra* experiment through to 1969 and the formation of an SPD-led government in Germany. What matters in the context of a discussion of 1964–65, however, is that the effect this leftward shift was to make the parties of the centre-Right still governing most of the Six acutely aware of the vulnerability of their position and even more sensitive than usual to the need to provide their electorates with that economic success and stability that the public had come to expect.

This had a mixed impact upon the integration process. To the extent that Alan Milward is correct to assert that European integration was driven by the need of governments to provide their public with a degree of affluence and welfare that only international economic cooperation could deliver, such a trend should, it is true, have reinforced the desire in each of the Six to press ahead with the EEC process.[44] To a large extent this does appear to have happened. But at the same time it also made member states acutely sensitive to any losses that might result from the development of the EEC and much less likely to accept incidental damage in the name of Europe. German intransigence on cereal prices mentioned above and the German and Italian sensitivity over the level of their contributions to the EEC budget which will be returned to below, are thus all partially explicable by this weakening of the centre-Right's hold on power. That 1965 was an electoral year in the Netherlands, Belgium, Germany and France only made this phenomenon that much more marked.

The third and most specifically EEC-centred of the broad trends was the changing nature of Community diplomacy.[45] This can best be described as the death of what had earlier been described as 'the Community spirit' and its replacement by a negotiating style in which national representatives were more ruthless in their defence of national interest and more willing to use high pressure tactics within an EEC context.[46] The most blatant example of the new negotiating style was of course the manner in which the French had threatened to leave the Community were their CAP desiderata not met in both 1963 and again in 1964. Such tactics were as unsubtle as they appeared to be effective. But it was not just the French. The Germans too had not only introduced into Community vocabulary a term – 'synchronisation' – that seemed to epitomise the new approach, but had also demonstrated a certain ruthless disregard of their partners' sensitivities in the course of the lengthy cereal price battle. And where the larger countries led, the others were showing strong signs of following.

Early in 1964 the Commission had grown sufficiently worried by this proliferation of hard-hitting diplomatic practice, for Hallstein to write to several government figures expressing his belief that 'the practice of attaching conditions to the implementation of tasks foreseen by the Treaty is contrary to this last and should be abandoned.'[47] He wrote in vain, however. Twelve months later, as the cereal price negotiations reached their climatic stage, a senior Eurocrat told *Le Monde* of the regrettable change that had come over Community diplomacy.

When one has followed the workings of European negotiations since 1958, one notes that it is by means of the 'pincer' movements as practiced by bewhiskered generals that Europe has advanced. On any given problem, three or four, sometimes five countries, have always ended up surrounding the one or two in the minority and obliged them to give way. But the coalitions were never identical: it was indeed inconceivable that one member state constantly won and never lost. And it was hence the memory of a gain already obtained or the hope of a future victory that on each occasion allowed the minority state to give way and accept the solution favoured by the majority: it knew that one day it would among the latter, and that the rules of the game were based on fair play.

This film of deliberate trust, of good faith, covered all issues, even the most contested, and allowed the Six to swallow them, each in turn, without pulling too much of a face. Over the last five years General de Gaulle has scoured this away. He has made this coating disappear, exposing nakedly the national interests, the shifting views, the doubts. He has rubbed Europe with an emery-board, and this is perhaps the most damaging blow that he has delivered. Negotiations are now no longer anything more than what they are: the brutal collision of conflicting material interests on a given problem, without future prospects, without a long-term aim in sight. Everyone is afraid of being the loser today, since no one has confidence in their partner tomorrow.[48]

Whether the General was entirely to blame was perhaps open to debate. What was clear, however, was that something in the manner of doing business had altered, which while not necessarily condemning the Community to stagnation – 15 days after this comment was printed the cereal price deal had been struck – did ensure that EEC diplomacy was that much more hard-fought and wounding than it had been in the past.[49] The outbreak of the empty chair crisis had much to do with the accumulation of wounds in the previous two to three years.

Grain, *grandeur* and growing unease

Had contemporary observers been asked to identify the EEC member state with the most troubled and problematic approach to European integration in the mid-1960s, most would have turned without hesitation and pointed towards France. Under de Gaulle's leadership, the French gave the impression of having become the malcontents of Europe – the country which felt most uneasy and uncertain about the extent to which it belonged within the European Community as constituted. An Italian cartoon of 1964 captured the feeling well, portraying the EEC as an elegant sailing boat, advancing at speed over a choppy sea, bedecked with national flags. As an observer on the quay with a telescope was shown commenting, however, 'the French flag? It keeps disappearing and reappearing ...'[50] *La construction européenne* might have been a process that the French prided themselves with having started, but there was seemingly little certainty in 1964–65 surrounding France's allegiance to that construction in its Community format at least. To his many critics, both within France and abroad, the General seemed intent upon either destroying, or at very least subverting, the European structures that his IV Republic predecessors had helped to create.

Paradoxically, however, Gaullist France was actually doing extremely well from its European involvement. France, it should be recalled, had been the most hesitant of the prospective EEC partners about the tariff liberalisation timetable foreseen in the Treaty of Rome. It had been largely to assuage Paris's concerns that the Treaty text included a large number of escape clauses, permitting member states to suspend or even reverse the liberalisation process should serious economic disturbance occur.[51] And yet in the event, the French economy had flourished under the EEC liberalisation regime, French exports to its Community partners growing faster than any other EEC member bar Italy (see Table 2.1).

Industrially, France had no incentive to rock the Community boat. Nor had the French agricultural sector paid the price of industrial success. On the contrary, the CAP as it existed, and as it seemed likely to evolve, was highly advantageous for France, contributing significantly to the resolution of the serious social and economic woes that had affected the sector in the early 1960s. France had seen its overall agricultural exports rise significantly since the CAP had begun operation in 1962, with the German market in particular representing a crucial outlet for French produce.

Table 2.1 Index of export growth to the rest of the EEC, 1957–69

1957 = 100	Bel/Lux	NL	Germany	France	Italy
1957	100	100	100	100	100
1958	94	104	96	89	96
1959	104	124	109	120	126
1960	127	163	122	149	208
1961	143	149	160	190	208
1962	169	165	180	213	258
1963	202	206	217	243	284
1964	241	251	236	274	357
1965	270	277	252	323	455
1966	294	291	292	362	514
1967	303	311	320	369	531
1968	359	372	373	428	643
1969	465	465	462	558	785

Source: Author's calculations based upon OECD, *Foreign Trade Statistical Bulletins, Series A, By Countries*, Paris: OECD, multiple years.

Table 2.2 Food and livestock exports to EEC partners, 1961–69

US$ millions	Bel/Lux	Netherlands	Germany	France	Italy
1961	117.3	564.2	72.9	291.4	266.1
1962	155.7	620	76.6	281.2	327.2
1963	203.4	695.9	94.7	391	299.1
1964	210.2	783.6	116.4	468.6	326.4
1965	276.9	935.9	143.6	604.5	433.6
1966	290.4	928.3	152	731.4	431.9
1967	372.9	1016.9	251.9	786.8	422.4
1968	466.7	1242.2	336.4	1008	413.7
1969	611.3	1490.8	451.4	1460.6	497.4

Source: OECD, *Statistical Bulletins, Series C, Trade by Commodities*, Paris: OECD, multiple years.

Already by 1965, the French were well on their way to overhauling the Dutch as the principal agricultural suppliers of their Community partners (see Table 2.2). Again, the French had every economic incentive to preserve what they had, and if possible push ahead with an integration process that was contributing significantly to the V Republic's economic success.

This success, moreover, was not even costing the French state much in terms of contributions to the EEC budget. The centrality of the CAP to Community expenditure in the mid-1960s and the way in which the first products to be covered by the policy were those – cereals, meat and dairy produce – most often produced by French farmers rather than their Mediterranean counterparts, meant that they, together with the Dutch, received the lion's share of CAP subsidies. With national contributions to the agricultural fund (FEOGA) tied to agricultural import levels meanwhile, the French, who were the most agriculturally self-sufficient member state, also paid in comparatively little. As a result, France was a major net beneficiary from the EEC budget in general and of the CAP in particular (see Table 2.3). Economically the whole Community experiment could scarcely work better for the French.

French negotiators had also fared well in Brussels. Whether the task in hand was the promotion of those aspects of the EEC that France did favour – the CAP most obviously, but also certain aspects of tariff policy and the association regime with (former French) Africa – or the prevention of developments not in line with Paris's priorities – Community enlargement or the increase in powers of the European Parliament – France had proved itself an extremely effective player of the Brussels game.[52] Its representatives at ministerial and at official level had become the most feared and respected operators within the EEC system, and its method of coordinating European policy was widely regarded as the most effective amongst the Community's founding members. Only in the field

Table 2.3 FEOGA contributions/payouts in 1964–65 (1 UC = 1 DM)

Member state	Contribution to FEOGA (Units of Account)	Receipt from FEOGA (UC)	Net contribution (UC)
Germany	28638413	5337600	23300813
Belgium	8285179	1184000	7101179
France	23772169	73208400	–49436231
Italy	27371400	3126600	24244800
Luxembourg	217869	9400	208469
Netherlands	9469970	14889000	–5419030
Total	97755000	97755000	

Source: ECHA, BAC 7/1973 No. 38, Commission de Contrôle, Rapport relatif aux comptes de l'exercise 1967.

of political union had it suffered a major setback with the 1962 collapse of the Fouchet Plan – and even this failure need not necessarily have been regarded as definitive once the late 1964 flurry of political proposals discussed above is taken into account. France in some ways ought to have been the most contented member state and not the least.

French unease centred, however, on how the Community agenda might evolve and how the system itself would operate in the future – the first and the second questions examined by this book. Regarding the focus of EEC activity, the French difficulty was that it feared that its partners might yet try to reclaim much of the ground they had given away, thereby denying France the prizes that were all but within its grasp. The CAP was felt to be particularly vulnerable. The danger seemingly came from two sources, the first of which was Germany. Bonn, as seen from Paris, had never been particularly enamoured of the way in which 'Green Europe' was evolving; the October 1963 attack on the progress of the CAP described in Chapter 1 had not been an isolated event, but instead part of a recurrent pattern. Also viewed with concern in Paris had been German recalcitrance during the first round of financial regulation negotiations in December 1961–January 1962, the excessively anglophile stance adopted during the 1961–63 enlargement negotiations, and the tactics Bonn had employed in 1964 in its attempts to delay the agreement on cereal prices.[53] Equally revealing had been the low priority accorded to CAP advance in the action plan of April 1963 and the German wish-list outlined in February 1964.[54] There was therefore every reason for Paris to believe that despite French successes so far, Germany would seek to renew its campaign to mutilate the Community's most expensive policy.

Germany's capacity to do so might be increased by potential cooperation with those whom the French saw as the other main enemies of the CAP – the Anglo-Saxon powers. British membership with all that it might have entailed for the CAP had admittedly been temporarily rebuffed, but the new nightmare scenario for the French was of Bonn teaming up with the Americans in order to use the Kennedy Round to undermine the CAP. The latest GATT negotiations were to make agriculture a much more central concern than in previous rounds, and it was widely known that the Americans hoped thereby to prise open the increasingly protected European market. German loyalty in any clash with the Americans over European agricultural liberalisation was not something which the French were willing to take for granted.[55] On the contrary, all other aspects of German behaviour – whether in the field of economics or security issues – seemed to indicate a degree of closeness (if not subservience) to Washington which might prove fatal to the CAP.[56] The negative way in which France reacted to the news that Erhard and Johnson had discussed agriculture in the aftermath of the December 1963 agreement is symptomatic of this unease.[57] Still more revealing were de Gaulle's reported comments to his spokesman in July 1964: '[The agricultural question] has not been sorted out because the Germans are not committed. They are having second thoughts, about the Danes, the British, the Kennedy negotiations. They are postponing the completion of the Common Market so that the Americans can swamp Europe with their agricultural produce.'[58]

Paris's negotiating achievements to date only increased French nervousness about what the future might hold. For a start, the French knew that some of their partners (not to mention outside observers) resented past French 'victories'. More importantly, Paris was well aware that the agricultural policy, although already functioning to France's advantage, was not yet complete. The December 1964 cereal price agreement in particular, while important in its own right, would not bear full fruit unless and until the French won definitive EEC agreement on the financing of the CAP. The comparatively high level of price set in December – entailing as it did a significant increase in the price French farmers would receive for their produce – was likely to provoke a surge in French production. This would almost certainly lead to substantial surpluses of cereals within France. In the absence of a fully-functioning financial regulation, stipulating that the costs of such surpluses would be covered by the Community budget and fixing member state contributions to this budget, the burden of supporting over-producing French farmers could yet fall upon the French state.[59] As a result, a definitive agreement on CAP finance – a French objective ever since the CAP discussions had begun – had become even more urgent in the light of the cereal price deal.[60] Nor did Paris have much sympathy for German complaints about the excessive cost of the CAP. Bonn had been repeatedly warned during the 1962–64 debate about the level of common cereal prices that the inevitable result of a high European price would be rising European production and hence ever greater support costs. The German government had nevertheless persisted in its dogged campaign to secure as high a cereal price as possible. It was therefore time for Bonn to pay the price of its earlier political choice.

The French thus entered 1965 determined to complement their cereal price triumph with rapid agreement on what de Gaulle described as the 'key-stone' of the whole European agricultural system – the financial regulation.[61] Past French successes also left Paris with few doubts about the wisdom of its negotiating tactics. In 1963 and 1964 the French had threatened Bonn and won; given the stakes they believed themselves to be playing for in 1965, it was unlikely that they would adopt a much more conciliatory approach.[62]

The second source of French discomfort was the mismatch between the way in which the Community was organised and General de Gaulle's publicly pronounced beliefs about supranationality. As was explained in the introduction, this divergence had long existed and had not prevented the French from playing the Brussels game under Community rules and doing extremely well. There were even occasions when the French had actively supported supranational arrangements so as to consolidate the gains they had made over the CAP.[63] And most of the key marathon negotiations had been characterised by a highly productive alliance between the French and the European Commission.[64] By the mid-1960s, however, there were signs that the French President at least was growing somewhat frustrated by the enduring federalist ambitions of the European Commission in particular. His public outbursts on the subject had grown more frequent.[65] His private mutterings, meanwhile, especially those directed at the pretensions of Hallstein as Commission President, were even more acerbic.[66] And French representatives in Brussels appeared to have been given instructions to follow up the President's words with actions – from the beginning of 1965 onwards there appeared to be a low-level guerrilla war in progress between France and the Commission on the Brussels institution's rights and prerogatives.[67] It is true, admittedly, that de Gaulle's ministers seemed consistently to advise the General not to move too radically against the EEC structures.[68] But whether their caution could be relied upon to restrain their leader was questionable. There was thus always the possibility that de Gaulle might be tempted to escalate his campaign against supranationality and seek a radical restructuring of the arrangements set out in the Treaty of Rome.

France was therefore not ready to bask in its comparative success at a Community level. It had done well out of the EEC so far, but it was neither content with its achievements to date, nor entirely certain that its partners would permit it to go on gaining so much. It therefore approached the 1965 round of negotiations with a strange mixture of anxiety, determination, and confidence that a reapplication of those tactics which had served it so well in the past would deliver the key prize of the financial regulation.[69] Whether it also sought to open a second front on the institutional development of the Community – and in particular attempted to block the introduction of majority voting in the Council due in January 1966 – was open to question.[70] The advice of the Quai d'Orsay seemed to be that there was no need: majority voting, a senior official predicted, would alter little in the way in which the EEC functioned in practice.[71] De Gaulle's readiness to accept such reassurance remained, however, to be seen.

Germany and the fear of de Gaulle

Germany's Community priorities were rather different. The Federal Republic's basic political commitment to European integration – discussed in Chapter 1 – had not altered. Nor had there been any change in Germany's economic desire to see commercial liberalisation pushed forward amongst the Six, across the rest of western Europe, and indeed on a global scale through GATT.[72] Bonn's commitment to Community enlargement had survived Britain's temporary loss of enthusiasm for EEC membership; for so long as London ruled out a second application, the Germans were content to press for a stepping-up of contacts with Britain through the WEU, a search for better overall relationship between the Community and EFTA, and a speedy and positive response to the Austrian request for association with the EEC.[73] But with Erhard's replacement of Adenauer in the autumn of 1963 and the somewhat fraught confrontation between Germany and its partners over cereal prices during most of 1964, three important changes had occurred in the Federal Republic's attitude.

The first, already mentioned above, was Erhard's determination to see some progress towards political union. Adenauer of course had also been favourable towards the idea and had responded positively to de Gaulle's 1960 and 1961 proposals.[74] Where Erhard broke new ground, however, was in his clear rejection of a purely Franco-German route to this end – the Elysée treaty was useful, but merely as a coordinating tool for wider European goals rather than as a political axis in the making – and in his readiness actively to initiate political union discussions rather than waiting for others to make the running. The November 1964 German proposals confirmed that the new activism of April 1963 had not been a one-off occurrence, but was instead representative of a much more generalised willingness to use the Community framework to seek out German goals. This activism, however, only increased Germany's need to gain some sort of reward for its initiative. Whereas in 1962 the Germans had been disappointed but passive spectators as the Fouchet plan ran aground, in 1964–65 their own prestige was much more tied up with the fortunes of political union. Success would enable the Chancellor to step out of the foreign policy shadow of his predecessor and silence those in the CDU, including Adenauer himself, who decried the deterioration in Franco-German relations that had occurred since 1963.[75] Failure by contrast would be a blow both to the Chancellor's self-esteem and to his standing in his party. Bonn thus entered 1965 keen to see real progress made towards effective foreign policy coordination amongst the Six.[76]

The second change was Erhard's sensitivity to public and parliamentary criticism of his European policy. Here too, part of the difficulty sprang from Adenauer's towering reputation – not to mention the former Chancellor's ability to go on making mischief for his successor from the position he retained as President of the CDU. Erhard was acutely aware of the need to achieve something significant at a Community level so as to be able to establish a strong independent reputation in the foreign policy field.[77] But, ironically for the father of the German *Wirtschaftswünder*, it also sprang from a degree of imbalance in the rapid growth of the German economy, with signs that inflation was growing and that country's export surplus was becoming too large. This meant that the Federal Republic needed to control its Community expenditure, increase its ability to bring in exports from outside the EEC, and advance towards a more coordinated approach to macro-economic policy within Europe.[78] There was also a greater threat than ever posed by the European alternatives offered by the SPD. Under Brandt, the German opposition party no longer espoused a radically different European line, critical of the Treaty of Rome and of the integration process, but instead promised a more successful rendition of the same *communautaire* theme.[79] Erhard thus had to look over his shoulder at opposition criticism of his European policy in a way that Adenauer had seldom had to do. With elections due in 1965, the CDU government could no longer remain confident that foreign policy was an area where its reputation would win large numbers of votes from the SPD. All of this meant that the new, more active, German stance in Brussels had to begin delivering tangible results.

The third change in German European policy-making was the way in which the temporary surge in mistrust of de Gaulle which had followed the crisis of January 1963 had been replaced with a deep-seated dissatisfaction with, and suspicion of, French Community diplomacy. Mistrust began at the top, where Erhard's relationship with de Gaulle fell far short of the closeness between Adenauer and the General.[80] The July 1964 meeting was a particular nadir, the two men lecturing each other at length, but failing totally to find common ground on any of the multiple subjects discussed.[81] De Gaulle also delivered a painful snub to his counterpart, pointedly spending more time than expected in his pre-summit meeting with the former Chancellor and therefore arriving late for the start of the official Franco-German encounter.[82] Schröder's relationship with Couve de Murville was also difficult, the two men reportedly going through phases when they were not on speaking terms with one another.[83] But the mutual suspicion spread into German officialdom as well, with de Gaulle's actions, whether in the EEC context, or on the broader issue of Europe's relationship with the US, being viewed with an extremely jaundiced eye. France was seen as being on collision course with the United States and determined to do all that it could to oblige the Federal Republic into making the painful choice between its links with Washington and Franco-German rapprochement.[84] This was something that Bonn wanted at all costs to avoid.

Against this backdrop, the events of early 1965 were very damaging indeed. The Germans believed themselves to have made a major sacrifice in having agreed to cereal prices on 15 December.[85] They had played what Schröder had tellingly referred to as their greatest trump card, and now expected to win something in return.[86] This expectation had only increased in January when the Rambouillet summit between Erhard and de Gaulle had gone unexpectedly well. France had given the strong impression that it was prepared to repay Germany's agricultural sacrifices by looking sympathetically at the 4 November, 1964 proposals, including political union.[87] Hopes had risen still further when the Italians – who shared Germany's desire for political advance – issued an invitation for the foreign ministers of the Six to gather in Venice for a meeting to discuss the various plans and to pave the way for a summit meeting later in the year. But in March, Couve de Murville had crushed German and Italian hopes, announcing that France would not participate in the Venice meeting since there was no real prospect of advance.[88] When pressed, the French relented somewhat and conceded that talks on political union were not necessarily futile. But progress would only be possible *after* an agreement had been reached on the CAP financial regulation.[89] What Bonn had expected as a reward for concessions already made, was now being held up as the possible result of future generosity towards France.[90]

Alongside this political union disappointment, Bonn also had to endure a series of French moves on East–West affairs, on the German question, and on the US's role in the world monetary system, all of which seemed designed to demonstrate the foreign policy divide between the French and the Germans.[91] It was therefore unsurprising that the pre-existing suspicions of de Gaulle amongst the German leadership soared to unprecedented heights. France, it seemed, was intent on behaving in a totally selfish fashion and would not hesitate to impose its unilateral priorities on the Community unless Germany could bar its path and force the French to allow others to pursue their Community objectives as well. Its best opportunity to try to do so were the forthcoming negotiations on the financial regulation, the one outstanding component of the CAP system. By early May, German officials had thus resolved to challenge France over the issue. As a report to the Chancellor explained:

> In yesterday's meeting of the State Secretaries' Committee, there was agreement that the finalization of the definitive financial regulation is the last major chance to compel France to support genuine progress in integration. This means above all the completion of the customs union, the elimination of fiscal borders – especially indirect tax borders – by 1.1.1970, the establishment of a common commercial policy, the strengthening of the position of the European Parliament,

and greater integration in the foreign policy field. The decision over the definitive financial regulation, and those on the remaining common agricultural prices, should under all circumstances be used to attain visible progress in the general area of integration. Were this opportunity to be missed, the Community's functions would be limited, on the basis of French aspirations, to a guaranteed market for French agricultural surpluses and a protectionist preferential zone. Such an outcome would be considered by German public opinion as a failure of the whole integration policy.[92]

Germany therefore entered the complex Brussels negotiations over the financial regulation with a determination to hold its line comparable to that earlier shown over cereal prices, but this time compounded by a sense that it alone could prevent de Gaulle from undermining the whole Community experiment. The stakes could scarcely have been higher.

Germany and France had been on collision course before and the Community had averted crisis. Central though this Franco-German disagreement would prove to be in the explanation of why the empty chair crisis occurred, a full analysis of what went wrong in May–June 1965 also requires the positions of three other players to be analysed: the Italians, the Dutch and the European Commission. For without the unexpected coalition of three member states determined to thwart French aspirations, and the miscalculation of the European Commission in providing the issue over which a dispute could occur, Bonn and Paris might still have been able amicably to resolve their differences. It is hence to these three further actors that this chapter must now turn.

A new Italian approach

For the Italians, a mixture of political and economic considerations seem to have lain behind their new, more muscular approach, to the Brussels negotiations. Italy had traditionally acted as one of the most important mediators amongst the Six. Although able at times to pursue its national interest with vigour, it had on many previous occasions decided that the advance of European unity outweighed too determined a defence of narrow sectoral interests. It had also decided that its best chance of influencing the outcome of Community negotiations had not necessarily been the forthright exposition of Rome's desiderata, but instead the timely intervention designed to nudge discussions towards a conclusion in line with the EEC and Italy's broader interest. It had thus shown itself to be remarkably skilful as an architect of compromise within the Community, advancing forms of words and mediating formulas, designed to bridge the gap between the poles of debate within the Council of Ministers. Such an approach had been of undoubted value in multiple previous Council negotiations and of great utility in the divisive enlargement negotiations of

1961–63.[93] The most consistent exponents of this brand of Italian diplomacy at a Community level had been Emilio Colombo – holder of various
ministerial portfolios between 1960 and 1964 – and Attilio Cattani, the
head of the Farnesina. It was therefore of some significance that in the
spring of 1965, Italy approached the financial regulation negotiations
without the involvement of either of these men. Colombo's place as the
chief ministerial negotiator was taken by the new Italian foreign minister –
and more senior rival of Colombo within the Christian Democrat party –
Amintore Fanfani, while Cattani had been forced into early retirement.[94]
A change of tone in Italian diplomacy was thus always likely. Furthermore, Fanfani clearly felt that there might be significant party political –
and perhaps foreign policy – advantages to be gained from adopting a firm
anti-Gaullist line.[95] As explained in the previous chapter, anti-Gaullism
was a useful rallying point for those political elements in Italy most
favourable towards the centre-Left experiment. Given Fanfani's personal
association with, and commitment to, the *centro sinistra* process, this too
was likely to weigh heavily in his calculations as he approached the Brussels talks. The key Italian negotiator thus had every reason to strike a very
different note in the forthcoming discussions from the soothing tones
typical of Colombo or Cattani.

Alongside such personality-centred and party political considerations,
however, there was also a very firm economic background for the harder
line Italian stance. Italy had generally done well out of the economic liberalisation brought about by the Treaty of Rome: since 1958 exports had
surged, contributing significantly to the Italian economic miracle of the
late 1950s and early 1960s (see Table 2.1 above). But the one dark cloud
had been the difficulties experienced by Italian agriculture. A greater per-
centage of the Italian population continued to work the land than that of
any other Community member state.[96] Despite the numbers of farmers
concerned, however, the Italians had not done well out of the early CAP.[97]
Much of Italian production was of commodities not covered by the early
agricultural regulations: CAP rules for olive oil, rice and wine were all
much delayed, and horticulture had initially been treated in a fashion
highly unsuitable for Italian would-be exporters. As a result, Italy had
not experienced the surge in farm exports enjoyed by the French (see
Table 2.4).

To make matters worse, one of the unexpected results of the country's
greater prosperity was that Italians had taken to consuming significantly
more meat, much of it imported from outside of the Community. Europe's
most agricultural country had in other words become a major net importer
of food (see Table 2.5). Under CAP finance rules, such third country
imports were heavily penalised, resulting in the perverse situation that by
1965 Italy, still at this point the poorest member state, had become the
largest net contributor to the Community's agricultural fund (see Table 2.2
above). Far from a source of income useful for modernising Italian agricul-

Table 2.4 Growth of food and livestock exports to EEC partners, 1961–69

1961 = 100	Bel/Lux	NL	Germany	France	Italy
1961	100	100	100	100	100
1962	133	110	105	96	112
1963	173	123	130	134	103
1964	179	139	160	161	112
1965	236	166	197	207	149
1966	248	165	209	251	148
1967	318	180	346	270	145
1968	398	220	462	346	142
1969	521	264	620	501	171

Source: Author's calculations based upon, OECD, *Statistical Bulletins, Series C, Trade by Commodities*, Paris: OECD, multiple years.

Table 2.5 Italy's agricultural trade balance, 1961–69

US$ millions	Exports	Imports	Balance
1961	559.8	763.5	−203.7
1962	639.4	787.3	−147.9
1963	613.8	1270.5	−656.8
1964	628.3	1304.7	−676.4
1965	765.9	1571.0	−805.1
1966	770.5	1718.6	−948.2
1967	807.3	1714.5	−907.2
1968	764.9	1859.1	−1094.1
1969	879.5	2115.3	−1235.9

Source: OECD, *Statistical Bulletins, Series C, Trade by Commodities*.

ture that some had expected, the CAP had turned out to be a major drain on Italian resources.[98] This was particularly unsatisfactory for the Italians at a time when the Italian economy was experiencing a temporary slow-down.

Italian discontent had been slow to manifest itself at a Community level. The first clear sign had been a long letter written by Aldo Moro, the Prime Minister, to Hallstein in June 1964, setting out Italy's qualms about the Commission's cereal price plans.[99] This had then been followed in November 1964 by an Italian memorandum submitted to the Council out-lining the problems with the status quo on agriculture.[100] In typically *com-munautaire* fashion, however, Italian criticisms of the CAP had been accompanied, in the same memorandum, by a declaration of Italy's readi-ness to accept the common cereal price regime.[101] The Italians were not, in other words, in open revolt quite yet. Significantly, both the French and the Germans took note, inviting Ferrari-Aggradi, the Italian minister of agriculture, to Paris and Bonn in the run-up to the final agricultural marathon.[102] Italian behaviour during the December 1964 agricultural marathon had also mixed determination with conciliation. Ferrari-Aggradi had put up a dogged fight for national interests. In particular, he had delayed the final agreement in order to obtain concessions on the price of hard wheat and maize – both of special interest to Italy – a promise of a rapid review of the horticultural regulation, and a temporary cap on Italian FEOGA contributions.[103] Despite this rearguard action, however, he had allowed a final deal to be done.[104] Rome it seemed had no immediate interest in replacing Bonn as the capital barring the way to CAP advance.[105]

Six months later, however, the Italian position was that much firmer. The Italians, like the Germans, felt strongly that France had not delivered the promised political counterpart to the 15 December accord. Furthermore, Fanfani felt personally affronted by French temporising over political union, since it had been his invitation to a meeting in Venice that the French had rejected and Couve had made public his refusal while on a visit to Rome.[106] To make matters worse, the promised review of the horticultural regulation had run into difficulties in April.[107] Finally, the Commission proposals on CAP finance did not seem to pay sufficient heed to Italian (and German) complaints about their excessive contributions. As a result, Fanfani and Ferrari-Aggradi would play a role in the May–June discussions far removed from Italy's normal mediating approach, matching Germany in open dissatisfaction with the development of the CAP, and willing to block agreement unless their concerns were met. The French in particular were to be badly wrong-footed by this dramatic change in Italian diplomacy in Brussels.[108]

Dutch democracy

The fourth key national player in the 1965 negotiations were the Dutch. The Hague's representatives were of course no strangers to forceful EEC diplomacy. The Dutch had pioneered the usage of cross-issue linkage in order to get their way on key Community negotiations – threatening to derail the planned acceleration of tariff reductions in 1961 were the principle of CAP levies not agreed by the end of 1960 – and had on numerous other occasions shown themselves to be strong-minded defenders of their national interest.[109] The Dutch were also renowned for their willingness to stand up to de Gaulle.[110] Nevertheless on CAP matters, the Netherlands' position as Europe's most efficient agricultural producer and exporter had tended to lead to a coincidence of interest between the French and the Dutch, greatly limiting the friction between the two delegations, and minimising the chances of The Hague joining forces with Bonn. Economic self-interest placed the Netherlands firmly on the side of the Commission and the French on most CAP discussions, and rendered deeply unconvincing Dutch efforts to adopt any other stance.[111] It was therefore unsurprising that Biesheuvel, the Dutch Minister of Agriculture, was much more conciliatory in his approach towards the financial regulation negotiations, both in Brussels itself and in the line he took back in The Hague, than Joseph Luns, his counterpart in the Ministry of Foreign Affairs.[112]

The Commission's March 1965 proposals, around which discussions would revolve in May and June, introduced into the finance regulation equation, however, a factor which all but ensured that the Dutch would not find themselves on the same side of the argument as the French, namely the role of the European Parliament. This had long been a matter of great importance to the Dutch. In the context of the fusion discussions mentioned above, it had been The Hague which had fought hardest to overcome French obstinacy on the issue. Dutch negotiators had even, at one point, threatened to block the whole fusion process were not some increase in Parliamentary powers agreed, despite the fact that the merger between the three Communities had originally been suggested by the Dutch.[113] In the event, they had backed away from this threat, contenting themselves with the thought that the question of the European Parliament's powers would surely be raised again. But once it was – this time by the Commission's finance regulation proposals – a further climb-down on the issue was all but unthinkable.[114] Neither the Dutch Parliament – a potent force on European policy at most times, but one which was particularly hard to ignore in the immediate aftermath of the lengthy two month negotiations which had preceded the formation of the latest Dutch government in April 1965 – nor the Dutch cabinet, were likely to forgive a negotiator who returned from Brussels empty-handed on this most symbolic of controversies.[115] New Franco-Dutch confrontation over Strasbourg's influence was all but guaranteed.[116]

Hallstein's gamble

The trigger for the confrontation between France, Germany, Italy and the Netherlands was of course the Commission's proposals for a financial regulation, submitted to the Council on 31 March. Traditional accounts of the crisis, indeed, have tended to portray the breakdown of 30 June, 1965 and its aftermath as a personal duel between de Gaulle and Hallstein – a duel that the French President is normally considered to have won.[117] By stressing the build-up of member state resentments and animosities and the way in which these contributed to the impasse this book has deliberately taken a very different line. But it is undoubtedly the case that the timing, content, and presentation of the Commission's financial regulation proposals contributed significantly to the way in which the crisis broke out, as did the manner in which the Commission chose to negotiate between April and June. No review of the principal players would therefore be complete without a section looking at Commission motivations in the spring of 1965.[118]

The financial regulations proposals were made up of three main elements.[119] The first covered the financing of the CAP and stipulated that from 1 July, 1967 full Community financing of the agricultural policy should come into force. It also, however, introduced a system of dividing the expenditure between the member states that was not based upon import levels – the system planned for the period after 1970 and a principle the French were very attached to – but instead used a fixed key. French and German contributions would thus be set at the same level for both years prior to 1967, with Italian contributions kept to below the ceiling set on 15 December. The second aspect of the proposals covered so-called 'own resources' – in other words the rules under which the money collected by the levy system would go directly into the Community budget rather than remaining with the importing member states. Radically, this part of the Commission proposal foresaw not just levy income but also the revenue from all industrial customs duties being allocated to the EEC from 1967 onwards. And the third part of the proposal suggested an amendment of the Treaty of Rome, increasing the budgetary control powers of the European Parliament and modifying the voting rules in the Council of Ministers so as to make it harder for member states to overturn budgetary alterations agreed by the Parliament and the Commission. Under the new system envisaged by the Commission, changes to the budget adopted by the Assembly and approved of by the Commission could only be rejected by the Council were five of the Six to vote against.

The three parts of the Commission proposal fitted together logically enough. Balancing the income derived from agricultural levies with other customs duties would avoid a situation in which agricultural importers paid almost exclusively for the Community, and there was also some sense in the way in which Parliamentary scrutiny at a European level would be increased to compensate for the way in which national parliaments would lose oversight powers once resources were transferred directly to the EEC.[120] It was also the case that, in the best traditions of Community 'package deals', the proposal contained something for everyone. The French would benefit from the completion of the CAP three years ahead of schedule; the Germans and the Italians would have the satisfaction of seeing a degree of redress provided for the financial imbalances of the early agricultural policy; and the Dutch would succeed in their long-standing campaign for greater European Parliamentary powers. But there was no denying that the ambitious proposals also represented a major gamble, and one which, if successful, would significantly strengthen Commission as well as European Parliamentary powers. A full implementation of the Commission's vision – especially when combined with the imminent introduction of majority voting – would have pushed the EEC significantly in the direction of a fully-fledged federation.

The proposals sprang from a combination of self-confidence and anxiety. The former is perhaps the most obvious: the belief that member states might agree to so radical a set of measures – and such an acceleration of the Treaty timetable – reflected the success of previous bold Commission initiatives, most recently the Mansholt Plan, and the good track-record of the Commission in brokering last minute deals in the Council. The initial request by the Commission President that Mansholt allow him to be personally involved in the preparation of the financial regulation proposal was, after all, made in the immediate aftermath of the 15 December deal.[121] It was probably also no coincidence that just days before the controversial text of the proposal was finalised within the Commission, Hallstein delivered a speech in London in which he boasted that 'all of the Commission's proposals to date – with a single unimportant exception – have been approved by the Council'. This he attributed to the Commission's expertise and its political skill in devising package deals acceptable to all the EEC members.[122]

Similar hubris is evident in the way in which a set of measures already bound to provoke serious controversy within the Council was allowed to become weighed down by additional provisions tacked on at the last minute. Jean Rey, the Commissioner responsible for external relations, was for instance permitted to add a clause to the draft requiring that Community approval be sought for all agricultural deals between EEC members and Eastern bloc regimes.[123] This was a response to a recent controversial agreement that the French had negotiated to sell substantial quantities of grain to the People's Republic of China – a state which several of the Six did not recognise diplomatically – but as such was bound to act as a red rag to the French bull. To make matters worse, it was also a provision that was likely to please the United States.[124] It could hence only reinforce French suspicions of the Commission's unduly close ties to Washington. Likewise, Hallstein's over-confidence (and ideological rigidity) partially explains why he chose to take the additional risk of presenting the proposals to the European Parliament *before* they were officially sent to the Council of Ministers, a significant alteration in Community protocol and another step which France more than any other member state was bound to resent.[125]

Just as important a source as this vein of over-confidence, however, was the European Commission's equally striking self-doubt. The timing of the proposal is the first clue in this respect. The fact that the Commission chose to use this piece of legislation as the vehicle for its evident ambitions reflected the fact it largely shared the German anxiety cited above that once de Gaulle had acquired a functioning CAP – and had won the elections scheduled for the autumn of 1965 – there would be no means of controlling French behaviour within the EEC.[126] The package thus reflected fear of France, as much as it did confidence vis-à-vis France. Likewise, the bid for 'own resources' reflected the multiple financial frustrations the Commission had encountered to date. The Brussels body had long complained about the inadequacy of the funds that the member states were prepared to allocate to cover its expenditure and its personnel and had sought to escape from this financial straitjacket; in July 1964, for instance, Hallstein had unsuccessfully suggested a major revision of the Community's budgetary procedure.[127] The categorical rejection of this request only increased the urgency of finding some other means of loosening the Commission's budgetary bonds. The acquisition of a substantial body of automatic EEC receipts would do so in definitive fashion. And even the early presentation of the proposals to the European Parliament may have reflected a naïve hope that a tidal wave of pro-European sentiment would help sweep the draft legislation past the inevitable member state objections.[128] Commission vulnerability was thus as important a factor behind Hallstein's unsuccessful gamble, as was over-confidence and a belief in the inevitability of Europe's progression towards a federal arrangement.

The Council breakdown

The combination of Commission audacity and the constellation of member state sentiment analysed above, was to prove disastrous for the EEC. There was nothing fundamentally different between the substance of the financial regulation discussions, and previous, tense, Community negotiations. Complex deals had been struck before, involving sensitive financial issues and important elements of national prestige. But never before had the Community encountered a situation in which so many national delegations had decided independently that the outcome of a particular negotiation was a vital issue of national interest and something on which compromise and concession might undermine the very bases of the integration process.

Nor had the EEC gone into a tense agricultural marathon with so many of its normal sources of mediation and compromise trapped by the partisan sentiments involved and therefore unable to play their usual facilitating role. The Council Presidency, normally one source of compromise, was held by the French who were clearly parti pris. The Italians, another usual mediator, had temporarily decided that rigidity rather than diplomatic finesse was the best way forward. And the Commission, so often the purveyor of last minute package deals, had taken a gamble and was determined to see how the game worked out rather than alter the cards it had placed on the table. Only the Belgians therefore remained in a position to craft bridging agreements, and even they were severely handicapped by a domestic political crisis which meant that they were without a government and therefore constitutionally debarred from entering into any commitment that might involve new financial expenditure. Belgian representatives were thus notable by their silence throughout the financial regulation talks, although Paul-Henri Spaak, the experienced foreign minister, did make an impassioned last minute intervention on the night of 30 June once he realised, too late, that his colleagues were heading for a potentially disastrous breakdown.[129]

The defining characteristic of the final weeks of negotiation was the divide between the French, who used their position as the Presidency to insist that agreement had to be reached, but only on the financial regulation narrowly defined and not on the accompanying measures sought by the Commission, and the Germans, Italians, and Dutch who tried to avert any such separation from occurring.[130] This is sometimes erroneously taken to imply that the Five were fully supportive of the Commission's ambitious proposals – something which it had been clear as early as May when COREPER had held a detailed discussion of the proposals was definitely not the case.[131] But Bonn, Rome, and The Hague were all extremely aware that to let France get away by the 30 June deadline with an agreement setting in place the financial regime without any quid pro quo, would probably be to abandon all hope of ever obtaining concessions from the French. Thus they decided tactically to cling to the indivisibility of the Commission's proposals, confident that come what may, France would not be able to accept some of the Commission's ideas. Once the 30 June deadline had passed, there could then be a much more general reckoning in which France's agricultural desiderata would be flanked by measures designed to make the funding system more equitable, to match agricultural advance with parallel movement on industrial liberalisation, and to introduce some measure of institutional reform. It was therefore suggested, by the Italians and Germans in particular but also by the Dutch, that the Six should seek only to agree a short-term bridging measure covering the financing of the agricultural policy for one or two years at most, thereby removing all urgency from the discussion.[132]

France did all it could to thwart this German, Italian, and Dutch ambition.[133] In mid-June, the French abandoned their initial hopes of establishing the CAP fully by July 1967, claiming that by so doing they made redundant the Commission's more ambitious ideas.[134] The bilateral Franco-German consultation mechanisms put in place by the Elysée treaty were also used to try to dispel any German impression that France owed its neighbour a debt for the cereal price accord and to forge consensus on the flaws in the Commission's proposals.[135] On 22 June the last in a series of meetings between Lahr and Olivier Wormser, a senior Quai negotiator, almost appeared to have bridged the gap, only for it to become apparent that both sides were guilty of hearing what they wanted to hear rather than what was actually said.[136] And on the night of 30 June, Valéry Giscard d'Estaing, the French Minister of Finance, descended on Brussels to unveil a package of financial measures specifically designed to buy off the Italians.[137] Such signals of French flexibility were meanwhile accompanied by an ever clearer chorus of threats about the dire consequences that might ensue should the Community not meet the 30 June deadline. Couve de Murville in particular defied all conventions about the impartiality of the Council chair in order to issue repeated warnings about the seriousness of a failure to agree.[138]

None of these tactics proved effective however. Whether spurred on by the painful memories of past Community defeats, or by the awareness that such a favourable alignment of forces against France was unlikely to recur, the Germans, Italians and Dutch held firm, ignoring both French blandishments and bluster. Fanfani, for instance, spoke dismissively of the financial regulation deadline, commenting during the night of 30 June itself that the date was 'not the year one thousand.'[139] The Commission meanwhile stood equally solidly behind its proposals, taking no steps to prepare a less comprehensive regulation in order to break the Council impasse. The late night meeting therefore drew to a close with Couve de Murville ignoring multiple suggestions that the clock be fictionally stopped, thereby allowing negotiations to continue into July, and insisting instead that the consequences of the failure to agree would now have to be faced.[140] The national delegations left Brussels without having agreed to meet again, and uncertain exactly what the implications of the Council deadlock were likely to be. As the next chapter will make clear, Paris would not take long before letting their partners know that the implications were extremely serious indeed.

Whatever their responsibility for the escalation of the crisis and for the selection of the empty chair tactics which would give the episode its name, the French had not conjured a Community confrontation out of nothing in order to pursue their long-term aims. Instead, the initial breakdown of 30 June, 1965 was the result of a prolonged build-up of tension within the Community – a build-up which not only had run in parallel to the apparent successes related above, but had in part been a direct consequence of earlier Community progress. As tangible results of European integration became progressively more apparent, long latent divisions about both the EEC's agenda, and its institutional balance, came much more clearly to the fore. And it had been disagreements about the former – about what exactly the EEC should do – which had been particularly acute. This build-up of tension goes a long way towards explaining the European Commission's disastrous haste and over-ambition in submitting a set of proposals on 31 March that were almost guaranteed to provoke deep divisions amongst the member states. But more importantly, it explains the member state tactics that transformed a negotiation centred upon a set of Commission proposals that no country really supported, into an ill-tempered confrontation and a failed exercise in brinkmanship that would plunge the EEC into the most serious crisis it had yet faced.

3   A careful confrontation

July–December, 1965

Awareness of quite how serious was the rift between France and its partners spread quickly, despite the determined efforts of all but Paris to present matters in the most positive fashion possible. The morning after the Council breakdown, Hallstein held a lengthy press conference in which he tried to persuade sceptical journalists that agreement amongst the Six was still within reach and that the negotiations over the financial regulation should continue. His refusal to use the word 'crisis' however, failed to convince, not least because of the gap between his sanguine analysis of the situation and the terse comments made a few hours earlier by Couve de Murville. Where the French Foreign Minister had spoken ominously about the need to face the consequences of a serious and deliberate breach in the Community's timetable, Hallstein tried to emphasise the goodwill with which all had conducted themselves during the lengthy negotiations and to point to other situations, notably December 1961, when the Community had been able to overcome a missed deadline without untoward consequences.[1]

Quite how correct the international press had been to reject Hallstein's strained optimism would become clear over the next few days as France outlined the way in which it would respond to the Council impasse. The first part of this chapter will therefore explore Paris's decision to adopt empty chair tactics, probe France's motives in escalating the crisis and explain how quickly the French made clear that at stake were not only the issues of Community finance upon which the preceding month's negotiations had centred, but also a series of fundamental questions about the mechanisms and institutions of the EEC. In the course of the summer of 1965, in other words, the main issue of dispute between the Six was to shift from what the Community should do, to how the EEC should operate. A second section must then turn towards France's anxiously watching partners, looking both at their analysis of what had gone wrong and at the steps they took to contain the effects of the French boycott. Finally the chapter will examine the diplomatic efforts made to resolve the dispute. These included the negotiations within the Community framework designed to remove the policy disagreements that had triggered the crisis, as well as the bilateral and multilateral attempts to engage with France so as to establish what exactly its grievances were and how it might be brought back to the negotiating table without wounding either the Community itself or the national pride of any of the states involved. Taken together, the three parts of the chapter should illustrate how the empty chair crisis, while unquestionably a serious disruption to the workings and development of the Community and a tense and uncertain intergovernmental row, was also a highly restrained confrontation in which each side did their utmost to avoid an irrevocable breakdown of relations amongst the Six. In essence, the dispute was always about how Europe should best be organised rather than about whether Europe should be organised at all.

Throwing down the gauntlet

The first confirmation that France intended to act upon its earlier threats came in the afternoon of 1 July, when, after an emergency meeting of the French cabinet, Alain Peyrefitte, the government spokesmen, announced: 'the government has decided to draw the economic, political and legal consequences, [of the situation] as it sees them … No new progress is to be expected for so long as all remains in stasis. As far as the Common Market is concerned there can be no question of a new meeting in July.'[2] This was followed on 6 July by the withdrawal of France's Permanent Representative to the Community, Jean-Marc Boegner, and by a message, sent to the Secretary General of the Council of Ministers making clear that French representatives would no longer take part in most Council meetings, whether at an official or a ministerial level.[3] No indication was given about when (or whether) French representatives might return. If the Five were not prepared to respect their engagements vis-à-vis France, the French were not prepared to participate at all in the Community process.

There are indications that the tactics of boycott had been identified by the French as a possible weapon some time before. Couve de Murville, for instance, recalled suggesting such an approach to de Gaulle in May of 1965, receiving the go-ahead, and participating in the fraught June negotiations certain in the knowledge that his country had a muscular response to any failure to agree.[4] And intriguingly, Manfred Klaiber, the German Ambassador to Paris, had warned his government as early as the previous October that if pushed too hard, France might adopt empty chair tactics.[5] This would suggest that the notion had been hatched within French government circles several months at least before it was employed in July 1965. But it is equally clear from French archival sources that the full implications of a Community boycott had not been thought through. In the course of the first fortnight after the Council breakdown, there was an intensive interministerial discussion in Paris about how complete the French withdrawal should be, what legal and practical consequences might be entailed by non-participation in the Community's work, and how

France should balance its desire to manifest its anger at the way the 1 July deadline had been disregarded with the need to protect its interests in Brussels.[6]

The outcome of these deliberations was a boycott that was much less complete than appeared at first sight. Thus while Boegner had gone, Maurice Ulrich his deputy remained, thereby ensuring that the French went on being extremely well informed about all that was discussed amongst the Five in the crucial COREPER encounters and giving the French an easy and direct channel through which to communicate with the Five. Furthermore, the French chair did not remain empty for all Council meetings. At official level a significant number of French representatives did take part in those working groups designed to manage ongoing Community business rather than push the EEC forward into new fields of activity.[7] And even where a French voice was not present, Paris showed itself willing to allow some decisions to be taken by means of the EEC's written procedure. Draft decisions would hence be signed in Paris and allowed to come into force despite the fact that the French had not participated in their formulation. France had too many interests tied up in the Community system to allow the institutions of the EEC to grind to a complete halt.[8]

If this less than total implementation of the French boycott appeared to suggest a degree of moderation on the part of de Gaulle's government, a quite contrary impression was conveyed by the decision to add a clear institutional dimension to the dispute between France and its partners. This is most famously associated with the General's press conference of 9 September – the latest in the French leader's rhetorical broadsides against supranationalism and the EEC – and to a lesser extent with Couve de Murville's speech to the French National Assembly a month later. In the former, de Gaulle placed most of the responsibility for the June breakdown on the shoulders of the European Commission and made clear his desire to see a radical reform of what he termed a 'technocratic, stateless and irresponsible Areopagus'.[9] He also outlined French unhappiness at the planned extension of those Council of Ministers' decisions that could be taken by qualified majority vote after 1 January, 1966. This too he implied ought to be rethought.[10] And he made clear that while both he and his country remained committed to a Europe grounded in 'common sense and . . . reality', France was ready to continue its boycott of the EEC for an indefinite amount of time.[11] The Five, it appeared, were being told that it was their responsibility to address the issues that had now been raised before France would resume its place at the Brussels table.

This was confirmed by the French Foreign Minister who in a lengthy speech before the French parliament on 20 October again attributed the outbreak of the crisis to an insidious combination of the Commission's ambition and ineptitude, and a degree of bad faith on the part of the Five. In these circumstances, Couve explained that 'a general revision was called for': such had been the gravity of the breakdown that the crisis had gone beyond the issues of CAP finance over which it had erupted and had become a dispute that could only be settled 'on a political terrain' and in negotiations between 'responsible governments'. The list of issues that France wanted addressed was again that of the Commission's role and powers, and the functioning of Council voting in phase three of the Community's transitional period, planned to start on 1 January, 1966.[12]

In fact, however, neither the President's eagerly awaited press conference nor Couve's combative speech to the National Assembly did more than amplify a French desire for institutional reform which had been expressed bilaterally to their partners within days of the Council breakdown. On 8 July, for instance, François Seydoux, the French Ambassador to Bonn, told Schröder that the whole way in which the Community worked, and in particular the functioning of the Commission, needed to be re-examined.[13] And by late July, Lahr was correctly predicting that de Gaulle would use his September press conference to present a set of institutional demands.[14] Pompidou had also warned the Germans on 2 September that the issue of majority voting would be raised alongside that of the Commission's behaviour and power.[15] What was significant about the two public French statements was therefore firstly their hard-hitting tone – both seemed to reject entirely the whole notion of supranationality – and secondly the fact that they overtly committed the French government, in an electoral year, to obtaining their institutional desiderata before returning to Brussels.[16] A purely agricultural solution was now out of the question.

A premeditated attack?

Why had France chosen to aggravate an already serious division by raising these institutional concerns? The combination of evidence that France had considered an empty chair approach prior to 1 July, 1965 and the rapidity with which Paris escalated the confrontation into an institutional quarrel as well as one about agriculture, might seem to support those who have argued that the 30 June breakdown was nothing more than a pretext for de Gaulle to launch a premeditated assault on the Community structures.[17] The French President's claim during his press conference that 'the crisis was, sooner or later, inevitable' implied much the same.[18] But there is no need to resort to such a theory in order to explain why France chose to raise institutional questions almost as soon as the crisis had begun. The issue upon which discord had centred in June – namely the future of the CAP – was quite important enough to have caused a major dispute. Instead it makes more sense to view the failure of the June negotiations as an occurrence that the French had genuinely sought hard to avoid, but to which they had to react forcefully – in other words by using the tactics Couve had suggested to de Gaulle. Once a stand-off had started, it then brought with it an opportunity to seek redress to some long-standing Gaullist objections to the Community system.[19] This was all the more so, since several of these very grievances had been accentuated by the manner in which the June deadlock had emerged. But the institutional escalation was a consequence of a pre-existing crisis rather than vice-versa.

It is admittedly true that there had long been an institutional dimension to the tension between France and its European partners. The repeated references in previous chapters to the fusion negotiations and to the argument over the powers of the European Parliament are ample demonstration of this fact. It is also the case that the importance of these apparently rather trivial institutional wrangles sprang from the way in which they were perceived as symbolising a more fundamental clash between federal and intergovernmental visions of European cooperation. To support an increase in Strasbourg's role thus became shorthand for a belief in a federal evolution of the EEC; to oppose it, by contrast, denoted a more intergovernmental approach. But it is equally clear from an overview of the 1963 to 1965 period that none of the member states, with the possible partial exception of the Dutch, saw much point in emphasising the divisions over this issue. Most Community governments were thus content to see a few token gestures made towards institutional reform (largely designed to satisfy national parliaments), while concentrating on the more profitable and seemingly less divisive question of determining the Community's policy agenda. The French had been very much part of this consensus: indeed as was explained in Chapter 1, Paris had even been prepared in 1963 to exchange a handful of minor institutional concessions in return for a resumption of forward movement on the CAP.

France, therefore, had made the first priority of its Community policy the advance of the EEC generally and of the CAP in particular. To this end, it had employed a variety of forceful tactics, including outright threats to leave the EEC. These were given added credibility by de Gaulle's known hostility to certain facets of the Community structure. But as long as the Community continued to make tangible progress, Paris refrained from making an issue of its institutional discontents. All changed, however, when this progress came to a sudden halt in June 1965. No longer was it worthwhile de-emphasising institutional disputes in the name of CAP and other policy rewards. Instead, the very outbreak of the crisis demonstrated the flawed nature of the Community set-up and the need to carry out significant reform before forward progress could be resumed. As de Gaulle asserted bluntly on 7 July, 'it is necessary to take advantage of this crisis to eliminate the political misgivings ... We should exploit the situation to revise the false notions that made us subject to the *diktat* of others.'[20] To put it in the terms used in the introduction, the failure of a strategy based upon seeking agreement on the Community's agenda refocused attention on the equally serious dispute about how the EEC should work.

The most obvious link between the outbreak of the crisis and French institutional grievances was the behaviour of the European Commission. De Gaulle's impatience with the self-styled Brussels 'executive' was of course nothing new. The French leader had repeatedly made public and private derogatory remarks, most famously perhaps in his press conference of 15 May, 1962.[21] He had also shown a degree of ruthlessness in the manner in which he had engineered the removal of Etienne Hirsch – adjudged to have been too power-hungry and supranationalist a president of the Euratom Commission.[22] As mentioned in Chapter 2, French representatives in Brussels had been engaged in a systematic effort to thwart the Commission's claim to represent the Community internationally since early 1965 at least. But events between late March and the end of June of that year had added fuel to an already smouldering relationship. For a start, the audacity and far-reaching nature of the Commission's finance proposals seemed to confirm all French suspicions about the power-hungry nature of the Brussels body.[23] To make matters worse, their timing seemed designed to take advantage of the French electoral calendar in a manner bound to enrage de Gaulle.[24] And Hallstein's decision to air his ideas to the European Parliament before submitting them formally to the member states could all too easily be seen as a calculated snub to French sensitivities.

Fundamentally, however, the key change was that the March–June 1965 talks were the first major CAP negotiation in which France and the Commission had found themselves on opposing sides.[25] In all previous agricultural marathons, any distaste felt in Paris about the pretensions of the European Commission had been kept in check by the recognition that a strong Commission was actively helping French interests. To attack Hallstein or Mansholt would thus have been to allow institutional qualms to undermine potential economic rewards. As a result, the French had tended instead to praise the Commission role, albeit grudgingly.[26] But in the run-up to the crisis this alliance of interest between Paris and the Commission had disappeared: not only did the French dislike the CAP financial arrangements that the Commission proposed, but the portmanteau nature of the March proposals actively seemed to encourage France's partners to make a deal on agricultural funding conditional on multiple other issues.[27] Furthermore, once the degree of division amongst the Six had become clear, the Commission had failed badly in its duties by holding firm to its original position rather than modifying its proposals in order to find an acceptable compromise. According to French analyses, this was one of the key reasons why the 30 June deadline had been missed.[28] Short-term resentment thus fused dangerously with long-term animosity, in an atmosphere and at a time when none of the conventional checks on France's quest for institutional reform applied. If a scapegoat for the crisis needed to be found, the Commission was the obvious choice.[29]

The targeting of majority voting also followed logically from the manner in which the crisis had broken out.[30] If majority voting was to work effectively, without infringing member states' sovereignty unduly, it needed to be based on trust. Each participating country had to feel secure that its needs and priorities would be respected and that it would not be ganged up against and forced to accept arrangements or legislation contrary to its vital national interests. As recently as May 1965, the Quai d'Orsay had seemed confident that this would indeed be the case after January 1966.[31] But in the wake of the financial regulation negotiations in which France felt that it had been badly let down by its partners, that vital element of trust had largely disappeared. From a French viewpoint, the Italians, the Germans and the Dutch had all behaved unacceptably, ignoring previous commitments to conclude the financial regulation by 1 July, 1965, attaching unconnected issues to prevent France from securing the desired agreement, and cynically exploiting a Commission proposal with which all profoundly disagreed as a mechanism to prolong the Council negotiations.[32] To make matters worse, the Germans also appeared to have gone back on promises to France made in the context of bilateral discussions between Paris and Bonn.[33] Only Belgium had behaved honourably in France's eyes.[34] This explains why Seydoux in his aforementioned discussion with Schröder defined the situation as a 'crisis of trust' – in such circumstances it was understandable that de Gaulle's long-standing misgivings about supranationality should override his officials' and ministers' concern not to damage the EEC.[35]

To make matters even worse, one of the key results of majority voting would be to increase the power of the European Commission. As de Gaulle indignantly noted in his September press conference, Treaty rules meant that as from January 1966, the Council would only be able to reject or amend a Commission proposal in the unlikely event of there being member state unanimity to follow this course. By contrast, the same Commission proposal could be passed by a majority and would become binding on the dissenting minority.[36] This would significantly increase the bargaining power of Hallstein and his colleagues in the context of Council debates. French acceptance of such an arrangement in the immediate aftermath of a crisis which Paris believed to have been precipitated by the Commission's lust for power was extremely unlikely. Both of the institutional issues raised by France were thus in part at least about the Commission's standing and influence.

A final, somewhat more speculative, link between the circumstances of the crisis and the formulation of France's institutional objections springs from the review of Community procedures that the French civil service carried out in the early stages of the boycott. This included, naturally enough, a number of legal studies designed to establish how France might be adversely affected by its non-attendance in Brussels. Such studies may well have brought home to the French government quite how far the integration process had gone in a legal sense. Amongst the conclusions, for example, were not only that France had no judicially acceptable means to leave the Community but also the worrying news that Community legislation, especially that subject to majority voting, decided upon in France's absence, might still carry legal force in France and would have to be applied by French courts, despite the absence of a French voice during its formulation.[37] It is possible – although unprovable from the materials so far released by the French archives – that such startling findings strengthened de Gaulle's determination to modify the Community's decision-making procedures and the use of majority voting in particular. Certainly there is evidence that some of the legal counsellors within the French civil service felt that the crisis was an opportunity to claw back some of the further-reaching legal aspects of the Community system as it had developed by 1965. In mid-July, for instance, one wrote:

> The crisis that broke out in Brussels on June 30 could be the opportunity for France to obtain the correction of the supranational interpretations that over the last seven years the Community institutions (Commission, Assembly and Court of Justice) have given to certain measures in the Treaty of Rome which were not intended by their authors to be so far reaching.[38]

If such advice was in any way heeded, it would mean that while Joseph Weiler is almost certainly wrong to assert that the origins of the empty chair crisis lie in a belated member state recognition of how much power they had ceded to the supranational system, his theory may carry some weight as far as the escalation of the crisis is concerned.[39]

Regardless of whether this last argument is sustainable, the appearance of an institutional dimension to the crisis did constitute a logical enough outcome of a serious crisis of trust between France and its partners, and still more, between France and the Community institutions. It also meant that any resolution of the crisis would now entail not simply the identification of some formula which could bridge divergent member state goals as far as CAP finance was concerned, but also an answer to French institutional grievances. It is to the efforts of the Five to respond to the French boycott, to contain the threat posed by the French action, and to identify a means of luring France back to its place within the EEC, that this chapter must now turn.

Holding the fort in Brussels

Amongst the Five remaining member states and the Community institutions, the progressive escalation of the crisis by the French was watched with some alarm.[40] Despite Spaak's perceptive warnings, few of his colleagues appear to have believed prior to 30 June that France would react so vigorously to their attempted brinkmanship and were correspondingly wrong-footed by Paris's new approach. But dismay and consternation did not lead to the immediate collapse of morale for which de Gaulle and his ministers must have hoped. On the contrary, from early July onwards, the Five showed a quiet determination to coordinate their positions, to devise means by which the dispute with France might be resolved, and, in the meantime, to find methods of work which allowed the Community to go on functioning. In so doing, the Germans, Italians and Dutch in particular seemed to be spurred on by that same resolution to thwart de Gaulle's plans for the Community which had had so much to do with the outbreak of the crisis.

The most immediate task to be confronted was that of working out how the Brussels institutions could function in the absence of one of their most influential member states. In practice, this meant deciding whether the Council and its various subordinate bodies such as COREPER could meet *à cinq*, what the legal status of such meetings were, and whether or not the Five were entitled to take formal decisions at such encounters. The sensitivity of this was clear from the very first gathering of the Five deputy permanent representatives when Dondelinger, representing Luxembourg, initially refused to take his place at the table at all. His instructions, he explained, forbade him to prejudge the outcome of the discussion of how to respond to France's absence that the permanent representatives were due to have later that day.[41] At the subsequent meeting both the Luxembourgers and the Belgians, supported intermittently by the Dutch, tried hard to convince their colleagues that the Council in all its manifestations should convene as infrequently as possible and should remain as inactive as it could when it did meet. All decisions, however innocuous, were to be avoided since these might deepen the rift with France.[42] Such views were, however, countered strongly by the Italian Presidency and the Germans, both of whom maintained that the Five should continue to work together intensely so as to avoid any paralysis of the EEC. If this required decisions, then these would have to be taken, although both delegations recognised the need to avoid provoking the French. The Commission sided with this line of argument.[43]

Over the weeks that followed, a pragmatic compromise emerged. The Council, COREPER and the multiple working groups did go on meeting, even when the French failed to attend, and functioned according to normal procedures. The Italians, as holders of the rotating Presidency, continued to chair each meeting; the Council secretariat went on, as usual, in its task of servicing each session; and the meetings were held in the usual location and at the usual times. But out of deference to Belgian and Luxembourgeois sensitivities, a number of meetings initially planned for the quiet summer period were cancelled – Community activity was abnormally low-level until mid-September.[44] Firm decisions were as far as possible avoided; even the Council minute-takers were instructed to use phrases that emphasised the provisional nature of the conclusions of each meeting.[45] And it was decided that after each meeting, the Presidency would provide the French, in the person of Ulrich, with a detailed account of proceedings.[46]

Importantly, these decisions were reached for political rather than legal reasons. Wisely, most of the Five rejected Belgian suggestions to conduct a full-scale legal exploration of the situation; to have done so would not only have added an extra layer of complexity to an already fraught situation, but it might also have ruled out a number of potentially useful courses of action in the name of judicial orthodoxy.[47] Instead, the Italians, Germans and Dutch seem to have decided that the best means of coordinating the position of the Five was to employ the tried and tested procedures of the Council structure without dwelling for too long on the exact legal status of either the meetings themselves or their outcomes.[48] It was the unity of the Five that mattered, not the precise means used to achieve this goal.

Resolving the CAP finance issue

Once a *modus operandi* had been devised, it was then up to the Five to begin to work out how France might best be persuaded to return. The first method identified was the continuation, on the basis of a new Commission proposal, of the discussions about CAP finance which had been broken off on the night of 30 June. This would serve several purposes. For a start, a quick agreement on a new financial regulation would vindicate the claim of the Five that a deal had been within reach at the end of June and that stopping the clock for a few weeks – as had been suggested repeatedly in the final hours of negotiations – would have sufficed to break the impasse. It would also counter French assertions that none of their partners had been serious in wanting the financial regulation agreed. A provisional agreement on the CAP would, moreover, underline to Paris the potential rewards of an early return. This would put pressure on the French government directly, and encourage French farmers to press their political leaders to abandon their boycott. And finally, a successful negotiation would demonstrate that Paris had not succeeded in its aim of paralysing the EEC and show the extent to which the Five had succeeded in preserving unity amongst themselves and safeguarding the operation of the Community system.

To this end, the Commission hurriedly recast its 31 March proposals, dropping some of the more contentious aspects of the earlier draft, and including a complex funding arrangement that was potentially more advantageous than ever for the French.[49] It was not a full capitulation to the French – it retained, for instance, an implied link between progress on the CAP financial regulation and a wider raft of Community advances. And there were passing references both to the issue of 'own resources' and to the question of European Parliamentary powers. But there was no doubting that the new system envisaged was much more congenial to Paris than that suggested on 31 March had been. Significantly, perhaps, Marjolin had been conspicuously active in its formulation, having been an isolated, dissenting voice when the earlier scheme had been devised.[50]

Hallstein presented the new Commission ideas to the Council meeting held in late July.[51] The Belgians in particular, however, were keen to avoid any detailed discussion at this point, once more primarily out of fear of provoking the French.[52] As a result, ministers did no more than take note of the new proposals and then postponed multilateral consideration of them until the autumn. Even at this later date, however, agreement amongst the Five proved highly difficult. Those basic divisions about the CAP that had so bedevilled the May–June negotiations remained largely unresolved – indeed in some ways with Germany in the midst of an election campaign and then a coalition-building process, Bonn's objections to the Community's agricultural regime had grown still more strident.[53] Furthermore, there was strong reluctance amongst all the Five to the prospect of paying twice for a CAP deal, first in the context of talks amongst the Five and then again once the resulting proposals were put to the French.[54]

As a result, multiple official level meetings in September and October failed to produce the hoped-for consensus.[55] Instead, as ministers gathered in Brussels in late October for the first Council meeting since the summer, they were confronted with the depressing prospect of having to admit publicly that no agreement on the CAP had been struck amongst the Five. Such a development would of course greatly encourage the French, since it would not only draw attention to the divisions amongst their opponents, but it would also confirm their claim that there had been no prospect of a CAP deal earlier in the year. At the Council, the Germans in particular were thus put under intense pressure to give way, with minister after minister urging Schröder to put the need for unity in the face of France above the particular interests of German agriculture and German government finances.[56] In the end, they were partially successful, the German foreign minister giving enough ground for a general statement of principles about the shape of a future deal to be issued.[57] A highly public demonstration of discord amongst the Five had been averted, but much room for disagreement remained concerning the detail of any new arrangements for agricultural funding.[58]

Institutional flexibility?

The second method used to try to resolve the crisis was that of discussing *à cinq* how best to conduct a negotiation with Paris over institutional matters. In order to do this, the Five had to decide what was and what was not negotiable; establish how best to make known their views to France; and determine how, in what context and when a multilateral discussion with the French could take place. Somewhat surprisingly, the most contentious of these issues did not prove to be the content of any eventual negotiations. On the contrary, a high degree of consensus quickly emerged, ruling out actual treaty change or any formal lessening of the Commission's powers, but ready to contemplate more subtle arrangements with regard to both the use of majority voting and the manner in which the Commission operated.[59] Within an EEC where so many important national interests were at stake, none of the member states were entirely happy with the prospect of too rapid a move to a much more federal arrangement with a powerful Commission able to disregard the weakened voices of the individual member states.[60] Instead, most of the Five were ready to see some of the Commission's ambitions reined in, provided that no change was made to the fundamental independence or to the the capacity to initiate the policy process of the Brussels body.[61] After all, the French were not alone in feeling that Hallstein and his colleagues had been guilty of serious lapses of political judgement in the run-up to 30 June.[62] A gentle reprimand, in the form of a non-treaty-changing arrangement, might therefore be acceptable in Bonn, Brussels or Rome as much as in Paris.[63]

Likewise on majority voting, few member states wished to see a situation in which the views of the minority were regularly disregarded by the majority within the Council of Ministers. Spaak for instance commented publicly that 'On major issues, a Community like the EEC cannot in reality function on any basis but unanimity.'[64] Most Community governments, it is true, had been sufficiently confident of the goodwill and self-restraint of their partners to regard the abuse of majority voting as an unlikely eventuality. This explains the agreement between Lahr and Colombo in Rome that the objections to majority voting raised by the French were a 'false problem', soluble by a reliance on the 'Community spirit'.[65] But if the French required some additional reassurance on this point, all but the Dutch seemed willing to contemplate some type of gentleman's agreement or informal interpretative deal.[66]

More problematic was the issue of how to discuss such matters with the French without seeming unduly weak.[67] Keenest to renew dialogue was Spaak: by mid-September, the Belgian foreign minister was advancing the idea of convening a Council meeting between the Six but without the presence of the Commission where the crisis could be discussed and French grievances explored.[68] Within days these Belgian suggestions had been set out in a memorandum, initially submitted to the Dutch and the Luxembourgers in the hope that it might become a joint Benelux document, and then when this proved impossible, put forward as a purely Belgian proposal.[69] The central idea remained that of an extraordinary Council meeting at which a means could be found to resolve a crisis situation which, if left to fester, could soon destroy the whole EEC. Both the Dutch and the Germans soon expressed doubts, however. For the former, the Belgian initiative was potentially dangerous, since it conceded the possibility of treaty 'interpretations', set an awkward precedent of the member states discussing matters in the absence of the Commission, and was too overt in its criticism of the Commission's role in the June breakdown.[70] Erhard too was sceptical about how far a Community dispute could be settled without the presence of the Commission – although Schröder had earlier been more positive.[71] And, needless to say, the Commission itself was deeply unhappy at its potential exclusion from the process of crisis resolution.[72]

By the October Council meeting, however, most of the hostility to Spaak's basic idea had faded. A vital breakthrough in this respect had been Belgium's willingness to acknowledge that the planned meeting would handle only the institutional questions raised by the French and would not include more debate about CAP finance. As Germany had long insisted, issues such as this last could not be discussed without the participation of the Commission.[73] Meeting privately over dinner on 25 October, Colombo, as Council President and the foreign ministers of the other four member states, were thus able to draft a Council communiqué which would formally invite the French to attend a Council meeting to discuss the crisis. Exceptionally, but within Treaty rules, the Commission would not be present. This statement was then followed up by a letter from Colombo to Couve de Murville reiterating the Five's willingness to explore France's institutional objections, but re-stating their continuing determination to rule out actual treaty change.[74] The underlying need to re-establish some type of dialogue with Paris had triumphed over the hesitations and divisions over the form that this dialogue should take.

Maintaining unity *à cinq*

The final priority of the Five was to maintain unity amongst themselves.[75] This did not prove to be an easy task. Behind the tactical disputes and the squabbles over CAP financing described above, lay a number of highly divergent interpretations of how serious the crisis was and how best it might be solved. At one extreme lay the Belgian viewpoint, most closely associated with Spaak himself, but also reflected in wider debate within the country.[76] This emphasised the extreme danger posed by France's empty chair tactics, highlighted the ongoing damage to the Community and to its standing in the world that even a few months of paralysis would cause, and drew attention to the possibility of unintentional escalation which might ultimately lead to the destruction of the Community experiment.[77] In such circumstances, Spaak and his Belgian colleagues sought to avoid too much debate about who was to blame for the outbreak of the crisis (although when they did talk about this, the tendency was to allocate it evenly between the French, the hard-liners amongst the Five and the Commission) and instead underlined the need to resolve matters as quickly as possible, even at the cost of some concessions. Until such a solution had been found, moreover, it was vital to avoid taking any precipitate actions within the Community structures that might deepen the rift with France – hence the extreme Belgian caution about taking decisions in five member state Council meetings.[78]

Paradoxically, however, this very pessimistic reading of the situation and its consequent emphasis on flexibility and emollience towards France in the short term, went alongside a willingness to think truly radically about what to do in the longer term should France not respond to overtures from the Five. The Belgian debate thus contained more references to the possibility of trying to build Europe without France, and possibly with the British drafted in as substitutes, than that in virtually any other of the member states.[79] So serious was the crisis that the unthinkable needed to be thought, although all should initially be done to resolve the dispute without any drastic steps being taken.[80] Indeed, British documents would indicate that as early as October 1965, Spaak had extended discreet feelers to London, exploring whether the British would be willing to enter the Community were the breach with France to become irreparable.[81] Although not going quite this far, Luxembourg seems to have had very similar views to Belgium throughout the crisis months.[82]

A rather different approach prevailed in Bonn – although as usual there was a multiplicity of competing viewpoints jostling for pre-eminence in the German capital. For the most hard-line of German observers – greatly in evidence in the Chancellor's own circle, but also present in the Foreign Ministry – the crisis, while serious, was unlikely to be life-threatening to the Community. France, it was felt, gained far too much from its EEC membership seriously to contemplate leaving the Community. Dr. Praß, one of Erhard's foreign policy advisors, noted in September, for instance, that 'France cannot easily do without the EEC. A failure would be a catastrophe for French agriculture, but would also be very dangerous for the French industrial economy.'[83] De Gaulle's tactics in withdrawing his ministers from Council meetings were no more than the logical continuation of those forceful tactics that France had employed since 1963 at least.

Germany's response, therefore, needed to be as firm as it had been in the run-up to June 1965; immediate concessions would simply encourage the General to continue with his bullying tactics. While some flexibility was possible, especially on the institutional level where the French and German positions were not impossibly far apart, Bonn was thus keen to press on as far as possible with the Community process, if necessary taking decisions by majority vote without the French.[84] Certainly, there was no question of bribing France to come back to the negotiating table with substantive concessions on CAP finance or the rest of the Community agenda. Nor, given the certainty that France would in due course return, was there any need seriously to contemplate dramatic remedies like discussions with Britain about EEC membership.[85] Instead it was best for the Five to hold firm, confident that time was as much on their side as it was on the side of the French. Such views were in a direct line of descent from that anti-

Gaullist anger, and irritation at the way in which Germany was being exploited by its western neighbour, which had had so much to do with Bonn's rigidity in May–June 1965.

Italy and The Netherlands, the two other countries to have adopted a hard-line towards France prior to the crisis, also retained a firm position once the new French policy was revealed. In the former's case, this had much to do with Rome's sense that the grievances that it had raised in the course of the finance regulation negotiations were fully justified; as with the Germans there was therefore an understandable reluctance to abandon a sincerely-held position simply because of the new extreme tactics of the French.[86] There also appears to have been a realisation that early concessions would break the unity of the Five and allow the French to dictate the terms of their return. It was therefore important that the two larger powers amongst the Five demonstrated their willingness jointly to resist de Gaulle.[87] And there were also party political pressures on Fanfani in favour of a defence of European orthodoxy and against any weakness in the face of the French.[88] The Italians therefore deployed their efforts as holders of the Council Presidency in favour of coordinating the Five and making certain that the Community continued to function.

The Dutch meanwhile combined rigidity with a profound sense of pessimism. In virtually all of the policy debates in Brussels, The Netherlands adopted the hardest line position of all, in favour of pressing ahead *à cinq* and deeply hostile to any tinkering with the institutions in order to woo back the French. In total contrast to the German case, however, this dogmatic stand co-existed with a deep sense of gloom about both French intentions and the ability of their partners to stand up to Paris.[89] Spaak in particular was regarded with great suspicion, but both the Germans and still more the Italians were watched anxiously for any sign of weakness.[90] Like the Belgians, the Dutch were therefore tempted into private speculation about how the Community might continue without France and whether the UK could be invited to join in its stead.[91] The disadvantages and dangers of such a course were, however, widely recognised.[92]

Remarkably, however, these highly divergent analyses of the crisis did not shatter the solidarity of the Five. Instead, despite a degree of mutual suspicion, the Five kept in step with one another and used the mechanisms of the Community to devise a common stance towards the French. The October 26 *prise de position* was followed by further Council meetings in November and December at which the basic principles of the Five's position – no treaty change but a willingness to debate the issues raised by the French at a Council meeting held without the Commission – were re-affirmed. Such high-level multilateral encounters were supplemented with periodic tactical discussions amongst the permanent representatives in Brussels and innumerable bilateral discussions.[93] The intensity of debate amongst the Five, indeed, contrasted strongly with the halting and inter-mittent nature of the dialogue with the French.

In order to explain the success of the Five in maintaining such unity it is tempting to look for one clear source of leadership. The obvious candidate to provide this would have been Germany – the only member state with the political clout and economic self-confidence fully to stand up to the French.[94] But while the Germans in general, and Schröder in particular, did play a significant role, credit for leading the Five deserves to be divided somewhat more equitably between Bonn, Rome and Brussels. At a diplomatic level, it is true that Germany proved energetic in reassuring its partners and in attempting to coordinate their position: within a month of the outbreak of the crisis, Schröder had met or spoken on the phone with all four of his counterparts.[95] Such meetings not only provided an opportunity for the causes of the crisis to be discussed and for joint tactics to be devised, but they also demonstrated to the Italians, Dutch and Belgians that Bonn was fully committed to their cause. In a tussle with France, it was immensely reassuring for the smaller or less wealthy European member states to know that they had the backing of the richest and potentially most powerful of the Six.[96] Schröder's series of bilateral encounters also calmed any residual fears that Bonn might have been intending to use the mechanisms of the *Elysée* treaty to come to a private and mutually advantageous deal with the French.[97] When the Council met in Brussels, moreover, Schröder attended (an event in itself) and played a prominent role.[98] As the next chapter will demonstrate, the same would be true in the Luxembourg meetings of January 1966.

Germany's capacity to lead, however, was limited by the rigidity of Bonn's position on most of the substantive issues that had to be debated amongst the Five. Hans-Georg Sachs, the German Permanent Representative, was thus a rather peripheral figure in most of the COREPER meetings *à cinq* condemned to marginalisation by instructions from his government which took no account of what was actually negotiable in Brussels.[99] And Schröder found himself in the dock at the October Council meeting, accused of threatening the unity of the Five and the strategy decided upon to resolve the crisis by means of his intransigence on the CAP.[100] Other sources of direction were therefore required in addition to that provided by Bonn.

Part of the need was met by the Italians who, as holders of the Council Presidency, were in a sense duty-bound to play a prominent part in the resolution of any Community deadlock. Doing so, however, was not made any easier by Fanfani who gave every impression of feeling that his destiny lay on the world, rather than European, stage. In quite an extraordinary demonstration of nonchalance (if not negligence), the official incumbent of the Council chair chose to spend a whole month of the EEC's most serious crisis touring Latin America – during which time his representatives in Brussels were left without instructions – and then, on his return, seemed more intent on securing a nomination to preside over the General Assembly of the United Nations than in helping to solve the Community's problems.[101] Fortunately for both Italy's standing and the EEC's development, the Foreign Minister's inattention was initially compensated for by the personal commitment of Antonio Venturini, the Italian Permanent Representative, who proved a dynamic chairman of the meetings between the Five, before being made irrelevant when Fanfani fell down some stairs in New York, injuring himself sufficiently seriously to need replacing as Council President.[102] Colombo, appointed in his stead, had a much firmer grasp of the Community's operation and confirmed his reputation as an extremely effective EEC operator both in the Council meetings with his four counterparts and in the personal diplomacy towards the French which he, as Council President, was asked to undertake on behalf of the Five.[103] From October onwards the Italians were thus able to play a key role in keeping the Five together and ensuring that discussions with the French were handled in the most *communautaire* of fashions possible.

A third, rather different, type of leadership was provided by Spaak.[104] The Belgian Foreign Minister, in what proved to be his swansong on the European stage, acted as a valuable counterweight to the hard-line German and Italian positions in his efforts to promote dialogue with the French and his search for creative formulas to allow this dialogue to take place. Similarly, the Belgian Permanent Representative, van der Meulen, can be seen as doing all of the Five a service in the way in which he advocated caution in the day-to-day crisis management in Brussels, dissuading his more impetuous colleagues from taking steps that might totally alienate the French.[105] Had the Five been utterly without leadership, such conciliatory tendencies on the part of the Belgians might well have been highly divisive, alarming the hard-liners and providing solace to the French. But in a situation where the Germans and Italians were already doing enough to maintain and demonstrate the resolve of France's partners, the softer Belgian line proved highly useful in demonstrating to Paris that dialogue was still possible and in avoiding a situation in which the divisions between Paris and other Community capitals were unnecessarily polarised.[106] The discreet dialogue that the Belgians appear to have maintained with Paris probably also served to lessen the chances of an irreparable breach.[107] The soft cop to Schröder's hard cop, Spaak would make one final valuable contribution to the EEC's development during the crisis months.

In striking contrast, Hallstein and the European Commission, despite having been major protagonists in the negotiations leading to the crisis, were largely marginalised during the months of the French boycott itself. They were not totally inactive: their role in devising a new set of proposals on CAP finance has already been mentioned and in other areas of activity too, the Commission went on discussing policy and where necessary advancing proposals. Their representatives, moreover, attended both most of the COREPER meetings where the day-to-day management of the crisis was discussed and the formal sessions of the various Council meetings amongst the Five. And Hallstein and his colleagues made a number of speeches analysing the crisis in the European Parliament and elsewhere.[108]

As far as devising a political way out of the Community's most serious dispute to date, however, the Commission found itself with next to no influence. To a limited extent this reflected a deliberate desire to keep a low profile so as to avoid further provoking the French; rather more worryingly, however, it had more to do with the Commission being systematically bypassed by the governments of the Five as well as the French. Thus, not only was it excluded from the intensive bilateral diplomacy being conducted amongst the Five, but it also found itself powerless to resist Spaak's suggestion that the key issues be debated with France in a Council meeting held without a Commission presence.[109] And to make matters worse, the Five showed signs of anticipating the 'exceptional' arrangements for the Luxembourg Council by meeting amongst themselves without the Commission present. Most of the key decisions about how to resolve the crisis were not taken in normal Council sessions with Hallstein and his colleagues present and able to intervene. Instead they were the products of mealtime discussions between the foreign ministers with the members of the Commission not even physically present.[110] Similar informal gatherings without Commission representation also became a feature of the crisis months at the level of the permanent representatives.[111] The Commission thus found itself largely debarred from playing a major part in resolving a crisis for the outbreak of which it was widely (if somewhat unjustly) blamed.[112]

The slow start of talks with the French

The dialogue with the French that Spaak had so desired did slowly begin. Indeed, given the multiple, overlapping fora of Western cooperation that characterised the mid-1960s, it was virtually impossible for ministers and senior officials from the Five and from France not to meet each other during the six months of Community stand-off, whether at the UN, NATO, WEU or more exotic occasions such as the official opening of the Mont Blanc tunnel or the closing ceremony of the Second Vatican Council. Furthermore, as explained above, France retained some official representatives in Brussels, to say nothing of the numerous French nationals who went on working for the Community institutions. They too could not help but meet their counterparts among the Five on a nearly daily basis and in the process allow plenty of information to flow between Paris and Brussels.[113] Each of the Six moreover retained the full panoply of diplomatic representatives in the other Community capitals. But despite this profusion of opportunities to talk, beginning a meaningful substantive negotiation about how the crisis might be brought to an end proved rather more difficult than might have been expected.

Part of the problem had to do with the remaining anger on both sides. Just as the last chapter sought to demonstrate that the empty chair crisis had not erupted out of nothing, so one of the themes of this one has been the way in which the mutual suspicion, resentment and even animosity that had given birth to the stand-off did not dissipate as soon as the confrontation began. On the contrary, the French escalation of the crisis only reinforced anxieties amongst the more pessimistic of the Five about what the General was seeking to achieve, while the unexpectedly firm response of the Germans, the Dutch and the Italians increased the conviction among some in Paris that an unreformed Community was a dangerous place for French national interests.[114] Furthermore, each side demonstrated some ability in convincing itself that time would work to its advantage. The German conviction discussed above centred on France's economic need; the corresponding belief on the French side had more to do with the inevitable disagreements and tensions that had surfaced amongst the Five.[115] De Gaulle, for instance, observed that 'as, in the final analysis, the Germans could not tolerate a situation in which there was no Common Market, they will eventually retreat.'[116] Any precipitate moves to begin dialogue were hence likely to be subject to fierce internal criticism and attacked as unnecessary weakness. Neither the French nor the Five could thus be seen to be talking to each other too early.

If the depth of suspicion between France and its partners was a major factor delaying the start of substantive talks, so too was mistrust amongst the Five. Here, the difficulty lay in the fact that, in the absence of a senior French presence in Brussels, the only way to talk to the French was bilaterally. This then raised the possibility of the French practising a policy of divide and rule, saying subtly different things to each of the Five. As a result, there was a high degree of nervousness about most forms of bilateral diplomacy, despite a sustained effort to share information about all contacts with the French.[117] There were also alarmist rumours of deliberate French disinformation and efforts publicly to attribute suggestions to individual members of the Five that had not in fact been made.[118] To counter this, the Five sought to coordinate their diplomacy towards France at Council meetings; policy towards the absent partner would be decided *à cinq* in Brussels and the conclusions conveyed to the French in writing by the Council Presidency. Unfortunately, the French were unwilling to reply in writing to such an approach – claiming that to do so would be to risk 'crystallising' the divide and so worsening the crisis.[119] And without anything on paper, the Five could do no more than rely on the Italians' accounts of their meetings with the French, before meeting once more to devise a new common position to be put to Paris.[120] With Council meetings only happening at a frequency of one a month, it scarcely needs saying that such a pattern of diplomacy was extremely slow.[121]

A third difficulty was the sensitivity of both sides to form and symbolism. At a time of heightened mistrust, but also at a moment when all of the governments involved were aware of being closely scrutinised by their respective political elites if not their overall electorates, it was of immense importance to each side that they were perceived as being in the right. Seemingly trivial issues thus became of great significance, none more so than the question of where any meeting of the Six might be held. For the French it was absolutely vital that they could not be portrayed as being forced to return to Brussels as *demandeurs*, seeking changes to the Community's working that their partners might or might not grant. Couve de Murville therefore resorted to increasingly unconvincing arguments about how Brussels was affected by a 'bad atmosphere' which would have a negative impact on any talks.[122]

For the Five it was equally important that the forum in which the institutional matters raised by the French were debated was a meeting of the Council of Ministers, properly constituted, albeit without the Commission. It was therefore highly desirable that such a meeting be where Council meetings normally occurred, namely Brussels. The eventual compromise solution of holding the Council in Luxembourg – not the normal location but nevertheless one of the three sites of major EEC institutions – was ingenious, but like many clever bridging formulas took some time both to devise and to become acceptable. Similarly, the Five refused adamantly to make any formal suggestions about institutional change to the French, despite holding innumerable discussions of this topic amongst themselves.[123] This reflected a reluctance to be seen in any way to have initiated a move which might result in a modification of the way in which the Community worked; if such a step were to be taken at all, it would have to be because the French asked for it and offered something in return. Unfortunately, the French were equally clear that they would not attend any meeting at which a deal of this sort might be done unless such a encounter were so well prepared that the terms of the deal were all but known in advance.[124] As a result, the Five had to go through the laborious and time-consuming process of providing countless hints about what they might be prepared to discuss and even grant without ever offering anything officially.[125] Again, the result was a significantly elongated negotiation process.

Worst of all, the diplomacy between the Five and the French was greatly complicated by the elections occurring in the Community's two largest member states in the course of the autumn of 1965. In the first months of the crisis, Germany's capacity both to lead the Five and to play down its dissatisfaction with the CAP so as to encourage the French to return were severely hampered by the general election scheduled for mid-September. German politicians in campaigning mode were even less inclined to restrain their criticisms of de Gaulle or of perceived French selfishness within a European context than would have been the case at a different point in the electoral cycle. Nor did the inconclusive outcome of the election help very much: Erhard remained as Chancellor (much to de Gaulle's displeasure) but the CDU performance had not been strong enough to dispel the impression that Brandt's SPD was the rising force in German politics or to spare Erhard the delicate task of constructing a new coalition.[126] There was thus neither the new approach that a different government or Chancellor might have brought to the crisis situation, nor the greater freedom of manoeuvre that Erhard might have enjoyed after a truly convincing electoral triumph.

No sooner had Germany completed its electoral process, than the build-up to the French Presidential contest of early December began. This too brought about an intensification of political rhetoric that seemed likely to deepen the divide between France and the Five. In particular, the multiple claims by de Gaulle's ministers that France bore no responsibility for the EEC crisis and that if necessary France could prosper without European integration, although primarily intended to rebut those French opposition politicians who accused de Gaulle of playing fast and loose with France's valuable European ties, were ill-suited to smooth relations with the Five.[127] Furthermore, having made its discontent with the existing institutional structure of the EEC so public, it was impossible for de Gaulle's government to enter into a dialogue with its partners which might result in an uneasy compromise rather than a clear victory before de Gaulle had been returned to power. The prospects of a Council meeting between the Five and the French before the year's end were greatly reduced as a result.

Nevertheless a halting dialogue did take place throughout the autumn. Particularly encouraging were the encounters between Couve and Klaiber in mid-October, that between Schröder and his French counterpart a month later, and the multiple contacts between the French and the Italian Presidency, whether represented by Fanfani, by Colombo or by Fornari, the Italian Ambassador in Paris.[128] At these meetings, the basic shape of a deal to solve the crisis – involving some type of interpretative document addressing France's institutional discontents but leaving the Treaty itself unaltered – gradually became clear. Too great a spread of optimism was however prevented by intermittent reminders of how raw emotions remained on both sides. The way in which the audience de Gaulle afforded to Baron Bentinck, the Dutch Ambassador to Paris, gained great notoriety because of the General's intemperate remarks about German power and his hard-line stance on the future of the Commission, as well as the stormy and ill-tempered lunch shared by Luns and Couve in December suggested that nothing yet could be taken for granted despite the apparent progress made.[129]

As 1965 drew to a close, however, both the French and the Five had strong incentives to try to end the impasse. The detailed internal examination which the French civil service had conducted in mid-October, designed to establish the significance of the EEC to the French economy and to examine potential alternatives should the crisis prove insoluble, had only underlined how much France had to lose in Brussels. That the paper prepared by the Ministry of Agriculture on how much France gained from the CAP supported this conclusion should perhaps not come as too much of a surprise – although the magnitude of the benefits drawn and the prediction that France's interests in the policy could only increase were hard for the government to ignore.[130] But what was still more compelling was the way in which the papers on the customs union, on prospects for complete economic union, and on the workings of the association regime with former French colonies in Africa, all came to much the same conclusion.[131] The European Community as it existed and functioned in 1965 was an extremely beneficial entity for France and one which Paris could not hope to replace elsewhere. While de Gaulle and his ministers were thus literally correct in their multiple assertions that France would survive without European cooperation, their rhetoric was fundamentally hollow since no government could lightly relinquish so advantageous a set of international arrangements.

The political dangers of too critical a line towards the European Community were also highlighted by the outcome of the French elections. Quite how significant a factor 'Europe' proved to be in the strong performance of the centre and centre-Left in the elections remains a subject of some controversy. Equally unclear is how many French farmers who might otherwise have voted for de Gaulle, abstained or voted for the opposition in protest at the way in which the General seemed to be taking risks with a system that served them so well. Nevertheless, the mere fact that de Gaulle had to go into an unexpected second-round run-off against François Mitterrand was an unwelcome jolt to the President's political self-confidence and a source of great encouragement to his many, pro-European critics. It was therefore in the interest of the General, once duly re-elected, to close off all those avenues of political attack that his critics had been able to exploit during the election campaign. The stand-off in Brussels was one such avenue and de Gaulle and his ministers thus moved swiftly to resolve the crisis as soon as the election was over. Crucial in this respect was their decision to accept the invitation to a meeting in Luxembourg – officially a Council, although the French would never use this name – to be held in mid-January.[132]

Fortunately for the French, a similar desire to solve the dispute as quickly as possible was spreading amongst the Five. One important source of pressure in this connection was the Kennedy Round. The way in which the whole timetable of the global trade negotiation was being put at risk by the paralysis of the Community – the Commission could be given no new negotiating instructions without French consent, and there was certainly no prospect of the EEC altering its stance on agriculture in the absence of France – was a source of considerable concern for all of the Five, and nowhere more so than in Bonn.[133] Any German tendency to feel that time was on their side began to fade once the GATT implications of Community deadlock became apparent.[134] Similarly, there were a number of important decisions that needed to be made before 1965 came to an end. These included the setting of the Community's budgets for 1966, the nomination of a new Commission to replace that whose mandate was due to expire on 31 December, and a number of delicate tariff questions. Particularly sensitive amongst these last was the issue of whether the EEC would be able to make permanent the 20 per cent cut in the external tariff that had been made – as a temporary gesture – in the context of the earlier GATT Dillon round.[135] In normal circumstances, the prolongation of this tariff cut might well have been expected to be virtually automatic. But without a French presence, it would be much harder to take the decision needed to avert an embarrassing situation in which the EEC raised its external tariffs by a substantial amount while the rest of the world was negotiating major tariff reductions. Here too, Bonn and The Hague, the two capitals most inclined to take a hard-line towards the French, were also those most sensitive to the international damage that such a situation would cause.

As the end of the year approached, the key question was thus whether the new desire to end the crisis apparent amongst both the French and the Five would prove strong enough to overcome the deep-running anger and irritation that still characterised both sides of the dispute. The likely components of any deal were already known. And the row about the location and character of the talks appeared to have been overcome. But such were the levels of sensitivity on each side that much could still go wrong. If confirmation of this were needed, it was provided on 24 December when the French announced, contrary to multiple hints that they had dropped earlier, that they were not ready to approve the EEC budget for 1966 by written procedure.[136] This meant that for the first part of the new year, the Community institutions would have to resort to an emergency financial mechanism that would leave them desperately short of funds. This news was extremely ill-received by the Five who had tended to believe the reassurances given by both Couve and Ulrich and regarded the sudden French change of direction as a deliberate provocation in the run-up to the Luxembourg Council.[137] The omens for the crucial Council meeting could scarcely have been less propitious.

In fact, however, the French decision over the budget, while certainly an indication that the General could overrule his subordinates' inclinations to rebuild relations with the Five, also demonstrated that fundamental element of caution that had characterised both sides' behaviour throughout the crisis. For according to a detailed account of the relevant French cabinet meeting leaked to the British, de Gaulle only insisted that a tough line be taken on the budget, *after* Couve de Murville had explained to him that the EEC did indeed have an emergency procedure to deal with a failure of its member states to agree a new budget.[138] The French move was thus a deliberate attempt to remind the Five that they should not go into the Luxembourg discussions expecting flexibility and concessions from the French. But at the same time it was a step that was only taken, once it had been made certain that no serious long term consequences were likely to ensue. France, like the Five, would head to Luxembourg, with strong views about what the outcome of the meeting should be, but with a basic commitment to ongoing European cooperation that would greatly limit the chances of total failure.

4 National interest and the rescue of the EEC

January–July, 1966

The Extraordinary Council meeting in Luxembourg scheduled for 17 and 18 January, 1966 would be 'the most important in the history of the EEC', Lahr told Dutch diplomats in mid-January.[1] The German State Secretary's assessment accurately captured the anticipation and nervousness with which most of those involved with the European integration process looked forward to the gathering of the six foreign ministers. A successful meeting could bring to an end six months of damaging French boycott; failure, by contrast, could call into question the whole continuation of the EEC in its existing form. This chapter must therefore begin by analysing the mood both amongst the Five and in Paris as the first multilateral encounter between France and its partners since 30 June, 1965 approached. It will then proceed to an examination of what happened at the two Luxembourg meetings themselves, before turning to the six months of careful and somewhat fraught diplomacy that followed the return of French representatives to Brussels. For it was only with the three successive marathon meetings of May, June and July 1966, and the agreements reached about the shape and timing of the CAP, the customs union and the Community's approach to the Kennedy Round of GATT negotiations, that it could truly be said that the EEC had recovered from its most serious crisis.

The second half of this chapter must then weigh the significance of what had happened. It will first explore the relationship between the waxing and waning of confrontation within the Community and the general evolution of West–West diplomacy during a period characterised by crisis within NATO and significant discord over East–West contacts. This will go some way towards assessing the extent to which the European integration process was just an element within the wider system of postwar international relations, or, instead, a fairly distinct phenomenon, subject to its own rules, dynamics and patterns of evolution. Returning to a more EEC-focused analysis, the chapter will next ask what the crisis and its resolution had indicated about the various national attitudes towards the Community experiment. This will lead logically into an exploration of the institutional outcomes of the empty chair crisis. Did the so-called Luxembourg compromise, reached after the second Luxembourg meeting, profoundly alter the functioning of the EEC as is frequently claimed?[2] Or were the Five right, by contrast, to assert their success in protecting the Community from de Gaulle's attack? Finally, an examination is necessary of the links between the institutional issues upon which so much attention had focused since the summer of 1965 and the seemingly more mundane agenda-related questions which had predominated both in the run-up to the crisis and in its immediate aftermath. This will suggest that the connections between the two separate disputes – the first and second questions around which this book is organised – were actually much tighter than is normally assumed, with each needing to be settled before the confrontation between France and the Five could truly be considered to be at an end.

On the eve of battle

The mood of most of the Five as 1966 began can best be summed up as angry defiance. A vein of deep irritation at French behaviour can, of course, be traced right through the crisis months and back into the negoti-ations about CAP finance which had triggered the confrontation. But such resentment had been greatly worsened by France's 24 December announcement, discussed in the last chapter, that it would not be prepared to approve the budgets of the EEC, ECSC and Euratom by written pro-cedure. This was regarded by most of the Five as an unwelcome escalation of the crisis by the French and, more seriously, as yet a further example of Paris failing to provide a quid pro quo for diplomatic concessions made by the other member states. For there is clear evidence that both the Germans and Dutch – normally the most hard-line of the Five – had tried to accommodate French sensitivities on the budgetary issue and had been rewarded by persistent hints from the French that the budgets would duly be approved.[3] That the French had ultimately disappointed such hopes seemed to reawaken all those suspicions about the basic trustworthiness of de Gaulle and his representatives that had been evident in the outbreak of the crisis. The mood amongst the Five darkened as a result.

The budgetary dispute added an element of radicalism to COREPER meetings in early January that would otherwise have been dominated by preparations for Luxembourg and discussion of how the crisis might be resolved. On 3 January and again three days later, four of the Five agreed that in the light of the French decision, the remaining members of the Community should now press ahead and adopt the budget by a qualified majority – the dissenting voice was, as in July, that of Belgium.[4] Such a step would significantly harden a dispute in which the Five had, hitherto, refrained from taking any firm Community decisions. As a worried Ulrich reported back to Paris after having been briefed by Borschette, the Lux-embourg chairman of COREPER, 'It appears that, as far as the legal debate is concerned, the German view allowing for the possibility of the

Council taking decisions even without one member whenever majority voting is permitted, has been largely accepted.'[5] A Council meeting was planned for the end of the month in order to approve the budget, whether the French participated or not.[6] If de Gaulle's decision had been taken in the hope of underlining France's determination and weakening the resolve of the Five before the crucial Luxembourg Council, it seemed to have had entirely the opposite effect.[7] A strong signal had instead been sent to Paris that unless a settlement were reached at Luxembourg, most of the Five were willing to press ahead with Community business *à cinq* if necessary.[8]

Such defiance was, however, often accompanied by gloom at the Five's prospects during the Luxembourg meetings. Spaak, for instance, spoke of going to the meeting with great pessimism, while Egidio Ortona, a senior official at the Italian foreign ministry, held that agreement amongst the Six was highly unlikely.[9] Much more probable outcomes were either a restatement by both the French and the Five of their differing viewpoints followed by two to three months of total stalemate, or the recognition by both sides that their opinions were irreconcilable and that cooperation was hence impossible.[10] As ever a significant source of pessimism amongst the Five was doubt as to whether their unity would hold once confronted with the French. As one internal Dutch memorandum noted: 'The crisis in the Community can be compared to a poker game, in which the outcome depends upon the staying power and the nerves of the players. In this respect, France is in a stronger position than the Five whose position can only be as strong as that of the weakest partner.'[11] The only remedies for this inherent weakness were careful preparation and coordination in the days before 17 January, a reaffirmation of the agreement that it was for France and not for the Five to put forward suggestions for institutional change, and mutual encouragement.[12] Luns thus met Schröder the day before the Luxembourg meeting, and Colombo the morning of the conference itself.[13] Somewhat worryingly for his partners, however, Spaak was believed to have timed his arrival from Brussels so as not to be included in this round of pre-Council diplomacy.[14]

The French, by contrast, were rumoured to be highly confident. Details of a French preparatory meeting before Luxembourg were leaked to the British and appeared to indicate that Wormser and his fellow negotiators believed the unity and the determination of the Five to be fragile and liable to crack, provided France held its ground.[15] Such an account would be very much in line with the normal, somewhat contemptuous Gaullist attitudes towards their EEC partners' negotiating prowess. Nevertheless, a number of Ulrich's reports from Brussels suggest that the French were uncomfortable with the development of discussions amongst the Five and aware of their collective 'ill-humour'.[16] By mid-January, French officials were also conscious of the toughening of attitudes that the budget issue had provoked.[17] And there are multiple hints in the Quai d'Orsay files that the French were keen to reach a settlement at Luxembourg and were prepared to scale down their demands in order to attain agreement. Certainly, Jean-Pierre Brunet ended his note to Ulrich about the tactics that the French should adopt at the Luxembourg Council with the observation that he was eager to solve this crisis 'that has lasted too long'.[18] The confidence noted by the British is thus likely to have been mixed with a strong element of caution and a recognition that a solution might well involve a degree of give and take.

The first Luxembourg meeting

Couve de Murville's opening stance at the first Luxembourg meeting reflected both facets of the French approach. The confident, not to say confrontational, aspect of French diplomacy was evident in the sheer number of issues raised by the French foreign minister on 17 January and the cumulative impact that the changes requested would have on the EEC. First of all France wanted an arrangement reached that would eliminate the possibility of any member state being outvoted on a major issue under the qualified majority voting rules due to come into action in stage III of the EEC's transitional period. And second, the French presented a ten point memorandum outlining the changes they deemed necessary in the Commission's mode of operation.[19] These would have obliged the Commission to consult member states before submitting legislative proposals, enjoined the Commission to draw up much more focused regulations rather than the wide-ranging directives that were the current norm, and subjected both Commission activities, notably in the information sector, and Commission finances to much tighter member state control. The Commission's ability to forge links with third countries and international organisations, and its ability to express political opinions, would also be sharply curtailed.[20] Couve further made clear his desire to see the fastest possible inauguration of the new, post-fusion, Commission, the Presidency of which should rotate frequently between all of the member states.[21] This last point underlined how unlikely were the French to accept Hallstein's re-appointment – the German had after all held the Commission Presidency since 1958.

The more cautious and conciliatory aspect of France's approach was, by contrast, evident from the distance between France's actual requests and the desire for radical change implied by the General's 9 September press conference or Couve de Murville's 20 October statement before the National Assembly.[22] Notable by their absence from France's Luxembourg desiderata was any real questioning of the notion of supranationality, any demand for treaty change, or any suggestion that the Commission be reduced to a mere civil service.[23] Instead, Couve made clear that the French would be content with a political arrangement about majority voting and a number of alterations to the Commission's behaviour that left intact the institution's basic independence and treaty-given rights. Indeed both the French decalogue – as the *aide-mémoire* on the Commission was immediately dubbed – and the foreign minister's own first speech at Luxembourg went out of their way to praise the Commission and to recall its contribution to EEC progress to date.[24] Even the drafting of the ten individual points was much less far-reaching than many had expected: Rutten, the Dutch deputy permanent representative, reportedly commented upon reading the decalogue that 'if this was what all the fuss was about there need be no crisis'.[25] And most welcome of all was the tone with which Couve's opening remarks were made. Although not all his audience was happy with the substance of his speech, there was a welcome absence of polemic or of outright criticism of any of the Five.[26] France had clearly arrived in Luxembourg ready to negotiate and therefore, by implication, ready to give some ground on its demands.

The Five took a while to respond in kind. The first afternoon and evening of the conference were dominated by multiple appeals to the French to trust the existing treaty provisions and by periodic outbursts that illustrated the underlying suspicion of the French. Spaak, for instance, voiced the widely-held fear that any understanding on majority voting would be vulnerable to abuse: 'If it is indeed true that each country would find it hard to accept being placed in a minority on an issue it believed to be of vital importance, it is equally true that the Community would find it hard to allow itself to be stopped by the will of one single country.'[27] The reluctance to break ranks and to offer the French any seeming encouragement also helps to explain the rather sterile afternoon session and the even more ill-tempered post-dinner unofficial talks.[28] But on the morning of 18 January the mood changed dramatically with Spaak and then Colombo, and finally Werner, all putting forward verbal formulae that might serve to address France's fears.[29]

As soon as this happened it became obvious that the Five were much more worried about the French attack on majority voting than they were about the decalogue.[30] The latter was despatched relatively quickly and with little acrimony. The French quickly accepted that the Council had no right unilaterally to impose changes on the Commission; any document agreed could therefore be no more than the Council's opening salvo in a discussion with the Commission to be held under article 162 of the Treaty.[31] And the Five were ready to acknowledge some substance in several of the individual points made by the French provided the language was altered and the suggested changes made more limited.[32] Within a couple of hours enough consensus had been reached for the text to be handed over to the permanent representatives with a strong chance that they would be able to devise a generally acceptable form of words. Majority voting, by contrast, proved much more contentious. Despite a general agreement that this facility needed to be used with care and tact, the Five were not ready to accept any document that ruled out the use of majority voting altogether where vital national interests were deemed to be at stake. None of the multiple formulae advanced by either side could bridge this gap.[33]

The real deterioration of the atmosphere, however, was not provoked by the inability to agree on majority voting but instead by the French decision midway through the second day of negotiation to submit a draft timetable for the resumption of EEC progress.[34] This was an ill-judged document that touched a number of very raw nerves. For a start, it called for the ratification procedure of the fusion treaty, which had been delayed by the crisis, to be completed by the end of March so as to allow the Six to finalise the personnel of the new Commission by mid-April. This suggestion was not only seen as a slight against the right of national parliaments to determine their own timetable (a point made with force by the Dutch), but would also undermine the authority of the existing Commission by setting so clear an end date for its term. Second, the idea that discussions amongst the member states of who should serve in the new Commission begin as early as 1 February, implied that these most sensitive of talks were likely to start before France had resumed its place in Brussels.[35] This was contrary to the very strong German and Dutch determination not to broach this topic under empty chair conditions.[36] And third, and almost worst of all, the only topics scheduled to be discussed in the weeks immediately following the reoccupation of the French chair in Brussels were the financial regulation and a series of tariff problems connected to the missed 1 January, 1966 deadline. Of the Kennedy Round, and the other issues known to be preoccupying most of the Five, there was no mention at all. The sole sweetener, the expressed French willingness to approve the Community budgets by written procedure in the course of February, was scarcely regarded as a concession at all, given the sense that France should have already done this.[37]

The timetable proposal undermined all the recovery of trust that had been apparent earlier in the day.[38] Schröder and Luns both made their annoyance very plain, and the Five then left the room for discussions amongst themselves, despite having earlier agreed to avoid as far as was possible confabulations without the French at Luxembourg.[39] On their return, further constructive discussion was manifestly not possible. Instead the Germans, Dutch and French exchanged a number of barbed comments. Werner, the Luxembourg chairman, hence quickly realised that he had no choice other than to adjourn the session and secure agreement to continue the Extraordinary Council ten days later.[40]

Both private and public reactions to the first two-day meeting were coloured by these ill-tempered final exchanges. Lahr's extraordinarily pessimistic account for the German government is a case in point, its gloomy predictions about the French seeking to impose their priorities on the EEC being almost entirely a product of the draft calendar row rather than the earlier, more promising discussions.[41] The Dutch, Italian and French internal assessments of the meeting similarly devoted much space to the dispute over the Community's future progress.[42]

There was also disquiet in both Germany and the Netherlands over the reliability of the Italians in the second round of Luxembourg negotiations. Not only was it widely rumoured that the French had sought to woo the Italians on the margins of the Luxembourg meeting with promises about the Commission Presidency, but the outbreak of a major governmental crisis in Italy made it less likely that Colombo would be in a position to stand firm when the Six met again.[43] And tempers became still more heated when the French press, acting, it was widely assumed, on official instructions, printed a number of stories placing all the blame for the deadlock on the German foreign minister.[44] As had been the case with the blocking of the budget, however, these attempts to bring extra pressure to bear on Schröder – if that is indeed what they were – proved entirely counterproductive. After a somewhat difficult Cabinet debate, the Erhard government responded by taking the unprecedented step of holding a full Bundestag debate on the eve of a major Community negotiation. The outcome, a remarkable cross-party consensus on the need for a firm German stance, greatly strengthened Schröder's position.[45] Germany also sounded out the Americans about the possibility of the Kennedy Round negotiations continuing between a Five member EEC and the US. The cautiously positive American response is likely to have further bolstered German resolve.[46] Schröder was thus able to travel to Luxembourg for the second half of the Extraordinary Council in a stronger position than he had been two weeks earlier.

Round two at Luxembourg

In the event, however, all this sabre-rattling prior to the second Luxembourg meeting was less significant than two lower key developments. The first of these, the solid progress made between the six permanent representatives in drafting a compromise document on Commission/Council relations, allowed the ministers rapidly to agree to a much milder 'heptalogue' in place of the French 'decalogue' when the Luxembourg Council resumed on 27 January. The compromise text picked up several of the main ideas of the original French draft, but moderated the language to such a degree that the Commission would scarcely be asked to do more than observe previous best practice.[47] Two of the more radical points in the decalogue – those that had targeted the Commission's overuse of broad directives rather than narrower regulations – were dropped entirely, while a third, which had asked the Commission to refrain from all public criticism of member state governments, was replaced by the agreement that the chairman of COREPER would have a discreet word with the Commission President about this issue.[48] And the whole text would be discussed with the Commission, under article 162, at some undisclosed point in the future. A few drafting quibbles aside, all of this was agreed with remarkably little argument, the entire process taking only an hour and a half.[49] The Six appeared to have rediscovered the ability to negotiate with one another.

Agreement on majority voting proved rather more difficult to achieve. Fundamentally, the Five continued to fear the tyranny of the minority whereas the French were more concerned with that of the majority.[50] But here, too, progress soon began to be made largely thanks to the second of the two developments referred to above. This was the indication by Couve de Murville that France would be willing to make its views about majority voting known not by means of an agreed text, but instead by using the tried and tested Community formula of a unilateral declaration.[51] With Spaak and others quickly picking up on this major French concession, discussions soon focused on the drafting of a two part statement on Council voting procedure. In the first, the Six members of the Community would reaffirm their shared belief that, when vital national interests were at stake, all reasonable efforts should be made to secure a consensus decision. And in the second the French delegation would outline its belief that in such circumstances no majority vote should be taken at all and that discussions should continue until a unanimous agreement was possible. A third and fourth paragraph would then note the agreement to disagree, but state that none of the Six believed this ongoing divergence of views sufficient to stop the Community from returning to its normal pattern of work. The outcome of the meeting would in other words be a *gentleman's disagreement* on majority voting rather than the gentleman's agreement that had been widely discussed.[52]

Finalising this form of words took some time. The first draft of the unilateral French declaration was much too radical for many of the Five. In particular, the reference to the 'serious difficulties' which might result were unanimity not achieved was felt to be uncomfortably close to the type of threatening language that Couve had employed in the run-up to 30 June, 1965. Colombo, Spaak and Luns had to combine forces to persuade the French to omit this phrase.[53] And there was a long and convoluted argument about whether or not the agreed statement should specifically exclude from the possibility of majority vote all of those issues that would have been settled under stage II rules (i.e. prior to 31 December, 1965) had the crisis not intervened.[54] Revealingly, on this issue it was the Germans rather than the French who seemed most worried about a series of important CAP decisions, including of course that on the financial regulation, being taken without a unanimity requirement. This resulted in an addition to the final communiqué which listed five major sets of CAP decisions that would certainly be taken by unanimous vote. But once the formula of a unilateral declaration had been identified, and the Five had thus realised that they would not be obliged publicly to renounce the possibility, however unlikely, of reaching a majority decision on an issue of vital national interest, a positive outcome of the meeting was almost guaranteed.[55]

With a settlement reached on the two institutional problems that France had posed, it then proved much easier to turn, in the final hours of the Luxembourg meeting, to the controversial issue of the EEC's timetable after France's representatives had returned to Brussels.[56] Here, too, the exchange of mutual concessions continued. Germany and the Netherlands thus agreed that the financial regulation should be made the priority once normal discussion resumed. In return, the French acknowledged that other matters would also have to be debated and they dropped their insistence that a firm date be set either for agreement on the membership of the new Commission or for the ratification of the fusion treaty.[57] The Six did agree to try and complete both by June 1966, but given the sensitivity that surrounded the question of whether or not the key members of the current EEC Commission should be allowed to retain their posts, and the firm insistence by the Five that the fusion treaty would not enter into force until the Commission personnel had been agreed, it was always likely that this target would prove aspirational rather than binding. In the relief surrounding the breakthrough over majority voting, however, nobody was in the mood to attach too much weight to such details. The 'most important' Council meeting in Community history was at an end.

Predictably perhaps, both the Five and the French claimed victory. Schröder, for instance, commented 'Those who wanted a veto right manifestly did not obtain one and the debates demonstrated clearly that the Five are firmly resolved to take decisions by majority voting if necessary.'[58] Colombo similarly emphasised that the Treaty and hence the right to take qualified majority voting remained intact.[59] De Gaulle by contrast used another of his press conferences in mid-February to assert that, on the contrary, the crisis had ended with a total victory for France.

> This agreement between the six governments is of great and felicitous scope. Indeed, for the first time since the Common Market process began, the fiction has been dropped that economic organisation of Europe should be carried out by agents other than states, with all their powers and responsibilities . . . As reason prevailed, one can anticipate that the economic negotiations will now proceed in favourable conditions.[60]

Internal government assessments were similarly divergent: Wormser's circular to all French diplomats failed to match the triumphalist tone of Lahr's memo to the German government but equally did not acknowledge defeat.[61] For the former, the key was that none of the member states had shown great enthusiasm for extensive majority voting; for the latter the essential feature of the agreement was the way in which it left the Treaty entirely unaltered. Both claims were accurate, but they do emphasise the extent to which the Luxembourg meeting had been about acknowledging an absence of agreement rather than devising a consensual viewpoint. Indeed, the main strength of the texts agreed was precisely their lack of the clarity on the contested issues of Commission powers and majority voting.[62] This allowed a situation in which, to quote Luns, 'There was neither victor nor vanquished: one can therefore be content.'[63]

What mattered was that the institutional dispute could be laid aside and the Community could resume the struggle about its future agenda. It had been this rather than the institutional issues that had lain at the heart of the June 1965 breakdown; and it was again the question of what the Community should do in practice, rather than the remaining points of institutional discord, that mattered as the Six sought to rebuild that trust which had evaporated in the spring and summer of the previous year. The empty chair part of the crisis was over, but neither the French nor the Five had done more at Luxembourg than agree to resume where they had left off seven months earlier. The return of French diplomats to Brussels – a process that began towards the end of the first week of February 1966 – was a major milestone in the evolution of the crisis between France and its partners, but it cannot really be considered its resolution. For that it would be necessary to await the triple marathon of May, June and July 1966 and the resultant compromise on parallel advance towards a customs union, a completed agricultural policy and a renewed Community engagement with the Kennedy Round negotiations. And it is this that the next part of this chapter must address.

Undoing the agenda impasse

The French return to Brussels was deliberately low-key. According to a Commission witness, 'The French representatives took their places at the table without any form of ceremonial. One is amongst well-mannered people, and the reunions took place without embraces, outpourings or general declarations. There was discreet satisfaction all round the table, but it was clear that everybody chose to act as if nothing at all had happened.'[64] The same observer noted a deliberate French effort to avoid 'all unnecessary provocation' and to tread carefully on issues such as the exact status of working documents produced by the Five during the empty chair period.[65] But there was no tactful way of avoiding the fact that there was still a yawning gap between the priorities of the returning French, for whom the key remained a rapid agreement on CAP finance, and the Germans and Italians, neither of whose misgivings about the whole agricultural policy had melted away during the crisis months.[66] The second COREPER meeting after the French return held on 17–18 February thus witnessed an angry exchange between Boegner and Sachs in the course of which the French Permanent Representative's seeming indifference to Community progress in fields other than agriculture provoked a fierce rebuttal from his German counterpart.[67]

The seriousness of this Franco-German disagreement appears much greater once the domestic development of Germany's European debate is taken into account. For behind the scenes in Bonn, pressure was mounting for Germany to adopt an ever harder line on the CAP. The details of the rather inchoate and very fractious internal debate need not detain us here. What mattered, however, was that those responsible for outlining Germany's stance in a set of Brussels negotiations which had to succeed were the crisis fully to be overcome, had to do so against a backdrop of fierce internal discord within the Erhard government.[68] One symptom of the disarray was the frequency with which the instructions sent to German negotiators changed, sometimes totally contradicting those that had gone before. Sachs, for instance, found himself rebuked by Hüttebräuker, State Secretary at the Ministry of Agriculture, for having taken the hitherto standard German line that all further progress forwards should be flanked by parallel advance on the Kennedy Round.[69] According to Hüttebräuker, the Permanent Representative should instead have argued that the financial regulation was dependent on a number of steps being taken towards German agricultural priorities. Maintaining a clear and constructive German line in such circumstances would not prove easy.

Nor was there much likelihood of the squabbling ministers and officials in Bonn being overruled by a Chancellor invoking his *Richtlinienkompetenz* in the name of Germany's wider political interest. Although this had been a frequent pattern in the Adenauer era it was extremely unlikely under his successor for at least three reasons. First of all Erhard had never been able to match the authority and clout of his predecessor and was still less able to exercise a strong leadership role at a time when Germany's previously unstoppable economic rise appeared to have stalled.[70] The temporary cessation of the *Wirtschaftswunder* could not but reduce the authority of the man generally credited with its start. Second, Erhard was himself in the vanguard of those complaining about the CAP and was hence ill-placed to dismiss 'economic' or 'technical' difficulties with the same type of Olympian disdain that Adenauer might have been able display. In both cabinet and coalition discussions, the Chancellor had become personally associated with the quest fundamentally to alter the CAP; abandoning such a stance would be correspondingly harder.[71] And finally, and perhaps most fundamentally, there seemed little reason to make concessions to a French government with whom relations had reached a seeming nadir with the outbreak of the NATO crisis in late winter, early spring of 1966.[72] The temporary thaw in Franco-German relations that had characterised the Rambouillet meeting between de Gaulle and Erhard in early February, had ended abruptly with the French President's announcement that he was to withdraw his country from the Alliance's integrated military command.[73] Understandably Germany, as a front line state in the cold war, reacted with particular concern to this move. Apart from anything else, the move cast doubt on the future of French troops in Germany. In such circumstances conciliatory German gestures towards Paris at a Community level seemed distinctly improbable.[74]

The troubled state of Franco-German relations at a Community as well as a general level seemed to be well summed-up by the meeting in March between Wormser and Lahr. The two men were regular sparring partners as well as central figures in their two countries' respective European policy-making. It was thus very disturbing that in the course of a two-and-a-half hour meeting, their first since Luxembourg, they succeeded in disagreeing on virtually every single substantive point that they broached.[75] They differed on the priority to accord the financial regulation, they disagreed on the date to set for the start of the customs union, there was no meeting of minds over the Kennedy Round, there was total discord over the legitimacy of Germany's request to set a ceiling for its CAP contributions, and there was deadlock over the Commission Presidency. Indeed, virtually the only point of agreement was their shared pessimism about the state of the Brussels negotiations. Lahr in particular regretted the deterioration of Community diplomacy:

> The EEC of today is no longer the same as that which took the acceleration decision, that which opened multiple membership and association negotiations, or that which came to an audacious resolution of the cereal price question. The difference is the following: the earlier progress of the Community sprang from political and economic motivations, with the political impulse proving decisive in the big decisions that were observed with astonishment throughout the world. Today such political motivations can no longer be detected. A Commission representative was very right to observe recently that Brussels now operates only on cash and no longer on credit. No delegation appears willing to pay an advance for the – alas unknown – political future of Europe. All that remains is the economic impulse, which may prove enough for the Community to survive upon. This means each member state will have to content itself with the economic advantages already obtained, and those that may be attainable in the future. The requirement for such a system, however, is that each partner has the conviction that any deal is economically advantageous from its point of view. Should this conviction disappear, it is very hard to see why any state should take the necessary steps to participate. It therefore follows that it is disastrous should any state insist that its interests must be addressed before all others. Only through well-balanced package deals does the EEC currently have a prospect of survival.[76]

Lahr's gloom, although understandable, was probably already out of date by late March, however. For by early spring 1966 there were clear signs that the negotiations in Brussels were regaining a degree of momentum and that accord was not as distant a prospect as Wormser and Lahr appeared to feel. As in 1963, this process was first observable at the level of the permanent representatives: the February row referred to above as a symptom of the malaise seemed to remind both Sachs and Boegner that they had little to gain from outright animosity.[77] In the course of the same meeting, aided and abetted by their fellow COREPER members, both retreated from the extreme positions and hectoring tone that they had initially adopted and began to take a more conciliatory approach.[78] Subsequent meetings of the member state ambassadors to the Community were much less acrimonious.[79] And the rebuilding of trust observable at the level of COREPER soon began to feed through both to the Council of Ministers and, still more gradually, to those parts of the national administrations entrusted with the making of European policy. The Council meetings in early March and then again a month later both made significant progress in bridging the gap between France and its partners over the financial regulation. Agreement was not yet at hand, but several of the main controversies were well on their way to solution. Germany's mood for instance was significantly improved by the completion in March of a general statement about the balanced development of the Community – a nod to Bonn's obsession with 'parallelism' or 'synchronisation' – and the near consensus achieved in April about a technical switch in the method of calculating agricultural trade which would mean that Germany was likely to receive a significantly higher amount of European subsidy in the future. Partly as a result, the German government took the very important step of deciding not to air in Brussels any of the ideas it was seeking to develop about the way in which the CAP might be substantially altered in the future. Internal discussions continued in Bonn, but no significant proposals were made at a Community level.

As negotiations continued in Brussels it also became increasingly clear that a number of important changes had occurred which made less likely a repetition of the previous year's breakdown. The first of these was the dissolution of the German and Italian axis of discontent towards the CAP. By 1966 neither country had overcome its basic unhappiness about the overall agricultural policy. Bilateral meetings between German and Italian ministers still provided the opportunity for shared complaints about the iniquities of the current system.[80] But nearly a year on from the outbreak of the crisis both governments had realised that a simple repetition of their earlier joint attempt to block CAP advance would be unacceptably provocative to the French. They had hence to look for ways in which the CAP could be pushed forward without hurting their national interests. And once this change of attitude had occurred, the solutions sought by Rome and Bonn became more often contradictory than complementary.

The Italians thus sought to solve their CAP problem by securing the rapid extension of European arrangements to commodities such as fruit and vegetables, olive oil, wine, or tobacco, in which they had a direct interest, and by maximising the amounts of money that the EEC would devote to the so-called 'guidance fund'.[81] CAP expenditure devoted to structural measures – in other words intended to improve the efficiency of European agriculture – were likely to be particularly useful in a country such as Italy with numerous, very technologically backward farmers. To German eyes, by contrast, both the establishment of generously-funded CAP support systems for Mediterranean produce and any increase in the size of CAP structural payouts, were simply aggravating factors at a time when the CAP budget was already threatening to spiral out of control.[82] For Germany the key was controlling expenditure and making certain that where the CAP did have to be extended, the new market regulations, like that proposed for sugar, included mechanisms other than price for controlling the Community's output.[83] In 1966, unlike a year earlier, there was therefore little chance of the French feeling cornered by a joint German–Italian assault on its agricultural interests.[84] Instead there were much better prospects of satisfying the Italians by means of financial inducements and winning the Germans round with 'parallel' progress towards the completion of the customs union and the Kennedy Round.

A second important change was that France's own approach was more tactful than it had been in 1965. For a start, the French were in less of a hurry to complete the CAP than they had been. By 1966, the French government was clearly extremely worried about the upward effect of high European cereal prices on both general domestic inflation and on French agricultural production. While the financial regulation and the establishment of an effective European mechanism to fund the surplus grain that French farmers were already beginning to grow remained imperative, the French were now rather less keen to see the immediate introduction of other European prices, since these too were likely to be higher than the French norm.[85] If common prices were agreed, the French would not object; but if this did not look likely, there was no need for Paris to push excessively. France was hence much better placed than it previously had been to accommodate other countries' hesitations about too rapid an establishment of the CAP.

The French also appeared to have learnt the dangers of too confrontational a style of negotiation. The 1966 talks were notable for the absence of the type of high pressure tactics that France habitually employed. At those rare moments when this was forgotten and French negotiators used threatening language – part of the discussion amongst permanent representatives on 24 February was an example – the rapid reappearance of a united front of the Five promptly reminded Boegner and his colleagues of why they had abandoned this approach.[86] And most important of all, Paris seemed to have recognised that it could only hope to advance by accepting much of the case for parallel progress to the CAP. Indeed, one of the great strengths of the French negotiating position in 1966 was that they rediscovered that they could win substantial credit in the eyes of their partners by taking steps that were actually in France's own national interest. An internal French analysis of the 4–5 April Council meeting for instance commented 'Our secret weapon, was our very real good will as far as the

Kennedy [Round] negotiations were concerned' – France in other words could give the impression of flexibility on the EEC's commercial diplomacy while in reality making no genuine sacrifices at all.[87] The combination of all three factors made France a much easier negotiating partner to deal with in 1966 than it had been in 1965.

A third change that facilitated the path to agreement was the way in which Germany won acceptance of a procedural ruse designed to get round the awkward clash between its desire for parallel movement and France's insistence that the devising of the financial regulation have priority over all other matters. This was the so-called 'Schubladentheorie' or 'drawer theory' – the idea that chronologically separate Council meetings handling different aspects of the overall package deal could be made conditional on the general success of all the individual negotiations.[88] Such an approach, which appears to have been initially suggested by the French, then enthusiastically espoused by the Germans and finally tacitly accepted by its partners, meant that Bonn could sign up to the outcome of a first set of negotiations centred on the financial regulation but still make it clear that it would not allow this agreement to be taken 'out of the drawer' unless and until a later Council meeting had successfully settled another package of measures connected to the Kennedy Round.[89] Staggering the negotiations in this way avoided the type of pile up of interlinked negotiations that might have seriously overloaded the Community machine.

A fourth beneficial change was the fact that Luxembourg rather than France held the Council Presidency. This not only meant that Borschette, a wily and experienced Community operator, took charge of the crucial COREPER preparatory work, but more importantly ensured that the Presidency could play an impartial role in the ministerial discussions. Luxembourg's interests in the CAP were much more limited and distinctly more easily accommodated than those of the French who had held the Presidency in the first half of 1965. It was therefore much easier for the Council chairman to devise compromise arrangements and broker deals than it had been in the equivalent negotiations 12 months before.

The final, and complementary, change was the return of the European Commission to a facilitating role in place of the politically controversial stance that it had adopted in the 1965 negotiations. The altered Commission approach was apparent from the very first meeting after France's return to Brussels and was to culminate with the Commission presenting vital package deals in both the May and July marathon meetings. For all the uncertainty that seemingly surrounded its post-crisis position, and despite the serious health problems that afflicted Hallstein and Mansholt, hitherto two of its most dynamic members, the Commission was thus able to play an extremely constructive role in the resolution of the agenda-centred aspect of the Community crisis. This went some way towards compensating for the institution's near total exclusion from the talks that had brought the institutional part of the crisis to an end.

All of these factors help explain how, a mere six months after both participants and outside observers had been speculating about the possible collapse of the integration process, the Six were able to conclude three successive marathon negotiations that all but secured the EEC's future. The agreements of 11 May, 14 June and 27 July mapped out the Community's internal and external development until the end of the transitional period on 31 December, 1969. The much delayed financial regulation was the centre piece of the first. This set out the way in which the costs of the CAP would be borne for the rest of the transitional period (until 1 January, 1970) but avoided firm decisions on either Community 'own resources' or any increase in the power of the European Parliament. France had, in other words, belatedly achieved that separation between the basic finance package and the extra items that the Commission had sought to add in March 1965 which France had long desired. Sweetening the pill for the Five, however, was the way in which the May deal also identified identical dates for the start of *both* the full CAP and the customs union for industrial goods. Bonn's quest for parallelism would be largely fulfilled on 1 July, 1968 when the industrial and agricultural markets would simultaneously come into operation. Likewise, the May deal contained timetables for the introduction of Community regulations for tobacco and wine designed to alleviate Italy's sense that the CAP ignored the needs of Mediterranean producers.[90]

There were further signs of a balanced compromise in June and July accords. The former devised the Community's stance on part of the agricultural chapter of the Kennedy Round negotiations – a breakthrough that assuaged German anxiety about the Community's failure to engage with the Geneva tariff negotiations, but also reaffirmed the Six's commitment not to allow global trade talks to undermine the structure of the CAP. And the latter combined a further set of internal agricultural provisions with more Community arrangements for the agricultural part of the Kennedy Round.[91] By the time the exhausted negotiators departed for their traditional August summer holidays, they had thus devised a new, parallel timetable for the introduction of free movement of both industrial and agricultural goods throughout the Community and allowed the EEC to resume the full involvement in the GATT negotiations which had been jeopardised by the French boycott. Despite a public and political response characterised by relief rather than elation, the crisis was truly over.

The significance of the crisis

The period between May 1965 and July 1966 had been amongst the most eventful and traumatic in the EEC's history. The Community had experienced an extremely acrimonious negotiating breakdown, a six month stand off between its single most influential state and the five other members of the EEC, an institutional 'compromise' in Luxembourg that appeared open to widely conflicting interpretations, and a set of complex and hard-fought negotiations which had ultimately produced the type of balanced package deal that had eluded negotiators in the summer of 1965. Such extreme circumstances revealed much about the basic functioning of the Community system. Faced with crisis, both Community members and onlooking outsiders such as the British and Americans, were more reflective than usual about the fundamental nature of the integration process. Furthermore, it is also frequently claimed that the events of the 1965–66 period, and in particular the institutional outcome of the January 1966 Luxembourg meetings, significantly altered the way in which the EEC operated. It is therefore essential that the second half of this chapter takes a step back from the detailed chronological description of what had happened in order to ask a series of important questions about the significance of the crisis period and the nature of the Community that had emerged from it by the summer of 1966.

The first, major issue that needs to be addressed, is how the empty chair crisis related to the broader struggle that appeared to be underway between Gaullist France and its Western partners. For by 1966, de Gaulle had seemingly led his country into a position of open revolt against most of the accepted orthodoxies, norms and institutions of the postwar Western system. The General had thus become a scathing critic of US policy, notably over Vietnam. He had adopted his own highly distinctive approach towards the Communist bloc recognising Mao's China at a time when other powers were minimising their links with Beijing and forging new links with the Soviet Union and the countries of Eastern Europe. And he seemed intent on launching a single-minded campaign to reform the institutions of Western cooperation. His 1964 attack on American plans for a multinational nuclear force (the MLF), had thus been followed by the 1965 tirade against the Bretton Woods monetary institutions, later in the same year by the boycott of the European Community, and in 1966 by his decision to withdraw his country from the integrated military command of NATO.[92] France, to many outside observers, seemed bent upon a Samson-like attempt to bring about the collapse of the whole Western economic and security apparatus, despite the potential harm to its own interests that such a collapse might entail.

The relationship within the EEC between the French and their partners could not fail to be affected by this wider confrontation. For a start, some of the General's own frustrations with EEC cooperation seemed to be traceable to his comprehensive dislike of American dominance. The institutions of the Community were, for instance, deemed to be partly US-inspired – Jean Monnet was routinely referred to as 'l'américain' in Gaullist circles – and to be unduly deferential to Washington's views.[93] The close links which the Hallstein Commission had built up with the Eisenhower, Kennedy and Johnson Administrations were prominent amongst the institution's faults.[94] And still worse was the way in which several of France's partner states seemed intent on acting as proxies for the United States. Dutch single-mindedness in thwarting the General's 1960–62 plans for European political union were seen as a product of The Hague's incurable Atlanticism and hence subservience to the Anglo-Saxons in general and the Americans in particular.[95] Similarly, Germany's enthusiasm for global trade liberalisation through the GATT and its hesitancy about the CAP were both felt to be as much a reflection of how close a path Bonn steered to Washington as it was of Germany's own national interests. Multiple Italian politicians, especially those like Fanfani on the left of the *Democrazia Cristiana* were also seen as being thoroughly under America's spell. In Belgium, Spaak, a former NATO Secretary-General after all, was equally suspect. Frustration at Dutch, German, Italian or Belgian opposition to French desires within a European context thus intermingled all too easily with the General's personal antipathy to any manifestation of US hegemony.[96] In August 1964, for instance, against a backdrop of German procrastination over the crucial cereal price decision, the General commented acerbically:

> Erhard and Schröder are the Americans' men, they don't like France. They hence feel obliged to strike a balance between the US alliance, in other words the obligation to comply with all that the Americans want, and the public's insistence on maintaining friendship with France. They would not be forgiven for breaking this last ... But on the major issues, as soon as there is a concrete problem, they always choose the American solution.[97]

Reactions amongst the Five to French European policy were also coloured by the wider crisis caused by de Gaulle. This of course had been true to a certain extent ever since the General's return to power. The Netherlands' determination to thwart the Fouchet Plan for instance can only be understood in the light of Dutch perceptions that the French intended to use any mechanism for European political union to lead the continent in foreign policy directions totally inimical to their own Atlantic beliefs.[98] But this phenomenon had become that much more acute in the mid-1960s as the French President's challenge to the Western system became increasingly strident. Those German anxieties about French European policy which had contributed significantly to the start of the crisis in June 1965 sprang, for example, not simply from the perceived maldistribution of the costs and benefits of the integration process (important though these undoubtedly were) but also from a deeper underlying anxiety about the direction in which the General was leading his country. The thaw underway in Franco-Soviet relations – illustrated for instance by the deal concluded in the spring of 1965 to sell French SECAM television technology to the Russians – and the signs of unwelcome French flexibility on the question of relations with East Germany were significant ingredients in the build-up of German alarm.[99] And when trying to make sense of why Germany's approach to the crisis seemed to harden in January 1966, the fact that the French leader had just announced his intention to visit the Soviet Union later in the year was almost certainly relevant.[100] In the light of these examples it is entirely comprehensible why Luns should have commented that as far as France was concerned 'policy towards NATO and European policy are nothing but communicating vessels.'[101]

A detailed examination of the Community crisis period also underlines, however, the limits of interconnection between tension within the EEC and tension within the wider Western system. After all, had Luns' metaphor of the 'communicating vessels' been entirely correct, no recovery from the crisis ought to have been expected in the spring and summer of 1966. On the contrary, the violent turbulence in the NATO vessel should have produced ever more agitated waters in the Community also. This would have meant no successful triple marathon. And yet, as was emphasised above, this concatenation of disputes in NATO and impasse in the EEC did not take place. Instead, relations between France and its partners within an EEC context appeared to have steadily improved at the very moment that those between France and many of the same countries within a NATO setting were reaching a nadir.

There are several possible explanations for the divergent evolution of Community and NATO affairs. One suggestion, put forward on several occasions by British and American observers, was that the French quite deliberately sought to avoid a situation in which they were involved in two major crises at once. A key reason indeed why de Gaulle and his lieutenants were content to accept much less than expected in January 1966 was precisely because the French President had decided that he wanted to launch his NATO *coup de théatre* early in the New Year and needed to wind up the Community dispute before this could be done. The EEC successes of May–July therefore reflected a conscious French strategy of giving ground in Brussels so as to avoid a diplomatic war on two fronts.[102] Whether this was in fact the case remains impossible to determine on the basis of French diplomatic documents relating to Community affairs. These contain next to no references to the gathering storm in NATO. But it is of course entirely possible that any calculation of this sort was carried out exclusively within the Elysée, the papers of which remain closed for the period in question. The silence of French documents does not therefore automatically disprove the Anglo-American contention. Even if true, however, a French decision of this nature would not of itself have been sufficient to explain progress at an EEC level, since for this to occur it was necessary for the Five to share France's belief that their disagreements over NATO should not be allowed to impede their cooperation within the Community.

Two further factors hence need to be taken into account. One of these is the realisation by most of the EEC member states that their interests would be harmed rather than served by any spill-over between the two institutional contexts. Such a conclusion had not been guaranteed. Schröder, for instance, had reportedly argued within the German cabinet that 'it was politically impossible to agree on agricultural financing involving large benefits for France at [the] same time [as the] French were attacking NATO'. But the German foreign minister had been overruled by his Chancellor, who had asserted that a 'temporary NATO crisis' should not be allowed to endanger a 'permanent European Community'.[103] And the four other Community governments appear to have reached a similar conclusion: the benefits that they derived from the EEC and the Community's lasting significance outweighed any tactical advantage that might be drawn from using pressure within the EEC to contain the French attack on NATO structures. The Community should hence, as one Commissioner put it, be 'insulated' from the wider dispute between the French and their Western partners.[104]

Such insulation was facilitated by the way in which European policy was carried out by most member state governments. By the mid-1960s, EEC affairs had already become a highly complicated and specialised policy-area. It was one, of course, within which foreign ministries and diplomats still played an important role. But the likelihood of it being affected by other foreign policy concerns was lessened both by the emergence within foreign ministries of Community-specialists who worked on little else but European policy and, more seriously, by the influence of other competing ministries less likely to be as sensitive to foreign policy pressures. German European policy for example was drawn up on a day-to-day basis by a state secretaries' committee on which the Auswärtiges Amt's influence was counterbalanced by that of the Ministry of Economics, the Ministry of Finance and the Ministry of Agriculture. It was thus entirely typical that opposition to Schröder's call for France to be punished in the Community for its NATO policies was spearheaded not just by the Chancellor, but also by Schmücker, the Minister of Economics.[105]

Furthermore, once discussions moved to Brussels they were again heavily influenced by out-and-out EEC specialists, whether within the Commission or in Council structures such as COREPER, all of whom recognised that multiple references to outside events would render their task that much more complicated. And even on those occasions where the final Council discussions involved the full foreign ministers, and not just more junior ministerial envoys, there were also multiple safeguards preventing extraneous factors from having too great an impact. Couve, Schröder, Harmel or Luns were all personally involved in the Atlantic dispute. But when they met in a Community context, they did so within the confines of a meeting, the agenda of which had been drafted so as to concentrate exclusively on EEC matters, their discussions were shaped by preliminary documents drawn up within the Community structure, and their briefs were already of sufficient complexity to deter loose references to unrelated concerns. Allusions to wider disputes were no doubt made in the corridors and in informal discussion between Council participants. But once formal exchanges began, the institutional context, the difficult and highly technical nature of the subject matter, and the intrinsic importance of the interests at stake all served to isolate Community discussions from the wider foreign policy context. The French, for instance, commented in the aftermath of the May ministerial meetings that 'The NATO crisis played no role, except perhaps in further stimulating the very evident desire on the part of all the Community member states to bring to an end discussions of the financial regulation.'[106]

Rather than communicating vessels, bound by immutable laws to respond in similar fashion to every event, the Community and NATO spheres were hence more like separate billiard balls, liable at times to touch and affect each other's advance but otherwise subject to independent stimuli and dynamics. The wider Atlantic crisis was relevant to both the Community's descent into impasse in 1965 and may have contributed to German determination and French moderation at Luxembourg. The mood of generalised mistrust between France and its partners was an important background factor throughout the 1965–66 period. And individual instances of national behaviour within the Community could take on a much more threatening appearance in the eyes of EEC partners when refracted through the prism of wider foreign policy disagreements. Atlantic divisions could, however, be kept from dominating discussions, provided that most of the participants wanted the Community to function. The months that followed the Luxembourg meeting thus demonstrated that outside events were not sufficient to prevent the Six from overcoming their internal divisions and reaching the vital series of agreements concluded in the summer of 1966. The EEC was capable of moving forward under its own rules, rather than simply being propelled, this way and that, by events elsewhere.

National interests

A second, general issue about the 1960s EEC, that can profitably be discussed in the light of the crisis period, is the importance of the integration process to each of the participating states. Paradoxically, this had been underlined rather than contradicted by a year during which the continuation of the Community had appeared open to doubt. For the outbreak, conduct and resolution of the crisis all provided vivid testimony to the desire on the part of each of the Six to safeguard what they had created. Thus in the spring and summer of 1965, the bruising nature of the diplomatic exchanges between France and its partners reflected the way in which Germany, Italy, The Netherlands and France had all separately decided that concession and moderation would be more dangerous to the Community and to their interests therein than bold diplomacy.[107] Similarly, the reluctance of both the French and the Five to retreat on issues of substance once the crisis began was largely due to their belief that the survival of the Community in the form they wished to see was at stake. The Five were forced into the awkward discipline of unity *à cinq* and the French were obliged to sacrifice some of their immediate interests in the smooth-running of the EEC by their respective conviction that softness and rapid compromise might undermine the whole structure of the Community they so valued.

Equally revealing, however, was the underlying prudence of both the French and the Five during the crisis months. The partial nature of the French boycott, the care taken by the Five to avoid reaching legally-binding decisions in France's absence, the constant use of discreet bilateral diplomacy and the restraint shown by both sides in their use of the superficially appealing but profoundly hazardous 'British card' all testify to the shared desire of all of the Six to avoid a situation in which the crisis escalated out of control.[108] Both the intensity of feeling provoked by the confrontation and the limitations that prevented such anger and irritation from degenerating too far thus illustrate member state awareness of how important were the stakes for which they were playing.

The messy and unclear institutional arrangements of January and the path to the triple marathon of the summer of 1966 also highlight the way in which each of the Six felt pressured into compromise by the importance of safeguarding the EEC. There was no great meeting of minds on institutional questions at Luxembourg. In many ways the documents produced by the Extraordinary Council raised more questions than they provided answers. But the reason why they sufficed to bring France back to the negotiating table in Brussels was that, by January 1966, both Paris and the Five had independently concluded that ongoing impasse within the EEC was more threatening to the Community and to their national interests than was the conclusion of a less than totally satisfying compromise accord. The challenge at Luxembourg had thus been to find a form of words that both sides could plausibly defend to their political class and general public. Once this was done the French and the Five could resume that cooperation that had appeared more threatened by the continuation of institutional paralysis than it was by divergent views about majority voting or even more deep-seated discord about supranationality and the *finalités politiques* of the EEC.

Likewise, in the months that followed the French return, a growing awareness of the potential dangers of a new failure to agree on the financial regulation and the EEC's parallel development, encouraged all of the participants in the February to July negotiation to retreat from their initially hard-line positions.[109] As usual such retreats were made easier to accept by compensatory gains elsewhere and were semi-disguised by the technical complexity of many of the issues being dealt with. But by late spring/early summer, all of the Six had evidently realised that agreement itself had become more important to the EEC and hence to their national interest than the individual details about agricultural finance or the Kennedy Round that still separated them. The triple marathon was thus characterised by a generalised willingness to compromise and to be flexible that had been signally lacking from the negotiations 12 months earlier.

The national interests tied up in the EEC were both economic and political. That each of the member states was partially driven by economic incentives is amply demonstrated by the crisis period. The vital importance to all of those involved of the balance struck between agricultural and industrial integration is one example of this. Had the EEC merely been an instrument for constructing a political Europe it would have mattered little whether the chosen vehicle was agricultural or industrial integration provided that it worked. All of the actions of the French, Germans, Italians, and Dutch in the 1965 to 1966 period underline how crucial this choice was, however, and how serious a blow to national interest it was deemed to be were integration in one sector to edge ahead of that in another. The form taken by Europe's economic integration was in other words intrinsically important rather than of simply instrumental significance. Similarly, the detailed SGCI investigation of the EEC's significance carried out in October 1965 stressed how much both French industrial and agricultural prospects were dependent on the Community's continuation and provided a highly significant set of economic arguments in favour of French moderation and flexibility in resolving the empty chair crisis.[110] Lahr's lament to Wormser about the changed nature of EEC diplomacy cited above also points in the same direction, with its assertion that even in the Community's darkest hour the integration process was likely to endure because of the remaining economic incentive to cooperate. Whatever the motives of Europe's founding fathers had been, the fortunes of the EEC experiment were, by the mid-1960s, profoundly affected by national calculations of economic interest.

It would be equally wrong, however, to believe that economics alone explains member state attachment to the integration process. On the contrary, as that same Lahr comment demonstrates, the EEC was a highly political enterprise. The whole thrust of the State Secretary's complaint was that something was going wrong with the Community if it had become entirely dependent on commercial self-interest. It therefore highlights the extent to which the undeniable national economic interests wrapped up in the Community project dovetailed with a set of equally important political motives. Indeed, the passions generated by the crisis are only comprehensible once the political significance of integration and the EEC's structures are grasped. A mere commercial treaty after all should scarcely have been affected by the disagreements about Europe's place in the world, East–West relations or the future of Atlantic cooperation which, as explained above, played so important a role in the build-up and escalation of the crisis.[111] Instead, a significant number of Europe's elected leaders, and the seeming majority of their political elites, believed that the EEC was already a deeply important political venture which both symbolised how far the continent had distanced itself from past conflict and had vested in it multiple hopes about much more extensive political cooperation and unity in the future.[112] It was hence something that had to be protected at all costs from a French leader who was feared to harbour very different political ambitions. Such views were particularly pronounced at a parliamentary level in almost all of the Five.[113] Indeed, the nervousness with which virtually all of the participants at Luxembourg regarded the way in which the meeting's outcome would be interpreted by their national parliamentarians is only comprehensible against the backdrop of such beliefs. Schröder, Luns, Colombo, and Spaak were very aware that they would have to convince their onlooking national political elites that the deal done in no way impeded the future political development of European integration.[114]

Also highlighted by the crisis months were some of the traditional political functions that the Community was meant to fulfil. That of a framework within which Germany's reviving power could be safely accommodated was particularly evident. Belgian and Dutch nervousness about a Community without the French and in which there would be little to counterbalance Bonn's political and economic weight, clearly showed that the pacific diplomatic track-record of the Federal Republic had not yet eradicated all European anxieties about German leadership.[115] More importantly, the Community framework also seemed to be that within which Bonn itself felt most comfortable flexing its largely untested foreign policy muscles. As in 1963, Germany had felt obliged to respond to seemingly threatening French behaviour during the crisis months, but preferred to do so acting with and through its Community partners rather than challenging de Gaulle directly. It was much easier for Schröder and his colleagues to take on their French counterparts as part of a united front of the Five rather than as German spokesmen bilaterally challenging the French.[116] This in part explains why the French had unsuccessfully sought to isolate Schröder in the aftermath of the first Luxembourg meeting. It also lay behind some of Germany's evident discomfort with bilateral diplomacy as a means to solve the crisis.[117] And it certainly explains the enormous retrospective satisfaction that German representatives seemed to derive from the fact that the unity of the Five had not cracked during the crisis months.[118] The 1960s EEC therefore continued to have an important function as a controlled environment within which the Germans could begin to reassert their burgeoning influence without either alarming their neighbours unduly or producing too much domestic political discomfort.

To the containment of Germany, however, there had arguably been added a further political role by 1966, namely the containment of France. For in the context of 1960s western Europe, the loose cannon that threatened to disrupt the existing system was no longer Germany but instead

Gaullist France. Any set of institutional ties that served to fasten France to the West and to prevent de Gaulle's dalliance with the Eastern bloc from becoming anything more than a provocative flirtation was of highly significant value. It was for this reason that Tuthill, the US representative to the Community, could write to Rusk, the US Secretary of State, of the 'heavy support within the Five for not invoking the NATO crisis in the EEC, and for moving ahead with Community business in order to enmesh de Gaulle more and more in European integration and preserve the Community structure for the post-de Gaulle period.'[119] The notion of *Westbindung*, of using integration as an institutional anchor designed to prevent dangerous movements in the international alignment of individual Western states, could now be seen as applying to France even more clearly than it still did to Germany.

The rejection of the institutional extremes

This combination of economic and political incentives to continue the integration process is vitally important for explaining the third major question that needs to be examined, namely the institutional outcome of the crisis. The exact significance of the 'Luxembourg Compromise' has been a subject of extremely polarised opinions ever since January 1966. For some it was a outcome of little weight, a reaffirmation of the known divergence of views on majority voting between France and its partners.[120] For others, by contrast, it was an explicit acknowledgement of the right of any member state to veto Community decisions on issues where vital national interests were felt to be at stake.[121] Many of those holding the latter view have therefore also seen it as a vital *caesura* between the vibrant and active Community of the early 1960s – the EEC which had outstripped all expectations in its development – and the stagnant, fractious entity that is normally held to have characterised the 1970s and early 1980s. De Gaulle's success in thwarting the federalist ambitions of Walter Hallstein and the Five were widely seen as having sapped the vitality from the Community institutions and condemned the Six to a lengthy period of frustration and disappointment.[122] 28 January, 1966 was thus a dark day in the history of supranational European integration.

Such simplistic views do not really stand up to a detailed historical examination of the crisis. The 1965–66 period clearly did matter institutionally. Never before had the functioning of the Community system, not to mention the arcane modalities of qualified majority voting, been so extensively discussed both within national governments and amongst the wider public. The vibrancy of this debate, furthermore, undermined the previous state of affairs where national governments had been able to exploit the comparative lack of knowledge about the functioning of the EEC to discuss the evolution of the system and their contribution to it in terms which had more to do with the state of national opinion about integration than it did with realities in Brussels.[123] Prior to 1966, the German, Dutch, Italian or Belgian governments had thus explained and justified their European policy to their own electorates and parliamentarians in radically more federalist terms than the French government, presenting the same set of events to the National Assembly in Paris. And yet in Brussels the way in which the different governments behaved and the extent to which they placed their national interests above too many abstractions about European interest was fundamentally similar.

The crisis of 1965 disrupted this comfortable state of affairs. The radicalism of Hallstein's 31 March proposals and still more the institutional grievances raised by the French after 30 June obliged the member states of the Community to assess what sort of European system they wanted and to reject much more explicitly than before what they did not wish to see. It also seemingly presented them with a clear institutional choice between the intergovernmentalism of de Gaulle – a system grounded on member state independence and with common institutions reduced to no more than a simple secretariat – and the federalism espoused by the Commission President. In this latter vision, power within the European Community would become ever more concentrated in the hands of the Commission and to a lesser extent the European Parliament, with the Council of Ministers gradually evolving into no more than the upper chamber of the Community legislature.[124] By January 1966, however, it had become abundantly clear that the Five rejected *both* of these competing visions and instead were wedded to an institutionally hybrid system that had gradually been emerging ever since the start of the Community system in 1958. The crisis months were hence more significant for the options that the Five did not take, rather than for any major change that did occur.

Pure intergovernmentalism held few attractions for any of the Five. In a system from which all supranational elements had been removed, in which the Commission had been turned into a largely subservient civil service, and in which member states retained the full right to block or opt out of any piece of Community legislation they disliked, there were only ever likely to be two types of political outcome. Either there would be ineffectiveness and institutional paralysis, a fate often compared to that of the OEEC – given the economic and political importance of the Community described above this was a highly unpalatable possibility – or, still worse, the defeat of supranationalism might mean dominance by the strong. None of the four smaller member states could look favourably on a set of institutional arrangements that made likely French leadership in the short and medium term and German dominance at a later stage. Nor were the Germans themselves pleased either with a system which gave too much power to France – something which would endanger many of the political and economic gains the Federal Republic hoped to make through integration – or one which put the onus of containing and then replacing French dominance on their shoulders. The genuine multilateralism of the existing

Community system was a much more appealing arrangement. And it is even possible to question how committed were the French to this vision. De Gaulle certainly seemed to want to move decisively in this direction – or so his rhetoric implied. The thrust of the initial decalogue, moreover, could be seen as seeking significantly to reduce the political independence of the Commission. But both the track record of those French negotiators who actually attended Community meetings and the pragmatism that Couve and his colleagues displayed when seeking a compromise at Luxembourg suggest that the real French desiderata fell a long way short of the maximalist stance adopted by the General in his 9 September, 1965 press conference.

Imminent federalism was every bit as unattractive as Gaullist intergovernmentalism. It would certainly prevent either French or German dominance, but it would do so at the cost of undue Commission power. The Hallstein Commission was respected by most of the Five (with a few reservations) but none of them wanted a situation in which it, rather than they, dominated Community decision-making. Nor was there great enthusiasm for the type of large-scale handover of funds to the Community budget to which Hallstein aspired. French objections that such a move would only encourage Commission profligacy had been largely accepted.[125] Furthermore, in a Council of Ministers where no constraints were placed on the use of majority voting, the risk would be ever-present of individual member states being outvoted and forced to accept deeply unpopular or damaging measures. The possible gains in the effectiveness of decision-making would, in other words, be outweighed by the risk of vital national interests being harmed. In an EEC which already had significant effects on important aspects of each member state's economic development, and which over time was likely to become that much more influential, such a degree of supranational control was not something that any of the Five were prepared to countenance.

Nor was it necessary for them to do so. Institutional radicalism might have held some appeal had the EEC of the 1960s been stagnant and ineffective. Faced with paralysis, member states might have gambled on a *fuite en avant* into federalism. But in 1965–66 there was no such need. On the contrary, the existing system had worked well and looked likely to continue to do so: it had delivered many of the hoped-for economic benefits and was likely to bring still more, provided that member states continued to operate effectively in Brussels. A few small moves in the direction of institutional reform had their supporters of course. Notable in this respect was the fusion of the executives that had already been agreed and some tentative steps in the direction of greater power for the European Parliament. And in the longer run all sorts of institutional arrangements could be contemplated under the general heading of European unity. The Treaty, with its built-in possibilities for future evolution, thus needed to be preserved. But few of those politicians and civil servants who had come to know the Community system as constituted eight years after the EEC's creation were in a hurry to alter the status quo radically. There was little appetite for a sweeping institutional overhaul of the Community in 1965 or 1966.

As a result all of the Six could accept the outcome of the Luxembourg meeting, since this essentially reaffirmed the existing state of affairs. The Heptalogue left unchanged the basic powers and prerogatives of the European Commission. Indeed, a careful analysis of the document by Emile Noël, the Executive Secretary of the Commission, highlighted the way in which most of the procedures outlined in the Council document corresponded to the way in which the Commission already behaved on most occasions.[126] The latter could hence go on playing that vital role in stimulating discussion amongst the Six that all of the member states, including the French in their less dogmatic moments, had come to appreciate. The mere fact that the member states had agreed to discuss its behaviour in the absence of Commission participation however sent a powerful warning to Hallstein and his colleagues that neither the ambition nor some of the political tactlessness that they had shown in the months prior to June 1965 could easily be tolerated. A modification in the Commission's behaviour was hence politically inevitable even if the Council statement had no legal force.[127] The prospects for any substantial shift in power from the Council to the Commission – prospects central to Hallstein's own vision of how the Community should and would evolve – were pushed back indefinitely.[128]

A similar lack of change was implied by the agreement to disagree over majority voting. Exactly how this would play out in practice remained unclear, of course.[129] Nevertheless, both the wording of the formula agreed and the tenor of the discussions at Luxembourg underlined two points, both of them essentially conservative in nature. The first was that the Five were determined to preserve, and the French prepared to accept, the legal sanctity of the Treaty and hence the continuing possibility of using qualified majority voting. The status of the Treaty of Rome as the unquestioned basis of cooperation amongst the Six was hence strengthened by the Luxembourg outcome. But once this important legal and political principle had been reaffirmed, all of the Six were prepared to show a strong degree of pragmatism about the way in which majority voting would be used in practice.[130] Indeed, as was shown by Germany's role in pushing for the list of major decisions that could not be taken by majority vote, France was not alone in regarding the possibility of majority voting with a degree of nervousness. It was therefore highly unlikely, despite the vagueness of the Luxembourg conclusions themselves, that the passage from stage 2 to stage 3 of the Community's transitional period would be accompanied by the type of institutional earthquake that some had anticipated.[131] Instead, the recognition by all of the member state governments that majority voting was a potentially dangerous device that would have to be deployed with caution and only in certain circumstances – a recognition that had arguably been there long *before* the crisis had begun – was made that much more explicit.[132] Again, the outcome made it likely that the Community would carry on as before rather than changing radically.

The type of hybrid Community, neither wholly federal nor wholly inter-governmental, that had been consolidated by the Luxembourg Council was well demonstrated by negotiations that led to the triple marathon. These made very clear the remaining influence and importance of the European Commission. Proposals tabled by the Commission formed the basis of most of the Council debate, Commission expertise, especially in the highly complex agricultural field, was frequently called upon, and the final Council meetings of both May and July were decisively shaped by package deals devised by the Commission.[133] Those parts of the talks devoted to GATT matters were even more striking: each debate began with a report by Jean Rey, the Commissioner in charge of external relations, about the state of play in Geneva, and the final outcome of both the June and July deals were mandates that would have to be implemented by the Commission as the Community's representative at the world trade talks.[134] These were not the workings of a traditional intergovernmental institutional system.

Equally apparent between February and July, however, was the extent to which the Community remained under the collective control of the member states. Central to all of the progress made was the huge volume of work accomplished by COREPER and its equivalent for GATT business, the Article 111 Committee.[135] Most of the vital substantive breakthroughs were made at, or just before or after, Council meetings, whether of agricultural ministers or of the foreign ministers, and the final successful outcomes of the three marathon meetings were largely attributable to the readiness to reach unanimous agreements displayed by all of the member state representatives involved and to procedural innovations, such as the *Schubladentheorie*, devised by the individual states themselves. The valuable contribution of the Luxembourg Presidency only further confirms this pattern of member state control. The European Community of 1966 was not the Commission-dominated entity described by early political science analysts like Leon Lindberg.[136]

None of this was new in 1966. Most of the patterns of behaviour described above had been emerging ever since the Community's inauguration eight years earlier. One of the first Commissioners, Robert Lemaignen, for instance, had lamented the rise of COREPER in the 1958–62 period.[137] The European Parliament had likewise expressed its unease at the multiplication of Council meetings and their growing impact in a report written in 1962.[138] The various hybrid procedures designed to retain member state control over areas where limited powers had been devolved to the Commission – mechanisms that had developed in fields as diverse as commercial negotiations with Third-World countries and European Community information policy – had been emerging piecemeal throughout the EEC's first years of existence.[139] Arguably indeed, the slippage away from Monnet's original vision of supranational power predated the Treaty of Rome and could be traced back to the negotiations that had led to the 1951 Treaty of Paris and then to the subsequent operational experience of the European Coal and Steel Community.[140]

What had changed, however, was that the gap between the rhetoric of federalism and the realities of cooperation in Brussels had been decisively exposed. Until Luxembourg it had always been possible for pro-Europeans, whether in the Commission or in member state parliaments, to disregard the growth in Council power, either by not noticing it at all or by dismissing it when it did become known as a temporary aberration from the inexorable federalist trend. This was made all the easier by the concentration of both media and academic attention on the Commission – viewed as the most original and hence most interesting of the EEC institutions – rather than on the Council structures.[141] After Luxembourg, by contrast, it was clear that none of the member states shared the belief in a rapid move towards federation characteristic of Hallstein, the vast majority of Members of the European Parliament, and a vociferous body of opinion within the Dutch, German, Italian and Belgian assemblies. It was true of course the Six states had also, at the same time, rejected any dangerous lapse into intergovernmentalism. But the way in which the Community had been spared this greater danger was not sufficient to prevent the spread of a wave of disillusionment and disappointment amongst many of those who had earlier been most prominent in their championing of the European cause.[142]

At the level of the Community's day-to-day functioning or its tangible achievements, however, this did not matter very much at all. On the contrary, one of the dominant themes of the crisis period was the way in which the controversy over how the Community functioned, though real, was always inextricably tied up with, and often subordinate to, the question of what the EEC could and should do. As argued in Chapter 3, the institutional element of the crisis had come to the fore largely because of the disagreement that had erupted over the Community's agenda. It was therefore logical enough that the Six should seek a means to accommodate their differing institutional viewpoints so as to be able to resume discussion on the issues that lay at the root of their divide. After all, from the point of view of most politicians and civil servants, the tangible gains that European integration would bring, whether economic or political, were of much greater national interest than the niceties of majority voting or the exact procedure followed for the accreditation of foreign diplomats to the EEC. The pragmatic deal struck at Luxembourg, while lacking the clarity that constitutional analysts would have liked, was thus fully in line with the basic national interests of those states which continued to dominate the integration process. France and its partners went on holding somewhat divergent views both about how the Community should work and on

Europe's place and role in the world. Their shared interest in the material and political benefits that integration could bring however proved sufficient in 1966 to override such disagreements and deliver a string of important compromises stretching from January, to May, June and July. National interest had triumphed over both institutional dogmatism and narrow sectoral advantage, and had allowed the Community to overcome the most important and serious crisis of its eight year history.

5 The return of the English question
September 1966–December 1967

In September 1966, as Brussels returned to life after the August break, Boegner composed a thoughtful telegram. The Community, he argued, was about to begin a new, rather different phase of development, 'a period of reflection and uncertainty'. Naturally, there was plenty of routine business to occupy those who worked in the European institutions. The Community's existing policies would continue to need fine-tuning and there were plenty of secondary controversies that were likely to arise. But, in marked contrast to preceding years, none of the immediate policy debates involved making fundamental choices: the great decisions of principle, whether concerning industrial trade or agriculture, had already been taken. Many in Brussels were therefore turning their attention to the Community's future agenda rather than being exclusively focused on the implementation of its first, treaty-defined, tasks. Such speculation was likely, the French permanent representative predicted, to change the spirit and tone of Community debate: 'it will be interesting to observe the manner in which the Common Market, after having for years progressed under the pressure of political imperatives and deadlines, copes with a period of living one day at a time without it being clear in what direction it is headed'.[1]

The first two parts of this chapter will confirm Boegner's analysis. Mistrust amongst the Six remained. The scars from a year and a half of confrontation had not vanished entirely in the August sun. And the wider relationship between Gaullist France and its partners, especially West Germany, continued to be fraught with difficulty. The exaggerated tones in which Erhard spoke of the threat posed by de Gaulle was still representative of what much of Germany's ruling elite believed to be the case.[2] But at a Community level at least, the heat appeared to have gone out of those central controversies that had done so much to destabilise the EEC since the spring of 1965. There was thus little immediate tension surrounding the agenda of the Community. The timetable agreed in May 1966 still had to be implemented, of course, and a lively debate had begun about where the EEC should go next. But neither the primarily technical tasks of realising both the customs union and the CAP by July 1968, nor the discussion about the future policy-agenda appeared likely to generate much passion, mutual suspicion or anger. Likewise, there was every sign that the Six had come to an institutional *modus vivendi*. Low level squabbles about the exact distribution of powers between the Community institutions rumbled on. There was ongoing deadlock about who should head the new single European Commission, due to replace the High Authority and the Commissions of Euratom and the EEC. And there continued to be sufficient disappointment about the Six's failure to extend their cooperation into the foreign policy sphere for new suggestions about how a political union might be launched to be always likely. But on a day-to-day basis that hybrid Community, neither wholly supranational nor purely intergovernmental, (the emergence of which was discussed in the previous chapter) appeared to be working well. Indeed, the biggest substantive issue of late 1966 and early 1967, the conclusion of the Kennedy Round of GATT negotiations, seemed only to underline the effectiveness of the existing institutional balance. Here too, Boegner seemed to be justified in his expectation of reduced controversy ahead.

The Community's steady recovery from crisis would, however, be disrupted by a sharp increase of discord surrounding the third of the great questions that the early Community needed to resolve, namely the matter of who should belong to the EEC. For as the last part of this chapter will demonstrate, it was the re-emergence of the issue of enlargement that was to turn what might have been a period of quiet reflection into one of renewed tension. A new British approach to the Community, culminating in the 2 May, 1967 application for membership, had a serious impact on the Community and reopened many of the old wounds left behind by the 1961–63 enlargement episode. Tension grew even higher as it became clear over the ensuing months that French opposition to early British membership remained as unmoving and complete as it had been at the time of the first veto. The year would thus conclude with the ill-tempered Council confrontation of 18–19 December at which both observers and participants spoke openly in terms of 'crisis' and the emotional ending of which appeared to suggest a return to the deep fracture between France and the Five that had been a feature of the empty chair crisis itself. Boegner's optimism of September 1966 had been shown to be sadly misplaced.

Towards a new community agenda

The 18 months that followed the successful conclusion of the triple marathon saw remarkably little discord amongst the Six about what the Community should do. The 11 May deal in particular, by setting a clear target date for both the completion of the CAP and that of the customs union, appeared to have drawn a line under the long-standing Franco-German dispute about the relative importance of agricultural and industrial advance within the EEC. The French, furthermore, appeared fully conscious of the need for the Community to participate constructively in the climatic stages of the world trade talks underway within GATT. Couve de Murville, Boegner and the new French minister of agriculture, Edgar Faure, thus threw themselves into the multiple Council sessions devoted to GATT matters in the latter part of 1966 and the first five months of 1967 with enthusiasm and commitment.

The consensus amongst the Six over the importance of the Kennedy Round did not of course mean that agreement was easily achieved on any of the substantive matters that needed to be discussed. On the contrary, negotiations within the Council continued to be hard fought and often frustratingly slow. In December 1966, for instance, the ministers of the Six found themselves disagreeing strongly not only on products that were well known to be sensitive within an EEC context – poultry and horticulture would be prime examples – but also over items like herrings that had not previously been the subject of Community impasse.[3] Significant differences remained too over the desired pace of advance in Geneva and the extent to which the Community should take seriously the United States' doom-laden predictions about how the Kennedy Round constituted the last chance to avert a new wave of global protectionism.[4] That same December 1966 Council meeting witnessed an impassioned speech by the German State Secretary, Neef, in which great alarm was expressed at the way in which several of the Community's partners had withdrawn some of the their earlier tariff offers, being countered by an equally forceful intervention by Couve emphasising how generous the Community had already been.[5] This Franco-German clash, moreover, was not a unique example of the ongoing differences in approach to the Kennedy Round in Paris and Bonn. French representatives were thus well to the fore of those who questioned how seriously the Community should take the deadline of 30 April which the US tried to set.[6] And predictably, Faure's dogged defence of French farm interests had much to do with the EEC's refusal to improve on the 90 per cent agricultural self-sufficiency level that it had offered to set itself as part of the agricultural chapter of GATT discussions.[7] On both issues, Germany's representatives had taken a very different line from the French.

None of these disagreements, however, went beyond those that were to be expected in any multilateral negotiation involving important national economic interests. France's efforts to defend its producers' interests were in no sense out of line with those of the Germans, Belgians, Dutch or Italians when their domestic economic factors were threatened. And several of the disagreements that arose between the more hesitant liberalisers like France and the enthusiastic Dutch or German partisans of the Kennedy Round reflected divergent tactical assessments rather than genuine arguments over substance. In both December and again in January, for instance, Boegner opposed too early a preparation of further EEC concessions on the largely justified basis that Brussels was so leak-prone that any such flexibility would become known to the Community's negotiating partners long before the Commission had a chance to table the improved offer in Geneva.[8]

Nor did the discussions create the type of rigid alliances of interest that might seriously threaten EEC unity. France and the Dutch, while poles apart on some GATT issues, were thus able to make common cause in their quest to widen the scope of the food aid programme that the United States had proposed as part of the deal.[9] Germany and Belgium, meanwhile, demonstrated the superficiality of any attempt to categorise the Six into pro- and anti-American camps by attacking Washington's whole notion of including food aid on the GATT agenda.[10] And most crucially of all, every single Community participant underlined its commitment to achieving a result in Geneva by showing a willingness both to make important substantive concessions and to entrust the Commission with the necessary authority to conclude a final deal. The GATT talks thus strengthened rather than undermined solidarity between the Six. Certainly they helped restore relations between the Five and the French. After all, the behaviour of Couve and his fellow French negotiators in Brussels largely confirmed what had long been apparent from internal French government documents, namely that Paris was acutely aware that a successful outcome in Geneva would serve its economic interests well whereas a breakdown, especially if attributable to French rigidity, might prove politically and economically disastrous.[11]

The Germans, meanwhile, seemed ready to reciprocate French flexibility over international trade by being more accommodating over the CAP. Admittedly, few in Bonn had lost their basic dislike of the Community's agricultural system; background rumbles about the illiberalism and cost of the policy would remain a feature of German political debate for years (and decades) to come.[12] But both the Erhard government and still more the Grand Coalition government that took its place in November 1966 seemed to accept that the CAP was a fact of Community life and that to impede its emergence would only be to invite French retaliation elsewhere. The programmatic statement that marked Willy Brandt's Brussels debut as the new German foreign minister thus contained none of the ominous references to CAP reform that had been a feature of earlier German action plans, notably that of 1963. Instead, his discussion of how the Community could move beyond being only a customs and agricultural union, seemed to imply a readiness to accept that the CAP was an unassailable part of the *acquis communautaire*.[13] Perhaps still more telling was the matter-of-fact manner in which a number of agricultural decisions were listed in an internal government document designed to identify the priorities of Germany's Presidency of the Community in the latter half of 1967.[14] Eighteen months or two years earlier, a comparable document would surely have discussed the possibilities of wide-ranging change to the

CAP or ignored agriculture altogether on the grounds that the CAP had already advanced too far, too fast. By 1967, however, the impossibility of either course had been recognised and Bonn was content to see its period of chairmanship used to advance towards the 1 July, 1968 deadline for the completion of 'green Europe'. French nervousness about the motives and European targets of their German partners was correspondingly reduced.[15]

As Boegner had recognised, the near completion of the Community's initial core agenda did mean that serious discussion could begin about what the next objectives should be. Brandt's statement referred to above was just one of multiple signs that this debate was underway. And any such airing of views about the Community's medium term development was bound to reveal a number of divergent priorities. The German foreign minister's enthusiasm for a joint Community approach to trade with the Eastern bloc was thus not something that was shared with the French, nor was his advocacy of multiple Mediterranean associations easy for the Italians to swallow.[16] German calls for fiscal harmonization meanwhile were looked at askance in several of its partners' capitals while Bonn's ongoing support for an effective common transport policy was guaranteed to provoke opposition from the Dutch.[17] In similar fashion, several of Italy's calls for future Community development were met with opposition elsewhere: Fanfani's suggestion of European technological cooperation, while well received by the Commission, caused deep divisions within the German government, with the powerful ministry of economics being especially hostile.[18] Italian suggestions for a greater Community role in the social field were still more unpopular, being systematically opposed by several of Italy's fellow member states, largely on grounds of cost. And even the European Commission's major policy initiative of 1967, namely the unveiling of Mansholt's ideas for structural reform of Europe's agriculture met with a polite initial response that belied the deep preoccupations to which the proposed scheme gave rise.[19]

None of these disagreements were particularly worrying, however. Debate on most of these questions was at so early a stage that the lack of consensus mattered little. What was important in 1966 to 1967 was that a debate about the EEC's future agenda had begun. No conclusions yet needed to be reached. Furthermore, the lines of disagreement varied so much depending on the exact issue under discussion that there was little risk of a serious rift developing amongst the Six. The Netherlands' opponent on one issue was likely to be its ally on the next, Italy's staunchest critic on the first of its enthusiasms a strong backer of the second. There was hence no short-term likelihood of disagreements about the future agenda of the EEC driving a wedge between individual members of the Six in the way that agenda-related issues had divided the French from the Germans, Italians and Dutch in the first half of 1965. The as-yet highly abstract speculation about the best future means of using the framework of European cooperation was much less divisive than the question of how to share the tangible benefits and costs of its existing policies. By 1967, the Community's agenda had thus temporarily ceased to be an issue which in any way threatened the unity and cooperation of the Six.

Institutional pragmatism

In similar fashion 1966 to 1967 could be described as a period during which the row over the Community's institutional shape also faded. This might at first seem a rather contentious suggestion. After all the whole of 1966 and the first months of 1967 were a time of total deadlock amongst the Six over the personnel of the new Commission – a dispute which long delayed the implementation of the 1965 merger treaty. This impasse, which centred on the question of whether or not Hallstein should have his term of office prolonged, seemed to defy resolution with multiple procedural ruses and compromise plans being tabled without result.[20] The rigidity of the French position on the issue appeared, moreover, to suggest that de Gaulle did not regard the January 1966 heptalogue as the end of his vendetta against the *apatrides* of Brussels. And the fact that May 1967 saw the first gathering of the Six Heads of State and Government for over five years, and the first ever EEC summit at which Community affairs as well as possible political cooperation were discussed, might seem, especially with the benefit of hindsight, to mark the start of a trend towards the institutionalisation of summitry which would in due course utterly transform the EEC. Surely this too was an institutional development that was both significant and controversial?

Upon closer examination, however, neither of these institutional issues really divided the Six in the way in which earlier confrontations over institutional matters had done. The dispute over the Presidency of the Commission was the more serious and did constitute a rather public embarrassment.[21] In reality, it was much more of a Franco-German trial of strength and an illustration of Erhard's determination to stand up to de Gaulle than it was a genuine battle about the strength or effectiveness of the European Commission. At the highest level, neither Paris nor Bonn showed great personal enthusiasm for Hallstein – in July 1966 Erhard and de Gaulle seemed to agree that the Commission President was over-ambitious and determined to build 'a Hallstein Community' rather than a truly European body.[22] Nor, once account is taken of the calibre of those discussed as potential replacements, does it seem likely that France any longer harboured a real ambition to reduce the Commission to an entirely subservient and quiescent civil service. A Commission led by one of the favourites – Colombo – was hardly likely to play this role.[23] Instead, the issue became part of both governments' efforts to persuade their publics that they had 'won' the European struggles of the previous year. As a result neither de Gaulle, nor a German Chancellor ever more beset by domestic and foreign policy difficulties felt able to retreat, despite the increasingly sterile nature of the dispute. In the end, only the change of government in Bonn broke the deadlock and even then, a few more months were necessary before the new Chancellor, Kurt Georg Kiesinger, felt confident enough of his standing to be able to scale down his support for Hallstein. Offended by the mere six month extension of his term that Bonn now called for, the Commission President then brought the row to a dramatic conclusion by resigning in April.[24]

Hallstein's departure did not however signal any major change in the standing or effectiveness of the European Commission. As explained in the last chapter, the more grandiose ambitions harboured by the outgoing President had not survived the member states' rejection of precipitate federalism. It was fully in keeping with the new mood of institutional pragmatism that the post-fusion Commission should be headed by someone less clearly associated with the Commission's earlier delusions of grandeur than with the practical achievements of the Brussels body. The selection of Jean Rey who had just proved his effectiveness as the Community's principal representative in the Geneva trade negotiations was therefore highly appropriate. An EEC insider, he had enough practical knowledge of the Community system to be able to oversee the process of merging the three separate institutions that were now to form the single European Commission; as a man with a party political background, he also helped demonstrate that the Commission remained a political body and not just a bureaucratic entity.[25] And as someone who had proved able to stand up to intense American pressure in Geneva, he was also unlikely simply to prove a pawn of the larger states. That he came from Belgium also helped reassure those worried about the undue dominance of France and Germany within a Council-centred EEC. On the other hand, the fate suffered by his predecessor, combined with the new consensus amongst the Six that the post of President should rotate much more quickly (normally every two years), acted as guarantees that Rey would not become as personally dominant as Hallstein had been. Instead, the Belgian was likely to be able to play a valuable role alongside national ministers in steering the Community without threatening member state control in the fashion that Hallstein had periodically seemed to do.

Nor should too much significance, in institutional terms, be read into the Rome summit. This was always intended as a one-off affair, designed to mark the tenth anniversary of the signature of the Treaties of Rome.[26] It was probably also a bid by the government of Aldo Moro and still more by his foreign minister, Fanfani, to rekindle Italian *europeismo* which had been dampened by the struggles with de Gaulle and by the cost of the CAP. But it was neither presented nor perceived as a significant change in the way in which the EEC should be run. The misgivings about the appropriateness of a gathering not foreseen by the Treaty of Rome handling EEC business were therefore fairly muted.[27] Furthermore, the decidedly limited outcomes of the meeting acted as an additional assurance that heads of government meetings were not likely soon to usurp the role of the Council of Ministers.[28] There was admittedly some limited talk about a new summit being held in December, primarily to resume the search for the still elusive political union.[29] But the notion of regular summitry as the missing ingredient in the Community's overall institutional make-up was almost entirely absent from member state debate before, during and after the Rome encounter. Whatever the longer-term significance of heads of government meetings in the Community's development, there was no sense of having witnessed a major alteration in 1967.

Instead, institutional change was very little discussed during this post-crisis period. Those still committed to the goal of a European federation were reluctantly forced to bide their time, aware that forward movement was all but impossible in the short-term and that impatience might well prove counter-productive. Their disappointment, often vigourously expressed, did much to colour the mood of the European debate. Journalists reporting from Brussels have always been very responsive to Commission disappointment and in 1967 were quick to fill their papers with stories outlining the 'malaise' affecting the European project.[30] But the undeniable gloom of those who wanted imminent federation was not particularly representative of national views. On the contrary, the majority of member states seemed reasonably content with the status quo.

After all, the Kennedy Round negotiations appeared to be just the latest indication that the system as constituted could deliver tangible rewards.[31] Rey and Theodorus Hijzen, the chief Community negotiator at an official level, had assumed a prominence in the Geneva talks that no representative of a single European country could have matched. Having a unified voice in commercial diplomacy thus clearly underlined the benefits that an effective supranational institution like the European Commission could bring. The Commission's effectiveness, moreover, demonstrated that the institution could still operate well despite the frustration of its further-reaching political aspirations. And yet at the same time the GATT talks had illustrated the extent to which the member states wished to retain a high degree of control over the integration process in all of its multiple manifestations. Rey and Hijzen had thus been subject to constant oversight from the Article 111 Committee, a Council body upon which sat representatives of each of the member states. Furthermore, most of the key decisions had been extensively discussed in meetings of the full Council, with ministers repeatedly demonstrating their willingness to enter into very detailed consideration of even comparatively minor products. As a result, the Commission negotiators in Geneva, while enjoying more freedom of manoeuvre than simple envoys with rigid instructions, were very much responsible for articulating a jointly-devised Community position rather than merely presenting Commission views in Europe's name. The successful outcome of the GATT talks and the impact that the EEC had been able to have upon it, were hence not merely a significant victory for the European Commission, but also a triumph for a Community system of which the Commission was a vital, but partial component.

With the institutions seemingly functioning well, with the short-term aims clearly defined and accepted by all, and with a complex, but as yet serene, debate underway about the medium-term future, it was not surprising that one former French official in Brussels should look back at the period following the empty chair crisis and the triple marathon as being one during which the EEC reached its 'cruising speed'.[32] This metaphor might also help explain the sense of disappointment felt by those who had been most exhilarated by the Community's rapid, if uneven and sometimes fraught, advance prior to 1965. The steadiness of a liner's progress, if dignified and perhaps satisfying for some of those aboard is scarcely an exciting prospect. But in reality, the smoothness of advance and the calm nature of the surrounding waters would soon prove illusory. For late 1966 and 1967 was also a time during which the Community would find itself having to navigate a safe-passage through a set of shoals, whirlpools and shallows which it hoped to have put behind it four years before. The reason for this renewed difficulty was quite simple: the issue of British membership had become relevant once more and gave no indication of having grown less problematic or divisive in the years since 1963.

The return of *les Anglais*

The disagreement over the desirability of EEC enlargement had of course been the original cause of open dispute between France and the Five. As Chapter 1 sought to demonstrate, the January crisis of 1963 triggered by de Gaulle's veto of Britain's 1961 EEC application was the first occasion on which the unilateral and peremptory nature of French Community diplomacy forced the other Community member states into an angry and defiant bloc. While never disappearing entirely, however, the issue of enlargement had progressively faded from view in the three subsequent years. Part of this reflected a conscious decision by the Six to avoid too much discussion of an issue that had shown itself to be highly divisive. With so much else to do, there was little point in dwelling unnecessarily on a largely insoluble difference of opinion. But more importantly, this ebbing of the British question reflected the seeming loss of UK interest in entering the EEC. The Labour Party, which was in power in London from October 1964 onwards, was after all still officially wedded to a set of conditions for EEC membership that stood little chance of being met and that had been devised in 1962 primarily to allow the party to oppose Macmillan's application without formally ruling out Community membership. During its first two years in power, Harold Wilson's government gave little indication of wanting to move beyond a purely 'paper' pledge about joining the EEC.[33] The disinclination amongst the Six to argue over the merits of British membership thus became even more pronounced in the light of London's own lack of enthusiasm. What would be the point of agonising over the issue, when the supposed beneficiary gave every indication of having lost interest in taking its place within the Community? The third of the questions upon which this book centres had thus been allowed to dwindle to not much more than a background disturbance – one of those issues of international diplomacy where all of those involved periodically reaffirmed their stance in principle but on which no one expected rapid change.

Change was, however, precisely what appeared to be underway in 1966. The exact reasons that led Wilson's government progressively to revise its view of European integration lie beyond the scope of a study focused upon the Six. According to the most detailed recent investigation of the subject, disillusionment with Labour's earlier policy choices, ever mounting economic pressure culminating in the July 1966 sterling crisis, and the presence within the government of certain departments – notably the Foreign Office – and certain individuals – George Brown would be the obvious example – whose belief in the virtues of joining the EEC had never diminished, all combined to push the Labour government towards a new approach to 'Europe'.[34] Electoral pressure from a Conservative party now led by Heath and deeply committed to taking Britain into the Community may also have been a factor.[35] But whatever its roots, the impact upon debate amongst the Six of the new more favourable, if still evolving, British attitude was immediate and profound.

Two meetings, three months apart, between Schröder and Couve de Murville illustrate the point well. In the first, held in February 1966 shortly after the Luxembourg Council, both the German foreign minister and his French opposite number seemed in agreement that the issue of British membership, while important, was not of any real urgency. Indeed, Couve felt relaxed enough about the whole affair to list a number of ways in which Britain's prospects for becoming European were gradually improving. He pointed, for instance, to the way in which the Commonwealth was becoming an ever looser grouping and as such a less significant obstacle to British EEC membership. And it was Schröder and not Couve who outlined his conviction that enlargement was not likely to be realisable for several years yet and that the Six should hence press ahead with developing their own cooperation. In so arguing, Schröder was admittedly preparing the ground for his suggestion that more be done by the Six to improve relations between the Community and EFTA – a plea to which Couve was largely unresponsive. An important gap remained, in other words, between German impatience to lessen the commercial divide between the Six and the rest of western Europe and relative French indifference to this issue. Nevertheless, there did appear to be a genuinely shared conviction on the part of both the French and the German ministers that British membership was a medium-term prospect only, and as such not something for which the Six had actively to prepare. At a time when France and Germany were liable to disagree about virtually everything else, the level of consensus between them on the question of Community enlargement was truly remarkable.[36]

By the time the two men met again in April, however, the situation had changed significantly. Britain's March election campaign had seen both main parties discussing the issue of EEC membership seriously. The Germans were correspondingly encouraged and Couve de Murville that much more defensive. Rather than being willing to list the ways in which British membership was becoming more realistic, Couve chose instead to emphasise those problems that still remained. Particular weight was, for instance, placed on the weakness of sterling and the way in which Britain might not be able to withstand the balance of payment pressures that early Community membership could bring. Schröder and his fellow German representatives seemed pleased, by contrast, at the way in which the issue had evolved and confident that despite the problems raised by France, a new British move was likely. Lahr, for example, rejected Couve's suggestion that the British problem was not likely to become acute for at least the rest of the year, arguing that it might become so as early as the autumn.[37] Long before the launch of the October 'probe', or the actual application in the spring of 1967, the British issue had started once more to become a source of discord rather than harmony between Paris and Bonn.

The French reacted to this incipient problem by doing their best to deter a new British approach. There had been some hope in London that Pompidou and Couve de Murville's visit to the UK in July 1966 might have offered an opportunity to avert a new Anglo-French clash over EEC membership. Some amongst the British political elite had long believed that the best way into Europe lay through a primarily bilateral bargain with the French and those who felt this way naturally looked to the presence in London of the French Prime Minister and Foreign Minister as a moment when some such deal might be struck.[38] Such hopes had been boosted by a number of public statements by the French earlier in the year that could have been taken as encouraging the British to apply.[39] The two French visitors had quite other ideas however. From the very start of their discussions, Pompidou and Couve made clear their reservations about any new British move towards the Community and their belief that the difficulties of sterling in particular all but ruled out EEC membership. To make matters worse, such sentiments were not confined to the privacy of governmental meetings; on the contrary, Pompidou expressed his doubts about the sustainability of sterling's global role and the compatibility of such a role with a European future in a press conference, thereby contributing to the mounting speculative pressure on the British currency.[40] Far from an opportunity to devise some means of averting future Franco-British difficulties, the meeting appeared to have been no more than the opening engagement in a further diplomatic row.

French determination to deter the British from applying was more than matched, however, by attempts by the Five to encourage the new trend in London's European policy. The Erhard government was particularly forward in this respect. As early as May 1966, the Chancellor urged the British to base their new approach to Europe upon the support of the Five rather than potentially misleading 'half-hearted' invitations from the French. Germany and Britain could, he suggested, undertake a joint study of the practical problems that enlargement might entail, secure the support of the four member states other than France, and then confront de Gaulle with a clear choice between accepting the UK or imposing a polit-ical veto. This latter option, Erhard believed, was not one which de Gaulle was strong enough to take in the face of unanimity amongst his partners.[41] Although Wilson demurred from the idea of Anglo-German studies, Bonn made clear that it would press ahead with its own internal review of the issues likely to arise from an eventual application.[42]

The Germans were also keen to rally the rest of the Five behind a new British approach. In early June, the German foreign minister spoke in radical terms to Fanfani about their two countries acting in concert to lead the Six towards a joint strategy on British membership – a declaration of goodwill by the EEC might, he suggested, have a great and beneficial impact upon Britain's own debate.[43] A month later Schröder was highly encouraging to Pierre Harmel as the Belgian foreign minister outlined the way in which his country and the Dutch intended to react to the negative line taken by Pompidou and Couve in London.[44] Even before the British had made up their own minds, the mere prospect of a new UK application appeared to divide the Five from the French in precisely the fashion that Couve had sworn earlier in the year to avoid.[45] Little wonder then, that by October a Quai d'Orsay report noted gloomily that 'in the final analysis, one cannot help feeling that the Germans are much more attached to the entry of the British into the Common Market than the British are them-selves'.[46]

The continuation of German pressure for enlargement was thrown into doubt in November, however, by the fall of Erhard and the coming to power of a Grand Coalition government led by Kiesinger.[47] The new government was still in favour of British EEC membership. Community enlargement was specifically referred to in the Bundestag speech with which the new Chancellor introduced his government's programme.[48] Brandt as foreign minister, moreover, went out of his way to stress to the British Ambassador that Germany's position had not altered.[49] And in a meeting with his British counterpart, the German leader was able, not without a slight trace of irony, to note that he had been a partisan of British Community membership long before Wilson had been.[50] But what had changed was the way in which the incoming German government was committed first and foremost to improving the very poor state of Franco-German relations and therefore had every incentive to avoid provoking a showdown with de Gaulle over the British question. Brandt's meeting with Sir Frank Roberts referred to above had significantly been immediately preceded by an equally friendly exchange with François Seydoux, the French Ambassador.[51] Still more revealingly, both his government's parliamentary policy statement and Brandt's meetings with the two ambassadors listed the new German West European priorities as being Franco-German rapprochement, Community advance, and EEC enlargement, in descending order of priority.[52] It was therefore clear that Kiesinger and Brandt would adopt a different approach from that of their French counterparts.[53] Compromise and gentle persuasion were likely to replace the more confrontational tactics espoused by Erhard and Schröder. As Kiesinger would comment at a somewhat later point of the row over British membership, 'Germany cannot play the role of a bull-dozer, since this would certainly prove counterproductive'.[54]

Neither the clear signs that France would once more seek to bar Britain's path, nor the worrying possibility that Germany would no longer fight as hard in the UK's cause, seemed to affect the direction of the policy debate in London however. The evolution of Britain's European policy has often tended to be more responsive to domestic developments and pressures than it has to events and trends on the other side of the Channel. The course of what would become Britain's second application fully fitted this pattern. In early November 1966 – at precisely the time that the first signs of change in Germany were emerging – the Prime Minister announced his intention to tour the capitals of the Six in order to 'probe' the prospects of British entry.[55] The exploratory visits then segued fairly quickly into a full-scale application, announced on 2 May, 1967, despite the fact that the Paris leg of Wilson's probe had largely confirmed de Gaulle's opposition to British membership.[56] Brown, in particular, continued to talk in terms of the Five being able to exercise decisive pressure upon Paris, totally disregarding Kiesinger's attempts to explain that this could not be done. A great deal of misguided political optimism thus underpinned Britain's 'second try'.

Reacting to Wilson

Misguided or not, the formal membership application from Britain, followed as it was by immediate Danish and Irish applications (and a somewhat delayed Norwegian bid), posed a serious challenge to the Community. For reasons that will be explored in greater depth in the next chapter, five of the Six remained firmly in favour of an enlarged EEC. They thus could not but welcome Wilson's decision to take the plunge. In the light of the expected opposition of the French, however, none of the Five were under any illusion that the British bid would easily be accommodated. Indeed, most of their fears appeared to be confirmed on 11 May when the latest de Gaulle press conference set out, with all the General's customary eloquence, the reasons why France did not believe that the immediate enlargement of the EEC was possible. Britain's approach, the General argued, would have one of three effects:

> Either it will have to be recognised that their [the British] entry into the Common Market, with all the exceptions that would inevitably accompany it, with all the quantitative and qualitative changes that it would entail, and with the participation of multiple other states that would certainly be its corollary, would amount to the establishment of entirely new entity, all but erasing that which has been built. And where, then, would this lead us other perhaps than the creation of a type of European free trade area, which would in turn lead to an Atlantic zone that would deprive our continent of any real personality.[57]

Or, Britain should be welcomed as an associate member. Or, finally, the UK would be asked to wait still longer while its slow internal evolution towards a European future completed its course. Confusingly, however, the French President also appeared to rule out any use of veto against Britain's application.[58] It was therefore left extremely unclear as to how the Six would be able to formulate a common response to the British and other applicants.

The sensitivity and complexity of the issue was very apparent from the early Community discussions of the topic. At the Rome summit and in the first Council exchange about enlargement in late June, the Six talked around the problem rather than having a wholehearted debate.[59] To a certain extent this reflected the genuine procedural complexity of any enlargement negotiation – and particularly one involving multiple applicants. Article 237 under which the British, Danes and Irish had applied was open to multiple interpretations as to how any negotiations with the candidate countries were to be conducted.[60] The seeming determination of all involved, moreover, to avoid repeating the mistakes made in 1961–63 meant that the most obvious procedural guide, namely the only previous membership negotiations that the EEC had experienced, was much less extensively used than might have been expected. And there were already signs that some of the Five hoped that the problem posed by France's stance could be finessed, were a sufficiently ingenious negotiating method to be devised.[61] A great deal of time was therefore lost in somewhat arcane discussions about who should negotiate, how much negotiation was needed, and when a decision for or against enlargement needed to be taken.

Just as important, however, in explaining the slow start of the talks, was French determination to keep its powder dry until a full Council debate of the subject was held.[62] While everybody thus knew that France was opposed to enlargement, nobody knew exactly what arguments against the membership of Britain and the other applicants the French were likely to deploy. As a result, ministers from the 'friendly Five' found themselves trying to rebut a French case against enlargement that, the General's Delphic press conference apart, had not yet been made. To make matters worse, the exact terms of Britain's approach were also unknown as the French had done their best to avoid arranging a Community forum to which the UK's opening stance could be set out. The June Council discussion was thus characterised by a strong air of unreality or even farce.[63]

Not even the French, however, could delay a full scale debate indefinitely. First of all the Belgians, encouraged by Brandt, sidestepped French obstruction to a British opening statement by suggesting that the UK statement be made to the Western European Union (WEU) and not to the Council of Ministers.[64] George Brown was thus able to explain why Britain desired to enter the Community in a speech to the WEU Assembly on 4 July that eclipsed even that of Heath in October 1961 in its ringing pro-European idealism.[65] Then Couve de Murville had no choice but to join his fellow foreign ministers for the Council meeting of 10–11 July at which the principal item on the agenda was that of enlargement.[66] The talks about talks, if not the full membership negotiations themselves, had begun.

As soon as this happened it became clear how radically the enlargement debate had evolved since 1961–63. For a start the new British approach was much less hesitant than that of the Macmillan government had been. No longer was the British application a conditional one – a bid memorably described by *The Economist* as being wreathed 'in a bower of "ifs" and "buts"'.[67] Instead, Wilson's letter to the President of the Council was a straightforward request for membership. Nor were the British asking to discuss nearly as many technical issues before joining. Some transitional arrangements would of course be needed were the UK to adapt to the EEC, but Brown's WEU speech raised far fewer difficulties than Heath's corresponding opening statement five and a half years earlier.[68] Its pro-European sentiments were hence not diluted by the vast array of special conditions that Heath had been obliged to request. And the impression that Britain was approaching the Community this time without the hesitancy that had characterised the 1961–63 application was further reinforced by the fact that the 1967 application was approved by the House of Commons by a sweeping 488 to 62 majority, with all three of the main English parties voting for EEC membership.[69] The British gave every indication of having decided wholeheartedly that their future lay inside the European Community.

All of this meant that French claims about the disruption that enlargement might cause were much less plausible in 1967 than they had been when Britain first applied. In 1962 it had been all too easy to believe that the UK was seeking to renegotiate the nascent CAP – indeed it is only a slight exaggeration to say that this is what Christopher Soames, the then

minister of agriculture had in effect asked for in February of that year.[70]
But five years on, not only were the Community's policies that much more
solidly established, but Britain seemed also to have accepted that the onus
of adaptation lay with the applicant and not with the existing member
states. It therefore seemed much more likely that the Community could be
increased in size without having significantly to reinvent itself in the
process. It would be the applicants and not the Six who would be forced to
change their ways.

Still more importantly, however, the French case was weaker than it
had been because de Gaulle had overtly stated his opposition to enlargement. In 1961 it had of course been widely suspected that the French
President was hostile to British membership in particular.[71] But the
General had cleverly kept everyone guessing until his January 1963 press
conference. As a result, French negotiators had been able to present the
arguments they raised during the membership negotiations as genuine
attempts to protect their national interests and the interests of the EEC
rather than as deliberate obstructionism. This they had done with great
skill, thereby allowing other members of the Six to feel perfectly legitimate
in siding with the French on multiple occasions. In 1961–63 it had thus
rarely been the case that the French had found themselves isolated; on
most subjects discussed either the European Commission and/or one or
more of the other Community members had adopted a near identical
stance.[72] In 1967, by contrast, the French were known to be against
enlargement from the outset, most probably for political reasons that most
of the Five believed to be unreasonable if not illegitimate. There was
hence much less willingness to view French arguments as *bona fide* anxieties about the exact manner in which Britain and others were admitted to
the EEC. Instead, they were seen as a figleaf of rational argument
designed to cover a nakedly political bid to preserve the political and economic advantages that France derived from the Community.[73] This meant
that it was much harder for the Five to back any aspect of the French
stance, even when their economic or material interests were similar. In
1967, France was therefore much more isolated than it ever had been
during Britain's first EEC application.

Couve de Murville, admittedly, did his best to present the French case
in a reasonable manner.[74] He was widely recognised as the Council of Ministers' most able debater and the course of the 11 July, 1967 intervention
only reinforced this standing.[75] As ever, his arguments were put together
with both eloquence and a degree of remorseless logic. And the sheer
number of points that he made, each designed to emphasise the way in
which enlargement would change the existing Community beyond recognition, was impressive in its way.[76] There was hence a brief silence in the
Council chamber when he finished talking, as each of his fellow ministers
digested the French case.[77] But once the counter-arguments began, it was
evident that few of Couve's points had really struck home. Brandt,

Fanfani, Harmel, Luns and Gregoire all did their best to refute each of the objections to enlargement that the French minister had raised, to highlight the positive aspects of British membership that Couve had ignored, and to advocate the immediate opening of negotiations with the applicants.[78] On few previous occasions had the validity or even the legitimacy of the French line been so clearly rejected in a meeting of the Council of Ministers.

For all its discomfort, however, the French position was in reality quite strong. With memories of the empty chair crisis still fresh in the minds of most of those around the Council table, none of the Five had a particularly strong appetite for another acrimonious confrontation with Paris. This was all the more so given that Bonn was generally known to have other reasons for avoiding a fight with the French and would thus be unable to reprise the central role it had played in 1965–66.[79] And still more importantly, it was all but impossible to deny that France did have the legal right to reject enlargement. Article 237 clearly stated that a unanimous decision was required before any new country could be admitted to the EEC; French acquiescence was hence essential if Britain or any of the other applicants were to join the Six. This meant that the situation was fundamentally different from that of empty chair crisis period. For in 1965–66 the Five had merely needed to defend the status quo and stand up to French requests for alterations to the Treaty of Rome or to the Community's *modus operandi*; in 1967, by contrast, it was they who wanted change and the French who sought to preserve the existing state of affairs. The respective strengths of their negotiating positions were correspondingly reversed.

This helps explain why the July meeting was almost entirely free from ill-temper or outright confrontation. Neither side had much sympathy for the other's case; both were determined to prevail in the end. But each was aware that in the short term, anger and hostility would serve little or no purpose. The Commission report on the meeting was thus able to comment that 'the debate was conducted with vigour and seriousness, but without bitterness'.[80] Furthermore, all of the participants were aware that the point of decision had not yet been reached. They were thus able to ask the Commission to proceed with the elaboration of the *avis* referred to in article 237 – a task that would take until late September at least – each hoping that in the meantime something would occur to avert the showdown that their incompatible positions implied. The first major Community discussion of enlargement thus ended in an honourable draw, but the depth of the divide between France and its partners had been uncomfortably clear to all of those present.

The Commission opinion, when it was completed on 27 September, did little to improve the situation.[81] Somewhat to Britain's discomfort it did include a fairly lengthy section on the woes of the British economy in general and of sterling in particular.[82] Unsurprisingly, it was on this that de

Gaulle chose to dwell in his immediate reaction.[83] But the main thrust of the report was deliberately intended to undermine the French case. The Commission thus decided to omit a section focusing on the possible 'institutional overload' that might result from enlargement and instead asserted boldly that the institutional system would be able to cope with the new member states.[84] Likewise, the sections on the CAP and on the Common External Tariff foresaw none of the adverse developments of which Couve had spoken.[85] And there were multiple references to how much Britain in particular could bring to the integration process. A lengthy section, for instance, outlined the way in which British membership would broaden the technological base of the EEC, thereby permitting a much more realistic attempt to close the industrial and scientific gap between Europe and the United States.[86] The concluding recommendation of the document, namely that the Six should open membership negotiations immediately with all four candidate states, was thus fully in line with all but the section on the British economy.[87]

This Commission *prise de position* further highlighted the way in which the enlargement debate had changed since 1961–63.[88] When Britain had first sought to enter the EEC, many in the Commission had been highly sceptical both about the UK's sincerity and about the desirability of new members joining. The Commission had also been very sympathetic to French attempts to protect existing Community arrangements during the 1961–63 talks – the relationship between the Brussels body and the French had been so close indeed that one observer had compared it to that between the Pope and the Holy Roman Emperor.[89] By 1967, however, the Commission had changed sides almost completely. It still sought to protect the existing Community of course. But it now appeared to feel that the interests of the EEC would be better served by the accession of new members rather than by a firm defence of the status quo.[90] It was hence prepared to use its *avis* as a means of putting further pressure on the French to allow talks with the British, Danes, Irish and Norwegians to begin.

Towards impasse in Brussels

French determination to prevent the opening of formal negotiations continued, however, despite the Commission's decision to side with the Five. In late October, Couve de Murville reiterated his country's opposition to any immediate membership talks at another Council meeting.[91] Little of substance was added to the French case, but the minister's refusal to accept any of the Commission's report other than those sections that dwelt upon Britain's economic travails came as a major disappointment to all of those in favour of Community enlargement. Both the Germans and Dutch seem to have regarded the French foreign minister's stance as a de facto veto.[92] And their impressions were confirmed just over a month later in the by-now familiar form of another rhetorical broadside from de Gaulle. On 27 November, the French President used the recent devaluation of the pound as further confirmation of his view that the UK, in its present state, was not in a position to enter the EEC without either destroying itself or the Community. It should therefore look to an alternative arrangement with the Six, perhaps taking the form of association.[93] The French veto of 1963 appeared to have been reiterated.

The British and their allies amongst the Five still refused to allow the French to draw a line under the issue of enlargement. Such was the indignation at any new, unilateral French attempt to shape the course of the EEC, that the Five fell back into the habit of meeting amongst themselves and without the French – a pattern of behaviour not seen since January 1963. There was at least one get-together of ministers from each the 'friendly Five' on 14 December and another immediately after the climatic Council debate of 19 December.[94] The Community thus seemed to be teetering on the brink of another round of confrontation as serious and as disruptive as the empty chair crisis had been. And once again it was Gaullist France that found itself severely isolated from its partners.

A careful analysis of what appears to have been said in these conclaves of the Five and what is recorded as having been argued in the 18–19 December, 1967 Council meeting, however, suggests that caution is needed about too easily accepting some of the rhetorical hyperbole about life-threatening divisions within the EEC. Emotions were undoubtedly running high. The Belgian Minister for European Affairs, for example, spoke to the press about the 'state of manifest crisis' in which Europe found itself.[95] In practical terms, moreover, there was an obvious split between France and its partners over the question of British membership. And it is all too clear that many of France's partners interpreted the new French veto as yet another example of the unacceptably hegemonic approach to European politics adopted by de Gaulle.[96] Such views only increased the longing of the Dutch or the Italians to bring Britain into the Community so as to counterbalance excessive French influence. But that same vein of caution commented upon as a feature of the 1965–66 crisis was also much in evidence in December 1967.[97] After all, Britain's desire to join the EEC would be little served were the existing members to tear the Community apart in their efforts to decide whether or not to allow new countries to join. Nor had the cocktail of economic and political motives that had led all of the Six to act with moderation during the French boycott of the Community vanished by 1967. Indeed, in the German case at least the need to avoid any serious disruption to the country's *Westpolitik* had only been strengthened by the advent of a government that planned to adopt a more imaginative approach to its Eastern policies. Stability in the Federal Republic's European and Atlantic bonds was a precondition for any new *Ostpolitik*.[98]

It was this desire to play down the gravity of the crisis that was most in evidence during the first part of the December Council meeting.[99] After a lengthy exchange of views about the state of the British economy that only confirmed the gulf between the French position and that of the Five, Karl Schiller, the German Economics Minister who chaired the session, set the tone by presenting a document designed to sum up the divergent views expressed.[100] Like the document that had emerged from the Luxembourg extraordinary Council of January 1966, this began by noting those points on which consensus existed (the acceptability of enlargement in principle for instance), went on to acknowledge those areas where the Five and the Commission held contrasting views to the French, and ended with a statement that stressed that EEC activity should go on despite this failure to agree. It would thus provide Britain with the clear answer that London sought, admit the difference of opinion that separated five of the member states from the (unnamed) sixth, but also suggest that the future held better prospects both for the internal development of the EEC and for the position of those countries seeking to enter the Community. This attempt to repeat the Luxembourg 'solution' nearly worked. Midway through day two ministers from all of the Six were deeply embroiled in a debate about the best wording of such a statement that seemed to imply that all had accepted that outright confrontation was in the interests of no one.[101]

The mood of the meeting was transformed, however, by a somewhat ill-judged intervention by Rey. The Commission President had for some time been intent on warning the ministers of the Six of the dangers that might result from a failure to agree on enlargement.[102] The language he chose to employ, however, with its multiple uses of the word 'crisis' and its explicit reference to the events of January 1963, introduced an element of emotion into a meeting the mood of which had previously been conspicuously subdued. Brandt was reportedly furious, describing Rey's intervention as 'maladroit' in an audible aside to Luns, and then seeking to undo the damage in a more general speech to his colleagues.[103] But the somewhat forced element of self-control that had hitherto prevailed had been irreparably destroyed. The Italians, the Belgians and the Dutch all gave vent to their feelings of frustration and anger at the way in which the applicants' paths had been barred once more, and the meeting ended with a series of unilateral statements of national discontent the like of which had not been seen in Brussels since 29 January, 1963 and the formal ending of the first enlargement talks.[104]

Thus, 1967 ended on an emotional and potentially worrying note. For the optimists, it was still possible to believe that the angry words of 19 December would soon be forgotten.[105] The motives to press on in Brussels with the Community experiment still remained after all and even the most malcontent amongst the ministers would continue to need to travel to the Belgian capital in order to defend his country's interests. There was therefore a strong chance that the 1963 situation would repeat itself, with the need to cooperate, and the desire to deepen the EEC, healing most of the wounds caused by the failure to widen the Community. For the pessimists, by contrast, a rapid return to normality was not nearly so likely in 1968 as it had been five years earlier. This was because de Gaulle's latest action, coming as it did on top of the crises of 1963 and 1965–66, undermined trust at a Community level to such an extent that any attempt to do more than keep the EEC alive would be fruitless. The EEC had been in a vulnerable state before; this latest veto was hence much more likely to block all further progress. Furthermore, those gloomy about the short-term future could also argue that the British question was much less likely to fade away than had happened in the aftermath of the 1963 breakdown.[106] This reflected both the new tripartisan consensus in the UK about the merits of EEC membership and the collapse of most of Britain's alternatives. The decision formally to leave the British and other applications lying on the Community table, was not therefore merely a matter of diplomatic politesse. It reflected the fact that peace was unlikely fully to return to the EEC until *la question anglaise* had been answered in a fashion acceptable to the applicants, to the Five and to the French.

6 The impossibility of progress à Six

January 1968–April 1969

The early months of 1968 were enough to demonstrate how deep were the divisions amongst the Six caused by the December 1967 breakdown over enlargement. As the first section of this chapter will make clear, any hope that the pattern of 1963 might repeat itself soon vanished. This time, the dispute between France and its partners over whether or not Britain and its fellow applicants should be allowed to join the EEC did not fade away and become an unthreatening background controversy. Instead, an intense but ill-tempered debate about enlargement went on amongst the Six for the whole of 1968 and the first half of 1969. Likewise, the multiple discussions between the British and their allies amongst 'the friendly Five' showed no sign of abating. The future size of the Community thus went on being as live and acrimonious an issue in 1968 and early 1969 as it had been in 1967.

It is also the case that the row over enlargement in the late 1960s proved to be much more disruptive of the EEC's forward momentum than the first Gaullist veto of British membership had been. The desire to see European integration advance did not disappear. Indeed, there were multiple declarations from all of the Community member states about how vital it was that the EEC continue to prosper and develop. But actual agreement about how this might happen and what concrete steps the Six could take without deepening the divide between themselves and the four would-be members was highly elusive. Progress in fact seemed less likely than regression, with the disagreement over British membership threatening to undermine the fragile truce amongst the Six over the agenda of the EEC. Little wonder then, that references to 'crisis', 'paralysis' and 'stagnation' recurred frequently in international exchanges throughout 1968 and early 1969.

So serious and intense had the row over British membership become that the second part of this chapter must probe why enlargement proved quite so contentious. This examination of the main national attitudes will underline the divergent reasons for pro-enlargement sentiment amongst the Five and expose the underlying causes of France's obstinate opposition. A detailed investigation of the French position, however, also highlights some of the pressures for a volte-face on British membership that were beginning to mount in Paris. These could not admittedly come to the surface at once. The celebrated Soames Affair of February–March 1969 – the lunch at which the French President was reputed to have offered the British Ambassador a mechanism by which France and Britain could work together to create a different 'Europe' – while perhaps a sign of some French movement towards Britain, also served as a reminder of how difficult it had become to advance on the issue for so long as General de Gaulle remained at the Elysée. But the gathering political and economic factors pushing Paris towards the lifting of its veto would of course become very much more important after the President's sudden resignation in April. The General's departure would open up the prospect of that genuine EEC advance towards both widening and deepening which had proved all but unobtainable during his last year-and-a-half in power.

National ideas but no Community outcome

1968 began with a flurry of member state suggestions as to how the deadlock over enlargement might be overcome. Three main categories of idea emerged. The first were proposals designed to maintain a degree of dialogue between the Community and the applicants. A Benelux memorandum of 19 January, for instance, spoke of using the Community institutions to ensure that the applicants and the Six did not drift apart.[1] Second were a variety of suggestions, again championed by the Benelux states and Italy, for the development of cooperative projects between the Six and the four applicants in areas not yet covered by the Treaty of Rome. This would allow firm ties to be established amongst the Ten, without this disrupting the patterns of cooperation that the Six had built up amongst themselves. The main fields envisaged for action of this type were technological cooperation and political union.[2] Third was the suggestion, first floated in the Franco-German communiqué of 16 February, of some kind of commercial 'arrangement' between the Six and the four would-be member states. This would involve a preferential trade deal between the EEC and the states that had sought to join, ostensibly designed to make enlargement itself more feasible in the medium-term.[3]

If this multiplicity of national proposals illustrated how keen were the Five (and seemingly the French) to move beyond the 19 December deadlock, it also inadvertently highlighted how divergent – and vague – were the solutions being considered. Although, strictly speaking, few of the ideas put forward were totally incompatible with one another, their variety did suggest a lack of consensus about the best way forward. And this lack of direction would become very apparent when Council level discussions began in Brussels on 29 February.

The Council debates about enlargement in 1968 and the first six months of 1969 were amongst the most sterile multilateral discussions on record in

Brussels. To the extent they had a substantive core, they centred on the Franco-German idea of a commercial 'arrangement'. The Germans submitted a more concrete proposal in early March explaining that in their view any trade agreement should provide for the gradual lowering of industrial tariffs between the applicants and the Community, with more extensive liberalisation possible in particular sectors, and should exempt some agricultural trade between the EEC and its would-be members from the usual array of protective levies and tariffs.[4] They also picked up Belgian ideas about technological cooperation including both current and future Community members.[5] But neither the commercial nor the technological strand of Germany's 7 March paper ever looked likely to gain unanimous support.

Part of the difficulty sprang from scepticism about the workability of Bonn's plan. As far as the notion of a trade arrangement was concerned, there were three areas of particular concern. The first was the question mark over whether any type of arrangement that fell short of full membership would be deemed compatible with GATT norms.[6] World trade rules permitted the establishment of fully-fledged customs unions, but were much less clear on more limited preferential tariff cuts. There was thus a serious danger that any formula designed to resolve Europe's trade division would be strongly condemned at a global level.

The second difficulty was the Commission's dislike of the initial French and German ideas for agricultural trade. Both in Council debates and in its 2 April commentary on the German plan, the European Commission criticised the whole notion of exempting certain quantities of agricultural commodities from the normal rules of the CAP.[7] To move in this direction would not only set a dangerous precedent by promising non-member states guaranteed sales in the Community market, but also evoked unpleasant memories in Brussels. During the first years of the EEC, the Commission had sought to conclude a number of commercial arrangements in agriculture using the long-term contract provisions of article 45 of the Treaty of Rome. These had not worked well and the Commission was unhappy about reintroducing a similar procedure a decade on. Mansholt in particular was therefore highly critical of Bonn's ideas – a damaging fact given the Commissioner's acknowledged expertise on CAP matters.

The third problem was the question of whether a commercial arrangement should, or could, be limited to the four applicant states. Both the French and the Germans seemed quite open to the idea that any deal concluded might also be extended to those other western European states that were known to want closer ties with the EEC but which had stopped short of applying for full membership.[8] This included the neutral states of Austria, Sweden and Switzerland, their fellow EFTA member, Portugal, and, somewhat more tenuously, Spain. By 1968 all of these states had sought with little success to establish privileged commercial links with the Community and all were likely to jump with some enthusiasm at an invitation to participate in the 'arrangement'. Were this to happen, however, the political significance of the commercial deal would be seriously diluted; rather than it being a privilege denoting a state likely soon to become a member of the EEC, it would instead become 'just another' international trade agreement albeit of a far-reaching type.[9]

By themselves, none of these objections need have been fatal to the Franco-German scheme. The German paper of 7 March set out only the bare outline of a commercial deal and there was every indication that Bonn would have allowed many of its ideas to be recast into a more acceptable form in order to win unanimous backing.[10] Unfortunately for the Germans, however, many of the 'technical' difficulties identified at the 9 March Council meeting and subsequently, were merely the visible manifestation of a much deeper hostility towards the Franco-German suggestion. There was hence little or no political will amongst the Council participants to overcome the initial difficulties raised. Instead, several ministers appeared to relish the opportunity to point out flaws in the plan. Germany's partners, it seemed, had come to Brussels to bury the 'arrangement', not to praise it.

To a large extent this reflected Britain's own dislike of the German scheme. The UK's tactics in the wake of the December 1967 disappointment were to isolate the French and through the Five to keep up steady pressure for the start of actual membership negotiations.[11] Neither of these goals would be furthered by an 'arrangement'. On the contrary, agreement amongst the Six on any such proposal would bring France back into the Community fold and lessen the commercial pressures for enlargement by raising the prospect of increased trade between the Six and the applicants even without membership. London therefore remained committed to an all-or-nothing approach: either it would be allowed to move swiftly towards full membership, or it would settle for no deal at all with the Six and direct its attentions elsewhere.

London's hostility to an 'arrangement' fed through directly into the stance of its main European allies. Throughout the 9 March Council meeting at which the German paper was first discussed, Fanfani, Luns and Harmel raised a succession of objections to the ideas tabled by Brandt.[12] All three admittedly were careful to avoid rejecting the German proposal out of hand. Fanfani, for instance, stressed how useful a contribution the Germans had made and urged that the suggestions be studied further.[13] But all made clear that the notion of an 'arrangement' needed to be seen as a possible complement to the Benelux and Italian papers and not as a substitute.[14] Only closer political contacts with the British and the other applicants would begin to address the fundamental difficulties raised by the failure of the enlargement process; commercial ties alone would not suffice.

Germany's predicament was not made any easier by the behaviour of the French.[15] When rejecting the accusation of having sold out to Paris,

German diplomats had been very keen to emphasise the way in which the 16 February communiqué represented an advance by the French towards those in favour of enlargement. This, they argued, demonstrated that patient dialogue could produce further French concessions and serve to unlock the whole enlargement affair.[16] Unfortunately, both inside and outside the Council chamber, the French adopted a grudging attitude that cast serious doubt on such German optimism. Couve de Murville's performances in Brussels, for instance, showed none of the enthusiasm that might have been expected had Paris really been determined to conclude a deal with the applicants.[17] Furthermore, the brutal fashion in which the French foreign minister exploited his role as the chairman of the Council to marginalise discussion of all but the Franco-German plan, not only angered the Italian and Benelux representatives, but also made it appear very doubtful that France would be ready to go beyond a minimalist 'arrangement'.[18] Germany's reward for having sought to engage the French in constructive dialogue looked ever more questionable as the Council debate wore on.

The submission on 2 April of a new Commission *avis* on the enlargement issue did not help matters either.[19] The Commission document conceded that an 'arrangement' might have economic and political benefits. But its rehearsal in some detail of all the technical objections to the scheme outlined above, provided yet more ammunition for those sceptical about the German proposal.[20] Still worse, when presenting the report, Jean Rey included a set of predictions about the length of time that it might take to conclude an 'arrangement' that made the prospect appear even less attractive.[21] Negotiating the type of deal envisaged by the French and Germans might require two full years, the Commission President estimated. Given that Bonn had suggested that the tariff reductions would then be staggered over five further years, this implied that the full benefits of the stop-gap solution would not be felt until 1975 – a date by which all of the Five hoped that Britain and its fellow applicants would be members of the EEC. Pressing ahead with the idea of an 'arrangement' might seem to imply a readiness to acquiesce in this time-table. This was not something that the Italians, the three Benelux states, or the applicants themselves were ready to do.

By the spring of 1968 the whole idea of a temporary solution to the enlargement issue was thus in some trouble. A combination of the energy with which the Germans had put forward their ideas, the actions of the French chairman, and the fact that a commercial arrangement was the scheme that most clearly fell within the Community's competence, meant that the idea of progressive tariff reductions and some type of matching agricultural deal had come to dominate discussions. Most of the Benelux and Italian ideas had temporarily fallen by the wayside, while the technological element of the German initiative had been hindered by the fact that the Six's own efforts to foster technological cooperation were being deliberately blocked by the Dutch.[22] But Bonn apart, nobody, either within the Community or amongst the applicants, gave much impression of being really enamoured with the planned commercial mechanism. There was thus scant chance of the Six being able rapidly to overcome the practical difficulties that any trade 'arrangement' would inevitably pose. Instead, the Council sessions devoted to enlargement appeared condemned to ever more frustrating impasse.

The Germans try again

Seemingly undeterred by the singular lack of success attained by their March 1968 suggestions, the Germans tabled a new set of proposals designed to break the enlargement deadlock in September. Presented to the Council by Brandt, these added a further layer of detail to the planned arrangement and, in a new tactical departure, sought to sugar the pill by adding a programme of internal Community developments that would become possible were the enlargement dispute to be resolved. The Germans were, in other words, seeking to exploit the growing level of frustration at the Community's inability to deepen in order to coax both the French and their four other partners out of their self-imposed rigidity on the widening of the EEC. Once again, however, Germany's diligent pursuit of a breakthrough received little encouragement from its fellow member-states.

The main change from the earlier German plan was the provision for much more consultation with the applicants.[23] Brandt called for the establishment of a working group consisting of the permanent representatives of the Six and the Brussels representatives of the candidates and, more radically, outlined the idea of an intergovernmental conference bringing together the foreign ministers of the Six and the Four.[24] This would permit a wide-ranging discussion of all of the various ideas for greater cooperation that had been put forward. As a gesture to French sensitivities, Brandt suggested that the foreign ministers' meeting should only take place *after* the Six had devised a joint approach.[25] But the whole thrust of the new German scheme was designed to convince both the applicants and Britain's closest allies amongst the Six that Bonn was working in their interests as well as those of Germany and France.

The second novelty was the way in which Brandt explicitly linked progress on enlargement with a series of specific internal Community developments. Earlier plans had included general statements about the way in which the EEC needed to go on evolving at the same time as establishing stronger ties with the applicants. But the Germans took this one step further by actually setting out their thoughts as to what particular policy areas should be focused upon. They thus suggested that the Six needed to do much more to coordinate their economic policies and especially their monetary policies, recommended an overhaul of Community finances, pointed to the need for CAP reform to address the growing problem of farm surpluses, and proposed a new effort to eliminate the need for frontier controls within the EEC.[26] This last move, Brandt argued, would be precisely the type of innovation that would actually affect the average European citizen and make them more aware of what was being done in Brussels.[27]

By establishing so clear a linkage between widening and deepening, the Germans clearly sought to send a double message to all of their partners, but especially to the French. On the one hand Bonn outlined what could be achieved were all to show the flexibility necessary to end the deadlock over enlargement. Several of the measures referred to by Brandt were in areas of Community cooperation known to be of great interest and importance to the French – monetary cooperation, the financing of the Community and CAP reform were three cases in point. But on the other hand, Brandt made clear that should the deadlock over relations with Britain persist, none of these internal developments could occur. The penalties of obstinacy were as evident as the potential rewards of flexibility.

In the short-term, Brandt's speech seemed only to worsen the deadlock. Clearly stung by Germany's move away from the joint Franco-German stance, Michel Debré, the new French foreign minister, energetically denied any 'parallelism' between the EEC's internal development and enlargement.[28] He also spoke in alarmist fashion about the 'mutation' of the EEC that would be the inevitable result of enlargement. In the face of such negative language it was difficult to see what remained of the 16 February communiqué and its acknowledgement by both Paris and Bonn that enlargement was 'desirable'.[29] The gulf seemed unbridgeable between the French and their partners, all of whom rallied behind the new German position as the barest minimum that could be done for the candidates.

Within six weeks, however, the French had switched from confrontation to attempted conciliation. Opening the discussion of enlargement at the 4–5 November Council meeting, Debré acknowledged the need to get away from the 'negativism' that had characterised the previous gathering and to this end set out a series of concrete French suggestions for a commercial arrangement and technological cooperation with the applicants.[30] The substance of the French proposals was much more limited than the existing German plan. It was therefore clear that French thinking would have to evolve much further were agreement with the Five to become attainable. But the change in tone since the 27 September meeting was nonetheless remarkable.

Quite why France had softened its position becomes clear once the discussions over enlargement are seen in conjunction with the rest of the 4–5 November Council meeting. For, in one of the other sessions, Debré had also presented a list of French Community priorities for the coming months.[31] France, he explained, wanted all of the EEC's common policies to advance, but was particularly aware of the urgency of harmonizing customs legislation, ending a series of technical obstacles to trade within the EEC and moving in the direction of tax harmonization. All three steps were necessary if the EEC's recently completed customs union was to function as intended. It was therefore essential that France and its partners begin work on all three questions at once.[32] In order to ensure that these relatively modest suggestions received a constructive welcome, the French had been obliged to give some ground in the enlargement dispute. Their actions hence tacitly acknowledged that parallelism that Debré had so fiercely denied only a month before.

This new softer French approach did remove some of the bitterness from the enlargement discussions. In November, December and January both the officials and the ministers involved in the debate were able to concentrate on the substance of a possible deal with the applicants rather than confronting one another in fierce exchanges about the very principle of enlargement. But the underlying differences remained and were sufficiently close to the surface to endanger any substantial progress made. As Borschette, the Luxembourg representative, noted rather wearily in January, as he summed up discussions for the benefit of ministers, no agreement on the exact content of an arrangement would be possible without consensus on the precise purpose of the deal. And unfortunately it was on the purpose of the 'arrangement' that opinions were most clearly divided, with the Five plus the Commission seeking a mechanism to facilitate enlargement, while the French desired only a means of improving commercial links between the Six and the four applicant states.[33] Until this fundamental difference of opinion was overcome, very little of substance was likely to emerge from the interminable Council and COREPER discussions of enlargement.

A frozen Community

By early 1969 when Borschette made these gloomy comments, the deadlock over enlargement was mirrored by a much more generalised paralysis of the whole Community system. In the first half of 1968 a semblance of forward movement had remained possible, largely because the Community still had to implement and follow up a number of earlier decisions. In April, for instance, the Community had agreed to accelerate its introduction of the Kennedy Round tariff cuts in response to strong American pressure.[34] A month later the Six had successfully concluded the CAP regulations for beef and for dairy products.[35] And on 1 July, both the CAP and the industrial customs union had entered fully into operation, a year and a half earlier than originally foreseen by the Treaty of Rome. All of these reflected earlier political decisions and were hence successes that said more about the state of the Community prior to 1968 than they did about the present. They nevertheless did help sustain the spirits of those involved in the integration process. The European liner, to resume the metaphor used in the last chapter, continued to plough forward, even though its propeller had all but stopped turning.

By the latter half of 1968, however, this forward momentum was beginning to run out. During the ill-tempered 27 September Council meeting, Rey had sought to bestir the six ministers with a passionate speech about the need to govern the Community. In the course of 1968, the Commission President argued, the EEC had progressed from its first stage of construction, to its second, and in the second the priority was government.

> Indeed, if during the first years it had been necessary to build the Community, the construction following in a fairly natural and progressive fashion along the lines set out in the treaty, the current task, now that a common external tariff, a common tariff policy and a common agricultural already exist, is clearly that of governing the Community. Now, without wanting to embark upon an analysis of inter-institutional relations or the treaties, it is clear, M. Rey stressed, that the principal decision-making organ is currently the Council. He would therefore say to the members of the Council, hoping in the process not to show any disrepect, that none of the ministers here present would accept that their own country be governed in the manner that the Community is currently governed. No national cabinet or ruling council in one of the six member states would allow itself to remain deadlocked for six months, a year or a year and a half, over an internal problem; ministers in such circumstances would come to agreement on a solution, whether permanent or temporary. M. Rey did not believe that the Council of the Community, given its responsibilities, could allow itself to remain blocked for so long; whatever the opinions that the delegations might harbour, a common solution must be found, given the need for the Community to be governed.[36]

As explained above, Germany and France had, moreover, tabled concrete suggestions in the course of the autumn about what decisions ought to be taken. This was followed, in March 1969, by a detailed Commission work programme setting out both the objectives at which the Community should aim over the following three years and the more urgent tasks that needed to be completed before the end of December 1969.[37] But neither appeals nor specific proposals had succeeded in reversing the gradual loss of speed.

At the heart of the problem lay a chronic inability to take bold new decisions. All of the Six were still prepared to participate in day-to-day decision-making about the Community's existing range of activities. To do otherwise would, as the French had discovered in 1965–66, have been to endanger the vested interests that all member states had acquired in the continuation of the CAP and the customs union. And all member states were also therefore prepared to accept that most discussions about current Community policies had to take place amongst the Six within the normal institutional framework. The candidate countries could certainly be consulted and express their views, but ultimately decisions about the EEC as it had come into being were the responsibility of the Six states that had built it and the Community institutions that had been established. But as far as new policy areas were concerned, the situation was much less clear.

This reflected the decision by the three Benelux states and the Italians to avoid any action that might deepen the divide between the Community and the applicants.[38] All four states appeared to interpret this pledge as permitting activities *à Six* designed to keep the Community ticking over but debarring any actions that might introduce new areas of common endeavour unless the four applicant states were involved from the outset. As a result, all initiatives designed to broaden the policy agenda of the EEC were vulnerable to obstruction from the Italians and Dutch in particular. Technological cooperation is a good example of this. Discussions about a common European approach to technological research – fuelled largely by the growing lag between Europe and the United States in most cutting-edge fields – had been launched in October 1967. A working group had been established to survey the field, under the chairmanship of the French scientist Maréchal. By early 1968 the Maréchal committee was all but ready to report, a step which would then have allowed further ministerial-level discussion. It proved impossible to finalise the report, however, because the Dutch (and initially the Italian) members of the working group refused to sign the document until ministers had agreed that any further debate would be among the Six *and* the four would-be members. This was totally unacceptable to the French, who argued instead that the existing Community member states needed to formulate a joint approach amongst themselves before then considering the possibility of including other European states in particular technological projects. These two positions proved impossible to reconcile and no advance was made in this area in 1968. The fundamental philosophical divide over enlargement had thus totally blocked a potentially exciting area of European integration. And regrettably for the Community what was true for technological cooperation also applied to multiple other fields of potential European activity. Euratom's inability to agree a new, long-term research budget had, for instance, left one of the original European Communities in a state of total paralysis that led many to question whether it had any future at all.[39]

As 1968 drew to a close, the seeming impossibility of action in any new fields of cooperation had become particularly serious. A couple of years earlier, the debate about the Community's new agenda had been relatively serene. Without the pressure of imminent deadlines, the Six had been able to exchange ideas about where the Community might go next without needing to become unduly concerned at the initial lack of consensus. By late 1968 and early 1969 the situation was very different. The CAP and the customs union were now complete and the EEC thus needed rapidly to discover a new central project upon which to focus its energies. Furthermore, the increasingly troubled global economic context had created pressures that threatened the EEC unless it could respond by developing new joint policies. Nowhere was this last point more true than in the field of monetary policy.

The late 1960s were a time of growing turbulence within the Bretton Woods system, the framework of monetary cooperation in the western world. The devaluation of the pound in November 1967 which had been employed by de Gaulle as a pretext for vetoing the second British application had been one, highly visible, symptom of the system's instability. But until 1968, the Six had been able to view such difficulties with a degree of detachment. The currencies under pressure, primarily sterling and the US dollar, were not their own, and the financial position of the French franc, the Deutschmark and the Italian lira appeared healthy. May 1968 and the subsequent French crisis had changed this situation, however. By the autumn of 1968, when a new currency crisis developed, the French franc found itself as much in the line of fire as sterling and the US dollar. The Germans meanwhile found themselves urged from all quarters to revalue the mark so as to relieve the pressure on the weaker currencies. Monetary instability had seemingly arrived in Europe of the Six.

This was not a development that the Community could afford to ignore. At the simplest level it was extremely frustrating for an entity that regarded itself as Europe's principal forum for economic cooperation to see itself largely marginalised during international discussions of monetary affairs in November 1968.[40] Two EEC currencies were centrally involved and yet the Community's own role in the affair was peripheral at best. The institutional framework was instead that of the Committee of the Ten. Still worse, an outbreak of monetary instability amongst the Six might seriously undermine the achievements of the Community's first decade. The customs union had been constructed during a period of remarkable monetary stability in western Europe: one upward movement of the Deutschmark in 1961 apart, there had been no change in parities amongst the Six since the French devaluation of 1958. A sudden alteration of this situation might call into question the commitment of all of the Six to the commercial liberalisation just completed. And the CAP was even more vulnerable to monetary disorder. The whole internal market system was based on the existence of a single price structure and might thus be jeopardised were the currencies of EEC members to begin moving significantly relative to one another. A coordinated European response to the world monetary crisis was hence not only desirable, but might actually be essential were the Community to avoid a situation in which its earlier successes were undermined by exchange rate fluctuation.[41]

In such circumstances the Community's inability to go forwards might well amount to a strong risk of sliding backwards. In the debate about European integration the analogy of the bicycle has been much over-used. Quite apart from anything else, the idea that a Community which ceased moving onwards would be a Community liable to fall over (if not apart) rather ignores the solid web of mutual interest that the development of the Community had created and which gave each participating state strong reasons to avoid any danger of collapse. But it is certainly the case that there were many in western Europe in the late 1960s who believed that a continuing failure to advance would not only be frustrating but actually dangerous. The need to break out of the sterile impasse over enlargement was correspondingly great.

By 1969 the dispute over British, Danish, Irish and Norwegian membership had thus developed into an extremely serious problem for the European Community. The discussions of enlargement themselves had become a time-consuming but almost entirely unproductive distraction – a charade which few any longer believed could produce results, but which all felt obliged to continue so as to demonstrate that the issue remained alive. Worse yet, the gulf between France and its partners over widening had spilled over into the other activities of the EEC, seriously compromising the Community's ability to progress and to adapt to the new and potentially more threatening international environment. And even bilateral links between the member states were being adversely affected. That the initially promising rapprochement between the German Grand Coalition government and the French had begun to falter was at least in part attributable to the row over British membership.[42] It was therefore no exaggeration to compare the impasse over the future size of the Community to the earlier deadlocks over the EEC's agenda and institutional make-up. The British question had become just as damaging to the progress of European integration as the issues of CAP finance, the powers of the European Commission, or the extent of majority voting had been. Indeed in terms of longevity the row over enlargement had already exceeded the empty chair crisis. It therefore becomes all the more important to establish quite why the disagreement amongst the Six on this issue had become so deep, so acrimonious and seemingly so insoluble.

The 'Three' not the 'Five'

Any analysis of General de Gaulle's impact on the European Community is almost bound to resort at times to the short hand of the Five versus the One. So much of French policymaking between 1963 and 1969 was controversial and distinctive that it is often possible to talk about the French position on many European controversies as being substantially different from those of their partners. And in their mixture of alarm, resentment and more than a hint of jealously, the reactions of the Five member states other than France did frequently possess strong elements of similarity to each other. It is nevertheless also true that dividing lines between Community member states were rarely as clear or as permanent as is implied by talk of a Five versus One split. On most individual questions France was neither as isolated, nor its partners as unified, as the standard formula might suggest. Instead, each of the Five tended to react to de Gaulle's policy in somewhat different fashions and to combine their policy responses to the General with their own individual approaches and priorities in European policy-making. The outcome was a debate about the Community and its future that while deeply affected by the maverick French leader was nonetheless much less crudely polarised than was suggested by references in the press and elsewhere to 'the friendly Five'. Discussions about enlargement fully conform to this rule.

To the extent that there was a unified bloc on the question of the British membership, it was made up not of the Five, but the Three: the Netherlands, Belgium and Italy. All three countries took a deeply political view of enlargement. Economic factors, while not altogether absent from the calculations of the Dutch and Belgians in particular, were nevertheless much less important than political considerations. All had lengthy track-records as partisans of closer ties between the Six and the British. And all three had seen their desire for an expanded EEC grow more acute as they became progressively disillusioned with de Gaulle's European policy. Their behaviour throughout the 1967–69 period was thus broadly similar on the enlargement question. There were times, indeed, when the closeness of their approaches in Brussels suggested that in addition to their shared starting positions and responsiveness to British pressure they were also doing much to coordinate their policies with one another bilaterally. At the March 1968 Council meeting, for instance, virtually all of Luns's interventions in the debate seemed to begin with a declaration of support for the position just adopted by Fanfani.[43] Despite their closeness, however, it still remains useful to examine each of the three national stances in a little more detail.

The most straightforward position in some senses was that of the Dutch. The Netherlands had been partisans of extensive British involvement in the integration process since well before the Schuman Plan of 1950. Their principal reservations, indeed, about European integration in the 1950s at least had been the absence of the United Kingdom. London's refusal to join the ECSC, the EDC and then finally the EEC had been the cause of much agonising in The Hague, even though in the end the impossibility of allowing the French, the Germans and their Benelux partners to proceed without them had overcome the reluctance to be parted from Britain.[44] Understandably, therefore, the Dutch had been elated when the British had changed their mind and applied to join the EEC – one Dutch paper spoke of the UK's volte-face fulfilling one of the key priorities of postwar Dutch foreign policy.[45] They had been the most outspoken advocates of British entry throughout 1961–63, and consequently the most upset by de Gaulle's veto.[46]

Dutch support for UK involvement in the European integration process was primarily political in origin. There certainly would be economic advantages for the Netherlands in an enlarged Community. The Dutch were major exporters of both industrial and agricultural goods, and not only looked forward to improved access to the markets of the four applicant countries, but also believed that the UK and its fellow applicants, once inside the EEC, would press for the type of liberal, free-trading Europe favoured by the Dutch. That several of the largest companies in The Netherlands were jointly owned by the British and the Dutch, was also a significant factor.[47] However, the principal reason that The Hague was so determined to see Britain take its place within the EEC was its hope and expectation that London would act as a powerful counterweight to both Bonn and Paris. In an enlarged Community, the Dutch would be much less likely either to find themselves marginalised by a Franco-German condominium or powerless to break the deadlock caused by disagreement between the Community's two largest member states. Furthermore, on most economic and political issues – with the solitary exception of the extent to which the EEC should be supranational – the Dutch expected that the British would adopt a line very close to their own. As one of the smaller member states, the Dutch looked forward with some anticipation to the presence of a new and powerful ally within the EEC.

This long-established pattern of pro-British sentiment combined powerfully in 1967–69 with an almost equally firmly rooted mistrust of de Gaulle. To the Dutch, the French President's faults were not confined to his blocking of British membership, grievous though this was.[48] Instead, de Gaulle was seen also as a threat to western Europe's political alignment with the United States and the opponent of the type of federal Europe that was still supported by the majority of the Dutch political elite. It was for this reason that the Dutch had been the main opponents of the French during the abortive Fouchet plan negotiations of 1961–62 and the hardest line of the Five during the empty chair crisis of 1965–66.[49] Their frustration at the second veto was thus all the stronger for the way in which de Gaulle's action appeared to confirm all of The Hague's worst suspicions about the French president.

This double source of dissatisfaction is important in explaining why the Dutch were to adopt quite so radical a stance in 1968–69. Five years earlier, the Netherlands' anger at France had been held in check by their equally strong desire to see the EEC advance. The sabotage policies initially adopted in the aftermath of the first Gaullist veto thus faded away very quickly and the Dutch had allowed themselves to be swept along with their partners in the seemingly irresistible forward movement of the European Community.[50] By 1969, however, such optimistic illusions had faded. Onward movement in Brussels no longer seemed either likely or credible, certainly for as long as de Gaulle was in power. There was thus little point, in Dutch eyes, of soft-pedalling their pro-British stance in the name of progress that was unlikely to materialise. Furthermore, so alien were the French President's priorities, that if forward movement did become possible while de Gaulle remained at the Elysée it was likely to be progress towards a type of future that the Dutch did not want to share.[51] Obstruction therefore became the least bad option. The Dutch would not destroy the Community as it existed: they after all gained much from both the trade liberalisation that the EEC had encouraged and from the CAP. But they would do their utmost to prevent it from developing in a manner contrary to their hopes. And they would do so confident that de Gaulle could not last for ever. The Dutch were in other words prepared to sit it out until the French position on British membership altered significantly.

The position of the Belgians had also evolved significantly since the first enlargement negotiations. Like their neighbours, the Belgians had been strong supporters of British Community membership ever since 1961 and had been deeply disappointed at the failure of the first UK entry bid.[52] But still more than the Dutch they had allowed their tactics both during the British negotiations and after the veto to be shaped by the need for Community advance. They had thus been more moderate than The Hague during the unsuccessful enlargement negotiations and had played a significant role in seeking to prevent the post-veto crisis from causing enduring damage to the EEC.[53] Similarly, when they had made tentative approaches to the UK in the course of the empty chair crisis, the Belgians had done so in a fashion that made quite clear that their first priority remained the survival and prosperity of the existing Community.[54] British entry in place of France was the *solution de désespoir* – a last resort that they very much hoped not to have to employ.

Much of this Anglophile and yet *communautaire* stance had been determined by the long-serving foreign minister Paul-Henri Spaak. As one of the key architects of the Treaty of Rome, the Belgian minister had had a peculiarly personal commitment to the EEC's survival.[55] He had also been highly aware that the Community might have to co-exist for some time with de Gaulle. And as a francophone Belgian politician, he had to make allowances for the sensitivity of his domestic public to French views.[56] His firm anti-Gaullism was therefore frequently moderated so as to avoid too total a breach with the French. To the recurrent despair of the Dutch, he had more often than not sought a mediating position designed to accommodate rather than to defy Paris.[57] And while most visible during the empty chair crisis, this balancing act between resistance to, and compromise with, the French had also been the hallmark of Spaak's approach to the issue of enlargement.

During 1967–69, however, Spaak had left government for the last time and the role of defining Belgium's stance on the question of British membership fell to his successor Pierre Harmel. The result was a much less cautious approach, closer to that of the Dutch and correspondingly further from the French position. The Belgians retained, of course, their commitment to the Community. The Benelux memorandum of January 1968 was quite clear on this point.[58] And the Belgians were more moderate than either the Dutch or the Italians when it came to obstructing the EEC's advance. But in areas where no clear rules for European cooperation yet existed – notably the arena of foreign policy coordination – the Belgians under Harmel were to play a game of brinkmanship with the French that they would surely have rejected had Spaak still been in charge. For it was Harmel and the Belgian government that bear primary responsibility for the spread of the EEC's crisis over enlargement to another European institution, the Western European Union (WEU).

The Harmel Plan of October 1968 was a somewhat improvised reaction to the way in which the Benelux and Italian ideas for political cooperation between the Six and the applicants had been sidelined during debate in the EEC Council of Ministers. By the autumn of 1968 it had become very clear in Brussels that the French would not allow any meetings about foreign policy coordination to take place between the Six and the applicants. The idea of proceeding without the French meanwhile, was systematically blocked by Bonn, for reasons that will be explored below. In the circumstances, the Belgian foreign minister decided to try to circumvent the deadlocked Council discussions, by suggesting foreign policy coordination between the Six and the British in a forum where they already met regularly, namely the WEU.[59] This would be much harder for Paris to oppose, since the WEU was an established institution, had long been used to permit dialogue between the British and the Community member states, and had a remit which included political as well as economic issues. The precedent of June 1967, when again at the suggestion of Belgium, a WEU meeting had been used as the occasion for George Brown's statement setting out the terms of Britain's second application, was also encouraging, since this too had been designed to side-step a French blockage of the normal Community processes.[60]

Belgian expectations were only increased when the French reacted in a very low-key fashion to the first airing of Harmel's ideas. At the Rome meeting in late October, the French representative responded cautiously to the Belgian proposal but did not reject it altogether.[61] Nor were the French that much more forceful in February 1969 when the Belgian plan was again raised at ministerial level.[62] It was only a few weeks later when, urged on by the British, the Belgians sought to convene a meeting in London to discuss the situation in the Middle East that French anger flared.[63] The WEU, they pointed out, was an organisation that habitually worked on the basis of unanimity. French consent should therefore have been obtained before any such gathering could take place and it had not been given. And yet the Five and the British went ahead and held the meeting without a French representative being present. Paris responded by announcing that it would boycott subsequent WEU meetings until the principal of unanimity was recognised by all. A re-run of the empty chair crisis, this time outside of the Community framework, appeared to have begun. The contrast between Harmel's role in precipitating this crisis, and Spaak's vain attempts to forestall the 1965–66 confrontation between France and the Five, did serve to underline the significant change in Belgium's approach to European diplomacy that had occurred by 1968–69.

A similar radicalisation of Italian European policy had been underway since the mid-1960s. The main reasons for this were explored in Chapter 2 and need not be reiterated here. What matters is that the combination of Italy's political dislike of Gaullist policy and its economic frustration at the workings of the CAP had not dissipated in the period since 1965 and had if anything grown yet more acute. They thus added steel to an Italian approach to enlargement that had previously been very similar to that of Spaak. In 1961–63, Italian negotiators, alongside their Belgian counterparts, had distinguished themselves as the main mediators amongst the Six, eager to see Britain join, but also anxious to prevent the Community from becoming too divided by the enlargement process.[64] Half a decade later, by contrast, Rome's priority had become forcing France to move, even at the risk of disrupting the EEC in the short term. As early as January 1967, before the British had even applied and well before France's renewed opposition had been confirmed, Pietro Nenni, the leader of the Socialist party, had called for the Five and the British to press ahead without France should it be necessary – a stance which had earned him an immediate rebuke from Brandt.[65] The strength of Italian views was as strong amongst Christian Democrats as it was amongst the Socialists. Thus Fanfani, the Italian foreign minister, had been the first to rebel against Germany's attempt to draw a line under the enlargement dossier on 19 December, 1967, and had gone on being one of the most outspoken critics of both the French and the German approaches during the Council discussions of enlargement in the first half of 1968.[66] Italy's desire to see the British take their place within the EEC seemed to match that of the Dutch.

Adding urgency to this pro-British activism was Italy's fear of being relegated to the second division of a Franco-German dominated EEC. This had long been a subject of concern, of course. The Italians had been amongst the most outspoken in their reaction to the honeymoon between de Gaulle and Adenauer in late 1962 and to the signature of the Elysée treaty in January 1963. One influential Italian politician indeed had gone so far as to suggest to the British that Rome and London should jointly respond by creating an Anglo-Italian axis to match that emerging between Paris and Bonn.[67] But in the mid-1960s such concerns had faded, as the relationship between France and Germany had grown ever more strained. There were even moments in the period between 1964 and 1966 when it made more sense to talk in terms of a special tie on Community matters between Rome and Bonn than it did to attach importance to the Franco-German relationship. By 1968, however, Italian anxieties had revived strongly. As Kiesinger and Brandt sought to rebuild German links with Paris, the danger of Italy being marginalised grew once more. And the Italian determination to bring in Britain as a countervailing force rose in parallel. It was hence a fundamentally political calculation that lay at the root of Italian support for British membership.

The uncomfortable mediator

For the Germans, by contrast, there was much closer balance between economics and politics in their assessment of Community enlargement. Bonn had always acknowledged that there was a political case for British membership.[68] At its most basic this reflected a belief that an expanded Community would also be a stronger Community, and hence a still firmer Western base for a Federal Republic whose position vis-à-vis the Eastern bloc was very much in a state of flux. But for many Germans there were also merits in having an alternative to the unpredictable and at times uncomfortable relationship with the French. As Kurt Schmücker had confessed to the British Ambassador in early 1966:

> His own personal conviction was that if a favourable decision on British membership had not been reached by the end of 1967 the EEC would probably break up or fade away. The reason he gave for this was the state of Franco-German relations and the impact on other members. During the short period when France and Germany had played a duet within the EEC this had disturbed the others. Now that Franco-German relations were more like a duel and likely to remain so this was even more fatal. Although resistance had to be made to the French and Germany was the only EEC country strong enough for this purpose it was politically undesirable in the wider sense that Germany should take such a lead. During last year's EEC crisis she had been able to work through the Belgians, the Italians and the Dutch in turn but this could not go on for ever. The EEC needed the UK as the essential balancing factor.[69]

That the Americans were also strongly in favour of British membership was a further political reason for Bonn to work for Community enlargement given Germany's dependence on the US security guarantee.[70] All of these factors help explain why Ludwig Erhard's government had been amongst the most active exponent of Community enlargement during the 1963–66 period.[71]

Under the Grand Coalition government, however, these political calculations in favour of an expanded EEC were matched by a series of equally political factors pushing Germany in the opposite direction. These centred on the new Chancellor's desire for better relations with France. As explained in Chapter 5, the essential support for British membership had not gone away, especially within the SPD and within the Auswärtiges Amt.[72] But Kiesinger was adamant that enlargement should not be brought about at the expense of Franco-German relations. This reflected his belief that good relations with Paris were both desirable in themselves and a source of popularity within the CDU. As a result, the German government systematically sought to oppose policy initiatives designed to isolate Paris.[73] British, Danish, Irish and Norwegian membership would be a positive outcome but only if achieved with France rather than against it. This was all the more true, given the Chancellor's firm conviction that Britain had no alternative but to join the EEC. An internal Kanzleramt report had concluded in November 1967 that 'EEC entry amounts almost to an economic existential question for Britain.'[74] There was hence no danger of the UK turning elsewhere if its wish to enter were not immediately granted.

The need to find a middle way between supporting the British and not alienating with the French also reflected Bonn's economic predicament. Economically, German exporters had flourished under the EEC. In the course of the 1960s, German exports had grown faster to their five Community partners than they had to other important markets elsewhere in Europe (see Table 6.1). By the end of the decade France had consolidated its position as Germany's most important foreign client, with the Netherlands outstripping the United States to become the second largest export market. The Federal Republic could hence ill afford economically to take risks either with the Community structures or with its rapport with Paris.

The pattern of German trade also explained, however, why the Federal Republic could not be content with the status quo in western Europe. Despite the export boom to its EEC partners, Germany still traded extensively with the British and the rest of EFTA. Even in 1969, after a decade of commercial preference in favour of the Six, 23 per cent of Germany's

Table 6.1 German export growth, 1961–69

German exports	Total	EEC	EFTA
1961	100	100	100
1962	105	125	103
1963	115	151	110
1964	128	165	123
1965	141	176	135
1966	159	204	141
1967	171	223	144
1968	196	261	157
1969	229	323	191

Source: Author's calculations based upon OECD, *Foreign Trade Statistical Bulletins, Series A, By Countries*, Paris: OECD, multiple years.

exports were sold to EFTA.[75] The underperformance of these markets relative to their EEC counterparts in fact only demonstrated how much Germany had lost from the commercial divide between the Six and the Seven. Were the artificial split to come to an end, and Britain and its fellow EFTA partners to take their place either within the EEC or closely linked to it, the Germans could expect to recapture some of their former dominance in these markets without losing any of their position amongst the Six. The economic rewards of European integration would in other words be much greater within an enlarged EEC than they were within a European Community limited to six member states.[76]

The German quest for an 'arrangement' was directly linked to these commercial pressures. Politically, Germany could tolerate the impasse in Brussels – delicate though its balancing act between London and Paris remained.[77] But economically, German industry would do very well were it to prove possible to devise a commercial stop-gap solution which in effect eliminated most of the Six/Seven tariff divide. Bonn's dogged persistence in pursuing this formula, despite the condemnation it received from the British, the ambivalence of its partners amongst the Five, and the seeming fickleness of its French co-sponsor, becomes much more comprehensible once the potential rewards of an 'arrangement' are appreciated. Brandt, Lahr and other German representatives did of course present their suggestions primarily as a way of helping all of the Community and the applicants out of the sterile deadlock in which they found themselves.[78] And such claims were no doubt sincerely meant. A successful bridging formula would also remove a constant irritant in the relationship between Paris and Bonn.[79] It nevertheless remained the case that a functioning Community plus an 'arrangement' was very much more in Germany's economic national interest than merely the continuation of integration *à Six*. If full enlargement was denied there was thus every reason for Bonn to go on pushing for something to make the delay much more economically tolerable.

The final member state committed to supporting an influx of new countries into the EEC was Luxembourg. Here too, the 1967–69 support for enlargement was in no sense a new policy. The Community's smallest member state had supported the first British membership bid and had joined its partners in condemning de Gaulle's veto.[80] Its main ministerial spokesman in the late 1960s, Grégoire, moreover, left his colleagues in no doubt as to the wide-ranging political benefits that he expected enlargement to bring.[81] But the tactics it espoused in its pursuit of British membership, reflected an understandable desire to avoid any action that put it too directly on a collision course with its two main neighbours, Germany and France. While a signatory to the January 1968 Benelux memorandum, the Luxembourgers subsequently backed away somewhat from the hard-line Belgian and Dutch positions, adopting a lower profile and less radical approach. By August for instance Bonn's assessment was that Luxembourg, unlike Belgium and the Netherlands, would no longer insist on there being any clear link between the internal development of the Community and its widening.[82] Benelux solidarity, although a useful device for maximising Luxembourg's impact in a Community context, had its limits after all.

The Five did therefore constitute something less than a totally united bloc on the enlargement issue. They were all in favour of British, Danish, Irish and Norwegian membership. This alone gave some validity to the label. And they all had profound misgivings both about the French position on enlargement and about de Gaulle's European policy more generally. But in the advantages that they expected to accrue from enlargement and in the tactics they adopted in pursuit of this aim there were a number of important differences between the three Benelux states, the Italians and the Germans. The latter in particular had adopted a highly distinctive approach which in trying to accommodate all of its existing and would-be partners often threatened to please none at all. As a result, the French, while isolated, were aware that their partners did not form the tight Anglophile cohort that London desired. There was much scope for Paris to seek to exploit the underlying differences of opinion amongst the Five.

An immovable obstacle?

French opposition to enlargement in general and British membership in particular was primarily to do with the preservation of French influence within Europe and hence also the protection of French interests within the existing European institutions. Or, to put it another way, Paris perceived enlargement to be a threat to its power. That France had done rather well out of the European integration process has been one of the themes of this book.[83] As far as economics were concerned, the French had seen both their industry and their agriculture grow rapidly within the emerging European customs union. But in the political sphere also, the French retained some hope that a more coherent European position might yet develop despite the frustrations of the Fouchet plan failure and the constant clash between Gaullism and Atlanticism.[84] Both actual and potential gains from a more united Europe might however be called into question, Paris believed, were the Community to be expanded too early from the Six to the Nine or the Ten.

The fate of the CAP within an enlarged Community was certainly one of the issues to preoccupy the French.[85] Neither the gains France made as a result of European agricultural policy, nor its perception that these benefits might still be vulnerable had changed fundamentally since 1965. The further consolidation of the CAP since the mid-1960s, plus the somewhat toned down nature of the German critique did mean, perhaps, that the total unravelling of the policy was no longer a genuine danger. But there was still enough evidence of both German and Italian disquiet with the mounting costs of the agricultural policy for the French to fear that the Six were unlikely to be uniformly committed to the agricultural *acquis*. Were the Community to expand to include the British who had an entirely different tradition of agricultural policy, who had never hidden their misgivings about many aspects of the CAP, and who were therefore likely to press for radical change as soon as they took their place at the Council table, there was thus a very real threat of the policy being substantially altered. Should this happen, France could expect to be the principal loser. The lessening of the value of the CAP to France was therefore one of the substantive concerns that lay behind Couve and Debré's alarmist talk of the Community ceasing to be itself in the wake of enlargement.[86]

France was, however, concerned with more than just agriculture. With the benefit of hindsight, French claims that enlargement might result in the erosion of the European customs union and its replacement by a much looser and more amorphous free trade area sound distinctly overblown. Most of the Five appear, moreover, to have felt that such predictions were fairly implausible in 1967–69.[87] But it is clear from French sources that this line of argument was not simply a rhetorical ploy, dreamt up to justify an opposition to Community expansion that was derived entirely from other factors. Instead, it was a genuine fear, based in part on Britain's free trading reputation and rhetoric (as the French were aware, actual UK industrial tariffs remained *higher* than those of the EEC) and also on the experience of the Kennedy Round in the course of which the US and the British had periodically placed joint pressure on the Community to cut its levels of protection.[88] Likewise, the French were genuinely worried that the applicants' readiness to welcome US inward investment might thwart any attempt to develop a Community policy designed to restrict the buying up of European companies by American competitors.[89] And there were multiple other fields of existing and potential Community policy where Paris feared that the British and the other newcomers would exert their influence in directions inimical to French interests. Keeping Britain, Denmark, Ireland and Norway out of the Community did thus appear to the French to be the most effective way of ensuring that the EEC would continue to correspond closely to the type of European project desired, and so far obtained, by Paris.[90] As Pompidou would put it in the course of a French cabinet meeting:

> The idea that Britain is part of Europe is gaining ground on the other side of the Channel. This is all well and good. But as far as we are concerned, our policy must only be shaped by the consideration of the advantages and disadvantages that British membership will have for us and for the Common Market.
>
> British membership will inevitably be followed by other new entries. Now, a Common Market with twelve or fifteen members would only be able to work by means of a strengthened European Commission. As we do not want this, the inevitable result will be the

falling apart of the Community and the CAP. This is really not our goal.[91]

The same calculation applied at a political level also. The non-appearance of a political Europe to flank the economic Communities was of course one of the great disappointments of Fifth Republic foreign policy.[92] None of the Five had shown any readiness to accept the Gaullist vision of a 'European Europe' and the Germans in particular had proved much too dependent on, and loyal to, the US to play the role that de Gaulle had envisaged for them. Such disappointments had not, however, entirely destroyed belief amongst many French politicians that some form of political Europe might yet emerge. In the late 1960s indeed there were a number of developments that made progress in this direction both more likely and more necessary.[93] For a start, the emergence in Bonn of a government better disposed towards Paris and less slavishly attached to Washington than the Erhard regime had rekindled the hope that the Elysée treaty might amount to more than a framework for regular inter-governmental meetings. Second, the spread across western Europe of criticism of the general direction of US foreign policy and its actions in Vietnam in particular, encouraged the belief that France was not alone in desiring a foreign policy voice distinct from that of the Americans. And third, the Soviet invasion of Czechoslovakia in August 1968 marked the near collapse of de Gaulle's independent policy of détente with Eastern Europe, to which France had initially turned as an alternative following the frustration of its hopes for political cooperation in western Europe. With French foreign policy back on the drawing board, the attractions of a political Europe were once more very apparent to the French.

British membership would however seriously impede any move towards a political Europe. UK entry, especially if accompanied by the Danes and the Norwegians, would reinforce the Atlanticist majority within Europe that had already proved so damaging to de Gaulle's hopes. Worse still, the British were likely to be even less amenable to French persuasion than the Germans and the other existing members of the Six had been. De Gaulle's selection of Germany as France's ideal European partner had always been based upon the expectation that, whatever its economic clout, the Federal Republic would not be able to match the foreign policy strength of France in the medium term.[94] In a partnership with Germany, the French, unencumbered with the same legacy of the past as Bonn, and possessing such trappings of power as nuclear weapons, a UN Security Council seat, and a global network of former imperial ties, were likely to remain the dominant party. Britain, by contrast, for all its disappointments in the course of the 1960s, still matched all of these French 'assets'. It was thus much less likely to allow Paris to rule the roost in quite the same way. Instead a European voice to which the British contributed was much less likely to express itself with the accent or the emphasis that France desired. As a SGCI note summarised the problem in November 1967, 'the enlargement of the Common Market raises political problems which call into question the whole notion of European unity and the place of western Europe in the world'.[95]

Taken together all of these factors helped create a strong consensus within the French government that enlargement would be deleterious to France and to French European interests. Most of the Quai d'Orsay seems to have believed this strongly, with French diplomats using the first months of 1967 to turn de Gaulle's basic opposition to Community enlargement into a series of precise arguments that Couve and then Debré could deploy in Brussels.[96] And what evidence exists about the tone of French cabinet discussions, suggests that few of de Gaulle's ministers diverged substantially from the General's views on British membership. Those misgivings that did exist seem to have centred primarily on the best tactics to employ in order to hold the British at bay.[97] The determination that the French would show in their discussions with the Five throughout 1967 and 1968 did therefore accurately reflect the strength of feeling within French policy-making circles.

Indeed, France's conviction that enlargement would harm its interests was arguably increased by the fraught diplomacy that surrounded Britain's second membership bid and its aftermath. Rightly or wrongly, French leaders perceived the hand of the British behind all of their partners' manoeuvring during the 1967 to 1969 period.[98] The way in which the Dutch, Italians, Belgians and even Germans and the European Commission acted in a pro-British fashion during the enlargement controversy acted as a frightening harbinger of what the Community would be like once the British were actually inside. Keeping them out thus seemed all the more imperative in the light of French discomfort during the two years spent discussing British membership. Likewise, the traumas that France endured in the aftermath of the *événements* of May 1968 seem only to have reinforced French obstinacy rather than weakened it. Certainly, Debré recalls having been persuaded by de Gaulle to accept the job of the foreign minister in the immediate aftermath of *Mai '68* on the grounds that France's opponents would exploit the crisis and that it would therefore need a doughty fighter to resist such pressure.[99] The behaviour of Couve's replacement during his year in office would appear to bear out this account.

Beneath the surface, however, a number of changes were taking place that began to call into question some of the building blocks of this French case against enlargement. The first was a growing awareness that those same French Community interests which might be threatened by Community expansion were also being endangered by the EEC deadlock caused by non-enlargement. This fear took some time to develop: as late as February 1969, SGCI documents were talking in resolutely upbeat fashion about the prospects of the French ideas for Community advance outlined the previous November by Debré.[100] But as the year advanced such optimism became ever harder to sustain. With even the European Commission seriously discussing the possibility of postponing the 31 December, 1969 deadline for the end of the EEC's transitional period it was all too clear that something serious was amiss.[101]

There were two main policy areas where impasse in Brussels began to cause Paris concern. The first was none other than the CAP, since 31 December, 1969 was not simply the planned end of the transitional period, but also the date at which the CAP's financial regulation, agreed after so much difficulty in May 1966, was due to expire. If the Community continued to suffer from a total inability to devise new agreements, there was thus a real possibility that whole CAP financial settlement which France had fought so hard to obtain would lapse at the year's end without a replacement having been negotiated.[102] This was a state of affairs that France could no more easily accept in 1969 than in 1965. Second, France had become much more interested in the possibility of Community action in the monetary field.[103] Now that its currency was the target of international speculators and adverse flows of capital, Paris had begun to call ever more insistently for some type of Community action in this field. The chances of meaningful progress in so delicate an area were slight however unless the deadlock over British membership could be broken.

The monetary turmoil of late 1968 also contributed to the second pressure for change in France, namely evolving attitudes towards Germany. November 1968 after all was widely seen as a moment when Germany had demonstrated its new found confidence and strength on the international stage.[104] Confronted with sustained American, British and French pressure to revalue the *Deutschmark*, the Germans had firmly refused to do so. They had taken this step, furthermore, while fully aware that it would almost certainly force France to devalue. In the event, de Gaulle had managed to defy those who predicted a devaluation and had maintained the French franc's parity.[105] But an important marker had nonetheless been laid down about both the relative strengths of France and Germany, and about Bonn's willingness to use its greater financial clout vis-à-vis its main European partner. There were many in France who duly took note. And the wider development of German foreign policy, especially towards the Eastern bloc, also seemed to confirm the trend towards a stronger, less passive Federal Republic. De Gaulle's rather unfair attempts to blame Bonn for helping to provoke the Soviet intervention in Czechoslovakia could not entirely mask the growing French anxiety that Germany rather than France was beginning to emerge as western Europe's key interlocutor with the East. As the Grand Coalition edged ever closer to a new, and much more far-reaching, *Ostpolitik*, the danger of France playing only a secondary role in any dialogue between the two halves of Europe grew more acute.

All of these signs of greater German self-confidence helped undermine the long-standing Gaullist assumption, analysed above, that Germany would prove a more emollient and comfortable partner for France than Britain. For the time being, of course, the pro-French attitudes of Kiesinger acted as a guarantee that Germany would not confront France too directly. One of the contributing factors to Franco-German discord during the monetary crisis of late autumn 1968, had been the fact that the French had been unable to make direct contact with the Chancellor who was at home recovering from illness.[106] The exception did therefore rather underline the rule about how far Kiesinger would try to go in maintaining harmonious relations between Paris and Bonn. But reliance on the Chancellor was not an entirely comfortable predicament at a time when the Grand Coalition was manifestly running out of steam and was generally believed to be unlikely to outlast the elections scheduled for late 1969. A Germany led either by Brandt or by a less Francophile member of the CDU would be a much less reliable ally. In such circumstances it could begin to be legitimately asked whether Britain, scarred by its own monetary and foreign policy crises, might not represent a useful counterbalance within the EEC to the newly assertive Federal Republic.

The third factor that could in time push France to review its position was the emergence of a possible economic case *for* British entry. A 1967 report compiled by the SGCI, while ultimately concluding against UK membership, already showed that the outlines of the opposite case were perceived in Paris. The section on agriculture, for instance, acknowledged that Britain would not only represent a valuable outlet for France's growing agricultural surpluses, but would also pay so much into Community budget that France's own contribution could drop substantially. Likewise the analysis of the dangers and opportunities that enlargement would present to French industry interspersed its overall caution with multiple admissions that British entry could prove economically beneficial to many types of French firm. It had taken a somewhat alarmist section on the possible harm that Britain could do to the EEC in the monetary field to tilt the report firmly in the direction of opposition to British entry.[107] Over a year later, with little sign that the subsequent devaluation of the pound had given British industry the major competitive advantage that France had feared, this conclusion looked somewhat questionable. Furthermore, in the light of France's own monetary difficulties it was harder for any Paris-based analyst to make a strong case against Community mutual assistance to a member state whose currency was under attack. On the contrary, to the extent that British membership might increase the pressure on the EEC to devise an effective system of mutual support in the monetary field, France as well as Britain would be the beneficiary. By 1969 it was therefore possible to envisage a similar report being drafted that came to the opposite conclusion and identified enlargement as something that was on balance likely to help rather than harm the French economy.

It is unclear how much any of these factors contributed to the celebrated 'Soames affair' of February 1969.[108] Indeed, it is far from certain whether de Gaulle's remarks to the British ambassador in Paris really represented any significant change in the French stance at all.[109] The General's supposed comments about the Community of the Six being replaced over time by a different type of wider economic grouping represented little more than a logical extension of the case against enlargement that France had been airing in Brussels since the summer of 1967. Similarly, there was scant novelty in de Gaulle talking dismissively about NATO. And even the suggestion of discreet bilateral discussions between London and Paris might have been no more than a reflection of how frustrated the French leader had become at a situation in which France believed itself to be negotiating with the British by proxy rather than directly. Much better surely to engage with London in a manner and a forum where none of the other member states or the Commission could interfere with the dialogue?

Debré's recollections of the affair do, however, suggest first that de Gaulle was making a genuine overture and second that this move reflected French discomfort with their EEC predicament and their belief that the best way to break out of it might well have been to engage the British in a bilateral bargaining process. The French foreign minister recalls pointing out to the General only five days before de Gaulle's lunch with Soames, that the imminent CAP deadline made France peculiarly vulnerable to blackmail from its partners amongst the Five. In the circumstances, there might therefore be advantages in talking to the British and exploring jointly the prospects of creating a substantially different Community with the UK rather than being forced to accept British entry into the existing, supranational, entity.[110] De Gaulle may therefore have been testing out this option in his discussions with Soames.

If the start of the 'affair' was perhaps the first sign of change in de Gaulle's opposition to British membership, its continuation underlined the near impossibility of any substantive progress while the General remained in power. For so strained had Anglo-French relations become that the British interpreted the French President's move as a trap rather than as a sign of genuinely new thinking.[111] They therefore decided first to discuss the General's comments with the Germans and then to leak a somewhat contentious account of de Gaulle's remarks to the press. What had begun life as a discreet feeler, therefore ended up in an acrimonious Anglo-French spat, in which both London and Paris accused each other of duplicity.[112] It was thus an eloquent example of quite how nasty the row over enlargement had become. Needless to say, no prospect of bilateral dialogue survived this very public dispute. Instead, Anglo-French relations grew even more frosty.

At the end of April 1969 the signs of an underlying shift in French hostility took on a new significance, however, when de Gaulle abruptly resigned. His departure from the Elysée, over an unrelated matter, suddenly raised the prospect of a resolution of the Community deadlock over enlargement. Dramatic change was not of course likely to take place overnight. In the very short term the General's resignation ushered in a period of uncertainty in French politics as the battle for his succession began. But once Georges Pompidou, the former Prime Minister, won the Presidential elections in June 1969, the Community found itself in a position where its lengthy deadlock could at last be brought to an end. It is to the manner in which the new French leader set about the pursuit of this aim, and the way in which his partners reacted, that the next chapter must turn. Any resolution of the crisis, however, would have to begin with a recognition of how serious the impasse over enlargement had become. So strong were the sentiments involved, and so lacking in trust were relations amongst the Six, that only an ambitious and far-reaching bargain was likely to end the affair. April 1969 and de Gaulle's resignation thus began a complex end-game in the Community's interlinked crises which would culminate eight months later at The Hague. It was a measure of how grave the situation had become, however, that only a change in regime in Paris could start the process of healing the divide.

7   The road to The Hague
June–December, 1969

Pompidou's victory in the French Presidential elections of June 1969 gave the Six a clear opportunity to resolve the crisis that had beset the European Community since late 1967. It was admittedly true that the new French leader was a man who presented himself to the French electorate as the candidate of continuity.[1] It was also the case that Pompidou had been de Gaulle's Prime Minister at the time of both the 1963 and the 1967 vetoes and throughout the empty chair crisis. This may well explain why several of the new President's fellow leaders had struggled to hide their preference for his electoral rival, the centrist and more reliably pro-European Alain Poher.[2] But so personalised and centred on de Gaulle had the row over Europe's future become, that any change of leadership in France was bound to have an impact. This was all the more so given the fact that Pompidou arrived at the Elysée with a reputation for moderation and pragmatism that contrasted strongly with that of his predecessor.[3] June 1969 therefore saw the start of six months of careful diplomacy designed to allow the existing Community member states to strike a comprehensive bargain over the membership, the agenda and the mode of operation of the EEC. It was this deal that would eventually emerge from The Hague summit of December 1969.

Central to any resolution of the Community's crisis would of course be an agreement over when and how the Six could start membership negotiations with the four countries that had submitted their applications in 1967. It was therefore highly encouraging for the Community that Pompidou had begun to show signs of flexibility on the issue of enlargement even before he had been elected. But as this chapter will go on to argue, a decision to begin the process of widening the EEC would not of itself suffice to overcome the Community's stagnation. Also needed was decisive action to redress the growing difficulties of the EEC's flagship policy, the CAP, and to identify the future policy priorities upon which the Community should focus during the 1970s. With the end of the Community's 12 year transitional period only months away, the question of what the EEC should do was once more as vital – and as controversial – as the still open issue of who should be allowed to join. Nor was it likely that any comprehensive settlement of the EEC's difficulties would be able to exclude institutional issues either. For while in 1967 it had been possible to talk of an apparent *modus vivendi* about how the Community should function, this agreement had been underpinned by the fact that the EEC seemed to be working well. By the second half of 1969, after two years during which the Community had manifestly *not* functioned smoothly, this was no longer the case. On the contrary there were many, both in Brussels and in the national capitals, who believed that one of the crucial ingredients in the Community's total inability to take important decisions was the inadequacy of its institutional structure. This too would be re-examined in the run up to The Hague summit. The final six months of 1969 would therefore be characterised by an eventful and far-reaching debate about the whole integration process – a debate which would eventually succeed in defusing the Gaullist challenge that this book has sought to trace from 1963 onwards.

The end of the enlargement impasse?

As had become abundantly clear in the course of the previous 18 months, no durable peace could return to the European Community unless and until the dispute over the British, Irish, Danish and Norwegian applications was resolved. Britain's desire to enter the EEC gave no sign of abating, despite the rise of domestic opposition to membership.[4] And for as long as the UK remained interested in Community membership, the Irish, Danes, and Norwegians were likely to remain equally committed. Nor did the Five seem likely to discontinue their pressure for enlargement. There were signs indeed that the three most resolutely pro-enlargement states identified in the last chapter – the Netherlands, Belgium and Italy – were increasingly likely to be joined in their determined approach by the Germans who had grown frustrated with the repeated failure of their mediation efforts. Certainly it was Brandt who reacted with the greatest speed and outspokenness when news reached him of de Gaulle's surprise resignation.[5] The German foreign minister would subsequently seek to retreat somewhat from his over-hasty prediction that with the General gone, talks with Britain could begin before the end of the year, but the fact that he had aired such thoughts in public did underline his relief at the apparent end of his country's awkward balancing act between Paris and London.[6] Bonn was unlikely to allow itself to be put back in this uncomfortable position by the new French government. The incoming French President would thus face concerted pressure from his European partners to soften his stance on Community enlargement.

To these external factors pushing France to alter its position, Pompidou had added a series of domestic pressures. These reflected the way in which he had campaigned for the Presidency and the composition of his first government. De Gaulle's former Prime Minister had made one of the central elements of his election strategy the attraction of support from prominent centrists such as Valéry Giscard d'Estaing and Jacques Duhamel.[7] Winning their backing would not merely help deliver the valuable votes of their numerous supporters, but would also ensure that any future government led by Pompidou would have a Parliamentary majority that stretched beyond the Gaullist UNR. Pompidou's tactics were hence focused on the so-called *élargissement de la majorité*. In order to achieve this aim, however, the Presidential candidate had to show a willingness to contemplate a very different *élargissement*, namely that of the European Community, for this was a cause espoused by Giscard and many other centrists.

As early as 2 May, Pompidou thus spoke publicly of Community enlargement as 'desirable'.[8] On 14 May, he admitted to a Parisian audience that 'It is dramatic to leave England outside of Europe'.[9] Later in the same speech he also stated that the sooner Community enlargement came about the better.[10] And on 20 May, the would-be President outlined his hope that France and its partners would soon be in a position to 'resume discussions with England'.[11] Furthermore, having won the election, Pompidou then included in his government several ministers, including Giscard and Maurice Schumann, the new foreign minister, believed to be sympathetic to British membership. The new President thus had powerful domestic incentives to lift his predecessor's veto.

Pompidou also did little to conceal his frustration at the Community paralysis caused by the disagreement over enlargement. In early July, the new French leader reacted furiously to an account of how the Dutch were making any advance in Brussels conditional on British involvement, scribbling a note to Schumann stating that 'In no circumstances should we allow anybody else to be involved in discussions that concern only the Six. England cannot be outside at one moment and inside by proxy at the next'.[12] Nor were such outbursts limited to an internal audience. A few days earlier, he told Brandt – his first major European visitor – that France had not had much luck with the British question over the previous few months. De Gaulle's last opening had been misunderstood and the whole affair had left 'several dark clouds and regrets.'

> Nevertheless, although none of this [past acrimony] can be wiped from the slate, we understand that the question is posed. It is posed by the candidacy of England and the others. It is posed by the more or less ardent attitude of our partners. It is posed by history and by geography. The relationship between Britain and Western Europe is an essential element of western political life and we are Europeans.[13]

Then still more significantly he indicated that France no longer had a closed mind on the issue.

We do not have a hostile attitude from the outset; it is simply, as I have already said, that we want the Community to progress into its definitive stage and for the Six to talk amongst themselves so as to establish a doctrine on how the issue should be approached. The question will then have to be handled with good faith and transparency, and we will need both. The more good faith and transparency that there is, the better able we will be to identify the difficulties ahead.[14]

By September, when he travelled to Bonn to meet the German Chancellor, the French President felt able to set out his views even more candidly. Responding to Kiesinger's suggestion that France ought to do something to ease Britain's position, Pompidou admitted:

The "English affair" has poisoned the atmosphere within the Community for all concerned. There are those who desire the entry of England and who are irritated by the French attitude whereas France is irritated that in the six-member Community the only topic of debate is a seventh state. I believe that this irritating rash should now be removed and that it is necessary to look at the problem as it stands.[15]

He then predicted that the moment of truth on this issue was now increasingly close and it would therefore be necessary to establish whether or not the British genuinely wanted to enter a functioning Community and whether the UK could accept the existing EEC rules. But he added 'We will not use a veto, of that you can be certain.'[16] The next day, he reiterated his desire to sort out the British issue, comparing the deadlock over UK membership to *L'Arlésienne*, a play by Daudet that centred on a woman who is constantly discussed without ever appearing on stage in person. 'Well I've had enough of Britain being the *Arlésienne*. Either she is present or she is not.'[17]

   In such circumstances it was therefore unsurprising that the new French government began to search for a means of resolving the British affair almost as soon as it had taken office. Pompidou himself had never been particularly dogmatic on the issue. While out of government in 1968, indeed, he had predicted to Geoffrey Rippon, subsequently the minister who would lead the successful British negotiations to join the EEC, that were he to become President he would allow the British to join.[18] This basic flexibility meant that he was much more likely to respond favourably to the pressures analysed above than his rather more dogged predecessor had been. But while privately acknowledging that France would have to open the way for Britain and its fellow applicants to join the Community, Pompidou had multiple reasons to move slowly and carefully in this direction rather than giving way at once.

   At the most basic level, Pompidou needed to be careful not to outrun opinion within his government and within his civil service. For if there were members of his cabinet who were known to support Community enlargement, there were others who would decry any quick betrayal of the General's legacy. Similarly, there were many French officials, especially within the Quai d'Orsay, who continued to harbour deep suspicions about Britain's real intentions and about the likely effects of premature enlargement.[19] Alienating those responsible for implementing his new foreign policy was not something that the President could afford to do. And it was even possible that were Pompidou to act too quickly or rashly, de Gaulle might break his self-imposed silence and condemn his successor's actions. This was not a scenario Pompidou was ready to contemplate so early in his term of office.

Even more important was the need to ensure that enlargement, if, or perhaps more accurately when it did happen, took place in a controlled manner. By 1969, France had become deeply suspicious of its European partners' pro-British sentiments. The Belgians, the Dutch, the Italians and even the Germans were viewed as much too responsive to London's every whim and liable to endanger much of the Community's fabric in their haste to let the British in.[20] There was thus a very real danger that were France to lift its veto and allow membership talks to begin without careful prior coordination amongst the Six, it would find its legitimate national interests swept aside by a stampede towards a Europe of Ten. The CAP, the level of customs tariffs, and the whole future direction of Community policies could be disastrously affected were this to happen. It was thus imperative for the French to commit their partners in advance to an orderly and *communautaire* negotiating procedure, designed to safeguard the Community and make certain that it was the applicants who adapted to the EEC rather than vice-versa.[21] Only in this way would it be possible to prevent the Community being transformed into the type of loose free trade area of which Couve de Murville and Debré had warned in the 1967 and 1968 Council debates.[22]

So keen indeed were the French to avoid a situation in which the Five and the applicants combined forces so as to push for a radically transformed and enlarged Community that Paris was even prepared to contemplate handing over the task of negotiation with the applicants to the European Commission.[23] The significance of this can perhaps best be gauged by recalling both France's 1961 attempt to exclude the Commission from involvement in the first enlargement talks and the persistent way in which France under de Gaulle had sought to limit the Commission's international role.[24] The scourge of Commission independence was demanding a greater and more autonomous contribution from the Brussels body. But this apparent volte-face did not signal that France had dropped its earlier dislike of undue Commission power.[25] Instead it reflected a belief that even the highly defensive negotiating procedure that the Six had employed in 1961–63 had not been enough to insulate France fully from its partners' desire to see the British join and their consequent readiness to be flexible about adaptations to the Community. Much better rather to hand the entire negotiating process over to the European Commission, an institution whose whole raison d'être was to protect the EEC as it existed and thus to ensure that enlargement did not come about at the expense of the *acquis communautaire*. France's institutional radicalism was hence purely tactical rather than reflecting a genuine change of heart about the way that the Community should normally function. But if France was to secure agreement to this, or any other defensive negotiating procedure, it needed to be in a position to bargain with the Five rather than simply announcing that the veto was no more and allowing membership talks to begin.

The French need to strike a bargain extended well beyond the way in which any talks with the applicants were to be conducted. Pompidou's government had much that it needed and wanted from the European Community. In particular, it wished to settle as soon as was possible the future organisation of the CAP and to push the integration process forward into a number of new fields of activity, notably monetary policy.[26] Its best hope of achieving these aims, and avoiding the weakness that inevitably sprang from being a *demandeur*, was to insist upon them as the price for EEC enlargement. The new French President may well have known that he was powerless to prevent British membership in the long or even medium term. But he was much too shrewd a politician to throw away the French veto without first obtaining the greatest possible quid pro quo. For this reason also, France had every incentive to hint that it might be willing to shift its position on the widening of the Community without actually going so far as to promise that it would happen. Uncertainty would make its bargaining position that much stronger.

The dispute over enlargement had thus reached an intriguing and delicate phase. In marked contrast to the final stages of de Gaulle's Presidency, there were now signs of movement aplenty from Paris. This was something that gave both the applicants and their multiple allies within the Community reasons to be optimistic. But the alteration of the French position – if such it was – occurred only slowly and cautiously. There would be no spontaneous throwing open of the Community's doors by the new leadership in Paris. Instead the Five and the candidate countries would have to probe carefully in order to establish what would be the full price of that opening which now looked possible but was as yet by no means guaranteed.

Saving the old agenda and settling the new

The second half of 1969 also witnessed a lively debate about the evolving agenda of the European Community. To a certain extent this reflected the continuation of that discussion of the Community's future activity referred to in both Chapters 5 and 6. This will be explored further below. Still more pressing however were the anxious exchanges provoked by the onset of serious difficulty within the newly-completed CAP. For by mid-1969 there were at least three distinct problems facing the Community's most ambitious and complex common policy.

The first problem, mentioned briefly last chapter, was that the 1966 agreement on CAP finance was due to expire at the end of 1969. The task of renewing the agreement and of establishing a financial mechanism that would apply to the post-1970 Community was bound to be a difficult one. Apart from anything else, the sums of money involved were sufficiently large for each of the governments to approach the talks with a strong desire to limit the extent of their commitment. But in 1969 there was an additional level of anxiety caused by memories of 1965. It had been the controversy over CAP funding after all that had precipitated the empty chair crisis.[27] To tackle the issue once more at a time when the French and the Five were already bitterly divided was a daunting prospect. This was all the more so since the Commission's legislative proposal, submitted to the Council of Ministers in July 1969, chose not to avoid the controversial aspects of the funding question in the way that the May 1966 accord had done.[28] Instead, the questions of 'own resources' (including the attribution of customs receipts to the Community and the allocation of additional powers to the Strasbourg Assembly) would again have to be discussed. The potential for bitter disagreement amongst the Six remained high.

This was all the more so given the apparent contradiction between the French and Italian approaches to the financial regulation. Rome's misgivings about the whole structure of the CAP were as strong in 1969 as they had been four years earlier. The Italians still believed that they did poorly out of the Community's agricultural policy and were as a result determined to use the expiry of the existing system as an opportunity to press for wide-scale reform.[29] This meant that they once again approached the Brussels negotiations intending to secure a substantial adjustment of national contributions.[30] If this could not be done before the end of 1969, the Italians were ready to settle for a short-term stop-gap regulation designed to remove the urgency from the financial regulation discussion and then to use the time gained to explore the possibilities of much further-reaching change.[31] France, by contrast, was intent on preventing either substantial change or delay. To allow the current regime to expire without agreement having been reached on a multi-annual replacement would, the French feared, raise a substantial doubt about the very continuation of the existing CAP system, especially with enlargement imminent. As one document put it, a failure to meet the 31 December, 1969 deadline would mean that 'at a political level, the agricultural policy would appear to have been called into question, made precarious and, destined to be profoundly altered, especially in the course of the negotiations with the countries that had asked to join the EEC'.[32] Given that French farmers were already over-producing substantially, the cost to the French state should European funding be significantly reduced or worse still not materialise at all was not something that Paris could take lightly. They thus approached the negotiations to renew the financial regulation with much of that same grim determination that they had displayed in 1965. Reconciling their stance and that of the Italians would not be easy.

The second difficulty was the explosion of European agricultural surpluses in the late 1960s. Overproduction had long been identified as one of the possible consequences of the CAP, especially once the common price set for grain was fixed closer to the high German level than to the much lower French one.[33] And there had been some small surpluses almost as soon as the common prices had entered into force. But it was only at the end of the decade that the problem had become really serious. As soon as it did, however, alarm bells rang across western Europe. Predictably perhaps the Germans were particularly worried.[34] They not only faced the prospect of paying the lion's share of the bill for disposing of Europe's unneeded agricultural produce, but as major industrial exporters were also amongst the most vulnerable to any world trade disruption that subsidised European farm exports might cause. There was hence genuine anxiety behind Brandt's references, in his conversation with Pompidou, to the unacceptable state of affairs in which the Community was being forced to rent deconsecrated churches in the Netherlands in order to store its growing food mountains.[35] Needless to say the Italians, as the other persistent critics of the CAP, were also outspoken in their condemnation of Community overproduction.[36] Similarly, Luns used a speech in London to highlight the problem.[37] But even the French were concerned, aware that such overproduction threatened the long-term viability of that European agricultural support from which they gained so much. It was admittedly true that they felt little culpability for the food surpluses – these were the inescapable consequences of the level of price upon which the Germans had insisted in 1964.[38] But there was a genuine readiness to try to tackle the problem, provided that this medium-term objective did not become an obstacle to their short-term priority, namely the finalising of the CAP's funding arrangements.[39]

Even more pressing was the impact of the monetary instability of 1969 on the Community's farm subsidy system. The theoretical problem that currency movements could pose to a centralised system like the CAP had long been recognised.[40] But in the latter half of 1969, theory became reality, with the French franc being devalued in August and the German mark moving in the opposite direction in October. The Community's reaction was a hasty but rather unsatisfactory piece of improvisation. First an unscheduled Council meeting, held deep in the usual holiday period, authorised the temporary imposition of export controls on France.[41] These would allow agricultural commodities to trade at lower prices in France than they did elsewhere in the Community. An expedient of this sort was deemed necessary since to allow domestic French food prices to rise –

which would have been the normal consequence of the French franc's fall – would have been to risk stimulating still further the already excessive level of French agricultural production.[42] And then in October, Bonn was allowed to introduce temporary subsidies for its farmers in order to compensate them for the drop in their revenue that devaluation would cause.[43] The upshot was that by the late autumn of 1969, only a little over a year after the start of the single European market for agricultural produce, both the continent's largest food producer and the continent's largest market for farm products had been forced to resort to temporary border controls that negated much of the liberalisation achieved. The blow to the credibility of the whole CAP project was very serious indeed. Although overblown in their conclusions, the comments by Walter Scheel, the German Foreign Minister, to the French Ambassador in Bonn did capture the seriousness of the problem: 'We find outselves in a critical situation . . .. It will be necessary to build a new agricultural policy'.[44] With more currency movement perceived as likely – there was much talk for instance of the Belgian franc changing parity – it was imperative for the Community to devise a more effective means of responding to monetary instability when it did occur, or, still better, preventing global currency movements from affecting the parities of those currencies within the EEC.[45]

These same currency movements had pushed the topic of monetary integration or at least coordination to the very centre of the discussion about the Community's future agenda. Some initial steps in this direction had already been taken. In July 1969, the Six reached agreement in principle to implement the so-called Barre Plan submitted by the Commission earlier in the year.[46] The fall of the French franc and the rise of the *Deutschmark* however soon made it apparent that the tentative steps towards macro-economic coordination foreseen by the Commission plan were insufficient to deal with the scale of the problem. Something rather more ambitious was required. In the latter half of 1969, a number of European governments were hence proceeding down the trail blazed by the Action Committee for the United States of Europe, Jean Monnet's influential pressure group, and actively exploring means of extending European integration into the monetary field.[47] Nobody was under any illusion that this would be an easy step; the events of 1969 had however convinced many that it was an essential one were the European Community to avoid being seriously damaged by currency movements amongst its members.

Alongside these putative ideas for monetary integration, there was also debate about other potential fields of Community advance. Technological cooperation remained one prominent topic, despite the difficulties experience by the Maréchal committee. Europe's general backwardness in this area had, after all, been all too graphically underlined by the culmination of the space-race with the American moon-landing in July 1969.[48] No western European country had yet developed a satisfactory satellite launcher, let alone a means of reaching the moon. But there was an awareness that the transatlantic technology gap was not confined to rocketry, but also included computers, nuclear energy, and military hardware. Closing this divide was a priority for the French and several other European governments. But Paris's ambitions also encompassed a full European industrial policy, including joint measures designed to control the level of US investments in Europe.[49] Similarly, the Italians' quest for the building of a social Europe had not stopped once free movement of labour had been achieved in 1968. Instead, Rome continued to press for a common approach to employment and the development of a regional policy.[50] This would help shelter the Italian *Mezzogiorno* from the harsher effects of economic integration.

Inevitably, the debate about the Community's future evolution also included multiple references to political union. Despite ten years of frustration in this field, the desire to see Europe able to act in a more unified fashion in the foreign policy arena was still strongly felt by many European leaders.[51] The new French President would appear, admittedly, to have been somewhat of an exception. Pompidou's reactions in 1969 to the notion of European foreign policy coordination seem to have ranged from the cautiously non-committal to outright scepticism.[52] But such was the enthusiasm of several of his European colleagues – Kiesinger would be one clear example, the Italian government another – that the French leader was unlikely to be able to rule it out altogether without risking another confrontation with his European partners.[53] This was all the more true if, as most hoped, the enlargement dispute was on the way to a solution, since it had been the question of British participation that had most bedevilled earlier efforts to coordinate the foreign policies of EEC member states.

Rethinking the EEC's institutions

The length and depth of the crisis over enlargement had also provoked widespread questioning of the EEC's institutional structure. Only two years earlier, those unhappy with the Community's move away from federalism and towards an ever-more Council-led system had been on the defensive, forced to concede that the rise of Council power had not led to the type of policy immobility associated with the OEEC. On the contrary, as was argued in Chapter 5, episodes such as the successful Kennedy Round negotiations, seemed to demonstrate that Council leadership had neither deprived the European Commission of a useful and high-profile role nor condemned Community decision making to endless lowest-common denominator decisions. The experience of 1968 and 1969 had strongly revived such fears, however. The EEC's total inability to rise above the division of opinion over British membership and the serious risk that it appeared to run of reaching the 1 January, 1970 deadline with many of the hoped-for decisions as yet untaken, did seem to vindicate the fears of those most unhappy with institutional developments brought into the open by the resolution of the empty chair crisis. Inevitably, therefore, calls for a return to the 'true path' of development gained new vigour.[54] Europe, it seemed, was broke and there was a clear need to fix it.

Part of the concern centred on the lacklustre performance of the European Commission under Jean Rey. Although few attacked Hallstein's successor personally, there were many who regretted his seeming lack of impact.[55] His multiple appeals for restraint in the enlargement row, for instance, seemed to have made no difference whatsoever to the course of Council discussions.[56] And his judgement also seemed suspect when the Commission managed to get itself embroiled in a minor, but unpleasant, spat with the new German government in the wake of the *Deutschmark's* revaluation in October.[57] To pick a fight with the Community's newest and potentially most powerful leader seemed an odd way of exercising that leadership function that many still hoped that the Commission might be capable of fulfilling. Furthermore, there were still doubts about the extent to which the administrative structure of the Commission had recovered from the turmoil caused by the 1967 merger of the EEC, ECSC and Euratom 'executives'. Virtually no part of the Commission had escaped from the sweeping changes that fusion had necessitated, and it took much longer than many had expected for the reorganised directorates general to begin to operate efficiently.[58] The flow of policy ideas and suggestions from the Commission was correspondingly reduced at the very moment when the EEC's need for new ideas was most acute. The way in which President Nixon pointedly refused to make time to see Rey when the Commission President visited Washington in mid-1969, whereas previous administrations had welcomed Hallstein to Blair House and given him extensive access to the President, seemed to symbolise well the much more general slippage in the Commission's authority, dynamism and political clout.[59]

The real problem institution in the late 1960s was the Council of Ministers, however. As Rey himself had conceded, it was at a Council level that real power lay within the EEC.[60] It was therefore the Council and not the Commission that was primarily responsible for the sterile deadlock of Community decision-making by 1969. Unsurprisingly, this led some to lament the non-use of qualified majority voting: both the Dutch and the Commission for instance indicated their belief that this was a contributory factor to the Council deadlock.[61] Others looked critically at the whole mode of Council operation. Brandt, for example, criticised the size of many Council meetings – with 200 plus people often present the gatherings were less a decision-making Council than a ponderous 'medium-sized popular assembly' – and regretted the lack of clarity about the division of powers between the Council and the Commission.[62] Also looked at negatively was the proliferation of sectoral Councils, bringing together ministers of agriculture or of social affairs and not involving the foreign ministers.[63] Clearly, the German foreign minister and then Chancellor believed that these made it harder for those involved in the Community negotiations to have any overall sense of what they were doing and where they were bound. Instead there needed to be greater continuity in the representation of each country including a still greater role for the permanent representatives.[64]

The powers and mode of election of the European Parliament had also become more topical again, primarily because of the link with the financial regulation. The Commission's proposals on CAP financing imitated those of 1965 by suggesting a redistribution of powers between the Commission, Parliament and Council so far as the Community's budgetary process was concerned.[65] Once again, the ostensible beneficiary was to be the Parliament, whereas in reality the Commission would also gain as much additional influence if not more. And once again the French would be attentively on guard for any significant reduction in the Council's ultimate power of decision.[66] But the major difference with 1965 was that the French were now ready to make some limited movement in direction of greater Parliamentary (if not Commission) influence.[67] This meant that another head-on collision between the eagerness of the Dutch, Germans and Italians for a greater role for the Strasbourg Assembly and total French obstinacy was much less likely. More probable rather was a procedure designed to give some new role to the Parliament while ensuring that the Council of Ministers remained firmly in charge. Less good, by contrast, were the prospects of Italy's determined campaign to re-examine the whole basis by which MEPs were chosen.[68] Direct elections, as sought by Rome, were perceived as much too dangerous by the French, since they would undermine the most compelling French argument for not giving the Assembly too much power. A directly elected body would have a much greater level of democratic legitimacy and would hence be much harder to deny revenue raising power.[69]

On institutional matters, as on the future agenda of the Community, there were plenty of ideas in circulation but little indication as yet as to whether any could attract the necessary consensus amongst member states. What was clear, however, was that de Gaulle's departure had aroused a widespread expectation that a resumption of Community advance might be possible. There was thus an inevitable contrast between the impatience with which many looked forward to the unfreezing of the EEC, and the caution with which Pompidou strove to change his country's position on enlargement in return for the maximum possible quid pro quo. Managing this contrast, and avoiding a situation in which his partners lost all patience with his careful diplomacy, was yet another challenge facing the newly installed French leader.

Proposing a summit

It was against this backdrop of somewhat impatient expectation that Pompidou launched his idea of a summit meeting between the Six.[70] At such a gathering, Europe's leaders would be able to discuss all three elements of the so-called triptych that Pompidou also declared his readiness to contemplate: *achèvement* or completion of the Community's initial agenda, *approfondissement* or deepening cooperation into new areas, and *élargissement* or widening the EEC's membership. Although there was to be no formal agenda at the summit meeting, the French were in effect signalling their readiness to discuss enlargement, provided that their priorities in the form of the other two elements of the triptych were also agreed upon. The Community could thus only afford to widen, if it completed all of those tasks that it was meant to finish in the course of the transitional period (including, of course, the financial regulation) and if it decided *à Six* what its priorities for future progress were. Such consensus would enable it to go into a well prepared negotiation with the applicants without there being too much of a danger that either the achievements of the Community or its future prospects would be undermined. The proposal for a summit and the announcement of the triptych thus sketched out for its partners the basic shape of the deal that France wished to strike.

From a French point of view there were a number of important advantages that could be achieved only through a summit meeting rather than through the normal process of Council meetings in Brussels. The first was quite simply that of holding out the prospect of movement without having to enter into any form of binding promise. The idea of a summit, especially when linked to that of the triptych, demonstrated that France meant business. It was also a means for the new government to thrust itself forward into the limelight and to set out its own ideas about how the Community's crisis could be resolved rather than letting others determine the timetable and manner of the crisis's resolution. But being simply a procedural suggestion, the proposed summit did not actually commit France to do anything more than talk about enlargement. Actual agreement would be dependent on France's partners approaching the summit in a reasonable mood and with a willingness to grant Paris some of its desiderata. It thus differed profoundly from something like Dutch suggestion, also put forward in the summer of 1969, that the Six should at once publicly declare their intent to enlarge the Community.[71]

The second advantage of a summit was that it was the only type of meeting that would have the necessary political authority to conclude the wide-ranging deal Pompidou sought. Before agreeing to open negotiations with the applicants, the French wanted to receive assurances that the financial regulation would be completed on time and in full, undertakings about the manner in which the Six would coordinate their position during any talks with the British, and some indication of consensus about the future agenda of the EEC. No normal Council meeting would, however, have an agenda broad enough or a set of participants senior enough to conclude an agreement about so many different topics. Instead, the ministers of agriculture and those of finance who might, together, be able to conclude some sort of deal on CAP funding would lack the authority to decide anything about the negotiating procedure in the membership negotiations, while the foreign ministers in their turn would be able to set the ground rules for the enlargement talks but would not have the collective power to settle the financial regulation or to talk about future monetary integration. A summit, by contrast, would bring together the only group of politicians in western Europe who could take so many interlinked decisions at once. And their word would be sufficiently powerful to oblige subsequent meetings of the various Councils of Ministers to implement the agreements reached according to whatever timetable had been set. Although the package deal had become a standard recipe for Community advance, that needed by the French in 1969 was so comprehensive as to require a negotiating procedure that went well beyond the normal pattern of EEC diplomacy. Only agreement amongst the Heads of Government would suffice to end the Gaullist challenge.

The third merit of a summit was that it would outflank the German suggestion of a summit bringing together the Six and the applicants.[72] A gathering of the Ten, or even just of the Seven, would be the worst possible scenario for the French, since it would subject the new President to the maximum possible pressure to allow enlargement to go ahead. It would also be an ideal opportunity for the British to practice the tactics of divide and rule at which the French believed London to be so adept.[73] Rejecting Brandt's idea without putting forward a counter-suggestion of their own would, however, have been a dangerous move, seemingly indicating that the French were as obstinate as ever. It would thus use up much of that credit with Bonn that the new French President possessed. And given that foreign minister Brandt was also SPD candidate for the chancellorship, it was doubly important for the new French government not to treat too cavalierly a solution advanced by someone who could be German leader after the elections in late September. It was therefore vital for France to be able to introduce their own procedural suggestions so as to reclaim the initiative from the German foreign minister without offending Brandt in the process.

A summit was, however, an extremely high risk occasion. In launching the idea, France was in effect indicating that it believed that the Community impasse could be overcome. A surge of optimism amongst its partners would almost certainly ensue. To fail to satisfy the multiple hopes induced by the holding of the summit would, however, be to provoke an even more serious crisis within the Community. A bad summit would be much worse than no summit at all.[74] It would be a failure, moreover, for which much of the blame would be attached to the French President personally. After a summit mishap it would not be possible to shelter behind the tactical blunders of the French foreign minister or those of some more junior negotiator. Instead, responsibility for any mistakes as well as any credit for advance would lie with the Elysée. It was therefore vital for the credibility of Pompidou's whole European policy that the summit which he had proposed achieved its aim and rescued the EEC from its 18 months of crisis. The new French President had personally committed himself to breaking the Community deadlock.

Preparing for The Hague

The best way of avoiding a damaging failure at the summit would be meticulous preparation. This was all the more so given the somewhat ambivalent response to the new French ideas in mid-July, when the Council of Ministers had its first opportunity to discuss both the triptych and the suggested meeting of European leaders.[75] Schumann's warmer and more flexible tone was appreciated by all. The new French foreign minister's Brussels debut was much less acrimonious than had been that of his predecessor, Debré. But only Brandt was unequivocal in his welcome of the summit idea. Harmel and Luns both expressed misgivings about using a procedure not foreseen by the Treaty of Rome, the Belgian recalling with evident displeasure the inconclusive Rome summit of 1967. Grégoire, moreover, seemingly spoke for many when he admitted his fear that the French suggestion might lead to the Community being put into a state of 'premature hibernation' until the leaders could meet.[76] Meanwhile, Zagari, the Italian representative, cited the domestic political crisis underway in Rome as a reason for not being able to formulate a clear response to the idea of convening a summit. Worryingly for the French, Brandt and Luns also continued to raise the idea of a summit level meeting of the Seven as well as that amongst the Six. The French proposal did not appear to have succeeded in pushing aside the earlier German initiative. And all of the Five were critical of the French insistence that enlargement talks could not begin until the Community had been completed.[77] Nobody in the Community of the late 1960s was ready to underestimate how difficult it might prove to finalise the financial regulation. Requiring that this be done before any talks could begin with the applicants might be tantamount to postponing membership negotiations for a substantial time to come.[78] Similarly, French calls for the Six to devise a common stance amongst themselves before beginning to bargain with the applicants might also lead to a lengthy round of pre-negotiations and to the yet further postponement of British, Danish, Irish and Norwegian entry.

This suspicion that the French were still playing for time was at the heart of most of the diplomacy in the run-up to the summit. By September when the Six discussed the subject again, the Five had begun a concerted campaign for first the recognition that completion, widening and deepening were interlinked processes that needed to run simultaneously and second for a start date to be set for actual membership negotiations.[79] Only in this way would both public and governmental opinion amongst the Five be able to accept further steps being taken towards French Community priorities. Paris's response, however, highlighted the depth of mistrust that continued to characterise Community exchanges. No formal linkage between completion, widening and deepening could be accepted, ostensibly since the first was a process required by the Treaty to occur before the year's end, whereas the other two were new targets the Community was contemplating setting itself.[80] In reality, however, the French determination to prevent any linkage sprang from the fear that were the financial regulation to become a subject of debate amongst the countries negotiating to join the EEC as well as amongst the Six themselves, the outcome might be a system of CAP finance very different from that sought by the French.[81] The triptych was hence to be realised successively not simultaneously. And a formal opening date for enlargement negotiations was also to be resisted, because Paris feared that this could be used by some of the Five as a means of escaping from too tight a prior coordination amongst the Six. As Pompidou privately explained in the days leading up to the summit:

> I am also totally opposed to the fixing of a date for the opening of talks with the United Kingdom. If a date is set, you will see that, as if by chance, M. Luns will be too busy, M. Moro will be in bed with a temperature, M. Brandt travelling. Time will pass and when the deadline arrives nothing will have been prepared and we will approach the British totally disunited amongst ourselves, able only to kowtow to the newcomers. This is moreover the scarcely veiled intention of some European governments.[82]

The September working lunch and a further preparatory meeting amongst the Six held in November thus saw no meeting of minds on this subject.[83] On the contrary, the gap remained as wide as ever between the Five's conviction that enlargement was the single most pressing issue that the EEC had to deal with, and the French belief that the Six should engage with the applicants only once their internal affairs were in order and they had decided upon a collective approach. Pompidou's repeated use of the metaphor of the EEC as a fortified city that should be entered through the city gate and not by means of a breach in its walls clearly underlined the ongoing defensiveness of the French.[84]

Fortunately for those hoping that agreement could be reached amongst Europe's leaders, the preparatory discussions fared rather better in establishing the ground-rules for the summit. As far as the venue was concerned, the Dutch government, which held the EC Presidency in the latter half of 1969, quickly assented to the French suggestion that they should host the event.[85] Similarly, a date in the first half of November was rapidly decided upon, although this would subsequently have to be changed to early December because Moro, the Italian foreign minister, fell ill.[86] And all seemed ready to accept the French suggestion that there be no formal agenda; so obvious were the key questions that the assembled leaders would have to discuss that the absence of a precise running order did not appear to matter that much. Rather more surprisingly, consensus was also established fairly quickly over the potentially awkward question of Commission participation. Although the French had initially seemed minded to try to exclude the Commission altogether, they rapidly gave some ground in the face of strong German and Dutch calls for Rey to take part.[87] By November it had been agreed that the Commission President was to be invited to the second of the two days of discussion.[88]

Even more important was the growing level of accord between the French and the new German government about what should be decided at The Hague. The bilateral dialogue between the two had not, it has to be admitted, begun in particularly promising fashion. In the course of the July 1969 meeting between Pompidou and Brandt cited above, it is clear that whereas the French were talking about a summit of the Six, the German foreign minister's response was based upon the idea of a gathering of the Seven or even the Ten.[89] But once the September elections in the Federal Republic had brought a new SPD-FDP coalition government to power and had promoted Brandt from the Foreign Ministry to the Chancellery, a much more constructive and focused discussion between Paris and Bonn could begin.

This might superficially appear surprising. After all, Brandt had often appeared far less close to the French than Kiesinger during the Grand Coalition years. Furthermore, the SPD had a long-standing suspicion of Gaullist France and a deep vein of enthusiasm for closer ties to Britain.[90] The departure of the strongly Francophile Kiesinger and the installation of an SPD-led government might therefore have been expected to disrupt Franco-German relations rather than lead to their improvement. But the new government moved swiftly to counter any such fears. Walter Scheel, the Foreign Minister, for instance reassured the French Ambassador on 4 November, 1969:

> The Federal government and the opposition are in agreement that European policy must advance. These advances are also necessary with regard to East–West relations; without these advances our Eastern policy will also be made more difficult, since this is grounded on our solid integration into the western Alliance system.[91]

Given the prominence that Brandt's new *Ostpolitik* had assumed in both the new government's self-image and the way it was perceived from abroad, the argument that the new line towards Eastern Europe was not merely compatible with Bonn's Western loyalties, but actually increased their importance, was highly welcome news to all of Germany's European partners.

Pompidou responded quickly to these German reassurances, sending word via Seydoux that he would like a dialogue between the two governments at a 'high but discrete [*sic*] level'.[92] To this end, Brandt sent Carlo Schmid, his newly appointed co-ordinator for Franco-German relations, to talk to the President in early November. Pompidou was in confident mood, first predicting that the conference would succeed, and then telling Schmid 'Once we have obtained what we want, we will not create any more difficulties. You can tell this to the Chancellor: we are open and cooperative, but we want the completion of the Common Market and the financial regulation.'[93] Brandt also wrote twice to the French President in the months leading up to the conference. The second of these letters, building upon the message conveyed by Schmid, made quite clear that Brandt would travel to The Hague fully aware of the need to grant France what it wanted on CAP finance in return for agreement to open membership talks with the applicants. Neither issue would be easy, the German chancellor predicted. But he left no doubt that Bonn was aware of the necessity, quite literally, to pay the price for the CAP. The paragraph devoted to completion conceded, 'I know that on this issue the Federal Republic must accept a financial burden.'[94] French internal documents from the days preceding the summit make it equally clear that Paris too knew what it was that needed to be done. Most obviously, the French would have to allow enlargement negotiations to begin in the course of 1970 – albeit perhaps without a firm date being stipulated in the conference communiqué.[95] Agreement seemed thus to have been reached between the Community's two most powerful member states before the leaders assembled in the Netherlands. It remained to be seen, however, whether unity between Paris and Bonn could be translated into consensus amongst all of the Six.

Starting badly, ending well

Day one of the summit underlined how much work needed to be done before trust could be rebuilt.[96] The first problem was that Pompidou's much awaited opening speech was a major disappointment. Far from a powerful rallying call designed to remind his partners of the constructive European role that France could play, it was short, unimaginative and grudging in its references to enlargement.[97] Brandt, who spoke next, came much closer to striking the right tone, despite dropping half of his planned intervention so as to avoid speaking for much longer than the French President.[98] A conference partially intended to demonstrate that France could once more aspire to European leadership, had instead opened with a set of statements that emphasised the new-found confidence and dynamism of the Germans.[99]

Then De Jong, the Dutch Prime Minister and hence chairman, made a disastrous attempt to focus debate on the issue of enlargement. Matters such as completion and deepening, he claimed, could be much more appropriately dealt with the next day when the Commission would be represented.[100] Pompidou was predictably furious and it needed emollient interventions first by Gaston Eyskens, the Belgian Prime Minister, and then by Brandt to rescue the situation. Not much more progress was made, however, even when it was agreed that completion was the logical topic to begin with. The main difficulty was the seemingly unbridgeable distance between France's desire for an agreement on the financial regulation by the start of 1970 which would then be all but unchangeable for a long period of time and the Dutch and Italian calls for adaptability (so as to be able to accommodate the needs of Britain) and greater financial equity.[101] Little wonder then that after the first day's formal session had ended, de Koster, one of the Dutch ministers to have attended the conference described proceedings as worse than the worst EC Council negotiations.[102] The summit had not started well.

The situation improved significantly over dinner that night. Crucial in this respect were a series of informal exchanges between the French President and several of his counterparts, in the course of which Pompidou reaffirmed his personal commitment to the enlargement process and expressed the willingness to see talks begin with the candidates by the summer of 1970.[103] This informal agreement cleared the air significantly and allowed the second day of discussions to be dominated by the issue of deepening rather than the lingering row over enlargement. The result was a much improved atmosphere and a surprising degree of consensus about what the Community's future priorities should be. Monetary integration was the principal concern for most of those present, and there was general agreement that Pompidou's call for more regular meetings of European finance ministers and Brandt's suggestion of a European Reserve Fund should both be pursued.[104] No details about the exact shape of European monetary coordination were settled, but the general willingness to move in this direction had been clearly demonstrated. Likewise, there was near consensus on the need to rescue Euratom from its ongoing budget crisis, on the usefulness of European technological cooperation, on the need to investigate an increase in the European Parliament's budgetary powers, and on the desirability of regular meetings amongst foreign ministers designed to coordinate the foreign policies of the Six.[105] By the end of the second morning it had become clear that the communiqué would be a document that signalled a general commitment amongst the governments of the EEC member states to relaunch the integration process.[106]

And so it proved. The public outcome of the conference, the communiqué upon which the foreign ministers had been working throughout the two day meeting and which was finalised amongst the heads of government on the afternoon of the second day, did confirm that significant steps forward had been taken on all three aspects of Pompidou's triptych.[107] As far as *achèvement* was concerned, paragraph 5 of the communiqué noted the commitment of all member states to the 31 December, 1969 deadline for both the end of the transitional period and the finalising of the CAP financing system and specified that the agreement to be reached on the latter would include the whole issue of EEC own resources. There was hence no question of the type of stop-gap regulation the Italians had sought. Furthermore, paragraph 7 stipulated that whereas adaptations to the financial regulation could be made in the future, they would not only require unanimity amongst the member states, but would also have to remain faithful to the basic principles of the funding system. France had thus secured most of the guarantees it was looking for as far as CAP finance was concerned. Paragraph 6 did admittedly refer to the problem of Community agricultural surpluses and mentioned the need to limit the budgetary weight of the agricultural support system. But with the financial regulation soon to be in hand and its basic principles sacrosanct, there was little danger that France would see a major reduction in the levels of European subsidy its farmers received.

In return, the French had to all intents and purposes lifted their veto on enlargement. Paragraph 13, the portion of the communiqué most clearly directed towards the widening of the Community, was, it ought to be acknowledged, somewhat vague in its wording. No date for the opening of talks was included. Furthermore the agreement 'in principle' to enlargement went little further than the statement drafted by the 19 December, 1967 Council or even the February 1968 Franco-German communiqué on the membership issue.[108] The rest of the paragraph, moreover, with its emphasis on the conditions that the applicants would have to fulfil and the preparations that the Six would need to make prior to opening talks with the British, Danes, Irish and Norwegians, could be read as defensive and even somewhat grudging.

Too jaundiced a reading would, however, be totally incorrect. For a start, paragraph 4 of the communiqué included a long passage which acknowledged that the widening of the EEC would strengthen rather than weaken the Community. The French had, in other words, publicly rejected the centre piece of their 1967–69 case against enlargement. Furthermore, Pompidou had not only assured his colleagues that he personally wished discussions with the applicants to open soon, but had agreed that De Jong should tell the press that membership talks were likely to open by June 1970. He also then authorised Schumann to comment to journalists: 'I see no reason why the preparatory work – that is, the definition of a common position – should require more than six months.'[109] France had thus accepted that membership talks should begin by mid-1970, but had done so in a fashion that avoided setting the type of rigid deadline that some of its partners might have sought to exploit.

It was of course true that the wording of the communiqué reaffirmed the need for applicants to accept fully all that the Community had decided

in the years prior to their entry. It also set out a very *communautaire* negotiating procedure, designed to maximise the unity of the Six and minimise
the scope for the would-be members to play off the existing members
against one another. The Hague outcome did thus confirm one of the main
lessons of the 1961 to 1963 enlargement discussions, namely that the onus
of adaptation lay fully with those states wishing to join the EEC, rather
than with the Community itself.[110] This would mean that Britain and its
fellow candidates would have to swallow a great deal of legislation that
they might, in ideal circumstances, have liked to have seen altered. But
given the complexity of the Community's internal bargains and the attitude that all of the member states had tended to adopt when collectively
talking about enlargement in the past this should not have come as a surprise to those states that had applied to join. What mattered was that the
Six had all agreed that the doors of the Community were now open and
that any applicant willing to step over the threshold could take its place
within. Pompidou's walled city was no longer an unassailable stronghold.

With some degree of unity restored over the question of enlargement,
the Six had also been able to progress as far as the future agenda of the
Community was concerned. Paragraphs 8, 9, 11, 12, 15, and 16 thus each
identified important new areas where the Community members could
deepen their cooperation. Understandably it was the section outlining the
importance of monetary cooperation that commanded the greatest attention in the press, even though the actual wording of the communiqué was
distinctly more cautious than some of the discussion amongst the heads of
government had been. But it also mattered that forward movement could
resume on a range of activities spanning technological cooperation, the
establishment of a European university, the furthering of European social
policy, and the creation of a European youth programme modelled on that
developed between France and Germany. Also potentially significant was
the public commitment to resume discussions of political union. While
none of these initiatives was guaranteed success, the list of new items
added to the EEC's agenda did reinforce the message of the communiqué's opening paragraphs that the Community was not destined to
remain just a customs union with an agricultural policy attached. The so-
called *finalités politiques*, or political goals, of the integration process had
been strongly reaffirmed.[111]

Finally, there was even some indication of movement at the institutional level. This claim may at first seem surprising. After all, one of the
main complaints aired by Rey in his retrospective analysis of the summit
meeting before the European Parliament was precisely that the heads of
government had failed to address the institutional issues that both Parliament and the Commission had urged them to consider.[112] Furthermore,
the multiple references during the summit to the need to improve the
workings of the Council of Ministers in particular were not acknowledged
by the communiqué.[113] But there were two areas in which an important

step forward had been taken. The first was over the European Parliament where even the French appeared to acknowledge that some alteration in its powers needed to be made. Full agreement on this would take time to emerge and consensus on the need to change the means by which the European Parliamentarians were elected remained even further away. But enough flexibility had been shown by Pompidou on this issue to make it extremely unlikely that the type of point-blank refusal to increase Strasbourg's powers that had been the hallmark of French policy under de Gaulle would reappear under the new French leadership. Since discussions at The Hague had also confirmed how much symbolic importance all of the member states other than France attached to the issue, any appearance of French flexibility on this question made an increase in the budgetary powers of the European Parliament a near certainty in the medium-term future.[114]

The second step forward was over the issue of summit meetings themselves. The six heads of government had certainly not set a date to meet again. On the contrary, in the run-up to The Hague several member states had been keen to emphasise that they did not regard summitry as something that should be resorted to on a regular basis.[115] The 1974 decision to institutionalise the European Council was still a long way off. Nevertheless, there had been strong indications in the course of the meeting that most of the participants did believe it to be right and proper for a forum other than the Council of Ministers to take Community decisions and to plot the EEC's course ahead. One of the few sour moments, indeed, of the second day of discussions, had been when Rey had tried to insist that it was not the job of the Prime Ministers to take decisions on the timing of enlargement that more properly belonged to the Community institutions meeting in Brussels.[116] This suggestion had been firmly dismissed by Brandt and by Eyskens, the former reminding his colleagues and the Commission President of the important step forward on enlargement that had been taken.[117] This willingness to override Council deadlock, especially combined with the very fruitful results of the summit meeting, made it probable that the Community member states would seriously consider meeting again whenever important path-setting decisions needed to be taken. Once successfully employed, the summit mechanism was unlikely to be set aside permanently.

The Gaullist challenge negotiated?

Overall then, The Hague summit did deserve both the press attention it received at the time and the prominence it has assumed in subsequent accounts of the Community's development. Many of the ideas that it set out would take time to be implemented. The financial regulation was not finalised until April 1970. The enlargement negotiations would last until late 1971 and Britain, Ireland and Denmark would not take their place within the Community until 1 January, 1973. Norway, meanwhile, chose not to join them after its population voted against Community membership in a 1972 referendum. And some of the monetary targets that were discussed at The Hague, if not specified in the communiqué, were arguably not attained until the late 1990s. Political union also would enjoy a difficult development, with a fully satisfactory process for devising a European foreign policy still proving elusive in the early twenty-first century. But The Hague's significance is probably more fairly measured by looking back to what had preceded the summit meeting than by scrutinising the path that lay ahead. For once the degree of deadlock and stagnation in the Community of 1968–69 is recalled, the leap forward made at The Hague becomes that much more remarkable.

Fundamentally, the summit marked the moment when the Community overcame what this book has described as the Gaullist challenge. French policy until 1969 had highlighted the difficult choices facing Europe over its policy agenda, its institutional make-up and over its membership. On all three issues, The Hague offered answers that, while not definitive, were firm enough to allow a strong degree of consensus to be rebuilt. In so doing it also allowed the Six to re-establish that level of mutual trust that had been amongst the first and most prominent victims of de Gaulle's European policies.

As far as the agenda is concerned, the summit consolidated the achievements of the 1960s and set down an important set of markers as to the future activities of the EEC. After The Hague, complaints and controversy would continue to surround the CAP. Reform of the agricultural policy indeed would prove a staple of Council and summit discussions for decades to come. But the basic fact of its existence and the main features of its operation had been reaffirmed in a manner and in a forum that were likely to calm French anxieties for many years ahead. The European Community would go on funding its farmers to produce, irrespective of the level of world commodity prices and of the surpluses that might result, for the indefinite future. The French nightmare of the Community becoming nothing more than a zone of industrial free trade could hence be pushed to one side.

Equally important, however, was the way in which The Hague also reassured those less attached to the CAP, that the Community would not become solely devoted to agricultural support policies. To a certain extent this had already been done with the completion of the customs union in mid-1968. Nevertheless, the frustration that had accompanied all attempts to find new areas of common activity in the months following this milestone had seemingly raised the prospect of a European construction whose day-to-day activity and whose future would be centred on the task of running the CAP and making occasional adjustments to the customs union, rather than anything more far-reaching or inspirational. This danger too had receded, however, now that the Six had jointly identified a series of ambitious new common targets upon which their future energies and deliberations could be focused and reaffirmed the fundamentally political nature of their enterprise. As mentioned above, it would take a long time for either monetary integration or foreign policy coordination to progress to the levels that some were already speaking of in December 1969. But the Community had identified a broad and exciting new agenda that would give the EEC a raison d'être that extended far beyond farm subsidies and the common external tariff. The slow transformation of the narrowly-defined low-policy Community of the 1958–69 period into the much broader-based high-policy Union of more recent times had begun.

Institutionally, The Hague also laid to rest many of the uncertainties raised by de Gaulle. As argued above, the summit did foreshadow two important elements of institutional change in the form of increased powers for the European Parliament and the greater use of summit meetings to overcome the leadership vacuum that had beset the Community of the later 1960s. It did therefore look forward to the emergence of the European Council and the first direct elections to the European Parliament held in 1979 – the two most important institutional changes that the Community was to undergo during the 1970s and arguably two of the most important changes it has ever experienced. But still more significant was what The Hague did not do. For, as Rey's lament appeared to acknowledge, the Six's failure to go any further on institutional reform signalled a willingness to live with the existing distribution of powers between Community institutions that was likely to impede hopes of a dramatic transformation of the EEC system for a long time to come. Despite the urgings of the Commission and of the Parliament, there was no widespread revolt against the Luxembourg compromise in December 1969. Nor was there any real talk of fundamental reform to either the Commission or the Council. Instead, that hybrid Community which had been brought to light in the wake of the 1965–66 crisis was confirmed almost by default. Power in the EEC of the 1970s would continue to lie primarily within the multiple manifestations of the Council of Ministers and yet the European Commission would retain a vital function as a progenitor of new policy ideas and as a negotiator within the Council debates. Federalism and traditional intergovernmentalism had both been decisively rejected.

The final certainty underlined at The Hague was that the European Community membership would grow. France had extracted a high price for its volte-face on enlargement. But Pompidou was now committed to permitting the widening of the EEC in a way which made any thought of future vetoes all but inconceivable. The awareness of how traumatic the row over de Gaulle's opposition to British membership had been, moreover, acted as a stark deterrent to any other state harbouring misgivings about Community expansion. Instead, the Six had laid down a set of rules about the way in which enlargement would be handled – primarily through their stipulation that the cost of adaptation should be borne by the candidates and not by the member states – that have continued to apply to this day. The corollary of these rules, however, was that any European country willing to pay this price is all but impossible to deny entry. The steady growth in size of the Community over subsequent decades was already predictable, although few in 1969 could have foreseen the scale of Union attained in May 2004.

December 1969 thus marked more than simply the end of the Community's transitional period. The resignation of de Gaulle eight months earlier, the cautious strategy of change mapped out by his successor and the two week postponement of the summit following Moro's illness combined to mean that the final month of the decade was also that during which the Community brought to an end a seven year struggle over its purpose, mode of operation and membership. The outcome was a European Community which had diverged somewhat from the path that some at least of its founding fathers believed it would take. It was nevertheless an institution that had demonstrated that it could accomplish the most important of the initial tasks set out by the Treaty, that had proved itself economically and politically indispensable to all of its member states, and that had revealed itself able to attract a high level of interest from its principal neighbours. And above all it had shown enough resilience to survive deep-rooted differences of opinion amongst those determining its evolution and course. All these qualities would stand it in good stead for the decades ahead.

Conclusions
The Gaullist challenge and its effects

The European policy of Charles de Gaulle is, and seems likely to remain, a subject of significant controversy. The General's ten years in power coincided almost exactly with the first and vital formative decade of the EEC. France, the country over which he ruled with such seeming dominance in the foreign policy field at least, had since 1950 acted as de facto leader of the integration process, doing much to determine both where 'Europe' went and where it did not go. These two facts combined ought to have meant that the first President of the Fifth Republic was the central figure in the Community's early development. And yet views remain polarised as to whether de Gaulle was a good 'European', a type of step-father of Europe who took over where the founders had left off and guided the EEC's development from treaty bargain to functioning reality, or instead an early Eurosceptic whose malevolent influence over the nascent European experiment was such as to divert the Six from the federal and political path to European unity upon which they had appeared to be bound.[1] Any study of the European Community during the 1963–69 period, when the General's challenge to the European status quo was most marked, must therefore assess where between these two extremes the actual truth lies.

A multilateral history of the Community cannot, however, focus its conclusions simply on one man, however enigmatic and fascinating. This final chapter will thus seek to move beyond an assessment of de Gaulle and include an investigation of how his European partners reacted to his policies. In particular, it will identify a number of strategies that were used to try to resist, divert and counter French European priorities. A further section will then explore what the clash between the French and their partners – and the manner in which it was contained and then resolved – indicated about the process of European integration in the 1960s. Who were the dominant influences in the Community between 1963 and 1969, how did the institutional structure of the EEC evolve, and how was the language and 'spirit' of the process affected by the repeated crises that characterise these years? And finally a concluding chapter must also include some assessment of how important the 1963–69 period is in the overall development of the Community. Were the seven years surveyed of intrinsic importance in the EEC's history, or are they simply a useful case-study of the integration process in action which matters primarily for what it reveals about the longer term transformation of Europe from a narrowly-focused Community of six to today's much deeper and wider European Union?

Barking but not biting?

Reaching a balanced assessment of de Gaulle's European policy is particularly difficult. For a start it is very hard entirely to separate the General's policy towards the EEC from his wider foreign policy concerns. Both his contemporaries and subsequent historians have tended, naturally enough, to perceive a degree of linkage between de Gaulle's actions at an EEC level and his more general rebellion against the institutions and norms of Western, American-led cooperation. The empty chair crisis or the vetoes of British membership are thus seen as products of the same basic attitude as the 1966 withdrawal from NATO's integrated military command or the 1965 verbal assault on the Bretton Woods monetary system. But as Chapter 4 sought to argue, there are also strong reasons for *not* regarding European integration merely as a sub-set of more general Western patterns of behaviour, but instead as an autonomous process which often responded to distinctive pressures and dynamics. Similarly, within France there were largely separate chains of command determining European policy and the French approach to NATO, the IMF or the general Western stance vis-à-vis the Communist bloc. There were also objectives that France could hope to attain through European cooperation that it could not expect to reach by means of its participation in other Western bodies. It is therefore as dangerous to assume that French policy in Brussels was entirely derived from a set of over-arching geo-political precepts as it is to go to the opposite extreme and maintain that economic calculations were the most important factor shaping French actions at virtually every point of the integration process. Instead it is necessary to dissect the internal logic of the General's actions on the European stage, while at the same time retaining an awareness that events and pressures seemingly unrelated to the integration process may well have affected both how French policy was determined and still more how it was received by the rest of the Six.

Equally problematic was the gap between what de Gaulle said about Europe and what he, or his representatives, actually did in Brussels. The French President was a master at ensuring that his words captured the attention of contemporaries and historians alike. His eloquence, his sense of drama, and his mastery of the striking yet ambiguous verbal formula, all helped ensure that a disproportionate number of his pronouncements impressed themselves upon the minds of his foreign counterparts, his ministers and civil servants, and the wider population both in France and beyond. And this trend has only been increased by the nature of the sources available to those seeking to assess his actions historically. For with the Presidential papers themselves firmly closed, most historians working on the period have been obliged to rely perhaps unduly on the massive outpourings of those who worked with the General and faithfully recorded his extensive wit and wisdom.[2] Second-hand accounts of what de Gaulle said have thus buttressed the already sizeable collection of the General's published speeches, press conferences and memoirs.[3] The prominence of an entertaining but deeply problematic source like the three Peyrefitte *C'était de Gaulle* volumes in the notes section of this book is a case in point.[4]

French policy as carried out in Brussels between 1963 and 1969 does not, however, necessarily correspond entirely to French policy as articulated by de Gaulle. Most obviously, French policy in practice appeared to accept a level of supranationality that had been verbally rejected by the General. Despite the 1965 clash, France went on allowing the European Commission to play a role in the EEC that went far beyond the type of secretariat that de Gaulle's pronouncements appeared to espouse.[5] And in legal terms the French never challenged the crucial series of European Court of Justice rulings that were to lay the foundations for European jurisprudence and to establish the superiority of European over national law.[6] Furthermore, there were times when the French appeared ready to allow flexibility on the knotty question of how the EEC functioned in order to press ahead in their quest to obtain a central and unchallenged place for the CAP on the Community's agenda. The 1963 softening of the French line on the fusion of the EEC, ECSC and Euratom 'executives' and the 1964 campaign to thwart a German-led attempt to reduce the Commission's role in the management committees that ran the CAP on a day-to-day basis are both good examples of this tendency.[7] But there are also repeated reminders in French behaviour in Brussels that Paris was not solely interested in the fate of the CAP as the General's rhetoric seemed often to imply. Agriculture certainly mattered to the French, but the Paris government was well aware that its economy depended more on the success of its industrialists than it did on the prosperity of its farmers; consequently it frequently intervened in Brussels to ensure that the level of the Community's external tariff or the EEC's approach to the Kennedy Round corresponded closely to its interests.[8] The General's repeated attempts to spread the notion that France was taking industrial risks in Europe and therefore deserved compensatory treatment for its farmers thus diverges from the reality of French policy in much the same way as his denunciations of the Commission and of supranational power.[9]

Quite how this discrepancy arose is hard to determine with any certainty. One factor may well have been the interplay between de Gaulle and his ministers and officials. So far as what the General said, there was little that Couve de Murville, the Quai d'Orsay or any other French representative could do, since the President wrote his own speeches and chose carefully what he wanted to say to the press. But once the issue became the implementation of French policy, the government and the civil service were much better placed to temper the full effects of de Gaulle's stance. Thus in 1965, the SGCI and the remaining French representatives in Brussels seem to have worked hard to soften the impact of the empty chair policy and to ensure that no permanent harm was done to those multiple interests France had wrapped up in the EEC.[10] Likewise Couve became adept at sounding and acting in a more *communautaire* manner in Brussels, than a strict interpretation of his master's original instructions would have implied.[11] On occasions, those responsible for transforming the General's sweeping statements about European policy into precise policy stances, may thus have quite deliberately added an element of restraint that was absent from the President's initial *prise de position*.

As important, though, and not at all incompatible, may well have been the General's own realisation that to speak loudly and act softly was tactically an astute ploy. It was particularly useful, for instance, to keep his partners guessing as to how committed to the integration process France really was. Such uncertainty gave an element of credibility to the 1963 and 1964 threats to leave the Community which, in the eyes of most French observers at least, played such an important part in forcing the Germans to give ground over the CAP.[12] And in similar fashion, de Gaulle's reluctance publicly to acknowledge France's growing interest in rising industrial exports allowed the genuine French willingness to see a successful Kennedy Round to be presented as a concession and hence exchanged for some type of quid pro quo from the Five.[13] Indeed, the apparent threat that the French might disown the whole process arguably strengthened the overall European negotiating effort in the GATT. De Gaulle may, in other words, have deliberately sought to unbalance his European and Transatlantic counterparts with the overblown nature of his verbal sallies against supranationality and commercial liberalisation, so as to facilitate the task of his negotiators in their efforts to attain a much more moderate array of French *desiderata* in talks in Brussels, Geneva and elsewhere. Such an approach would fit well with the similar double-strategy of shock words and practical pragmatism described in Frédéric Bozo's analysis of de Gaulle's policy towards the Atlantic Alliance.[14]

The exact balance to strike between these two possible explanations and the question of whether there were other factors at work in creating this gap between the rhetoric and reality of French European policy, will probably only be possible to determine once the records of both the Elysée under de Gaulle and French cabinet meetings have been made public. In the meantime, however, it is already feasible to outline enough broad features of the Gaullist challenge, both verbal and actual, to be able to establish how serious a threat it posed to the workings of the EEC and to France's role within it. Doing this suggests that while the panic and anger of the Five about de Gaulle were comprehensible, the actual danger of France destroying or withdrawing from the European Community was much less acute than was sometimes feared.

De Gaulle was well aware of how much France gained from the integration process. His sensitivity to his country's potential weakness in the wake of May 1968 and the ensuing economic crisis clearly illustrates how conscious he was that the state of the French economy was a central component of France's ability to play the type of international role to which he aspired.[15] *Grandeur* and economic underperformance were incompatible. As a result, bailing out of a process of economic integration that, as his government's own internal studies confirmed, was vital to the continuing growth of the French economy was never really an option.[16] But there was no particular need to proclaim this fact aloud. On the contrary, it was much more fitting for a country and a ruler publicly committed to retaining *les mains libres*, to pass over in silence the fact that economically its hands were to all intents and purposes bound. Furthermore, as argued above, there were distinct tactical advantages in keeping his partners uncertain about France's commitment to the Community. To admit dependency on Europe would be to forfeit the ability to threaten withdrawal and to concede that in multiple Brussels negotiations France was a *demandeur* rather than a free agent able if necessary to commit its allegiance elsewhere. It therefore made much more sense to go on talking about France's total independence even while aware of the unrealistic nature of this claim.[17]

In institutional terms, de Gaulle did have strong views about the way in which the Community should work. He appeared to have a genuine dislike of the European Commission, especially when it seemed to aspire to a clearly political role.[18] Hallstein's love of the trappings of power as much as of power itself got under the skin of a French leader so attuned himself to the symbolism of sovereignty and of power. And there are hints amongst some of de Gaulle's outbursts against the European Commission of a real, if somewhat exaggerated, fear of the Commission being able to acquire yet more power by stealth and by exploiting the weakness and lack of vigilance of national governments.[19] De Gaulle could occasionally sound as convinced (albeit fearfully) of the process of *engrenage* or spill-over as the most enthusiastic neofunctionalist. Likewise, there can be little doubt that the vociferous defender of French independence disliked the idea of widespread majority voting in Brussels and would have found it hard to accept a situation in which his ministers could be systematically put in a minority in Council votes.[20]

Such views were, however, held in check by a strong streak of pragmatism (which again may be partly attributable to his staff). Until 1965, at least, de Gaulle therefore showed a willingness to use supranationality instrumentally, whenever it appeared to be in French interests so to do.

His distaste at some of the Commission's pretensions was outweighed by the recognition that France's ability to acquire what it sought in Brussels were greatly improved by the formidable negotiating partnership it was able to build up with the self-styled executive.[21] And he probably shared the *Quai*'s confidence that majority voting would be used sparingly after January 1966, if at all.[22] Germany's misgivings over majority voting and the setting of cereal prices had, for instance, demonstrated that France was not alone in resisting a situation in which its interests could be seriously harmed by a contrary Council vote.[23] It was therefore only when both his partners and the Commission overplayed their hand in the run-up to the 30 June, 1965 deadline for the financial regulation agreement, that de Gaulle lost this willingness to tolerate the Community system as it existed. The outbreak of the empty chair crisis and the highlighting of France's institutional grievances in the President's September press conference does therefore constitute a significant turning point in the General's approach to the EEC.[24]

Nevertheless, enough pragmatism remained for de Gaulle to accept a settlement of the crisis that fell far short of his original aims. Having raised the issues of majority voting and Commission power, the General was almost certainly thinking in terms of a rather further-reaching response than the Gentleman's Disagreement on the former and the non-binding Heptalogue on the latter. Given the mood of the Five, however, to have pressed for more might have been to risk a serious aggravation of the crisis – something which the French had sought to avoid throughout the June 1965 to January 1966 period. It was also the case that the accounts of the Luxembourg meeting that he received emphasised that none of France's partners had shown any great enthusiasm for precipitate federalism or the extensive use of majority voting.[25] A partial reversion to the tactic of relying on the self-restraint of the Germans or of the Belgians thus seemed possible. Post-Luxembourg, de Gaulle therefore dropped his earlier campaign to impose an institutional settlement on the Community, and instead contented himself with the systematic blocking of any initiatives that might alter the status quo. If there was one lesson that could be learnt from the trial of strength between the French and the Five during the latter half of 1965, it was that preserving the Community as it existed was much easier than forcing through change. French vigilance was therefore likely to suffice to prevent any rapid increase in the powers of the Commission or the European Parliament or any attempt to use majority voting much more extensively.

De Gaulle's challenge to the EEC was therefore never quite the existential issue that it sometimes seemed. At no point was it ever likely that the French would either destroy a Community from which they gained so much, or cease to be a member. What they were prepared to do, however, was to conduct Community diplomacy with a forcefulness that had seldom been encountered before, to dispense with the veneer of European rhetoric that had tended to characterise earlier bargaining amongst the Six, and to resist the process of gradual institutional change that was seen by many as a vital aspect of the Community system. Still worse, for some, was the fact that de Gaulle did little to hide his opposition to British membership of the EEC and was twice prepared to use a veto to debar the UK's path. Ultimately, of course, it was this last aspect of the Gaullist challenge that France's partners would find impossible either to accept or to forgive.[26] Forcing France to change its mind would not, however, be an easy business and it would only be after de Gaulle had left office that the last great controversy raised by the General could finally be resolved.[27]

Standing up to the General

None of France's partners of course enjoyed the benefit of hindsight when attempting to measure the seriousness of de Gaulle's challenge. On the contrary, most found their assessment coloured by the General's seeming determination to attack all of the structures of Western cooperation. Could a man who had withdrawn his troops from NATO control, or shocked the West with his sudden recognition of Communist China really be regarded as a trusted partner in a European context? In Italy, Germany and Belgium, moreover, the alarm of the political leadership was only compounded by the way in which de Gaulle's critique of Atlanticism and integration seemed to strike a chord with an influential minority of politicians within each country.[28] *Le défi français* was hence not merely a foreign policy problem but one with a significant domestic dimension also.

The genuine alarm, however, did not translate into an immediate disavowal of European cooperation with France. Much of this reflected the commitment of each of the Five to the European integration process. To attempt to proceed without France might be to endanger the whole European experiment and was therefore not a risk worth taking.[29] But, as argued in Chapter 4, it also sprang from the recognition that France gained greatly from the integration (too much indeed according to some national assessments) and was hence less likely to break with the Community than with other Western fora.[30] Involvement in the EEC therefore imposed limits on the extent to which France could disown the West and act upon its occasional implied threat to seek closer links with the Eastern bloc. The key therefore became that of devising a response to de Gaulle within the Community system, thereby both preserving the EEC and the ties that bound France to the West.

In the course of the 1963 to 1969 period, France's partners would experiment with at least three different types of response. The first, most obvious in 1963, but also apparent during the 1966 post-crisis *reprise* and Brandt's September 1968 effort to break the impasse over enlargement, was that of trying to lure France out of its self-inflicted isolation by emphasising the potential rewards of cooperation.[31] CAP advance was the favourite bait, for obvious reasons. But also important was the promise of resuming business as usual in Brussels and the chance to break out of periods of crisis that were open to strong political criticism within France and were likely to damage a broad range of French interests within the EEC. The tangible benefits of the integration process could hence be used as one means of protecting the Community system from the General's assault.

Rather different was the second strategy, that of counter-attack. In its simplest form this could be no more than a systematic attempt to frustrate French policy preferences within the EEC and replace them with a different set of priorities. This was what the Germans, Italians and Dutch were trying to do in 1965 – thereby helping to precipitate the empty chair crisis.[32] And as such it was no more than an effort to imitate the forthright pursuit of national self-interest pioneered by the French. Somewhat more complex, by contrast, were the attempts to transform the Community so as to render it less susceptible to French dominance. One way of doing this, favoured by some in the Dutch Parliament and still more by the European Commission, was to alter the institutional shape of the EEC so as to dilute the power of the larger states through ever-greater helpings of supranationality. It was this tactic that lay at the heart of Hallstein's financial regulation proposals of 31 March, 1965 and still more in the Commission President's fervent support for majority voting.[33] It also explains his continuing anger at the partial non-implementation of the Treaty's majority voting provisions in the wake of the 1966 agreement to disagree.[34] And the other means of attaining the same end would be to enlarge Community membership by bringing in the British to counter French power. This was the method preferred by Luns and most of his governmental colleagues in Holland, by the Italians, by the Belgians and by large portions of the German political elite.[35]

Finally, some of the Five also experimented with a policy of pure containment – a refusal to accept French EEC preferences even at the expense of widespread Community paralysis. This was nobody's preferred option.[36] The costs of deadlock in Brussels ranged from lost material benefits to political criticism and frustration on the part of those most committed to integration's advance. But by the late 1960s this was the course of action that Italy, Belgium and Holland had turned to, convinced that it was the only means of frustrating de Gaulle.[37] And in a sense they were to be vindicated. For while the short-term result was a stagnant period that damaged the morale and the confidence of all of those involved in the formation of the EEC, it is undoubtedly the case that the desire to break the impasse in Brussels was one important ingredient in Pompidou's careful and calculating volte-face on enlargement.[38] Of course, it is possible to argue that by 1967–69 the Gaullist challenge was much less dangerous than the Dutch, Italians and Belgians tended to assume. They might thus have been able to prevent serious damage to the Community and pressurise de Gaulle's successor into altering his position on British membership without having to resort to such systematic blocking of advance in Brussels. But that three states, all of whom remained strongly committed to the EEC, were prepared to go to such lengths to counter the Gaullist challenge is an eloquent reminder of how alarming and dangerous the European policies of the French President appeared to many of his counterparts. The French may have been initially convinced of the successful nature of its forceful approach to European issues, but by the later 1960s the cumulative effect of Gaullist diplomacy had been to force several of France's partners into a stance of dogged resistance that threatened to block all future Community gains and might begin to erode Paris's earlier achievements.

A transformed Community?

The struggle between France and the other Five member states during the 1963 to 1969 period was to have a number of important effects on the nature of the EEC. The first, mentioned in Chapter 2, was the transformation of the language and tactics of Community diplomacy. Gone were the niceties of negotiations between partners in a joint enterprise and the language of common endeavour in the name of Europe; in their place was the forceful, even brutal pursuit of national interest. While the institutional context remained distinctive, the etiquette and vocabulary of Brussels diplomacy had thus become much more akin to those of a traditional intergovernmental negotiation in the GATT, the UN or the IMF. The much vaunted *esprit communautaire* was no longer much in evidence.

It can admittedly be questioned how much of a change this represented. National interest had never been far beneath the surface in European negotiations from 1950 onwards, however frowned upon was the overt reference to an individual country's desires. The ferocity of argument during the original Treaty of Paris negotiations about such seemingly petty topics as the site of Community institutions is a reminder of how thin and fragile was the layer of European rhetoric.[39] And it can also be legitimately asked how helpful in the long run were those instances where countries did allow their immediate interests to be set aside in the pursuit of a common European goal. The clearest single example of this happening – the way in which Italy soft-pedalled its own particular agricultural needs between 1958 and 1962 in order to facilitate the emergence of a CAP deemed vital for the advance of 'Europe' – had clearly backfired by 1964, turning Italy from acquiescent 'good European' into a semi-permanent agricultural dissident.[40]

Nevertheless, an important change had occurred after 1963. Community negotiations in the mid- to late-1960s were much more ill-tempered and tense affairs than some of the earlier discussions had been. Furthermore, the range of tactics employed by the participating national representatives grew ever more extreme. The 1963 and 1964 agricultural negotiations thus saw the near ubiquitous use of so-called 'préalables' – in other words the linkage between seemingly separate issues – flanked by the deployment by the French of naked political threats to leave the Community were their aims not granted.[41] In 1965, this escalation went several steps further, with three at least of the member states quite deliberately approaching a negotiation with tactics designed to ensure that an important internal deadline would be missed and a fourth reacting to the success of such an approach by (partially) withdrawing its representatives from the Community.[42] Filibusters and boycotts had thus joined the range of options resorted to amongst the Six. Furthermore, the terms in which the negotiations were discussed, both in Brussels, but still more within each participating country, resorted ever more to the basic vocabulary of profit and loss or victory and defeat rather than the emphasis on shared gains and future potential that had accompanied earlier Community milestones.[43] As a result, the clash of national interests in Brussels became progressively more confrontational and potentially wounding, while the domestic pressures placed upon each national negotiator also sharply increased. Deals that satisfied all were correspondingly harder to find.

This change was not solely a consequence of de Gaulle. Indeed, it is possible to argue that the earlier tinge of idealism would have been hard to sustain once the Six had to start dealing with material benefits and costs of integration rather than the basic shape of their future enterprise. National parliamentarians, for instance, could be blandly reassured in the early stages of integration with references to the political and symbolic importance of advances in Brussels; once the bills for the CAP began to arrive in each national capital, or the farmers lobbying parliaments and ministries of agriculture began to feel the impact of altered cereal prices, such vague words of comfort were much less likely to be effective. But it is undoubtedly the case that the manner in which the French pursued their national interests, and the climate of uncertainty that de Gaulle's rhetoric induced, added significantly to the more confrontational tone of Community diplomacy in the mid to late 1960s. The 1965 breakdown is the clearest example of this, since the Germans, Dutch, Italians, and the European Commission all felt that their more aggressive and high-risk approach to the financial regulation talks was justified because of the gains that France had made in the past and because of the threat that an unchecked de Gaulle would pose to the Community structure.[44] June 1965 thus constituted the high-water mark of this new, more nationalist diplomacy.

In the wake of the empty chair crisis there was a certain retreat from the more brutal tactics, driven by the realisation of how dangerous they had proved. The 1966 negotiations, the final stages of the Kennedy Round and even the first enlargement discussions of 1967 were all characterised by a partial return to a more conciliatory and balanced form of debate.[45] But the basic unease caused by de Gaulle was never far from the surface and both the new hard-line tactics and the fear that underpinned them quickly reappeared in the wake of the second veto. The behaviour of the Belgians, Dutch and Italians in the course of 1968 and early 1969 thus bore all the hallmarks of the more aggressive style of bargaining.[46] Couve's questionable use of the chair in the first months of 1968, and Debré's outspoken bluster in the summer and early autumn of the same year, reciprocated meanwhile for the French.[47] The post-de Gaulle Community would thus have much to do in order to recapture the level of mutual trust and shared excitement at future prospects that had been a feature of the EEC during the 1958 to 1962 period.

The second significant change that occurred during this period was the temporary shelving of the leadership ambitions of the European Commission. This was not, it must be emphasised, the direct result of the French attempt to shackle the supranational institution. As explained in Chapter 4, de Gaulle failed in his attempt to obtain a legal alteration of the Commission's prerogatives. The Heptalogue moreover was both fairly mild in its content and not legally binding. But what could not fail to curtail the ambitions evident during the Hallstein presidency was the clear reluctance of all of the member states apart perhaps from the Dutch to sanction any substantial transfer of power away from the Council and towards the Commission. Thus in 1963 none of the member states responded positively to Hallstein's plea that the Commission and not the Permanent Representatives be entrusted with maintenance of relations between Britain and the EEC, and no one protested that it had been a member state and not the Commission that had put forward the work programme which had eased the EEC out of crisis.[48] In 1965, all of the Six were deeply reluctant to accept a situation in which the Commission would receive an income from 'own resources' that substantially exceeded its existing spending.[49] And in 1966 all proved willing to accept a system of more frequent rotation for the Commission Presidency which would place fairness to each member state well above the type of continuity of office that would have been necessary for the Commission to exercise real political leadership.[50]

To make matters worse, the Commission itself had manifestly failed to have a decisive impact during any of the Community's recurrent political crises. On the contrary, the experiences of 1963, 1965–66, and 1967–69, all appeared to suggest that when the controversies became political as opposed to technical, Commission influence melted away. Hallstein and his colleagues had thus found themselves largely marginalised during the fraught diplomacy that followed the first veto of British membership.[51] They had again all but disappeared during the months of the empty chair crisis, excluded from many of the coordinating meetings amongst the Five, and absent from the Luxembourg Councils at which the dispute was finally settled.[52] And Rey had had little success in trying to urge his colleagues to behave in a restrained fashion as the row over enlargement had flared again in late 1967.[53] Indeed, the Commission President's clumsiness had been identified by some at least as a contributing factor to the acrimonious end of the December 1967 meeting of the Council of Ministers.[54] That sureness of touch and ability to identify compromise formulas which characterised the Commission's contribution to so many of the agricultural marathons or discussions about tariffs and trade, seemed to desert both Hallstein and his successor when the Community had encountered more overtly political disagreement.

None of this meant, of course, that the Commission had ceased to matter or had simply become a type of European civil service. In the day-to-day life of the European Community, the Commission had repeatedly shown itself to be a fertile source of policy ideas and proposals, an adept seventh voice around the Council or COREPER negotiating table, and an eloquent and tireless promoter of the European idea. The impact of Sicco Mansholt on the emergence of the CAP, of Robert Marjolin and then Raymond Barre on Europe's first halting steps towards monetary coordination, and of Rey on the Kennedy Round was there for all to see. The Commission's technical expertise meanwhile could make or break member state policy initiatives, as was demonstrated by Mansholt's dismissal of Germany's 1963 call for CAP reform.[55] And the way that Britain's second application in 1967 was accompanied by the type of systematic campaign to woo the Commission that had been entirely missing in 1961–63 was a testament to how the outside world had come to recognise the importance of the Brussels body.[56]

Such evident successes, however, could not conceal the fact that the Commission of the mid-1960s was not, as it had sometimes appeared to believe, en route to becoming the dominant force within the EEC.[57] Rather the reverse, it had been the Council and its subsidiary bodies such as COREPER, which had seen their authority and influence grow in the course of the Community's first decade. The Commission meanwhile had lost even its role as the main arbiter of the Community's agenda. The sinking without trace of its 1962 action plan was thus followed by the decidedly limited impact of the much touted 'Initiative 1964', and the increasing tendency of member states to arrogate to themselves the right to plot the Community's future course.[58] By 1969, the Commission's effort in March of that year to mark out where the EEC was bound was, by its own admission, little more than a compilation of all the various national proposals that had been submitted over the preceding months.[59] The once-confident helmsman had become the messenger boy, reduced to relaying plans devised in national capitals rather than in Brussels. Similarly, the Commission's *aide-mémoire* of November 1969 had done little to shape the agenda-setting decisions taken at The Hague.[60] These again had been the work of national governments and especially those of France and Germany.[61] Thus while the Commission remained an important player within the Community system, it could no longer harbour short term aspirations to lead the integration process. Responsibility for this duty lay elsewhere.

One contender for the task of leadership, to introduce the third main change brought about by the Gaullist challenge, was West Germany. Prior to 1963, Germany had been highly reluctant to play a prominent role in Brussels. It mattered, of course. Access to its economy was the central prize of the EEC customs union; access to its market the main attraction to France and the Netherlands of the CAP.[62] And in political terms, many viewed the whole integration process as a mechanism for controlling Germany's re-emergence.[63] But under Adenauer, Bonn had been deliberately self-effacing when it came to Community diplomacy.[64] The way in which Germany was forced to respond to de Gaulle's first veto had lasting effects, however.[65] For, having been woken from self-imposed passivity, the Germans appeared to have acquired a taste for Community activism. The 1963 action plan was thus followed by another programmatic statement in January 1964, a set of proposals for political union in November of the same year, and an unprecedentedly forthright role in the run-up to the empty chair crisis.[66] Schröder was also prominent in the diplomacy of the crisis months themselves and of particular importance at Luxembourg.[67] Nor did this activism fade when the Erhard government fell from power. On the contrary, Brandt marked his Brussels debut with yet another attempt to set out a European vision for his colleagues, played a key if controversial role in efforts to resolve the enlargement crisis, and, in the wake of his 1969 electoral triumph, was the dominant figure at The Hague.[68] De Gaulle had seemingly woken the sleeping German giant.

The actual success rate of this German activism was, it must be acknowledged, somewhat mixed. The 1963 plan had largely achieved its objectives (albeit with a bit of help from Luxembourg), but neither of the 1964 efforts nor Brandt's first attempt had accomplished much. Germany's role in the empty chair crisis had also been of patchy effectiveness, with Schröder and Sachs often isolated amongst the Five by the rigidity of Germany's position on agricultural finance. Nor was everybody in Bonn entirely happy with Germany's new, more central role. Schmücker's wistful appeal to the British to hurry up and join, thereby taking from the Federal Republic some of the responsibility for standing up to de Gaulle, was probably not unique.[69]

The most important limitation on German leadership was, however, their very strong reluctance to clash too directly with the French. Bonn, indeed, seemed most at ease when its Community initiatives were designed to build bridges to Paris, rather than to rally the Five against France. The 1963 action plan, or the 1969 diplomacy in the run-up to The Hague was thus altogether more satisfying (and successful) than the 1965 or 1966 attempts to lead a *fronde* against French dominance and to maintain the unity of the Five in the face of the French boycott. Confrontation with de Gaulle, while perhaps unavoidable given the distance between France and Germany throughout the Erhard years was always controversial within the German political elite and subject to continuous sniping from the many influential partisans of Franco-German rapprochement.[70] It was therefore already predictable that with a more moderate President in the Elysée, the Germans would seek to act in concert with the French. Multilateral or bilateral action remained greatly preferable to unilateral German initiatives; action with France much better than action against.

The ongoing hesitations of Bonn, the legacy of mistrust surrounding French dominance, and the ever more apparent weakness of the Commission did mean, however, that the Community of the late 1960s faced a clear leadership vacuum. On a day-to-day basis this probably did not matter too much. When attention needed to be directed towards routine affairs the potential influence and impact of the Commission has already been noted.[71] And each of the smaller member states was able to make a contribution that could at times affect the path of the EEC's development as significantly as that of their larger neighbours. The role of the Luxembourgers in rescuing Schröder's action plan, the importance of Italian and Dutch anger in the run-up to the empty chair crisis, the personal contribution of Spaak to the resolution of the crisis and the impact of Harmel in the row over enlargement, all illustrate clearly how difficult it is to analyse the course of the EEC without frequent references to the role of the smaller or politically less powerful member states.[72] The recurrent conceit, much employed by modern political scientists, but also popular amongst those journalists seeking to explain Community (or now Union) affairs, that only a handful of big players matter and hence need to be discussed, while tempting and at times unavoidable is a gross simplification and should seldom be used for long.[73] Instead the pattern of EEC development can only adequately be explained by an analysis that factors in not only all of the member states – no matter how small – but also the contributions, both positive and negative, made by the Community institutions themselves. The workings of a supranational system can only be fully dissected by an analyst willing to acknowledge the multiplicity of actors and influences within the EEC.

This very complexity did, however, make some source of leadership all the more essential either at times of crisis or on those occasions when the Community needed to move beyond routine actions and identify major new targets or ambitions. This had been all too apparent during the lengthy impasse over British membership and was also highlighted by the unsatisfactory nature of the pre-Hague summit debate about the EEC's future agenda. Finding a new means of giving the Six a clear sense of direction had therefore become one of the more pressing medium term institutional objectives. But if the Gaullist challenge had been responsible for highlighting this difficulty (although not really for causing it), the manner in which the crisis was resolved at the end of 1969 also drew attention to one important mechanism with which to address it. For as argued at the end of Chapter 7, the success of The Hague summit in healing many of the divisions caused by de Gaulle and in identifying a number of new fields into which the integration process could venture, only increased the likelihood of future summits being used to fill the leadership gap. 1974 and the institutionalisation of the European Council as a form of collective leadership was a logical, if indirect, consequence of 1969.

The struggle to contain the Gaullist change had therefore had a number of transformative effects on the EEC. The French had certainly not succeeded in subverting the Community in the way in which many of their partners feared that they might do. Indeed, as argued above, it is more than likely that this had never really been the General's intention. But the six year tussle over the agenda, institutions and membership of the Community had left a profound mark on the language and style of EEC negotiation, on the political ambitions of the European Commission, on West Germany's willingness to act at a European level, and on the whole question of who should direct the EEC. These changes alone justify a detailed investigation of the 1963 to 1969 period.

A period of consolidation

The years between the first veto and The Hague conference were not just marked by the confrontation between France and the Five, however. It was also a period rich in joint achievements. Most notably, it was an era that saw the steady advance and then completion ahead of schedule of both the customs union foreseen by the Treaty of Rome and the CAP. The latter in particular was a remarkable achievement, especially given the vagueness of the Treaty provisions regarding agriculture. In the space of eight years, the Six had put together an ambitious legal and administrative framework, with a sizeable budget, a complex range of policy instruments, and the capacity to affect, for good or for ill, the lives and livelihoods of millions of European farmers. That they had argued fiercely amongst themselves about how exactly the policy should work, and that the policy has remained controversial over the ensuing four decades, should not be allowed to obscure the fact that this was arguably the furthest-reaching experiment in international economic cooperation that the world had ever seen. Furthermore it had been a challenging test-bed for the Community's institutional structure, and one which had on the whole demonstrated the effectiveness of the Treaty of Rome design. The success in devising a common policy for agriculture did therefore underline to all of those involved in the integration process, as well as to those watching from the sidelines, that the EEC was much more than a simple customs union. As the post-1970 Community turned its attention to other, equally ambitious new tasks, it was important that this point had been clearly made.

Institutionally, the six year period surveyed by this book also mattered greatly. The 1965 merger treaty apart, few formal institutional modifications had been made. But what mattered was that the balance of institutions that had emerged over the Community's first years of operation had been tested by crisis, had survived largely unscathed, and had been strengthened as a result. Within this structure, the Commission remained an important player and the Parliament had done enough to ensure that it was likely to receive greater powers in the future. But the two institutions that had performed better than expected were the Council and the Court. The former had consolidated its position as the key nexus of decision-making with the EEC, able to perform effectively even without majority voting, provided some degree of consensus existed about the overall direction of the Community's advance. At ministerial level, both the assembled foreign ministers and the proliferating sectoral Councils had shown a capacity to reach decisions even in circumstances where most of the national capitals had expected impasse. At an official level, moreover, COREPER had repeatedly shown itself to be an invaluable tool for building consensus amongst the Six, for managing the day-to-day operation of the Community system, and for ensuring that national bureaucracies were quickly and accurately informed of the direction of debates within Brussels. The formal recognition of the Committee's role contained within the merger treaty was only a belated official acknowledgement of perhaps the single most striking institutional success story of the early EEC.

The ECJ meanwhile had continued a tradition of judicial activism that had begun under the European Coal and Steel Community, taking a series of landmark decisions that laid the foundations of European law. The doctrines of Direct Effect – essentially the principle that Community decisions were not simply something to which states could refer, but instead rules that were binding on and accessible to their citizens also – and of the Superiority of EC Law confirmed the potential scope of the Community experiment and the degree of change that member states had opened themselves up to by signing and ratifying the Treaty of Rome.[74] But fundamentally, the main institutional lesson of 1963 to 1969 was that Council-led period of the Community's existence was not a brief, chrysalis like phase, out of which Europe would quickly emerge as a much more exotic, federal butterfly. Instead it was an institutional structure that could certainly be improved in the future but which was likely to endure in its essentials. To some this was undoubtedly a disappointment; for multiple others it was instead a relief.

Finally the 1963 to 1969 period had been deeply marked by the uncertainty over the membership of the EEC. The degree of division and controversy that the prospect of enlargement had caused has been one of the central themes of this book. De Gaulle's vetoes in 1963 and 1967 were responsible for two of the three great crises of the period reviewed and had left a legacy of mistrust and suspicion over the whole question of who should belong to the EEC that would take years to dispel. It is nevertheless only fair to note that by the end of the 1963 to 1969 period, the issue did appear to have been resolved. The Hague summit had taken a clear political decision about the openness of the EEC to Britain and the other applicants that was binding on all of the Six. Were the applicants to maintain their resolve through the lengthy and complex negotiations ahead, there was thus no longer any doubt that the door to the Community was open. An enlargement of the Community that might in other circumstances have taken place in 1964 or 1965 was now a near certainty at some point in the early 1970s.

Overall, then, 1963 to 1969 could be described as the period in the course of which the EEC had confirmed its ability to implement much of the limited initial agenda set out in the Treaty of Rome. In the process it had also shown that its institutions could function, albeit with an enduring doubt about their ability to provide clear political leadership. And by the end of the period, a vital agreement had at last been reached over the question of enlargement. The seven years upon which this study has concentrated were thus of some intrinsic importance in the Community's early growth and consolidation.

They also constitute a revealing case-study of the EEC in operation. Most of the existing literature on the first decade of the EEC has focused either on a rather narrower chronological period or on a single policy or institutional actor.[75] This study has quite deliberately adopted a more comprehensive approach, so as to highlight not only the interplay between different member states and different institutions, but also the evolution of Community diplomacy over time, and the extent to which advance came to be distributed over different policy areas. Several important conclusions result.

The first is the way in which so much of member state behaviour in any given Community negotiation reflected lessons learnt, debts accumulated or animosities provoked by previous episodes in the EEC's development. The cast of those involved with the European integration process altered only slowly during the 1963 to 1969 period. Ministers like Couve de Murville, Luns, Lahr or Fanfani or Commissioners like Rey or Mansholt thus accumulated a wealth of Brussels experience which inevitably affected their subsequent appreciation of what any individual situation required. Similarly, at official level, some of those civil servants who handled EEC affairs remained in the same post for lengthy periods of time. Boegner, the French Permanent Representative, is one good example, Spierenburg, his Dutch counterpart another, and Noël, the Executive Secretary of the Commission, a third.

This meant that few Community negotiations can be entirely understood without a knowledge of what had gone before. Neither French nor German behaviour in the spring and early summer of 1965 is thus fully comprehensible without an understanding of the bruising first round of CAP negotiations which had ended in January 1962, the lengthy battle over cereal prices in the course of 1963 and 1964, and the short and ill-starred life of Germany's November 1964 proposals for political union. Similarly, the strength of the Belgian, Dutch and Italian reactions in

December 1967 only really makes sense in the light of the January 1963 precedent. And French tactics and anxieties in the run-up to The Hague summit were deeply shaped by the negative lessons about both the 1961–63 enlargement talks and the way France had been ambushed over CAP finance in 1965. The brief history of the Community since 1958 was already full enough to act as a rich source of warnings, salutary examples, and disturbing parallels.

A second fact that becomes apparent from a comprehensive overview of a sizeable period of Community history is the way in which most member states combined a strong streak of institutional pragmatism with a deep underlying commitment to the political nature of the EEC project. The resolution of the empty chair crisis is obviously the clearest example of this phenomenon in that what mattered most to all of the Five were not the exact rules for majority voting or the precise details of the Commission's role, but instead that the EEC quickly resumed operation and that the long-term possibilities opened up by the Treaty of Rome remained in place. But there are multiple other instances when countries diverged from their habitual institutional beliefs when it was in their interest to do so. Thus, the Germans sought restrictions on the use of majority voting in the setting of cereal prices and tried to curtail the Commission's influence over day-to-day CAP management, while the French countered both of these German ambitions in the name of effective agricultural decision-making.[76] Likewise, in 1969 the French were prepared to contemplate handing over the task of negotiating with the British and other applicants to the European Commission, so as to minimise the opportunity for the Five to gang up against Paris and seek to smooth Britain's path into the EEC.[77] And even the Dutch were prepared temporarily to postpone their quest for greater European Parliamentary powers so as to be able to secure agreement to the merger treaty in early 1965 and to acknowledge that their belief in a more supranational Europe was unlikely to be helped by the accession of the UK.[78] Each of the member states did have strong views about how the Community should be run. The constancy of such attitudes did not, however, mean that the exact institutional shape of the EEC was always the most immediate priority. On multiple occasions, questions about what the Community did, or who should belong to the EEC, took precedence over institutional beliefs.

What was less flexible, by contrast, was the enduring belief in a political dimension to the EEC. One of the surprises in studying the 1963 to 1969 period is the remarkable resilience of the political union idea.[79] Although seemingly dead and buried after the acrimonious failure of the Fouchet Plan in 1962, the notion of closer foreign policy coordination amongst the six re-emerged with remarkable regularity throughout the seven years surveyed. It is true, of course, that only at The Hague was a decisive step taken towards this end – and that even this advance was condemned as inadequate by some.[80] But the way in which not even the obvious foreign policy discord between de Gaulle and his fellow European leaders could kill the idea, is a remarkable testament to its enduring appeal. As soon as the dust had settled from each European crisis, or as soon as a world event erupted which underlined western Europe's less than central position in global affairs, one of the leaders of the Six would float the idea and suggest convening a meeting of foreign ministers to debate the prospect.[81] The eventual emergence of European Political Cooperation in the early 1970s thus had a lengthy, if frustrating, pre-history throughout the previous decade.

The ongoing appeal of political union links well with the third and final conclusion that can be drawn from a multi-issue examination of the Community over a seven year period, namely the way in which the EEC attracted support for several, very different reasons. One of the tendencies of much recent writing on European integration history has been an attempt to identify the main motivation behind the process.[82] What a study of the Community between 1963 and 1969 would suggest, however, is that different politicians and civil servants rallied behind the EEC for extremely different reasons. Thus for some – a minority no doubt, but a vociferous, well-organised and influential one – the Community experiment was an ideological venture, a means of transforming postwar Europe in the most profound way possible and creating a genuinely united and fully federal entity.[83] It was those sharing this view who reacted most violently to de Gaulle's very different beliefs and similarly it was the same group who did much to create the mood of disappointment and frustration that was apparently lifted by The Hague breakthrough.

A second group, meanwhile, viewed the Community in slightly more pragmatic but equally political fashion, valuing its structures for the bonds they created between individual member countries, for the balance that they ensured between Europe's larger and smaller states, and for prospects they opened up of a more united Europe able to make itself heard in world affairs. Someone like Kiesinger would be a good example of a political leader who showed little affection for a traditional federal vision of Europe's future (in the short term at least), but who did believe that a Community framework was not only useful for the Federal Republic as it slowly regained its political influence in the postwar world but was also a way of ensuring that the Six were not condemned to be perpetual bystanders in future global crises or emergencies.[84] And finally, there were those whose attachment to the integration experiment was primarily caused by the material and economic benefits that it was perceived to bring. Here too, of course, there were divisions between those who wanted to prioritise a relatively liberal and free-trading vision and those who believed that Europe should hold the trade amongst its members to be more immediately important than that with the world beyond. But regardless of their exact economic philosophy, there was a widespread consensus amongst western Europe's political elite that the Community was a vital component in Europe's existing prosperity and an essential tool in confronting future economic challenges.

Far from a weakness, this triple source of allegiance was an important element of strength. For it meant that neither an economic downturn, nor the short-term frustration of those harbouring a more political vision of Europe's future would destroy the EEC's political base. Instead, the varied nature of the support that the Community enjoyed, together with the institutional resilience that had been demonstrated by the Six's ability to overcome the Gaullist challenge, would stand the EEC in good stead as it began the difficult and lengthy task of widening both its agenda and its membership. The 1970s would not be an easy decade for the European experiment. The strength gained from the crises as well as the successes of the 1960s would, however, give the Community the greatest possible chance of surmounting the difficulties ahead.

Notes

Introduction

1 See, e.g. R. Marjolin (1986) pp. 304–21.
2 On the teething problems, see Lemaignen (1964). For an overall assessment, N.P. Ludlow, 'A Supranational Icarus: The European Commission and the Quest for Independent Political Role', in A. Varsori (2005).
3 H.-J. Schlochauer, 'Der Gerichtshof der Europäischen Gemeinschaften als Integrationsfaktor', in E. von Caemmerer (1966); S. Scheingold (1965).
4 *Le Monde*, 1–2 April, 1962.
5 M. Camps (1964) pp. 253–62; H. von der Groeben (1984) p. 110.
6 von der Groeben (1984) p. 61.
7 Milward (1992) pp. 224–317; Noël (1988).
8 Knudsen (2001).
9 Marjolin, (1986) p. 304.
10 Lundestad (1997).
11 Winand (1993).
12 See White (2003) pp. 111–31.
13 Milward and Deighton (1999).
14 Débats de l'Assemblée Parlementaire Européenne 1961–2, vol. II, p. 78.
15 Connelley (2002) pp. 215ff.
16 Steineger (2001).
17 Vaïsse (1993).
18 Contrast Spaak (1969) pp. 73–100 and Snoy et d'Oppuers (1989).
19 Massip (1963).
20 Marcowitz (1996) pp. 11–36.
21 R. Poidevin, 'De Gaulle et l'Europe en 1958', in Institut Charles de Gaulle (1992) vol. 5, pp. 79–87; Boegner (1992) pp. 28–36.
22 Moravcsik (2000) pp. 3–43.
23 De Gaulle (1970) vol. 3, pp. 404–9.
24 Bange (2000) pp. 25–9.
25 Gerbet, P. (1987) 'The Fouchet Plan negotiations 1960–2', in R. Pryce (1989) pp. 105–29.
26 Marjolin (1986) pp. 322–53.
27 A typical and recent rendition of the Community's own view of its history is Olivi (1995) also published in French as *L'Europe difficile. Histoire politique de la Communauté Européenne* (Paris: Gallimard, 1998).
28 Rhenisch (1999); Laschi (2000); Soutou (1990). The same single country approach characterises the best recent political science analysis of early European integration: Parsons (2003).

29 See Becker and Knipping (1986); di Nolfo (1992); Schwabe (1988); Serra (1989); Milward and Deighton (1999); Loth (2001) and Deighton (1995).
30 Milward (1984, 1992, 1993).
31 Moravcsik (1998, 2000); Giauque (2002). Much less impressive, although ostensibly multinational in focus is Gillingham (2003).
32 Trachtenberg (1999).
33 Varsori (1988); Guderzo (2000); Guasconi (2004).
34 On France and Germany see, e.g. Lappenküper (2001); Soutou (1996); Bitsch (2001); on Anglo-German: Schaad (2000); on Anglo-French: Decup (1998); on Italian-French: Bagnato (1995); and on Dutch-German: Wielenga (1997).
35 The early neo-functional works include: Haas (1958); Lindberg (1963, 1965); Scheingold (1965).
36 See, e.g. Heyen (1992); Loth, Bitsch and Poidevin (1998); Dassetto and Dumoulin (1993); and Dimier (2001).
37 Poidevin and Spierenburg (1993).
38 The only previous historical study to have made use of as many national and Community archival sources was focused solely on the emergence of one sectoral policy (albeit the most important). Knudsen (2001). There are one or two further Ph.D.s in the pipeline in Florence that also try to trace a single policy area using a broad range of national and supranational archives.
39 The first use of this term, to my knowledge, was by Laursen (2002) pp. 5–10.

1 Back from the brink

1 Public Record Office (henceforward PRO), PREM 11 4524, Codel 103, Heath to Macmillan and Home, 29 January, 1963. See also Müller-Armack, (1971) pp. 139–40; Lahr (1981) p. 373; *Documents Diplomatiques Français 1963* (2000) (henceforward *DDF 1963*), Paris: Imprimerie Nationale, vol. 1, document 47.
2 See Chapter 6.
3 Dumoulin (1999) p. 652.
4 On the enlargement negotiations see Ludlow (1997); Milward and Deighton (1999); Wilkes (1997).
5 For Britain's welcome, see Ludlow (1997) pp. 43–8.
6 Political archives of the Auswärtiges Amt (henceforward AAA). Bestand B150, Bestellnummer 2, Abteilung 1 (IA2), Bd. 144, Lahr Aufzeichnung, 19 January, 1963.
7 See *Débats de l'assemblée parlementaire européenne 1962–3*, vol. 2, pp. 25–32; Marjolin (1989) p. 338.
8 See Council of Ministers Archives, Brussels (henceforward CMA) RU/M/73/63, Enlargement negotiation minutes, 28–29 January, 1963.
9 See Spaak's interview with *Le Peuple* 4 February, 1963.
10 For views of the threat posed by de Gaulle see, for instance, Nuti (1999) pp. 574–8; *Foreign Relations of the United States, 1961–1963 West Europe and Canada* (henceforward *FRUS*) (1994), Washington: United States Government Printing Office, pp. 487–91.
11 PRO, PREM 11 4524, Codel 103, Heath to Macmillan and Home, 29 January, 1963.
12 *Le Peuple*, 4 February, 1963; *Akten zur Auswärtigen Politik der Bundesrepublik Deutschland 1963* (henceforward *AAPD 1963*) (1994), Munich: R. Oldenbourg Verlag, document 63; European Commission's Historical Archives, Brussels (henceforward ECHA), PV 215, 2e partie, 28–30 January, 1963; PRO, PREM 11 4524; Tel. 148, Ward to FO, 14 February, 1963.
13 Müller-Armack (1971) p. 240. See also Ministero degli Affari Esteri (1987) p. 112.

14 On American support, see Winand (1993); Lundestad (1997).

15 ECHA. PV 215, 2e partie, 28–30 January, 1963.

16 *Ibid.*

17 ECHA. PV 217, 2e partie, 13 February, 1963.

18 Ibid. and PRO, PREM 11 4524; Tel. 148, Ward to FO, 14 February, 1963.

19 Harkort to AA, 4 February, 1963 reprinted in *AAPD 1963*, document 78.

20 PRO. FO371 171420; M1091/180, Robinson to Keeble, 8 February, 1963. Cf. ECHA, BDT 214/1980, G/101/63, Noël to Commission, 1 February, 1963.

21 ECHA, BDT 214/1980, G/122/63, Noël to Commission, 8 February, 1963.

22 For French relief: *DDF 1963*, vol. 1, document 71.

23 For the context, see Koerfer (1987) pp. 709–25.

24 Nuti (1999) pp. 575–6.

25 Ministero degli Affari Esteri (1987) pp. 111–16.

26 W. Asbeek Brusse. 'Alone Within The Six: The Dutch Cabinet and the British Application for EEC membership', in Griffiths and Ward (1996) p. 134.

27 ECHA, BDT 214/1980, G/101/63, Noël to Commission, 4 February, 1963; CMA, R/169/63, Council minutes, 25–26 March, 1963.

28 *Ibid.*

29 PRO, PREM 11 4524; Tel. 148, Ward to FO, 14 February, 1963.

30 ECHA, BDT 214/1980, G/101/63, Noël to Commission, 4 February, 1963.

31 Ministero degli Affari Esteri (1987) p. 115.

32 CMA,R/169/63, Council minutes, 25–26 March, 1963.

33 *Ibid.*

34 *Ibid.*

35 See Bange (1997).

36 Herbst (1989); Müller-Roschach (1974); Wurm (1995).

37 Rhenisch (1994) esp. pp. 254–8; M. Schulte, 'Challenging the Common Market Project: German Industry, Britain and Europe 1956–63', in Deighton and Milward (1999) pp. 167–83.

38 On the international pressure on Bonn, see Ludlow (1997) pp. 221–2; Bange (2000) pp. 151–5; Holscher, W. 'Krisenmanagement in Sachen EWG: Das Scheitern des Beitritts Großbritanniens und die deutsch-französischen Beziehungen', in Blasius (1994) pp. 9–44.

39 See, e.g. *AAPD 1963*, document 49.

40 Cited in Minstero degli Affari Esteri (1987) p. 114.

41 On the stakes for Germany, see Schulte in Deighton and Milward (1999) pp. 169–71 and Ludlow, N.P. 'Constancy and Flirtation: Germany, Britain and the EEC, 1956–1972', in Noakes, Wende and Wright (2002) pp. 97–100.

42 Kleiman (1965) p. 122.

43 *AAPD 1963*, document 78.

44 Cited in Marcowitz (1996) p. 83.

45 *AAPD 1963*, document 67.

46 *AAPD 1963*, document 70.

47 *AAPD 1963*, document 71.

48 *AAPD 1963*, document 87.

49 PRO, PREM 11 4524, Tel. 228, Reilly and France to FO, 1 March, 1963.

50 PRO, PREM 11 4524, Tel. 223, Roberts to FO, 4 March, 1963.

51 See also Rothschild (1997) p. 279.

52 *AAPD 1963*, document 115; on the background to this hard-line French approach, see Archives Nationales, Fontainebleau (henceforward ANF), SGCI files, Versement 870662, Art. 24, Note 'Perspectives du marché commun', 11 February, 1963.

53 *AAPD 1963*, document 134.

54 ANF, SGCI files, Versement 900638, Art. 25, Boegner to Couve, No. 23/DE, 'Le marché commun depuis la crise de Janvier jusqu'aux accords de Décembre', 3 February, 1964.
55 See Bundesarchiv, Koblenz (henceforward BAK), Bundeskanzleramt files (henceforward BKA), B136/2589.
56 Adenauer tried in vain to obstruct this review. BAK, BKA, B136/2589, Selbach note, 20 March, 1963, Erhard to Globke, 21 March, 1963 and Globke to Erhard, 22 March, 1963.
57 See BAK, BKA, B136/2589, AA/BMW memo 'Richtlinien unserer Politik in der Europäischen Gemeinschaft', 14 March, 1963.
58 Hölscher, in Blasius (1994) p. 38.
59 CMA. R/295/63 Council minutes, 1–2 April, 1963.
60 *Ibid.*
61 The French were pleased: *DDF 1963*, vol. 1, document 123.
62 CMA. R/295/63 Council minutes, 1–2 April, 1963.
63 BAK, BKA, B136/2589, 'Arbeitsprogram der Gemeinschaft für die nächste Zeit', 19 April, 1963.
64 The length was a result of each German ministry adding its own priorities. BAK, BKA, B136/2589 assorted documents.
65 See BAK, BKA, B136/2589, No. 645, Harkort to AA, 25 April, 1963; for a French assessment see Ministère des Affaires Etrangères (henceforward MAE), Serie DE-CE 1961–66, Carton 432, SGCI note, 'Programme de la communauté économique européenne pour 1963', 22 April, 1963.
66 See BAK, BKA, B136/2589, No. 645, Harkort to AA, 25 April, 1963.
67 CMA, R/423/63, Council minutes, 8–9 May, 1963.
68 As Boegner had predicted: see *DDF 1963*, vol. 1, document 155.
69 ECHA, BDT 214/1980, G/449/63, Herbst to Commission, 6 May, 1963.
70 CMA, S/346/1/63, Council minutes, 8–9 May, 1963.
71 ECHA, COM(63) PVs 228 (7 May, 1963), 232 (19 June, 1963) and 235 (10 July, 1963).
72 CMA, S/346/1/63, Council minutes, 8–9 May, 1963.
73 See e.g. *DDF 1963*, vol. 1, document 133.
74 BAK, BKA, B136/2589, Praß to Adenauer, 3 May, 1963; CMA, R/621/63, Council minutes, 10–11 July, 1963.
75 CMA, R/621/63, Council minutes, 10–11 July, 1963.
76 *AAPD 1963*, document 219 and *DDF 1963*, vol. 2, document 6.
77 CMA, R/621/63, Council minutes, 10–11 July, 1963.
78 This was only guaranteed because of Colombo's intervention on the Commission's behalf. *Ibid.*
79 *AAPD 1963*, document 230.
80 The WEU was London-based in the 1960s. See also *DDF 1963*, vol. 2, document 18.
81 MAE, Serie DE-CE 1961–66, Carton 432, SGCI note, 'Programme de la communauté économique européenne pour 1963', 22 April, 1963.
82 Ministero degli Affari Esteri (1987) p. 126.
83 See, e.g. Massip (1963).
84 MAE, Serie DE-CE 1961–66, Carton 432, SGCI note, 'Programme de la communauté économique européenne pour 1963', 22 April, 1963.
85 MAE, Serie DE-CE 1961–66, Carton 577, Note de la sous direction d'Europe occidentale, 27 July, 1963.
86 ANF, SGCI files, Versement 900638, Art. 24, 'Perspectives du marché commun', 11 February, 1963.
87 CMA, R/792/63, Council minutes, 23–24 September, 1963.
88 Figures cited in CMA, R/423/63, Council minutes, 8–10 May, 1963.

89 For the claim that 'disparities' were a largely French invention see Zeiler (1992) p. 168.

90 CMA, R/423/63, Council minutes, 8–10 May, 1963.

91 See also *AAPD 1963*, document 219.

92 de Gaulle (1970) vol. 4, pp. 128–9; see also *DDF 1963*, vol. 2, document 253.

93 CMA, 1368/63, Council minutes, 15 October, 1963.

94 See *DDF 1963*, vol. 2, document 6.

95 Talbot (1978).

96 Boegner interestingly attributed Lahr and Hüttebräuker's interventions to a purely tactical desire to delay the agricultural talks until more progress had been made on the slower than expected GATT negotiations. This was not the first or last time that the French failed to comprehend their partners' genuine anxiety about the CAP. ANF, SGCI files, Versement 900638, Art. 25, No. 23/DE, Boegner to Couve, 3 February, 1964.

97 CMA, 1496/63, Council minutes, 12–15 November, 1963.

98 *Ibid.*

99 As will become clear, this constitutes a significant theme of this book. See also Keeler (1987) pp. 62–77; Moravcsik (2000) pp. 3–43.

100 The clearest example of this line of thought (albeit from a slightly later period) is Hallstein's comments to the US government about the way each new Community deal constituted a further 'thread' binding France into the EEC. *FRUS 1964–8*, vol. XIII, p. 112.

101 For the first signs of Italian malcontent see *DDF 1963*, vol. 2, document 244. But they were much less forceful than they would become in 1964 and 1965.

102 *DDF 1963*, vol. 2, document 207.

103 Knudsen (2002) pp. 308–11.

104 PRO, FO371 171451, No. 792, Dixon to FO, 12 December, 1963.

105 PRO, FO371 171451, No. 387, O'Neill to FO, 13 December, 1963.

106 BAK, BKA, B136/2589, Kurzzusammenfassung der Ergebnisse des Minister-rats der EWG, 4 January, 1964.

107 BAK, BKA, B136/2589, Vorläufige Stellungnahme zu den Ergebnissen der Ratstagung der EWG vom 16–23 December, 1963, 2 January, 1964.

108 *Ibid.*

109 BAK, BKA, B136/2589, Sitzungen des EWG-Ministerrats vom 18 bis 23 Dezember 1963, 4 January, 1963.

110 ANF, SGCI files, Versement 900638, Art. 25, No. 23/DE, Boegner to Couve, 3 February, 1964.

111 de Gaulle (1986) *Lettres, notes et carnets. Janvier 1961–Décembre 1963*, Paris: Plon, 1986, p. 403.

112 The December negotiations did act as a reminder, however, that on some aspects of the CAP, the Germans could be every bit as protectionist as the French.

113 See MAE, Serie Europe 1961–5, Carton 1976, Luns letter, 3 January, 1964.

114 ANF, SGCI files, Versement 900638, Art. 25, No. 23/DE, Boegner to Couve, 3 February, 1964.

115 For Commission disatisfaction, ECHA, COM(63)235 final, 2ème partie, 10 July, 1963.

116 ECHA, CEAB 2, No. 2589, S/859/63, Rapport des Représentants Permanents sur les aspects et problèmes de la fusion, 18 December, 1963.

117 See Ducci and Olivi (1970) pp. 348–88.

2 From the cereals agreement to Council breakdown

1 See Knudsen (2002) pp. 277–376; A.C. Knudsen, 'Creating the Common Agricultural Policy: Story of Cereals Prices', in Loth (2001) pp. 131–54; H. Delorme, 'L'adoption du prix unique des céréales', in Gerbet and Pepy (1969) pp. 269–96.
2 Knudsen (2002) pp. 158–224.
3 Knudsen (2002) pp. 239–53.
4 For December 1961 to January 1962 see Knudsen (2002) pp. 267–76; for December 1963 see Chapter 1.
5 Cited in Knudsen, in Loth (2001) p. 131.
6 Archivio Centrale dello Stato (ACS), Ministero del Bilancio e della Programmazione Economica (MBPE), vol. 93, 'Politica Agricola della CEE', undated (but clearly early to mid-1964).
7 PRO. FO371 177353; M1087/271, O'Neill to FO, Tel. 202, 17 December, 1964.
8 For the sense of euphoria see *Le Monde*, 16 December, 1964 and 17 December, 1964.
9 The problems that the issue caused for Italy will be discussed later in this chapter.
10 See Freisberg (1965) p. 185.
11 For a flavour of the internal German debate, see *AAPD 1966*, document 76.
12 Knudsen (2002) pp. 318–19.
13 See for instance, CMA, R/402/64, Council minutes, 13–15 April, 1964.
14 *Ibid.*
15 Knudsen (2002) pp. 328–47.
16 *Le Monde*, 22 October, 1964. For the background see Peyrefitte (1994–2000) vol. 2, pp. 265–6. For Erhard's reaction, *FRUS, 1964–8*, vol. XIII, 1995, pp. 90–1.
17 *AAPD 1964*, document 307.
18 CMA. 1666/64. Council minutes, 30 November and 1 December, 1964; for the ensuing negotiations, CMA, 1667/64 and CMA, R/1269/64. See also Mansholt (1974) pp. 108–15.
19 Most telling were German reactions. See Lahr (1981) pp. 412–13.
20 *Le Monde*, 16 December, 1964.
21 Cited in *Le Monde*, 30 December, 1964.
22 PRO. FO371 177353; M1087/271, O'Neill to FO, Tel. 202, 17 December, 1964.
23 CMA, R/1210/64, Council minutes, 10–15 November, 1964.
24 PRO. FO371 182299, M1063/1, O'Neill to Gordon Walker, Annual report on the European Communities for 1964, 2 January, 1965. For multiple German anxieties on this score, see below.
25 For de Gaulle's attitude see Peyrefitte (1997) vol. 2, p. 267.
26 M.T. Bitsch, 'La création de la commission unique: réforme technique ou affirmation d'une identité européenne?' in Bitsch, Poidevin and Loth (1998) pp. 327–47.
27 See, e.g. CMA, I/38/64, Council minutes, 28–30 July, 1964.
28 CMA, I/16/64, Council minutes, 25 March, 1964.
29 CMA, I/16/64, Council minutes, 25 March, 1964.
30 *Ibid.*
31 CMA, I/41/64, Council minutes, 16 June, 1964.
32 C. Germond, 'Les projets d'union politique de l'année 1964', in Loth (2001) pp. 109–30.
33 *AAPD 1964*, document 14. See also documents 27 and 59.

34 See BAK, BKA, B136 2590, various documents; CMA, R/1210/64, Council minutes, 10–15 November, 1964.
35 For Spaak's views, see Smets (1980) vol. 2, pp. 975–83.
36 See Parr (2002).
37 See, e.g. *AAPD 1964*, document 44.
38 PRO. FO371 18299, M1063/1, O'Neill to Gordon Walker, 2 January, 1965.
39 See, e.g. Schwabe (2001) pp. 18–34.
40 Trachtenberg (1999).
41 See Couve de Murville's speech to the National Assembly, 16 June, 1965. Couve de Murville papers, Sciences Po, Paris (henceforward CdM), vol. CM/2.
42 See, for instance, Gray (2003).
43 On the emerging security divide, see Bozo (1996); Conze (1995); and Guderzo (2000).
44 See Milward (1992) pp. 2–3.
45 For earlier patterns, see Ludlow, 'Diplomacy With Different Rules. Learning to negotiate in the EEC' in Bitsch, Poidevin and Loth (1998) pp. 241–55.
46 Smets (1980) p. 975.
47 ECHA. COM (64) PV 259 final, 2e partie, 29 January, 1964.
48 *Le Monde*, 1 December, 1964.
49 See also PRO. FO371 177328; M1063/18, Memo by UK delegation to the European Communities, 24 September, 1964.
50 Reprinted in Jouve (1967) p. 856.
51 van Tichelen (1981) pp. 335–6.
52 Moravcsik (2000) pp. 3–43.
53 For 1961–62 see Knudsen (2002) pp. 265–6 and 271–3; on French fears in the context of the enlargement negotiations see Ludlow (1997) pp. 186–7; on December 1964 see above.
54 For the April 1963 plan see Chapter 1; for Schmücker's presentation of Germany's 1964 priorities, see CMA, R/121/64, Council minutes, 3–5 February, 1964.
55 See *DDF 1964* (2002) vol. 1, document 79, Brussels: Peter Lang.
56 *DDF 1964*, vol. 2, document 154.
57 PRO, FO371 177352; M1083/5, Melville to Marjoribanks, 7 January, 1964; ECHA, COM(64) PV 256, 2e partie, 8 January, 1964.
58 Cited in Peyrefitte (1997) vol. 2, p. 263. See also *AAPD 1964*, document 273.
59 MAE. Série DE-CE 1961–66, Bte. 432, Note, 22 April, 1965.
60 See *AAPD 1964*, document 207.
61 Cited in Peyrefitte (1997) vol. 2, p. 273.
62 Peyrefitte (1997) vol. 2, p. 272.
63 See for instance the long-running battle fought throughout 1964 by the French and the Commission to repulse a German-inspired move to dilute the authority of the Commission-chaired management committees that ran the CAP on a day-to-day basis. ECHA, BDT 214/1980, Coreper reports, multiple documents.
64 See for instance Chapter 1.
65 For example, *Le Monde*, 12 June, 1965.
66 Peyrefitte (1997) vol. 2, pp. 282 and 286.
67 See ECHA, BDT 214/80, G(65)227, Sigrist note, 29 May, 1965; COM(65) PV 316, 2e partie, 5 May, 1965; BDT 214/80, S/0 22959/65, Sigrist to Rabot, 6 May, 1965.
68 For an indication of the phenomenon, albeit one reported in a fashion designed to show the General at his most crushing, see Peyrefitte (1997) vol. 2, pp. 265, 266 and 271. For an earlier example, Ludlow (1997) pp. 157–8.

69 For French preparations, see ANF, SGCI archives, Versement 870662, Art. 65, SGCI note, No. CE/4200, 27 April, 1965 and SGCI note, 26 May, 1965; MAE, Série DE-CE 1961–66, carton 402, various documents; carton 412, various documents; carton 581, various documents.

70 The Americans were openly predicting that he would. See *FRUS 1964–8*, vol. 13, p. 111.

71 MAE. Série DE-CE, 1961–66, Carton 402, Brunet note, No. 107/CE, 21 May, 1965.

72 See *DDF 1964*, vol. 1, document 226 and vol. 2, document 121.

73 See CMA, R/121/64, Council minutes, 3–5 February, 1964.

74 Mayer (1996) pp. 39–59; Soutou (1990) pp. 149–201.

75 For a French analysis, see *DDF 1965*, vol. 1, document 262.

76 *AAPD 1965*, document 22. See also Lappenküper (1991) pp. 103–12.

77 On the Atlanticist/Gaullist struggle within the CDU/CSU, see Granieri (2003) pp. 191–227.

78 For Erhard's financial woes, see Zimmermann (2001).

79 Marcowitz (1996) talks about the SPD acting as a government-in-waiting during this period; p. 223.

80 For contrasting views of this, see J. Vanke, 'The European Collaborations of France and Germany, 1963–1966', in Loth (2001) pp. 93–108, and Soutou (1996) pp. 272–7.

81 *AAPD 1964*, documents 180, 183 and 187; see also Lappenküper (1991) pp. 106–8 and *DDF 1964*, vol. 2, documents 6, 9, 11 and 12.

82 Peyrefitte (1997) vol. 2, pp. 257–8.

83 Vaïsse (1998) p. 563.

84 See for instance, *AAPD 1964*, document 210.

85 BAK. BKA, B-136, Bd. 2590. III A 2 report, 'EWG (gleichgewichtige Fortentwicklung in allen Bereichen)', 7 January, 1965.

86 *AAPD 1964*, document 347.

87 *AAPD 1965*, document 22; *DDF 1965*, vol. 1, documents 35 and 41.

88 *Le Monde*, 30 March, 1965.

89 *AAPD 1965*, document 157.

90 See *DDF 1965*, vol. 1, document 144.

91 For more details see Ludlow (1999) pp. 240–3.

92 BAK. BKA. B-136/2590. Praß to Erhard, 12 May, 1965.

93 See A. Varsori, 'The Art of Mediation: Italy and Britain's Attempt to Join the EEC', in Milward and Deighton (1999) pp. 241–55; and Ludlow (1997) pp. 162–5 and 237–8.

94 Galli and Torcasio (1976) pp. 85–6.

95 *Ibid.* p. 86.

96 The figures for 1965 were: Germany 11 per cent of the total workforce, France 17.4 per cent, Italy 24.69 per cent, The Netherlands 7.91 per cent, Belgium 6.9 per cent and Luxembourg 13.5 per cent; Knudsen (2002) p. 441.

97 See, for instance, ACS, MBPE, vol. 93, Resoconto sommario della XXXIV riunione del comitato ristretto dei direttori generali di ministeri tecnici incaricato delle questioni CEE e dei rapporti con i paesi terzi, 20 November, 1964.

98 Galli and Torcasio (1976) pp. 71–2.

99 ACS, MBPE, vol. 93, Moro to Hallstein, 6 June, 1964.

100 For the background see ACS, MBPE, vol. 93, Resoconto sommario della XXXIV riunione del comitato ristretto dei direttori generali di ministeri tecnici incaricato delle questioni CEE e dei rapporti con i paesi terzi, 20 November, 1964.

101 Galli and Torcasio (1976) pp. 78–9.

102 *Ibid.*

103 CMA, R/1269/64, Council minutes, 15 December, 1964.
104 For the immediate Italian assessment, see ACS, MBPE, vol. 93, Venturini to Rome, 21 December, 1964.
105 See ACS, MBPE, vol. 93, Resoconto sommario della XXXIV riunione del comitato ristretto dei direttori generali di ministeri tecnici incaricato delle questioni CEE e dei rapporti con i paesi terzi, 20 November, 1964.
106 *DDF 1965*, vol. 1, document 139.
107 *Le Monde*, 18 March, 1965.
108 See, for instance, SGCI, Versement 870662, Art. 66, Fourcade note pour le Ministre, 29 June, 1965.
109 Neville-Rolfe (1984) pp. 207–8.
110 Luns' memoirs even contain a chapter proudly entitled 'My "No" to De Gaulle'! Luns (1971) pp. 139–63.
111 See Ludlow, in Bitsch, Poidevin and Loth (1998) pp. 245–6.
112 A. Harryvan and B.J. van der Harst 'For Once a United Front. The Netherlands and the "Empty Chair" Crisis of the Mid-1960s', in Loth (2001) p. 176.
113 CMA, I/16/64, Council minutes, 25 March, 1964.
114 For an analysis of the Commission's proposals, see below.
115 For Dutch parliamentary pressure, see Lambert (1966) pp. 197–8.
116 See also *DDF 1965*, vol. 1, documents 80 and 270.
117 See, for instance, H. Götz, 'Die Krise 1965/66', in Loth, Wallace and Wessels (1995) pp. 189–202.
118 See also M. Schönwald, 'Walter Hallstein and the "Empty Chair" Crisis 1965/66', in Loth (2001) pp. 157–71.
119 ECHA. COM(65) 150, 31 March, 1965.
120 *Le Monde*, 11 May, 1965.
121 ECHA. COM(64) PV 298, 2e partie, 16 December, 1964.
122 ECHA. Speeches collection. Hallstein address to the British Institute of International and Comparative Law, London, 25 March, 1965.
123 ECHA. COM(65) PV 311, 2e partie, 22 March, 1965.
124 See Guderzo (2000) p. 226.
125 Loth, 'Les implications du conflit Hallstein-de Gaulle en 1965', in Bitsch, Poidevin and Loth (1998) pp. 410–11. See also *DDF 1965*, vol. 1, document 137.
126 BAK. BKA. B-136/3546. Praß memo. 6 April, 1965.
127 CMA, 1146/64, Council minutes, 7 July, 1964.
128 For an earlier example of Hallstein contemplating a *fuite en avant*, see *DDF 1964*, vol. 2, document 107.
129 CMA. R/850/65, Council minutes, 28 June–1 July, 1965.
130 For an atmospheric account of the final weeks of negotiation see L'Ecotais (1976) pp. 18–28.
131 ECHA, BDT 214/80, SEC(65) 1618, Sigrist note to Commission, 25 May, 1965.
132 CMA. R/850/65 and R/673/65, Council minutes, 14–15 June, 1965. For the German instructions going into this meeting, BAK, BKA, B-126, Bd. 2591, Prass Vermerks, 28 June, 1965 and 30 June, 1965.
133 La Serre (1970) esp. pp. 406–9; M. Vaïsse, 'La politique européenne de la France en 1965: pourquoi la "chaise vide"?' in Loth (2001) pp. 201–11.
134 CMA. R/673/65.
135 See Historical Archives of the European Communities, Florence (HAEC), Wormser papers, MAEF 368, vol. 122–3, 189, Note pour le Premier Ministre, 2 June, 1965.
136 BAK. BKA. B-136 3546, Ergebnis des Gesprächs zwischen Lahr und Wormser, 22 June, 1965 and Vermerk, 23 June, 1965; MAE. Série DE-CE 1961–66, carton 402, Quai to Bonn 4691/470, 23 June, 1965.

137 CMA. R/850/65.
138 *Ibid*. See also *AAPD 1965*, document 248.
139 Cited in Lambert (1966) p. 209.
140 CMA. R/850/65.

3 A careful confrontation

1 CMA. 07.352, La rupture par le Gouvernement français des négociations concernant le financement de la politique agricole, dossier 1. Texte de la conférence de presse tenue par le professeur Walter Hallstein, 1 July, 1965. For Couve's assessment see Jouve (1967) vol. 1, p. 427.
2 Cited in Jouve (1967) pp. 441–2.
3 CMA. 07.352, La rupture par le Gouvernement français des négociations concernant le financement de la politique agricole, dossier 1. Council press release, 6 July, 1965.
4 Vaïsse, in Loth (2001) p. 207.
5 *AAPD 1964*, document 307.
6 ANF, SGCI files, Versement 900638, Art. 25, various documents in subfolder entitled 'Crise du Marché Commun. Participation française aux travaux des Communautés Européennes'.
7 See ECHA, High Authority microfiche, No. 3482, SEC(65) 222, Sigrist note to Commission, 19 January, 1965.
8 See especially ANF, SGCI files, Versement 900638, Art. 25, unsigned note on 'Les conditions de participation française aux travaux des Communautés Européennes', 3 July, 1965. See also Cointat (2001) p. 163.
9 De Gaulle (1970) vol. 4, p. 379.
10 *Ibid.* pp. 380–1.
11 *Ibid.* p. 381.
12 *Débats de l'Assemblée Nationale* (1965) pp. 3889–92.
13 *AAPD 1965*, document 270.
14 BAK, BKA, B-136 2591, Praß note, 30 July, 1965; see also *FRUS 1964–8*, volume XIII, pp. 225–6.
15 *AAPD 1965*, document 339.
16 For domestic French reactions, see *Le Monde*, 17 September, 1965. For German complaints, PRO, PREM 13/904; Roberts to FO, Tel. 1127, 22 October, 1965.
17 Examples include Newhouse (1967) pp. 21–4; Lindberg (1966) p. 245; Jaumin-Ponsar (1970) pp. 111–16; Bitsch (1996) pp. 161–2; Roussel (2002) pp. 774–7.
18 De Gaulle (1970) p. 377; see also PRO, PREM 13/904, M1099/178, Marjoribanks to Stewart, 2 August, 1965 and *FRUS 1964–8*, vol. XIII, pp. 225–6.
19 For a similar line of argument see Vaïsse in Loth (2001) pp. 213–14.
20 Cited in Peyrefitte (1997) vol. 2, p. 292.
21 De Gaulle (1970) vol. 3, pp. 404–9; for reactions, Vaïsse (1998) pp. 187–8.
22 Braun (1972) pp. 174–6.
23 MAE. Direction Europe 1961–65, carton 1976, Note, 10 May, 1965.
24 Peyrefitte claims de Gaulle had predicted this tactic (1997) vol. 2, p. 281.
25 *Le Monde*, 11 May, 1965.
26 See, e.g. Peyrefitte (1997) vol. 2, p. 273.
27 CDM, CM8, Draft tel., Couve to Seydoux, 6 July, 1965.
28 ANF, SGCI files, Versement 900638, Art. 25, Dromer to de Gaulle, 1 July, 1965 and Brunet circular No. 27/CE, 15 October, 1965.
29 ANF, SGCI files, Versement 900638, Art. 25, Note du Conseiller Juridique, No. 479, 28 July, 1965.

30 MAE, Série DE-CE, 1961–66, carton 402, Exposé sur les règles de majorité du Traité de Rome, 15 September, 1965.

31 MAE. Série DE-CE, 1961–66, carton 402, Brunet note, No. 107/CE, 21 May, 1965.

32 ANF, SGCI files, Versement 900638, Art. 25, Dromer to de Gaulle, 1 July, 1965.

33 *Ibid.*

34 Peyrefitte (1997) vol. 2, p. 289.

35 *AAPD 1965*, document 270; see also ANF, SGCI, Versement 900638, Art. 25, Brunet circular No. 27/CE, 15 October, 1965.

36 De Gaulle (1970) vol. 4, p. 381.

37 ANF, SGCI archives, Versement 900638, Art. 25, Conseiller Juridique, Note 444, 13 July, 1965 and Note 478, 27 July, 1965.

38 ANF, SGCI archives, Versement 900638, Art. 25, Conseiller Juridique, Note 443, 13 July, 1965.

39 Weiler (1991) pp. 2423–4.

40 See, e.g. ECHA, COM(65) PV 330, 2e partie, 22 September, 1965 and BDT 214/80, G(65) 431, Sigrist note on COREPER meeting, 16 September, 1965.

41 ECHA. BDT 144/1992, Carton 588, G(65) 339, Sigrist note on the COREPER I meeting, 8 July, 1965.

42 ECHA. BDT 214/80, G(65) 347, Sigrist note on COREPER meeting, 8 July, 1965.

43 *Ibid.*

44 ECHA. BDT 214/80, G(65) 364, Sigrist note on COREPER meeting, 15 July, 1965.

45 CMA. 07.352. La rupture par le Gouvernement français des négociations concernant le financement de la politique agricole, dossier 1. Troffaes to Fricchione, 9 July, 1965.

46 ECHA. BDT 214/80, G(65) 367, Sigrist note on the COREPER meeting, 15 July, 1965. See also SGCI archives, Versement 900638, Art. 25, unsigned note for Dromer, 14 July, 1965.

47 On the contrasting Belgian and German approaches, see *AAPD 1965*, document 307.

48 Revealingly, most of the governments involved do seem to have commissioned legal opinions. But these were kept for internal use, rather than being systematically compared in any meeting of the Five. See, e.g. Netherlands Foreign Ministry (NLFM), 996.0 EEG, box 175, DIE to DGES, 6 October, 1965 and Historical Archives of the European Communities, Florence (HAEC), Emile Noël papers, EN-8, G(65) 353, Note du Service Juridique, 13 July, 1965.

49 ECHA. COM(65) 320 final, 22 July, 1965.

50 See ECHA. BDT 144/1992, box 1036, 'proposition de compromis', 2 July, 1965 and COM(65) PV 326 final, 2e partie, 19–22 July, 1965. The French Commissioner did eventually vote against the new draft, largely in protest at the vague nature of its reference to the European Parliament. He acknowledged, nevertheless, that it was a major improvement on the March text.

51 CMA. 3.07.352, Remplacement des contributions financières des Etats membres par des ressources propres (1965/6), Déclaration de M. Hallstein au sujet du Mémorandum.

52 HAEC, Noël papers, EN-343, Etienne note to Narjes, 12 January, 1966.

53 See BAK. BKA B-136, Bände 2591 and 2592, multiple documents.

54 ECHA. BDT 214/80. G(63) 433, Sigrist note on COREPER meeting, 21 September, 1965.

55 ECHA. BDT 214/80. Multiple reports on COREPER meetings.

56 CMA. 1304/65, Council minutes, 25–26 October, 1965.

57 CMA. Annexe to R/1062/65. T/418/65. Lignes directrices pour le financement de la politique agricole commune, 26 October, 1965.

58 For French awareness of divisions amongst the Five, SGCI, Versement 900638, Art. 25, Tel. 1016/24, Ulrich to Couve, 26 October, 1965.

59 The full text of the agreement reached at the October Council meeting is in BAK, BKA, B-136, 2592. See Lambert (1966) pp. 218–19.

60 See, for instance, Erhard's comments cited in Chapter 2.

61 See *AAPD 1965*, document 369.

62 Spaak's speech on 27 September is a demonstration of this. Smets (1980) pp. 988–97.

63 Even the Dutch recognised Commission errors: *AAPD 1965*, document 378.

64 Cited by Jaumin-Ponsar (1970) p. 100.

65 *AAPD 1965*, document 397.

66 See, e.g. CDM, CM2, Conversation entre le Ministre des Affaires Etrangères de la République Française et le Ministre des Affaires Etrangères de la République Fédérale d'Allemagne le 13 novembre 1965. Also *AAPD 1965*, document 416. For the Dutch position: *AAPD 1965*, document 378; NLFM, 996.0 EEG, box 175, Tel. 80, Luns to Rome, 16 November, 1965.

67 ACS, MBPE, vol. 94, Venturini to Fanfani, 2 August, 1965.

68 See ECHA, COM(65) PV 330, 2e partie, 22 September, 1965. Also Smets (1980) pp. 993–4, and Werner (1991) p. 65.

69 NLFM, 996.0 EEG, box 175, Tel. 106, de Vos van Steenwijk to MBZ, 5 October, 1965.

70 NLFM, 996.0 EEG, box 175, Tel. 266, Van de Block to Luns, 7 October, 1965.

71 *AAPD 1965*, documents 379 and 303.

72 ECHA, COM(65) PV 330, 2e partie, 22 September, 1965; see also *AAPD 1965*, document 283.

73 *AAPD 1965* document 369.

74 BAK, BKA, B-136, Bd. 2592, Vermerk Westricks, 26 October, 1965; see also MAE, Série DE-CE 1961–66, Carton 402, Ulrich to Quai, Delfra No. 1035/39, 26 October, 1965.

75 ACS, MBPE, vol. 94, Venturini to Fanfani, 2 August, 1965.

76 A detailed analysis of the Belgian approach is in HAEC, Noël papers, EN-343, Etienne note to Narjes, 12 January, 1966. See also Dumoulin (1999) pp. 659–64.

77 NLFM, 996.0 EEG, box 175, Tel. 106, De Vos van Steenwijk to MBZ, 5 October, 1965.

78 See *AAPD 1965*, documents 303 and 307.

79 See, e.g. NLFM, 996.0 EEG, box 175, Savelberg to MBZ, 26 October, 1965.

80 NLFM, 996.0 EEG, box 175, De Vos van Steenwijk to MBZ, 4 November, 1965; see also *AAPD 1965*, document 360.

81 PRO, PREM 13/904, Barclay to FO, Tel. 36 saving, 29 October, 1965.

82 NLFM, 996.0 EEG, box 175, Luxembourg aide-mémoire, 14 October, 1965; see also Werner (1991) pp. 64–73.

83 BAK, BKA, B-136, Bd. 2592, Praß note, 24 September, 1965.

84 T. Oppelland, '"Entangling Alliances With None" – Neither de Gaulle Nor Hallstein. The European Politics of Gerhard Schröder in the 1965/6 Crisis', in Loth (2001) pp. 241–2.

85 BAK, BKA, B-136, Bd. 2591, AA memo, 'Die Lage der Europapolitik', 21 July, 1965.

86 ACS, MBPE, vol. 94, Venturini to Fanfani, 2 August, 1965.

87 See *AAPD 1965*, documents 269, 379, 397 and 462.

88 See A. Varsori, 'Italy and the "Empty Chair" Crisis (1965–6)', in Loth (2001) pp. 218–19.

89 Harryvan and van der Harst, in Loth (2001) pp. 182–3.
90 See NLFM, 996.0 EEG, box 175, Luns to MBZ, 1 October, 1965 and Tel. 364, Van Ittersum to MBZ, 6 October, 1965.
91 Harryvan and van der Harst, in Loth (2001) pp. 183–5; see also NLFM, 996.0 EEG, box 176, Tel. 623, Bentinck to MBZ, 25 November, 1965.
92 NLFM, 996.0, EEG, box 175, Directeur-Generaal van de Buitenlandse Economische Betrekkingen to Luns, 4 November, 1965.
93 See Newhouse (1967) pp. 132–4.
94 Newhouse (1967) pp. 129–30.
95 *AAPD 1965*, documents 269, 276, 303.
96 *AAPD 1965*, document 379.
97 See *AAPD 1965*, document 303.
98 The Dutch for instance praised his firmness: NLFM, 996.0 EEG, box 176, Tel. 132, Spierenburg to MBZ, 2 December, 1965.
99 Unwisely Bonn chose to all but ignore a long despatch from their deputy Permanent Representative, Bömcke, which had warned in early July that the German position on CAP finance was unsustainable. BAK, BKA, B-136, Bd. 2591, Bömcke note, 9 July, 1965.
100 See above.
101 See Varsori in Loth (2001) pp. 218–20; ECHA, BDT 214/80, G(65) 364, Sigrist note on COREPER meeting, 15 July, 1965 and G(65) 469 add. 1, Sigrist note on COREPER meeting, 12 October, 1965.
102 Varsori, in Loth (2001) p. 219; for Venturini's role, see ECHA, BDT 214/80, multiple COREPER reports.
103 For Colombo's earlier reputation, see Ludlow (1997) pp. 164–5; from French documents it would appear that Fanfani did his best to undermine his replacement; his inability to attend meetings, however, proved too great a limitation to be easily overcome. MAE, Série DE-CE 1961–66, Carton 402, Wormser note for Couve, 12 November, 1965.
104 See Dumoulin (1999) pp. 659–64 and SGCI, Versement 900638, Art. 25, Tel. 985/89, Ulrich to Quai, 15 October, 1965.
105 See, e.g. ECHA, BDT 214/80, G(66)8, Sigrist report on COREPER meeting, 6 January, 1966.
106 For French appreciation, SGCI, Versement 900638, Art. 25, Tel. 1211, Ulrich to Quai, 15 October, 1965.
107 See Dumoulin (1999) p. 662; ECHA, BDT 214/80, G(65)502, Sigrist note on COREPER I meeting, 22 October, 1965; MAE, Série DE-CE 1961–66, Carton 402, unsigned note, 29 November, 1965.
108 See ECHA speeches collection: Hallstein speech to the Düsseldorf CDU/CSU meeting, 8 July, 1965, Hallstein's speech to Bayerischen Rundfunk, 5 November, 1965 and Levi-Sandri's speech to delegation of Italian MPs, 8 November, 1965.
109 The absence of high level contacts between the Commission and the German government was very striking. For Commission displeasure at Spaak's ideas, ECHA, COM(65) PV 330, 2e partie, 22 September, 1965.
110 See, e.g. *AAPD 1965*, document 470.
111 ECHA, BDT 214/80, G(65)487, Sigrist note on COREPER meeting, 13 October, 1965.
112 The Commission's near-disappearance is noted in 'The EEC after Luxembourg', working paper C-1 of the Istituto Affari Internazionali, Rome. Reproduced in *Lo Spettatore Internazionale*, vol. 1, No. 2, 1966, p. 33.
113 SGCI, Versement 900638, Art. 25, Note pour M. Dromer, 9 July, 1965.
114 Lahr (1981) pp. 425–32; see also *AAPD 1965*, document 395.

115 MAE, Série DE-CE 1961–66, Carton 402, annex to Brunet to Wormser, 30 September, 1965.
116 Cited in Peyrefitte (1997), vol. 2, p. 300.
117 The Spaak memorandum, for instance, spoke of the misunderstandings that could arise. MAE, Série DE-CE 1961–66, Carton 402, Spaak memorandum, 5 October, 1965.
118 NLFM, 996.0 EEG, box 176, unsigned note, 19 November, 1965.
119 *AAPD 1965*, document 416.
120 See CMA, R1136/65, Council minutes, 20 December, 1965; also *AAPD 1965*, document 470.
121 The Belgians had originally hoped that a meeting with France could be arranged well before the French Presidential elections. See *AAPD 1965*, document 382.
122 Spaak dismissed French arguments about this as childish! NLFM, 996.0 EEG, box 176, Tel. 130, De Vos to MBZ, 29 November, 1965.
123 On the hazards of bilateral diplomacy, MAE, Série DE-CE 1961–66, Carton 402, Seydoux to Quai, Tel. 6350/54, 16 November, 1965.
124 CDM, CM2, Conversation entre Couve et Schröder, 13 November, 1965.
125 *Ibid.*
126 De Gaulle rather pointedly refused to send Erhard the customary message of congratulation after his election win. U. Lappenküper. '"Ein Europa der Freien und der Gleichen". La politique européenne de Ludwig Erhard', in Loth (2001) p. 87. See also Peyrefitte (1994–2000) pp. 304–5.
127 See Roussel (2002) p. 783.
128 *AAPD 1965*, documents 388 and 416; CDM, CM9, Tel. 2389/96, Couve to Quai, 30 September, 1965 and Tel. 5671/81, Wormser circular, 9 November, 1965; ACS, MBPE, vol. 83, telespresso 46/26774, Foreign Ministry circular, 30 December, 1965.
129 NLFM, 996.0 EEG, box 175, Tel. 552, Bentinck to MBZ, 19 October, 1965; for Luns' lunch, NLFM, 996.0 EEG, box 176, Tel. 623, Bentinck to MBZ, 25 November, 1965.
130 SGCI, Versement 900638, Art. 26, dossier 'Bilan et situation dans les Communautés Européennes', Annex 2, 'Bilan de la politique agricole commune', 1 October, 1965.
131 See *ibid.*, annexes 1 and 3.
132 CDM, CM9, Tel. 5930/32, Wormser circular, 24 December, 1965.
133 CMA, R/1063/65, Council minutes, 29–30 November, 1965.
134 One source of mounting pressure, closely linked to the GATT impasse, was the *Bundesverband der deutsche Industrie* (BDI). BAK, BKA, Bd. 2592, Berg to Westrick, 24 November, 1965.
135 ECHA. BDT 214/80, G(65) 556, Sigrist note of COREPER meeting, 10 November, 1965.
136 CDM, CM9, Tel. 5933/36, Wormser circular, 24 December, 1965. For earlier French indications that it would accept the budget, see BAK, BKA, Bd. 2592, Tel. 1926, Sachs to AA, 7 December, 1965.
137 NLFM, 996.0 EEG, box 176, Tel. 143, Spierenburg to MBZ, 28 December, 1965.
138 PRO. FO371 188375; M10836/4, Robinson to Hugh-Jones, 6 January, 1966.

4 National interest and the rescue of the EEC

1 NLFM, 996.0 EEG, box 177, van Ittersum to MBZ, 14 January, 1966.
2 For a review of some of the primarily political science literature that has built up about events in January 1966, see N.P. Ludlow, 'The Eclipse of the Extremes. Demythologising the Luxembourg Compromise', in Loth (2001) pp. 247–64.

3 MAE, Série DE-CE 1961–66, Carton 402, Ulrich to Brunet, 4 October, 1965 and unsigned note, 13 November, 1965. See also BAK, BKA, Bd. 2592, Tel. 1926, Sachs to AA, 7 December, 1965 and ACS, MBPE, vol. 83, telespresso 46/26774, Foreign Ministry circular, 30 December, 1965.

4 NLFM, 996.00 EEG, box 177, Spierenburg to MBZ, 4 January, 1966 and 6 January, 1966; ECHA, BDT 214/80, G(66)8, Sigrist report on 6 January, 1966 meeting; BAK, BKA, B-136, Bd. 8319, Praß note, 3 January, 1966.

5 CDM, CM9, Ulrich to Quai, Tel. 9/23, 7 January, 1966.

6 *Ibid.*

7 NLFM, 996.0 EEG, box 177, Bentinck to MBZ, Tel. 1735, 26 January, 1966.

8 PRO, FO371 188375, M10836/32, Marjoribanks to Statham, 10 January, 1966.

9 NLFM, 996.0 EEG, box 177, de Vos to MBZ, Tel. 3, 5 January, 1966.

10 NLFM, 996.0 EEG, box 177, Vredenburch to MBZ, Tel. 9, 11 January, 1966. See also Ortona (1998) p. 106.

11 NLFM, 996.0 EEG, box 177, D.I.E. memo, F/319/66, 13 January, 1966.

12 NLFM, 996.0 EEG, box 177, Spierenburg to MBZ, Tels. 4, 6, and 13, 14 January, 1966.

13 NLFM, 996.0 EEG, box 177, Ministerraad van het Koninkrijk, 21 January, 1966.

14 PRO. FO371 188375; M10836/37, Garran to O'Neill, 20 January, 1966.

15 PRO. FO371 188375; M10836/8, Marjoribanks to FO, Tel. 6, 13 January, 1966.

16 MAE, Série DE-CE 1961–66, Carton 402, unsigned note, 29 November, 1965.

17 MAE, Série DE-CE 1961–66, carton 402, Note 'Affaires budgétaires des Communautés Européennes', 12 January, 1966.

18 MAE, Série DE-CE 1961–66, carton 402, Brunet to Ulrich, 3 January, 1966.

19 CMA, C/12/66, Council minutes, 17–18 and 27–28 January, 1966.

20 MAE, Série DE-CE 1961–66, carton 402, aide-memoire, 17 January, 1966.

21 CMA, C/12/66, Council minutes, 17–18 and 27–28 January, 1966.

22 See Chapter 3.

23 The gap was even more notable between the decalogue and internal French government documents. See ANF, SGCI Versement 900638, Art. 25, SGCI note, 'le rôle de la Commission', 8 January, 1966.

24 CMA, C/12/66, Council minutes, 17–18 and 27–28 January, 1966.

25 PRO, FO371 188375; M10836/41, Galsworthy to Statham, 21 January, 1966.

26 CMA, C/12/66, Council minutes, 17–18 and 27–28 January, 1966; see also PRO. FO371 188375; M10836/42, Garran to FO, 28 January, 1966.

27 CMA, C/12/66, Council minutes, 17–18 and 27–28 January, 1966.

28 Luns apparently left the latter commenting to an Italian official 'Nothing doing', Ortona (1998) p. 110.

29 CMA, C/12/66, Council minutes, 17–18 and 27–28 January, 1966.

30 This rather contradicts Lindberg (1966) p. 256.

31 For the Commission this was an absolutely vital French concession. ECHA, COM(66) PV 345, 2e partie, 19 January, 1966.

32 PRO. FO371 188375; M10836/37, Garran to O'Neill, 20 January, 1966.

33 CMA, C/12/66, Council minutes, 17–18 and 27–28 January, 1966.

34 ANF, SGCI, Versement 900638, Art. 25, 'Projet de calendrier', 18 January, 1966.

35 ACS, MBPE, vol. 83, telespresso 46/1566, Foreign Ministry circular, 21 January, 1966.

36 NLFM, 996.00 EEG, box 177, Van Voorst to MBZ, Tel. 1, 17 January, 1966.

37 NLFM, 996.00 EEG, box 177, Bentinck to MBZ, Tel. 1735, 26 January, 1966.

38 The atmosphere in the meeting was reportedly frostier than outside, where it was minus 15! Ortona (1998) p. 111.

39   Ulrich had been informed of this agreement amongst the Five. MAE, Série DE-CE 1961–66, carton 402, Ulrich note, 14 January, 1965.
40   CMA, C/12/66, Council minutes, 17–18 and 27–28 January, 1966.
41   *AAPD 1966*, document 12.
42   See NLFM, 996.00 EEG, box 177, Spierenburg to MBZ, Tel. 1520, 19 January, 1966; ACS, MBPE, vol. 83, telespresso 46/1566, Foreign Ministry circular, 21 January, 1966; MAE, Série DE-CE 1961–66, carton 402, Wormser to Delfra Brussels, No. 6/20, 20 January, 1966.
43   PRO. FO371 188375; M10836/27, Marjoribanks to FO, Tel. 3 saving, 21 January, 1966; NLFM, 996.00 EEG, box 177, Ministerraad van het Koninkrijk, 28 January, 1966; the Italians for their part were worried about German rigidity: ACS, MBPE, vol. 83, telespresso 46/1566, Foreign Ministry circular, 21 January, 1966.
44   NLFM, 996.00 EEG, box 177, Ministerraad van het Koninkrijk, 21 January, 1966; PRO. FO371 188375; M10836/27, Marjoribanks to FO, Tel. 3 saving, 21 January, 1966. Wormser had certainly singled out Schröder's role, MAE, Série DE-CE 1961–66, carton 402, Wormser to Delfra Brussels, No. 6/20, 20 January, 1966.
45   Newhouse (1967) pp. 110–11; for the context Granieri (2003) pp. 196–214.
46   *FRUS 1964–8*, vol. XIII, p. 302.
47   For the agreed text, see Salmon and Nicoll (1997) pp. 94–5.
48   On the radicalism of these demands NLFM, 996.00 EEG, box 177, Hartogh briefing to Luns, 21 January, 1966 and PRO, FO371 188375; M/10836/26, Everson to Statham, 20 January, 1966.
49   CMA, C/12/66, Council minutes, 17–18 and 27–28 January, 1966.
50   A formula employed by Werner, in the Council chair. *Ibid.*
51   *Ibid.* The extent of this concession can be gauged by looking at earlier French internal documents that had aspired to restrict majority voting by means of a formal alteration of the Council of Minister's internal regulations. MAE, Série DE-CE 1961–66. Carton 402, SGCI note, 'le problème de la majorité qualifiée', 3 January, 1966.
52   Lahr (1983) p. 226.
53   CMA, C/12/66, Council minutes, 17–18 and 27–28 January, 1966.
54   *Ibid.*
55   For the agreed text see Salmon and Nicholl (1997) p. 94.
56   CMA, C/12/66, Council minutes, 17–18 and 27–28 January, 1966.
57   *Ibid.*
58   Cited by Jaumin-Ponsar (1970) p. 135.
59   *Ibid.* See also ACS, MBPE, CEE 1, Ministero degli Affari Esteri circular, telespresso 46/2333/e, 1 February, 1966.
60   de Gaulle (1970) vol. 5, pp. 20–1.
61   CDM, CM9, Wormser circular, No. 32, 31 January, 1966; *AAPD 1966*, document 25.
62   Kobbert (1966) pp. 119–22.
63   Cited in Jaumin-Ponsar (1970) p. 135.
64   HAEC, Emile Noël papers, EN 343, Etienne to Noël, 22 February, 1966.
65   *Ibid.* See also Cointat (2001) pp. 162–3.
66   See ACS, MBPE, vol. 84, appunto, 18 February, 1966.
67   CMA. 3.07.515 Verbatim de la 373ème réunion du Comité des Représentants Permanents (17–18 February, 1966).
68   BAK, BKA, B-136, Bd. 8319, multiple documents and *AAPD 1966*, documents 76, 92, 112 and 118.
69   BAK, BKA, B-136, Bd. 8319, Hütterbräuker to Sachs, 25 February, 1966.
70   Even the Americans, who appreciated Erhard's instinctive Atlanticism, grew

exasperated at his inability to take a firm foreign policy decision. Schwartz (2003) pp. 114–15.

71 BAK, BKA, B-136, Bd. 8319, unsigned Vermerk on 'Ergebnis der heutigen Kabinettsitzung', 24 February, 1966 and *ibid*. Geberth Kurzvermerk über Koalitionsgespräch, 28 March, 1966.

72 On the NATO crisis see Haftendorn (1996) esp. pp. 1–24; Bozo (1996) pp. 151–66; Soutou (1996) pp. 287–301.

73 For the Rambouillet meeting see *AAPD 1966*, documents 34 and 36.

74 See Seydoux (1977) pp. 67–79.

75 BAK, BKA, B-136, Bd. 8319, Lahr Vermerk, 1 April, 1966; MAE, DE-CE 1961–66, Carton 402, Wormser note, 26 March, 1966.

76 BAK, BKA, B-136, Bd. 8319, Lahr Vermerk, 1 April, 1966.

77 For the 1963 situation, see Chapter 1.

78 ECHA, BDT 144/92, SEC(66) 558, Noël report on the COREPER meeting, 17–18 February, 1966.

79 ECHA, BDT 144/92, multiple COREPER reports.

80 BAK, BKA, B-136, Bd. 3546, Herwarth to AA, Tel. 91, 5 February, 1966.

81 Galli and Torcasio (1976) pp. 105–19.

82 BAK, BKA, B-136, Bd. 8319, Praß Vermerk für die Kabinettsitzung, 19 January, 1966.

83 BAK, BKA, B-136, Bd. 3546, Praß memo, 'Morgiges Koalitionsgespräch über den Fortgang der EWG-Verhandlungen', 2 May, 1966.

84 Indeed in the aftermath of the May deal, Italian analyses identified Germany as having been Italy's main opponent in most of the discussions. ACS, MBPE, vol. 94, Resoconto sommario della 66.a riunione ristretto dei direttori generali incaricato dei problemi CEE e delle relazioni con i paesi terzi, 13 May, 1966.

85 MAE, Série DE-CE 1961–66, carton 432, SGCI note on 'Orientations françaises pour les négociations relatives au financement de la politique agricole commune', No. CE/1093, 11 February, 1966.

86 ECHA, BDT 144/92, SEC(66) 589, Noël report on COREPER meeting, 23–24 February, 1966.

87 MAE, Série DE-CE 1961–66, carton 402, unsigned and undated note on 'Conseil des 4 et 5 avril 1966'.

88 See BAK, BKA, B-136, Bd. 8319, Hornschu 'Vermerk für die Kabinettsitzung', 19 July, 1966; the idea emerged much earlier in the year. See *ibid*. Vermerk Geberths, 'Ergebnis der Tagung des EWG-Rats vom 4/5 April 1966', 6 April, 1966.

89 The inspiration for the German tactic seems to have been a comment made by Edgar Faure in his March meeting with Höcherl. BAK, BKA, Bd. 8319, Praß note, 16 March, 1966.

90 ACS, MBPE, vol. 94, Resoconto sommario della 66.a riunione ristretto dei direttori generali incaricato dei problemi CEE e delle relazioni con i paesi terzi, 13 May, 1966.

91 For the details of all three see CMA. R/609/66 Council minutes, 4–5 and 9–12 May, 1966; R/612/66, Council minutes, 13–14 June, 1966; R/926/66, Council minutes, 23, 24 and 26–27 July, 1966; see also Cointat (2001) pp. 181–99.

92 See Vaïsse (1998).

93 On Monnet see for instance Peyrefitte (1994) vol. 1, p. 362.

94 De Gaulle's reputed annoyance at the fact that Hallstein had stayed at Blair House when in Washington is likely to have sprung not simply from the fact that this confirmed the Commission President's over-exalted view of his own status, but also from the way in which it indicated a US desire to encourage this delusion.

95   Couve de Murville (1971) p. 380.
96   Peyrefitte (1994) vol. 1, pp. 366–8.
97   Peyrefitte (1997) vol. 2, p. 264.
98   Vanke (2001) p. 98.
99   *AAPD 1965*, documents 107 and 196.
100 Camps (1967) p. 110.
101 *AAPD 1966*, document 61.
102 See for instance *FRUS 1964–8*, vol. 13, p. 355.
103 *FRUS 1964–8*, vol. 13, p. 400.
104 *Ibid.*
105 *Ibid.*
106 MAE, Série DE-CE 1961–66, Carton 432, 'Accord du 11 mai 1966', undated.
107 See Chapter 2.
108 All of these factors are discussed in Chapter 3.
109 See, e.g. *AAPD 1966*, document 235.
110 For discussion of the French dossier, see Chapter 3.
111 For de Gaulle's celebrated dismissal of the Treaty of Rome as 'un traité de commerce' see R. Poidevin, 'De Gaulle et l'Europe en 1958', in Poidevin (1992) vol. 5, p. 82.
112 Even the French admitted as much. See *DDF 1965*, vol. 1, document 238.
113 See for instance the useful surveys of parliamentary opinion in Germany, France and Italy published in the *Revue du Marché Commun*, Nos. 108, 111 and 116 (1967–68).
114 The Luxembourg minutes are distinctive for the number of references to the parliamentary pressure many of the participants felt themselves to be under. CMA, C/12/66, Council minutes, 17–18 and 27–28 January, 1966.
115 PRO. PREM 13/04, Barclay to FO, No. 36 saving, 29 October, 1965.
116 For a retrospective German admission of this, see PRO. EW 5/8, Roberts to FO, Tel. No. 95 saving, 2 May, 1966.
117 See Chapter 3.
118 *AAPD 1966*, documents 25 and 180.
119 *FRUS 1964–1968*, vol. 13, p. 356.
120 Newhouse for instance talks about the dispute over majority voting having been 'simply shunted aside', Newhouse (1967) p. 157.
121 For a denunciation of those who have misunderstood the Luxembourg outcome in this manner, see Lahr (1983) pp. 226–8.
122 Taylor (1983) p. 20; Duchêne (1994) p. 332; Tsebelis and Kreppel (1998) pp. 60–7.
123 A 1962 survey of European views about and knowledge of the workings of the European Communities underlined the high level of popular ignorance. ECHA. CEAB 2, No. 2174, 1962, 'L'Opinion Publique et l'Europe des Six.'
124 The clearest exposition of what Hallstein believed ought to have happened, and would he was certain still occur, is in Hallstein (1972).
125 See Chapter 2.
126 HAEC, Noel papers, EN 343, 'Note sur les conclusions du Conseil relatives aux rapports avec la Commission', 1 February, 1966.
127 The Commission attached great importance to the non-legally binding nature of the heptalogue. See Jaumin-Ponsar (1970) pp. 141–2.
128 Commission disappointment is explored further by Ludlow, in Loth (2001) pp. 254–6.
129 Even Lahr's otherwise bullish assessment acknowledged as much. *AAPD 1966*, document 25.
130 See Chapter 3.

131 See ECHA, speeches collection, Hallstein speech to the British Institute of International and Comparative Law, 25 March, 1965.

132 MAE. Série DE-CE 1961–66, Carton 402, Brunet note, No. 107/CE, 21 May, 1965.

133 Even the French acknowledged the Commission's contribution: MAE, Série DE-CE 1961–66, carton 432, 'Accord du 11 mai 1966', undated.

134 The most extensive exploration of the Commission's role in the Kennedy Round remains Coombes (1970) pp. 168–216.

135 For COREPER's emergence see Newhouse (1967) pp. 162–5; E. Noël and H. Etienne, 'The Permanent Representatives Committee and the "Deepening" of the Communities' in Ionescu (1972) pp. 98–123, and Lassalle (1968) pp. 397–401; on the Art. 111 committee see Coombes (1970) pp. 190–1.

136 Lindberg (1963).

137 Lemaignen (1964) pp. 85–8.

138 The Deringer Report of 5 October, 1962, document 74, *European Parliament Reports 1962–3*, pp. 36–8.

139 On information policy, see N.P. Ludlow, 'Frustrated Ambitions: The European Commission and Formation of a European Identity, 1958–1967', in Bitsch, Poidevin and Loth (1998) pp. 307–25.

140 Poidevin and Spierenburg (1993) esp. pp. 649–55 and Gillingham (1991) pp. 299ff.

141 See, e.g. Braun (1972) p. 1.

142 Jaumin-Ponsar's study (1970) both cites many examples of federalist disappointment, and is a typical specimen, esp. pp. 150–71.

5 The return of the English question

1 ANF, SGCI files, Versement 900638, Art. 25, Boegner to Quai, No. 780–91, 28 September, 1966.

2 *FRUS 1964–8*, volume XIII, pp. 412–13.

3 CMA, R/1528/66, Council minutes, 21–22 December, 1966.

4 Preeg (1970) p. 140.

5 CMA, R/1528/66, Council minutes, 21–22 December, 1966.

6 CMA, R/374/67, Council minutes, 7 March, 1967.

7 CMA, R/601/67, Council minutes, 10–12 April, 1967.

8 CMA, R/1528/66, Council minutes, 21–22 December, 1966 and R/178/67, Council minutes, 12 January, 1967.

9 CMA, R/601/67, Council minutes, 10–12 April, 1967.

10 *Ibid.*

11 See, for example ANF, SGCI files, Versement 900568, Art. 26, SGCI note, 'Les négociations multilatérales au GATT', 10 October, 1966.

12 See for instance *AAPD 1967*, document 394.

13 CMA. 467/67. Brandt speech, 10 April, 1967.

14 BAK, BKA, B-136, bd 8318, Aufzeichnung, 'Schwerpunkte der Arbeiten der EWG während der deutschen Präsidentschaft', 19 September, 1967.

15 *Le Monde*, 2 June, 1967.

16 E. Calandri, 'To Be or Not to Be: Bilateral Association and the External Role of the EEC 1958–1963', in Varsori (2005).

17 See CMA, R/601/67, Council minutes, 10–12 April, 1967.

18 BAK, BKA, B-136, bd. 8318, 'Institutionelle Fragen der Zusammenarbeit auf dem Gebiet der wissenschaftlichen Forschung und Technologie in den europäischen Gemeinschaften', 18 April, 1967. See also *AAPD 1967*, document 8.

19 CMA, R/1898/67, Council minutes, 16–17 October, 1967.

20 P. Gassert, 'Personalities and the Politics of European Integration: Kurt Georg Kiesinger and the Departure of Walter Hallstein, 1966/7', in Loth (2001) pp. 265–84. See also *AAPD 1966*, documents 116, 211, 230, 234, 405 and 411 and *AAPD 1967*, documents 15, 17 and 33.
21 *AAPD 1966*, document 323.
22 *AAPD 1966*, document 230.
23 Colombo was actually offered the job in May 1967 but turned it down. CMA, C/112/67, IGC minutes, 5 June, 1967.
24 Gassert, in Loth (2001) pp. 274–82.
25 See *AAPD 1966*, document 211 and *AAPD 1967*, document 33.
26 *AAPD 1967*, document 8.
27 Harmel did express some disquiet, but his desire to discuss political cooperation seems to have overridden such concerns. See *AAPD 1967*, document 62.
28 On the Rome summit see *AAPD 1967*, documents 194, 197 and 205. See also Nenni (1983) pp. 68–9.
29 *Le Monde*, 31 May, 1967.
30 ECHA, speeches collection, Hallstein's speech to the Organization of European Journalists, Brussels, 14 April, 1967.
31 *AAPD 1967*, document 170.
32 Cointat (2001) pp. 201–17.
33 Camps (1967) pp. 140–4 and 157–95. Camps speaks about a revival of British interest from 1965 onwards; it would take time, however, both for Labour's conversion to gather pace and for it to be detected amongst the Six.
34 Parr (2002). See also Daddow (2003) pp. 149–65.
35 Camps (1967) p. 189; on the Conservatives, see also P. Lynch, 'The Conservatives and the Wilson Application', in Daddow (2003) pp. 56–74.
36 *AAPD 1966*, document 37.
37 *AAPD 1966*, document 113.
38 Parr (2002) pp. 120–1.
39 The most famous had been de Broglie's statement to the WEU in March 1966.
40 Parr (2002) pp. 121–2.
41 *AAPD 1966*, document 158.
42 PRO. EW5/8, Roberts to FO, Tel. 960, 3 July, 1966 and *ibid.*, Tel. 987, 6 July, 1966.
43 *AAPD 1966*, document 180.
44 *AAPD 1966*, document 234.
45 *AAPD 1966*, document 37.
46 Cited in G. Bossuat, 'De Gaulle et la seconde candidature britannique aux Communautés européennes (1966–1969)', in Loth (2001) p. 513.
47 See also K. Böhmer, '"We Too Mean Business": Germany and the Second British Application to the EEC, 1966–67', in Daddow (2003) pp. 211–26.
48 Kiesinger (1979) pp. 22–3.
49 *AAPD 1966*, document 392.
50 *AAPD 1967*, document 363.
51 *AAPD 1966*, document 391; see also Seydoux (1977) pp. 81–3.
52 *AAPD 1966*, document 391 and 392.
53 For Italian–German disagreement on this, see Nenni (1983) pp. 10 and 114.
54 *AAPD 1967*, document 345.
55 Parr (2002) pp. 153–70.
56 For the meeting with de Gaulle, Parr (2002) pp. 192–206.
57 de Gaulle (1970) vol. 5, pp. 168–74.
58 *Ibid.*
59 *AAPD 1967*, document 197; ECHA, BDT 144/92, bte. 179, G(67)139, Rapport sur la 224ème session du Conseil (26–27 June, 1967).

60 See, e.g. ECHA, BDT 144/92, bte. 179, G(67) 116, Demande d'adhésion de la Grande-Bretagne. Note du Service Juridique, 26 May, 1967.

61 ECHA, BDT 144/92, bte. 179, G(67)139, Rapport sur la 224ème session du Conseil (26–27 June, 1967).

62 See ECHA, BDT 144/92, bte. 179, G(67)139, Rapport sur la 224ème session du Conseil (26–27 June, 1967); SEC(67) 3011, Sigrist note on the Coreper meeting, 10–11 July, 1967.

63 ECHA, BDT 144/92, bte. 179, G(67)139, Rapport sur la 224ème session du Conseil (26–27 June, 1967).

64 *Ibid.*

65 ECHA, BDT 38/84, bte. 341, SEC(67) 3108, Compte Rendu de la Réunion des Ministres de l'UEO, 4 July, 1967. On Heath, see Ludlow (1997) pp. 74–9.

66 CMA, I/4/67, Council minutes, 10–11 July, 1967.

67 *The Economist*, 5 August, 1961.

68 ECHA, BDT 38/84, bte. 341, SEC(67) 3108, Compte Rendu de la Réunion des Ministres de l'UEO, 4 July, 1967.

69 Lynch, in Daddow (2003) p. 68.

70 Ludlow (1997) p. 103.

71 *Ibid.*, p. 157.

72 *Ibid.*, esp. pp. 157–61 and 238–40.

73 See *AAPD 1967*, document 366.

74 N.P. Ludlow, 'A Short-Term Defeat: The Community Institutions and the Second British Application to Join the EEC' in Daddow (2003) pp. 137–8.

75 On Couve, see Spaak (1969) vol. 2, pp. 365–6.

76 On the background see L. Badel, 'Le Quai d'Orsay, la Grande-Bretagne et l'élargissement de la Communauté (1963–1969)', in Catala (2001) pp. 235–60.

77 ECHA, BDT 144/92, bte. 179, G(67)207, Compte rendu de la 2ème réunion du Conseil du 11 juillet 1967, 14 July, 1967.

78 CMA, I/4/67, Council minutes, 10–11 July, 1967.

79 For German caution, see *AAPD 1967*, documents 261 and 262; on why this happened, PRO, EW 5/8, Roberts to FO, Tel. 269, 9 February, 1967.

80 ECHA, BDT 144/92, bte. 179, G(67)207, Compte rendu de la 2ème réunion du Conseil du 11 juillet 1967, 14 July, 1967.

81 ECHA. COM(67)750, Avis de la Commission au Conseil concernant les demandes d'adhésion du Royaume-Uni, de l'Irlande, du Danemark et de la Norvège, 29 September, 1967.

82 PRO. FCO 30/103, Marjoribanks to FCO, Tel. 247, 30 September, 1967. British diplomats did acknowledge, however, that the rest of the report was very encouraging from their point of view.

83 *AAPD 1967*, document 335.

84 ECHA. COM(67) PV3, 2ème partie, 18 July, 1967.

85 ECHA. COM(67)750, Avis de la Commission, 29 September, 1967.

86 *Ibid*; see also J.W. Young, 'Technological Cooperation in Wilson's Strategy for EEC Entry' in Daddow (2003) pp. 95–114.

87 ECHA. COM(67) 750, Avis de la Commission, 29 September, 1967.

88 See Ludlow, in Daddow (2003) pp. 141–3.

89 Cited in Beloff (1963) p. 123; for details on the Commission in 1961–63, see Ludlow (1997) pp. 165–6 and 240–1.

90 See ECHA, BDT 144/92, bte. 179, G(67)201, Document de travail des services de la CEE sur l'élargissement de la Communauté, 7 July, 1967.

91 CMA, I/14/67, Council minutes, 23–24 October, 1967.

92 *AAPD 1967*, documents 364 and 373.

93 De Gaulle (1970) vol. 5, pp. 241–5.

94 *AAPD 1967*, documents 420 and 441. See also Brandt (1978) p. 59.

95　Cited in *Le Monde*, 21 December, 1967.
96　See, e.g. *AAPD 1967*, document 366.
97　See Chapter 3.
98　See Brandt (1978) p. 154.
99　CMA. I/17/67, Council minutes, 11–12 December, 1967.
100　*Ibid.*
101　*Ibid.*
102　ECHA, COM(67) PV 18, 2ème partie, 13 December, 1967.
103　ANF, SGCI files, Versement 900639, Art. 75, Brunet circulaire No. 314, 23 December, 1967; see also *AAPD 1967*, document 442.
104　CMA. I/17/67, Council minutes, 11–12 December, 1967.
105　ANF, SGCI files, Versement 900639, Art. 75, Brunet circulaire No. 314, 23 December, 1967.
106　*AAPD 1967*, document 449.

6　The impossibility of progress *à Six*

1　CMA. 07.151 Propositions concernant l'élargissement éventuel de la Communauté. Aide-Mémoire Benelux. Ministère des Affaires Etrangères press release, 19 January, 1968. See also *ibid.*, Aide-Mémoire presenté par la délégation italienne, 23 February, 1968.
2　*Ibid.* See also *AAPD 1968*, document 74.
3　CMA. 07.151 Propositions concernant l'élargissement éventuel de la Communauté. Texte intégral déclaration franco-allemande, 16 February, 1968. See also *AAPD 1968*, documents 59, 60 and 62.
4　CMA. I/5/68, Council minutes, 9 March, 1968.
5　*Ibid.*
6　*Ibid.*
7　CMA. I/7/68. Council minutes, 5 April, 1968; ECHA, COM(68)210, Avis de la Commission au Conseil concernant certains problèmes consécutifs aux demandes d'adhésion du Royaume-Uni, de l'Irlande, du Danemark et de la Norvège, 2 April, 1968.
8　CMA. I/5/68, Council minutes, 9 March, 1968.
9　*Ibid.*
10　*AAPD 1968*, document 72.
11　Pine (2004).
12　CMA. I/5/68, Council minutes, 9 March, 1968.
13　*Ibid.*
14　*Ibid.*
15　*AAPD 1968*, document 71.
16　*AAPD 1968*, document 68.
17　CMA. I/5/68, Council minutes, 9 March, 1968; see also *AAPD 1968*, document 68.
18　CMA. I/7/68, Council minutes, 5 April, 1968.
19　ECHA, COM(68)210, Avis de la Commission, 2 April, 1968.
20　*Ibid.*
21　CMA. I/7/68, Council minutes, 5 April, 1968.
22　See below.
23　CMA. I/12/68. Council minutes, 27 September, 1968.
24　*Ibid.*
25　*Ibid.*
26　*Ibid.*
27　*Ibid.*
28　*Ibid.*

29 *Ibid.*
30 CMA. I/13/68. Council minutes, 4–5 November, 1968.
31 CMA. R/2111/68, Council minutes, 4–5 November, 1968.
32 *Ibid.*
33 CMA. I/5/69. Council minutes, 27–28 January, 1969.
34 CMA. R/753/68. Council minutes, 9 April, 1968.
35 CMA. R/1025/68. Council minutes, 27–29 May, 1968.
36 CMA. I/12/68. Council minutes, 27 September, 1968.
37 ECHA. COM(69)250, Programme de travail des Communautés, 20 March, 1969.
38 See, e.g. CMA. Aide-mémoire presenté par la délégation italienne, 23 February, 1968.
39 *Deuxième Rapport Général sur l'activité des Communautés 1968*, Bruxelles: European Commission, 1969, pp. 15–16.
40 *Ibid.*, p. 16.
41 For the Commission's initial response to the crisis, dubbed the Barre Plan, see ECHA, COM(69)150, Mémorandum de la Commission au Conseil sur la coordination des politiques économiques et la coopération monétaire au sein de la Communauté, 12 February, 1969.
42 Seydoux (1977) pp. 108–9 and 134.
43 CMA. I/5/68, Council minutes, 9 March, 1968.
44 Bouwman (1993); Griffiths, R. 'The Schuman Plan' and 'The EEC', in Griffiths (1990) pp. 113–35 and 183–208; Kerstens, A. 'A Welcome Surprise? The Netherlands and the Schuman Plan Negotiations', in Schwabe (1988) pp. 285–304; van der Harst (1986).
45 *Nieuwe Rotterdamse Courant* cited in the *Guardian*, 2 August, 1961.
46 J. Molegraaf and R. Dingemans, 'The Netherlands and the Common Agricultural Policy, 1958–1963', in Milward and Deighton (1999) pp. 151–65; N.P. Ludlow, 'Too Close A Friend? The Netherlands and the First British Application to the EEC, 1961–3', in Ashton and Hellema (2001) pp. 223–39.
47 *AAPD 1968*, document 15.
48 Luns (1971) esp. pp. 139–86.
49 Vanke (2001) pp. 95–112; Harryvan and van der Harst, in Loth (2001) pp. 173–91.
50 See Chapter 1.
51 *AAPD 1968*, documents 15 and 306.
52 Spaak (1969) pp. 397–406; Dumoulin (1999) esp. pp. 635–7 and 651–4.
53 Ludlow (1997) pp. 44, 156–7 and 235–6.
54 See Chapter 3.
55 For Spaak's role in the original negotiations, see Dumoulin (1999) pp. 507–28.
56 HAEC, ENP, EN-343, Etienne note to Narjes, 12 January, 1966.
57 See, e.g. *DDF* 1964, vol. 2, document 171 and NLFM, 996.0 EEG, box 175, Luns to MBZ, 1 October, 1965.
58 CMA. 07.151 Propositions concernant l'élargissement éventuel de la Communauté. Aide-Mémoire Benelux. Ministère des Affaires Etrangères press release, 19 January, 1968.
59 *AAPD 1968*, document 336.
60 See Chapter 5.
61 *AAPD 1968*, document 362.
62 *AAPD 1969*, document 50.
63 *AAPD 1969*, documents 60, 61 and 65; Debré (1993) pp. 265 and 669; Dumoulin and Rémacle (1998) pp. 84–5.
64 A. Varsori, 'The Art of Mediation' in Deighton and Milward (1999) pp. 241–55; Ludlow (1997) pp. 45–6, 162–4 and 237–8.

65 *AAPD 1967*, document 15; Nenni (1983) p. 10.
66 CMA. I/17/67, Council minutes, 11–12 December, 1967. For the 1968 discussions, see above.
67 L. Nuti, 'Italy, the British Application and the January Débacle', in Griffiths and Ward (1996) pp. 112–13.
68 N.P. Ludlow, 'Constancy and Flirtation', in Noakes, Wende and Wright (2002) pp. 100–2.
69 PRO. EW 5/8. Roberts to FO, No. 95 Saving, 2 May, 1966.
70 For the context, Schwartz (2003); Zimmermann (2001).
71 A revealing cartoon from 1963 depicted Erhard and de Gaulle, with the German Chancellor smoking a cigar the smoke from which formed a cloud shaped like the British Isles hanging directly in front of the General's face. Jouve (1967) vol. 2, p. 843.
72 Marcowitz (1996) pp. 278–9.
73 See for example, *AAPD 1968*, document 352 and *AAPD 1969*, document 35.
74 BAK, BKA, B-136, bd. 14926, Exposé über das Procedere der Gesprächsaufnahme über die EWG-Beitrittsgesuche Großbritanniens, Irlands, Dänemarks und Norwegens zwischen der EWG und den Antragstellern, 27 November, 1967.
75 Author's calculation on the basis of OECD trade figures.
76 For an example of German industrial pressure on Bonn, see PRO, EW 5/8, Translation of a BDI report, 27 January, 1967.
77 *AAPD 1969*, documents 67 and 70.
78 See, e.g. CMA. I/12/68. Council minutes, 27 September, 1968.
79 For examples of the strain, see *AAPD 1968*, documents 71 and 144.
80 Ludlow (1997) pp. 154–5.
81 CMA, I/7/68, Council minutes, 5 April, 1968.
82 BAK. BKA, B-136, bd. 8318, Aufzeichnung Poensgens, 2 August, 1968.
83 See for instance Chapter 2.
84 For the context, see Bozo (1996).
85 Moravcsik (2000) esp. pp. 4–34.
86 Peyrefitte (1994–2000) pp. 266–74.
87 CMA, I/4/67, Council minutes, 10–11 July, 1967.
88 For an indication of how persistent this fear proved, see ANF, SGCI papers, Versement 900568, Art. 386, MAE note, No. 181/CE, Elargissement de la Communauté, 15 November, 1969.
89 This was a long-standing French concern: see ANF, SGCI papers, Versement 900638, Art. 24, unsigned note, 'Perspectives du marché commun', 11 February, 1963. But it had become all the more so since the autumn 1968 when a set of unilateral measures taken by Paris had been strongly condemned by the Commission: ECHA, COM(68) PV 52, 2ème partie, 16 October, 1968.
90 AN, Pompidou papers, 5AG2/1001, SGCI note, 'Réflexions sur l'évolution de l'Europe des Six', 27 September, 1966.
91 Peyrefitte (2000) vol. 3, p. 269.
92 See Couve de Murville (1971) pp. 347–84.
93 The Germans certainly believed that France had renewed its interest in political union. *AAPD 1969*, document 91.
94 Vaïsse (1993) pp. 231–2.
95 ANF. SGCI files. Versement 900639, Art. 73, SGCI note 'Les aspects économiques d'une éventuelle adhésion de la Grande Bretagne au Marché Commun', 2 November, 1967.
96 Badel, in Catala (2001) pp. 235–60.
97 Peyrefitte (2000) vol. 3, pp. 266–74.
98 The French suspicions were not entirely groundless: Pine (2004).
99 Debré (1993) vol. 4, p. 228.

100 ANF, SGCI files, Versement 900568, Art. 386, Note SGCI 'Programme relatif au renforcement des Communautés européennes', 28 February, 1969.
101 ANF, SGCI files, Versement 900638, Art. 4, Bernard to Couve de Murville, 14 April, 1969.
102 For Debré's awareness of this, see below.
103 For earlier French interest in monetary cooperation, see AN, Pompidou papers, 5AG2/1035, Pompidou note to de Gaulle, 26 December, 1967.
104 *AAPD 1968*, document 389.
105 Amouroux (1986) pp. 102–20.
106 *AAPD 1968*, document 396. See also Seydoux (1977) pp. 128–32.
107 ANF. SGCI files. Versement 900639, Art. 73, SGCI note 'Les aspects économiques d'une éventuelle adhésion de la Grande Bretagne au Marché Commun', 2 November, 1967.
108 For details see Pine (2005); Kitzinger (1973) pp. 45–58; Newhouse (1970) pp. 337–41; Bossuat, G. 'De Gaulle et la seconde candidature britannique aux Communautés européennes (1966–1969)', in Loth (2001) pp. 529–35.
109 See, e.g. Kiesinger's reaction: *AAPD 1969*, document 56.
110 Debré (1993) vol. 4, pp. 265–6.
111 Kitzinger (1973) pp. 50–5.
112 See *AAPD 1969*, document 77.

7 The road to The Hague

1 Roussel (1994) p. 282.
2 See for instance *AAPD 1969*, document 165.
3 *Le Monde*, 18 May, 1969.
4 Pine (2004).
5 *Le Monde*, 7 May, 1969.
6 *Le Monde*, 8 May, 1969.
7 J.R. Bernard, 'L'élargissement de la Communauté vue de Paris' in Association Georges Pompidou (1995) p. 238.
8 *Le Monde*, 3 May, 1969.
9 Cited in Fontaine (1981) p. 159.
10 M. Vaïsse, 'Changement et continuité dans la politique européenne de la France', in Association Georges Pompidou (1995) p. 34.
11 *Ibid.*
12 AN, Pompidou papers, 5AG2/1035, Pompidou note, 8 July, 1969.
13 AN, Pompidou papers, 5AG2/1010, Entretiens entre le Président de la République et M. Willy Brandt, Ministre des Affaires Etrangères de la RFA, 4 July, 1969.
14 *Ibid.* See also *AAPD 1969*, document 221.
15 AN, Pompidou papers, 5AG2/1010, Entretien en tête à tête entre le Chancelier Kiesinger et le Président Pompidou, 8 September, 1969.
16 *Ibid.* See also *AAPD 1969*, document 279.
17 AN, Pompidou papers, 5AG2/1010, Entretien en tête à tête entre le Chancelier Kiesinger et le Président Pompidou, 9 September, 1969. Curiously the German record of the meeting referred to *L'Arlésienne* as an opera by Bizet! Pompidou's underlying meaning had been fully understood, however. *AAPD 1969*, document 279.
18 Fontaine (1981) p. 159.
19 Badel in Catala (2001) pp. 251–4.
20 AN, Pompidou papers, 5AG2/1014, Compte rendu de l'audience accordée par le Président de la République à l'Ambassadeur d'Angleterre, 10 October, 1969.

21 ANF, SGCI files, Versement 900568, Art. 386, Brunet to major embassies, circulaire No. 474, 25 November, 1969.
22 See Chapters 5 and 6.
23 ANF, SGCI files, Versement 900568, Art. 387, SGCI note, 'Reflexions sur les problèmes européens (fond et procédure)', 13 November, 1969.
24 On former see Ludlow (1997) pp. 58–9; on the latter see Chapter 4.
25 For ongoing French dislike of undue Commission power, see ANF, SGCI files, Versement 900639, Art. 76, Bochet to Delfra, Tel. 124/26, 17 June, 1969.
26 See ANF, SGCI files, Versement 900568, Art. 386, unsigned note, 'Renforcement du Marché Commun', 10 July, 1969.
27 See Chapter 2.
28 ECHA, COM(69)700, Communication de la Commission au Conseil concernant le remplacement des contributions financières des Etats membres par des ressources propres et l'accroissement des pouvoirs budgétaires du Parlement européen, 16 July, 1969; see also ECHA, COM(69) PVs 83, 85 and 86, 2ème partie (24–25 June, 9–10 July and 15–16 July, 1969).
29 On the basis of French figures, of the US$800 million that was raised by agricultural levies, France contributed a mere 7.4 per cent, Italy 38.6 per cent. Given that French farmers also received much more by way of European subsidies than their Italian counterparts, the divergent attitudes of the two countries becomes none too surprising. ANF, SGCI files, Versement 900568, Art. 387, Bernard note, 'Note sur le financement du Marché Commun agricole', 4 July, 1969.
30 AN, Pompidou papers, 5AG2/1036, Raimond to Pompidou, 'Voyage à Rome de M. Schumann', 27 November, 1969.
31 ANF, SGCI files, Versement 900568, Art. 386, Burin des Roziers to Quai, Tel. 2119/33, 13 November, 1969; see also Galli and Torcasio (1976) p. 147.
32 ANF, SGCI files, Versement 900568, Art. 387, SGCI note, 'Règlement financier pour la période définitive du Marché Commun', 23 September, 1969.
33 PRO. FO371 177353; M1087/271, O'Neill to FO, Tel. 202, 17 December, 1964.
34 *AAPD 1969*, document 352.
35 AN, Pompidou papers, 5AG2/1010, Entretien entre le Président de la République et M. Willy Brandt, Ministre des Affaires Etrangères de la RFA, 4 July, 1969; see also *AAPD 1969*, document 221.
36 ANF, SGCI files, Versement 900568, Art. 386, Boegner to Quai, Tel. 1281/94, 11 November, 1969.
37 ANF, SGCI files, Versement 900568, Art. 386, Courcel to Quai, Tel. 4344/51, 20 November, 1969.
38 AN, Pompidou papers, 5AG2/1035, Gaucher to Lemerle, 14 September, 1969.
39 ANF, SGCI files, Versement 900568, Art. 386, Brunet to major embassies, circulaire No. 474, 25 November, 1969.
40 See Chapter 2.
41 CMA, R/2416/69, Council minutes, 11–12 August, 1969.
42 *Ibid.*
43 CMA, R/24240/69, Council minutes, 27 October, 1969.
44 ANF, SGCI files, Versement 900568, Art. 386, Seydoux to Quai, Tel. 5627/38, 4 November, 1969.
45 CMA, R/24240/69, Council minutes, 27 October, 1969.
46 CMA, R/1457/69, Council minutes, 17 July, 1969. For Barre's original proposal, ECHA, COM(69)150, Mémorandum de la Commission au Conseil sur la coordination des politiques économiques et la coopération monétaire au sein de la Communauté, 12 February, 1969.

47 I. Maes and E. Buyst, 'Triffin, the European Commission and the Project of a European Reserve Fund', in Dumoulin and Van Laer (2005).
48 CMA, I/13/69, Council minutes, 22–23 July, 1969.
49 ANF, SGCI files, Versement 900568, Art. 386, unsigned note, 'Renforcement du Marché Commun', 10 July, 1969.
50 Guasconi (2003) p. 107.
51 CMA, I/13/69, Council minutes, 22–23 July, 1969.
52 *AAPD 1969*, document 279; AN, Pompidou papers, 5AG2/1035, Note de M. de Lipkowski à la suite de son entretien avec le Président de la République, 6 January, 1970.
53 See *AAPD 1969*, document 279.
54 *AAPD 1969*, document 319.
55 PRO. FCO 30/560 96652; MWE 2/5, Marjoribanks to Stewart, European Communities Annual Review for 1968, 9 January, 1969.
56 For one such appeal see Chapter 6.
57 *AAPD 1969*, document 306.
58 The scale of the administrative upheaval can best be appreciated by scanning the innumerable meetings of the Commission in 1967 and 1968 devoted primarily to the bureaucratic reorganisation. For a good example: ECHA, COM(68) PV28, 2ème partie (6 March, 1968).
59 ECHA, COM(69)83, 2ème partie (24–25 June, 1969).
60 See Chapter 6.
61 European Commission (1969) p. 19.
62 Brandt (1978) p. 158.
63 *AAPD 1969*, document 358.
64 *Ibid.*
65 This time the proposals on Parliament's powers were submitted separately, however. See ECHA, COM(69) PVs 95 and 96, 2ème partie (21–22 and 26–30 October, 1969).
66 ANF, SGCI files, Versement 900568, Art. 387, Bernard 'Note pour le Premier Ministre', 7 August, 1969.
67 ANF, SGCI files, Versement 900568, Art. 387, SGCI note 'Proposition de la Commission concernant les pouvoirs budgétaires de l'assemblée parlementaire européenne', 20 November, 1969.
68 ANF, SGCI files, Versement 900568, Art. 386, Burin des Roziers to Quai, Tel. 2119/33, 13 November, 1969.
69 ANF, SGCI files, Versement 900568, Art. 387, SGCI note 'Proposition de la Commission concernant les pouvoirs budgétaires de l'assemblée parlementaire européenne', 20 November, 1969.
70 M.T. Bitsch, 'Le sommet de la Haye. La mise en route de la relance de 1969', in Loth (2001) pp. 540–2.
71 *AAPD 1969*, document 229.
72 *AAPD 1969*, document 194. See also Bitsch (2003) p. 541.
73 Roussel (1994) p. 335.
74 CMA, I/13/69, Council minutes, 22–23 July, 1969.
75 *Ibid.*
76 *Ibid.*
77 *Ibid.*
78 *AAPD 1969*, document 353.
79 *AAPD 1969*, document 294.
80 *AAPD 1969*, document 352.
81 AN, Pompidou papers, 5AG2/1035, Gaucher to Pompidou, 'Etat actuel des problèmes européens', 24 June, 1969.
82 Cited in Roussel (1994) p. 337. See also *AAPD 1969*, document 358.

83 ANF, SGCI files, Versement 900568, Art. 386, Boegner to Quai, Tel. 1281/94, 11 November, 1969.
84 AN, Pompidou papers, 5AG2/1014, Compte rendu de l'audience accordée par le Président de la République à l'Ambassadeur d'Angleterre, 10 October, 1969. See also *AAPD 1969*, document 352.
85 AN, Pompidou papers, 5AG2/1036, Gaucher to Pompidou, 29 August, 1969.
86 Bitsch (2003) pp. 547–8.
87 CMA, I/13/69, Council minutes, 22–3 July, 1969.
88 ANF, SGCI files, Versement 900568, Art. 386, Boegner to Quai, Tel. 1281/94, 11 November, 1969; for the Commission's reaction ECHA, COM(69) PV 98, 2ème partie (11–12 November, 1969).
89 AN, Pompidou papers, 5AG2/1010, Entretiens entre le Président de la République et M. Willy Brandt, Ministre des Affaires Etrangères de la RFA, 4 July, 1969.
90 Marcowitz (1996).
91 *AAPD 1969*, document 343.
92 Cited by Hiepel (2003) p. 72.
93 *Ibid.*
94 *AAPD 1969*, document 380.
95 AN, Pompidou papers, 5AG2/1036, Schumann note, 'Ouverture des négociations sur l'élargissement', 25 November, 1969.
96 Most of what follows is based upon two detailed records of the talks: AAA, Bestand 1, Band 334, Aufzeichnung 'Gipfelkonferenz in Den Haag am 1./2. Dezember 1969' (kindly supplied by Claudia Hiepel); ANF, SGCI files, Versement 900568, Art. 386, MAE note, No. 19, 6 December, 1969.
97 ANF, SGCI files, Versement 900568, Art. 386, MAE note, No. 19, 6 December, 1969.
98 AAA, Bestand 1, Band 334, Aufzeichnung 'Gipfelkonferenz in Den Haag am 1./2. Dezember 1969'.
99 *Le Monde*, 2 December, 1969.
100 AAA, Bestand 1, Band 334, Aufzeichnung 'Gipfelkonferenz in Den Haag am 1./2. Dezember 1969'.
101 *Ibid.*
102 Cited in A. Kersten, 'Das europäische Gipfeltreffen in Den Haag 1969', in Wielenga (1997) p. 47.
103 Harryvan and van der Harst (2003) p. 38.
104 ANF, SGCI files, Versement 900568, Art. 386, MAE note, No. 19, 6 December, 1969.
105 *Ibid.*
106 ANF, SGCI files, Versement 900568, Art. 386, Unsigned and undated note 'Commentaires succincts sur le communiqué de la Conférence au Sommet'.
107 See Salmon and Nicoll (1997) pp. 105–7.
108 See Chapters 5 and 6.
109 *Le Monde*, 4 December, 1969.
110 Ludlow (1997) pp. 249–50.
111 See esp. paragraphs 3 and 4.
112 *Débats du Parlement européen. Session 1969–70*. Séance du jeudi 11 décembre, 1969, pp. 167–8; for the Commission and Parliamentary calls for greater institutional ambition see European Commission (1970) pp. 516–20.
113 Brandt, De Jong and Rumor had all spoken of the need to improve the workings of the Council.
114 Rumor, Brandt, Eyskens, De Jong and Werner all stressed the need for an increase in the European Parliament's powers. AAA, Bestand 1, Band 334, Aufzeichnung 'Gipfelkonferenz in Den Haag am 1./2. Dezember 1969'.

115 CMA, I/13/69, Council minutes, 22–23 July, 1969.
116 AAA, Bestand 1, Band 334, Aufzeichnung 'Gipfelkonferenz in Den Haag am 1./2. Dezember 1969'.
117 *Ibid.*

Conclusions

1 See Vaïsse (1998) and Institut Charles de Gaulle (1992) vol. 5. Rather more critical are Roussel (2002); Loth and Picht (1991); and Lucas (1992).
2 See Jouve (1967). Amongst the more personal accounts see Maillard (1990); Pisani (1974); Kusterer (2001) and Burin des Roziers (1986).
3 Most crucially de Gaulle (1970).
4 Peyrefitte (1994–2000).
5 See Chapters 2, 4 and 7.
6 For evidence that they were tempted to do so, see Chapter 3.
7 See Chapter 1 for the former. For the latter ECHA, BDT 214/1980, multiple reports, e.g. S/01633/64, Sigrist note on COREPER meeting of 4 June, 1964.
8 See Chapters 2, 3 and 5.
9 Pisani (1974) p. 64.
10 See Chapter 3.
11 Couve's attempts to pose as the defender of the Community against the danger of being swamped by enlargement would be a case in point. For his unsuccessful 1967 attempts to do this see Chapter 5; for the more successful use of the same tactics in 1961–63, see Ludlow (1997) esp. pp. 158–60.
12 See Chapters 1 and 2.
13 See Chapter 4.
14 Bozo (1996).
15 See Chapter 6.
16 See Chapter 3.
17 Such claims were to reach their apogee during the 1965 election campaign: see Chapter 3.
18 See Chapter 2.
19 See, for example, *DDF 1963*, vol. 1, document 207 and *DDF 1965*, vol. 1, document 275.
20 See Chapter 2.
21 *Ibid.*
22 *Ibid.*
23 *Ibid.*
24 See Chapter 3.
25 See Chapter 4.
26 See Chapter 6.
27 See Chapter 7.
28 See Koerfer (1987); Marcowitz (1996); and Nuti (1999).
29 See Milward (1992) p. 223.
30 *AAPD 1964*, document 307.
31 See Chapters 1, 4 and 6.
32 See Chapter 2.
33 See Chapter 2. For an earlier example, see PRO, PREM 11 4524, Ward to FO, Tel. 148, 14 February, 1963.
34 Hallstein (1972) pp. 68–9.
35 See Chapter 6.
36 For the rapid disappearance of this policy in 1963, see Chapter 1.
37 See Chapter 6.
38 See Chapter 7.

39 Poidevin and Spierenburg (1993) pp. 44–52.
40 See Chapter 2. See also Laschi (2000) pp. 269ff.
41 See Chapters 1 and 2.
42 See Chapters 2 and 3.
43 The internal German debate about the CAP both before and after the crisis would be a case in point: see Chapters 2 and 4.
44 See Chapter 2.
45 See Chapters 4 and 5.
46 See Chapter 6.
47 *Ibid.*
48 See Chapter 1.
49 See Chapter 2.
50 See Chapter 4.
51 Bange (2000) pp. 151–5; Holscher, in Blasius (1994) pp. 9–44; and Ludlow (1997) pp. 200–30.
52 See Chapters 3 and 4.
53 See Chapter 5.
54 *Ibid.*
55 See Chapter 1.
56 Ludlow, 'A Short-Term Defeat', in Daddow (2003) pp. 141–3.
57 See ECHA speeches collection, Hallstein speech to the British Institute of International and Comparative Law, 25 March, 1965.
58 CMA, R/964/64, Council minutes, 12–13 October, 1964; CMA, R/850/65, Council minutes, 28 June–1 July, 1965.
59 ECHA, COM(69) 250, Programme de travail des Communautés, 20 March, 1969; CMA, R/505/69, Council minutes, 25–26 March, 1969.
60 *Troisième Rapport Général sur l'activité des Communautés 1969*, pp. 518–20. See also Ludlow (2003) pp. 11–25.
61 See Chapter 7.
62 Milward (1992).
63 R. Poidevin, 'Le facteur Europe dans la politique allemande de Robert Schuman (été 1948 – printemps 1949)', in Poidevin (1986) pp. 311–26.
64 Schaad (2000) pp. 102–6.
65 See Chapter 1.
66 See Chapter 2.
67 See Chapters 3 and 4.
68 See Chapters 5, 6 and 7.
69 PRO. EW 5/8. Roberts to FO, No. 95 Saving, 2 May, 1966.
70 Granieri (2003) pp. 191–227.
71 See above.
72 See Chapters 1, 2, 3 and 6.
73 Moravscik (1998); Mahant (2004); and Giauque (2002).
74 Schlochauer, in von Caemmerer (1966); Weiler (1991) pp. 2410–31; J. Gerkrath, 'La Cour de Justice des Communautés européennes, la constitution-nalisation du traité de Rome et son impact sur l'émergence d'une identité européenne', in Bitsch, Poidevin and Loth (1988) pp. 451–74.
75 For examples, see Loth (2001).
76 See Chapter 2.
77 See Chapter 7.
78 For the former, see Chapter 2.
79 For my earlier, incorrect belief that the idea had died in 1962–63, see Ludlow (1997) pp. 229–30.
80 Débats du Parlement européen. Session 1969–70. Séance du jeudi 11 décembre, 1969, p. 167.

81 See, e.g. *AAPD 1967*, document 241.
82 Milward (1992) p. *xi* arguably started this trend. Moravcsik (1998) took matters several steps further.
83 Hallstein was perhaps the single most articulate leader of this group, but others were scattered throughout the Community institutions, national Parliaments, and, occasionally, national governments.
84 See Kiesinger (1969) pp. 187–201.

Bibliography

Archival sources

Community archives

Council of Ministers Archive, Brussels

Council minutes 1963–69.
Dossiers on the empty chair crisis, enlargement and the Hague Council.

Commission Archives, Brussels

Commission minutes 1963–69.
Commission reports on COREPER meetings, 1963–69.
Marjolin *cabinet* papers.
Mansholt *cabinet* papers.
Commission de contrôle budgetary reports.
Speeches collection.
Annual activity reports 1963–69.

European Community archives, Florence

Emile Noël papers.
Olivier Wormser papers.
Oral History collection of interviews. Online.
    Available HTTP: <http://www.arc.iue.it/oh/OralHistory.html>.

French archives

Ministère des Affaires Etrangères, Paris

Série Europe 1961–66.
Série DE-CE 1961–66.

Archives Nationales, Paris

Georges Pompidou papers.

Archives Nationales Contemporaines, Fontainebleau

SGCI files 1963–69.

Archives de la Fondation Nationales des Sciences Politiques, Sciences Po, Paris

Maurice Couve de Murville papers.

German archives

Auswärtiges Amt, formerly Bonn, now Berlin

Ministerbüro files, 1963–66.
Referat IA2,1963–65.
Referat IA3, 1964–65.

Bundesarchiv, Koblenz

Bundeskanzleramt files, 1963–69.
Karl Carstens papers.

Dutch archives

Ministerie van Buitenlandse Zaken, Den Haag

Archief EG, 1965–74.

Italian archives

Archivio Centrale dello Stato, Rome

Ministero del Bilancio e della Programmazione Economica files.

British archives

Public Record Office (now National Archives), London

Foreign Office files (mainly FO371 and FCO30).
Prime Minister's files (PREM 13).
DEA files (EW 5/8).

Published documents and statistics

Akten zur Auswärtigen Politik des Bundesrepublik Deutschland, multiple volumes, 1963–69, Munich: R. Oldenbourg Verlag.

Documents diplomatiques français, multiple volumes, 1963–65, Paris: Imprimerie Nationale/Brussels: Presses Interuniversitaires.

Foreign Relations of the United States, 1961–63, vol. XIII, and 1964–68, vols VIII, XII, and XIII, Washington: Government Printing Office.

Débats du parlement européen, 1963–69, Luxembourg: European Communities.

OECD (1961–70) *Statistical Bulletins, Series C: Trade by Commodities*, Paris: OECD.

OEEC/OECD (1958–70) *Foreign Trade Statistical Bulletins, Series A: By Countries*, Paris: OEEC/OECD.

Salmon, T. and Nicoll, W. (1997) *Building European Union: A Documentary History and Analysis*, Manchester: Manchester University Press.

Memoirs

Adenauer, K. (1992) *Teegespräche 1961–1963*, Berlin: Siedler Verlag.

Alphand, H. (1977) *L'étonnement d'être : journal, 1939–1973*, Paris: Fayard.

Blankenhorn, H. (1980) *Verständnis und Verständigung: Blätter eines politischen Tagebuchs 1949 bis 1979*, Frankfurt: Verlag Ullstein.

Brandt, W. (1978) *People and Politics: The Years 1960–1975*, London: Collins.

Carstens, K. (1993) *Erinnerungen und Erfahrungen*, Boppard: Harald Boldt Verlag.

Cointat, Michel. (2001) *Les couloirs de l'Europe*, Paris: L'Harmattan.

Couve de Murville, M. (1971) *Une politique etrangère 1958–1969*, Paris: Plon.

de Gaulle, C. (1970) *Mémoires d'espoir*, vols I–II, Paris: Plon.

de Gaulle, C. (1980–86) *Lettres, notes et carnets*, vols IX–XII, Paris: Plon.

de Gaulle, C. (1970) *Discours et messages*, vols IV–V, Paris: Plon.

Debré, M. (1988–93) *Trois républiques pour une France*, vols 2–4, Paris: Albin Michel.

von der Groeben, H. (1984) *Combat pour l'Europe; la construction de la communauté européenne de 1958 à 1966*, Brussels: CECA-CEE-CEEA, p. 110.

Hallstein, W. (1972) *Europe in the Making*, New York: Norton.

Harmel, P. (1993) *Temps forts: entretiens avec Jean-Claude Ricquier*, Brussels: Editions Racine.

Kiesinger, K.-G. (1969) *Stationen, 1949–1969*, Tübingen: Rainer Wunderlich Verlag.

Kiesinger, K.-G. (1979) *Die Grosse Koalition 1966–1969*, Stuttgart: Deutsche Verlags-Anstalt.

Kusterer, H. (2001) *Le général et le chancelier*, Paris: Economica.

Lahr, R. (1981) *Zeuge von Fall und Aufstieg. Private Briefe 1934–1974*, Hamburg: Albrecht Knaus.

Lemaignen, R. (1964) *L'Europe au berceau: souvenirs d'un technocrate*, Paris: Plon.

Luns, J. (1971) *'Ik herinner Mij . . .'*, Leiden: A.W. Sijthoff.

Maillard, P. (1990) *De Gaulle et l'Allemagne: le Rêve Inachevé*, Paris: Plon.

Mansholt, S. (1974) *La crise: Conversations avec Janine Delaunay*, Paris: Editions Stock.

Marjolin, R. (1986) *Le travail d'une vie: mémoires 1911–1986*, Paris: Robert Laffond.

Marjolin, R. (1989) *Memoirs 1911–1986*, London: Weidenfeld & Nicholson.

Monnet, J. (1976) *Mémoires*, Paris: Fayard.

Müller-Armack, A. (1971) *Auf dem Weg nach Europa: Erinnerungen und Ausblicke*, Stuttgart: Rainer Wunderlich Verlag.

Nenni, P. (1983) *I Conti Con La Storia: Diari 1967–1971*, Milan: SugarCo Edizioni.

Ortona, E. (1998) *Gli Anni della Farnesina:Pagine del Diario 1961–1967*, Rome: SPAI.

Osterheld, H. (1986) *'Ich gehe nicht leichten Herzens–": Adenauers letzte Kanzlerjahre: ein dokumentarischer Bericht*, Mainz: Grünewald.

Osterheld, H. (1992) *Außenpolitik unter Bundeskanzler Ludwig Erhard, 1963–1966: ein dokumentarischer Bericht aus dem Kanzleramt*, Düsseldorf: Droste.

Peyrefitte, A. (1994–2000) *C'était de Gaulle*, vols 1–3, Paris: Fayard.

Pisani, E. (1974) *Le général indivis*, Paris: Albin Michel.

Rothschild, R. (1997) *Un Phénix nommé Europe: Mémoires 1945–1995*, Brussels: Editions Racine.

Seydoux, F. (1977) *Dans l'Intimité Franco-Allemande: une mission diplomatique*, Paris: Editions Albatros.

Snoy et d'Oppuers, J.-C. (1989) *Rebâtir l'Europe*, Paris: Duculot.

Spaak, P.-H. (1969) *Combats inachevés. De l'espoir aux déceptions*, vol. 2, Paris: Fayard.

Werner, P. (1991) *Itinéraires luxembourgeois et européens: Evolutions et Souvenirs 1945–1985*, vol. 2, Luxembourg: Editions Saint-Paul.

Books, articles and theses

40 ans des Traités de Rome ou la capacité des Traités d'assurer les avancées de la construction européenne, Brussels: Bruylant, 1999.

Le rôle des ministères des finances et de l'économie dans la construction européenne (1957–1978), Paris: Comité pour l'histoire économique et financière de la France, 2002.

Amouroux, H. (1986) *Monsieur Barre*, Paris: Robert Laffond.

Ashton, N. (2002) *Kennedy, Macmillan and the Cold War: The Irony of Interdependence*, London: Palgrave.

Ashton, N. and Hellema, D. (2001) *Unspoken Allies: Anglo-Dutch Relations Since 1780*, Amsterdam: Amsterdam University Press.

Association Georges Pompidou (1995) *Georges Pompidou et l'Europe*, Brussels: Editions Complexe.

Badel, L. (2002) 'Deux administrations françaises face à la construction européenne', *Matériaux pour l'histoire de notre temps*, 65–66: 13–17.

Bagnato, B. (1995) *Storia di un'illusione europea: Il progetto di Unione Doganale italo-francese*, London: Lothian Foundation Press.

Bange, O. (1997) 'Picking up the pieces: Schröder's working programme for the European Communities and the solution of the 1963 crisis', unpublished Ph.D. thesis, University of London.

Bange, O. (2000) *The EEC Crisis of 1963: Kennedy, Macmillan, de Gaulle and Adenauer in Conflict*, London: Macmillan.

Barman, T. (1963) 'Behind the Brussels breakdown', *International Affairs*, 39(3):360–71.

Becker, J. and Knipping, F. (1986) *Power in Europe: Britain, France, Italy and Germany in a Postwar World 1945–1950*, Berlin: Walter de Gruyter.

Beloff, N. (1963) *The General Says No*, London: Penguin.

Berstein, S. (1995) *La France de l'expansion*, vols 1–2, Paris: Editions du Seuil.

Bette, A. (1967) 'Euratom: difficultés transitoires?', *Revue du Marché Commun*, 98:19–23.

Bitsch, M.-T. (1996) *Histoire de la construction européenne*, Brussels: Complexe.

Bitsch, M.-T. (2001) *Le couple France-Allemagne et les institutions européennes*, Brussels: Bruylant.

Bitsch, M.-T. (2003) 'Le sommet de La Haye. L'initiative française, ses finalités et ses limites', *Journal of European Integration History*, 9(2):83–99.

Bitsch, M.-T., Poidevin, R. and Loth, W. (1998) *Institutions européennes et identités européennes*, Bruxelles: Bruylant.

Blasius, R.A. (1994) *Von Adenauer zu Erhard: Studien zur Auswärtigen Politik der Bundesrepublik Deutschland 1963*, Munich: R. Oldenbourg Verlag.

Bloes, R. (1970) *Le 'Plan Fouchet' et le problème de l'Europe politique*, Bruges: College of Europe.

Boegner, J.-M. (1992) '1958, le général de Gaulle et l'acceptation du traité de Rome', *Espoir*, 87:28–36.

Bossuat, G. (1996) *L'Europe des français*, Paris: Publications de la Sorbonne.

Bourrinet, J. (1964) *Le problème agricole dans l'intégration européenne*, Montpellier: Editions CUJAS.

Bouwman, B. (1993) 'The British dimension of Dutch European policy (1950–1963)', unpublished D.Phil. thesis, University of Oxford.

Bozo, F. (1996) *Deux stratégies pour l'Europe: De Gaulle, les Etats-Unis et l'Alliance Atlantique 1958–1969*, Paris: Plon.

Braun, N.C. (1972) *Commissaires et Juges dans les Communautés Européennes*, Paris: R. Pichon et Durand-Auzias.

Braun (Condorelli), N. (1967) 'L'opinion allemande et le Marché commun, a travers les débats du Bundestag', *Revue du Marché Commun*, 108:596–613.

Braun (Condorelli), N. (1968) 'Les débats sur l'Europe au parlement français', *Revue du Marché Commun*, 111:645–52.

Braun (Condorelli), N. (1968) 'La politique européenne de l'Italie vue a travers les débats parlementaires', *Revue du Marché Commun*, 116:899–909.

Brugmans, H. (1967) 'Les prolongement européens de l'administration moderne', *Revue du Marché Commun*, 103:336–43.

Burgess, M. (2000) *Federalism and the European Union: the Building of Europe, 1950–2000*, London: Routledge.

Burin des Roziers, E. (1986) *Retour au sources, 1962, l'année decisive*, Paris: Plon.

Caemmerer, E. (1966) *Probleme des europäischen Rechts: Festschrift für Walter Hallstein zu seinem 65 Geburtstag*, Frankfurt: Klostermann.

Calandri, E. 'Italia e communita europea 1963–1965', unpublished paper.

Camps, M. (1964) *Britain and the European Community 1955–1963*, Princeton: Princeton University Press.

Camps, M. (1967) *European Unification in the Sixties: From the Veto to the Crisis*, Oxford: Oxford University Press.

Catala, M. (2001) *Histoire de la construction européenne: cinquante ans après la déclaration Schuman*, Nantes: Ouest Editions.

Cerny, P. (1980) *The Politics of Grandeur*, Cambridge: Cambridge University Press.

Charlton, M. (1983) *The Price of Victory*, London: BBC.

Chiarini, R. (1992) 'La fortuna del gollismo in Italia: l'attacco della destra alla "Repubblica dei partiti"', *Storia Contemporanea*, 23(3):385–424.

Connelley, M. (2002) *A Diplomatic Revolution: Algeria's Fight for Independence and the Origins of the Post-Cold War Era*, New York: Oxford University Press.

Coombes, D. (1970) *Politics and Bureaucracy in the European Community: A Portrait of the Commission of the EEC*, London: George Allen & Unwin.

Conze, E. (1995) *Die gaullistische Herausforderung: die deutsch-französischen Beziehungen in der amerikanischen europapolitik, 1958–1963*, Munich: Oldenbourg.

Curli, B. (2001) 'Questioni monetarie e costruzione europea, (1955–1962)', *Europa Europe*, 10(1):94–119.

Daddow, O. (2003) *Harold Wilson and European Integration: Britain's Second Application to Join the EEC*, London: Frank Cass.

Dassetto, F. and Dumoulin, M. (1993) *Naissance et développement de l'information européenne*, Brussels: Peter Lang.

Decup, S.M. (1998) *France–Angleterre: les relations militaires de 1945 à 1962*, Paris: Economica.

Dehousse, J.-M. (1965) *La fusion des communautés*, The Hague: Martinus Nijhoff.

Dehousse, J.-M. (1967) *La fusion des communautés européennes au lendemain des accords de Luxembourg*, The Hague: Martinus Nijhoff.

Deighton, A. (1995) *Building Postwar Europe: National Decision-Makers and European Institutions, 1948–1963*, London: Macmillan.

Deighton, A. and Milward, A. (1999) *Widening, Deepening and Acceleration: the European Economic Community 1957–1963*, Baden-Baden: Nomos.

Delorme, H. and Tavernier, Y. (1969) *Les paysans français et l'Europe*, Paris: Armand Colin.

Diallo, T. (1992) *La politique étrangère de Georges Pompidou*, Paris: Librairie générale de droit et de jurisprudence.

Dimier, V. (2001) 'Leadership et institutionalisation au sein de la Commission Européenne : le cas de la Direction Générale Développement, 1958–1975', *Sciences de la Société*, 53.

Dimier, V. (2003) 'L'institutionnalisation de la Commission européenne (DG Developpement): du rôle des leaders dans la construction d'une administration multinationale 1958–1975', *Revue études internationales*, 34(3):401–27.

Donat, M. (1975) *Brüsseler Machenschaften: dem Euro-Clan auf der Spur*, Baden-Baden: Nomos.

Ducci, R. and Olivi, B. (1970) *L'Europa incompiuta*, Padova: Cedam.

Duchêne, F. (1994) *Jean Monnet: The First Statesmen of Interdependence*, New York: Norton.

Dumoulin, M. (1999) *Spaak*, Brussels: Editions Racine.

Dumoulin, M. and Van Laer, A. (2005) *Les réseaux économiques dans les processus de construction européenne*, Brussels: Peter Lang.

Dumoulin, A. and Rémacle, E. (1998) *L'Union de l'Europe occidentale: phénix de la défense européenne*, Brussels: Bruylant.

Eckes, A. (2000) *Revisiting US Trade Policy: Decisions in Perspective*, Athens: Ohio University Press.

European Commission (1969) *Deuxième Rapport Général sur l'Activité des Communautés 1968*, Brussels: EEC.

European Commission (1970) *Troisième Rapport Général sur l'Activité des Communautés 1969*, Brussels: EEC.

Fontaine, A. (1981) *Un seul lit pour deux rêves: histoire de la "détente"*, Paris: Fayard.

Freisberg, E. (1965) *Die Grüne Hürde Europas. Deutsche Agrarpolitik und EWG*, Cologne: Westdeutscher.

Galli, R. and Torcasio, S. (1976) *La partecipazione italiana alla politica agricola comunitaria*, Rome: Istituto d'affari internazionali.

Gerbet, P. (1983) *La construction de l'Europe*, Paris: Imprimerie Nationale.

Gerbet, P. (1995) *La France et l'intégration européenne: essai d'historiographie*, Berne: Peter Lang.

Gerbet, P. and Pepy, D. (1969) *La décision dans les communautés européennes*, Brussels: Presses Universitaires de Bruxelles.

Giauque, J. (2002) *Grand Designs and Visions of Unity: The Atlantic Powers and the Reorganisation of Western Europe, 1955–63*, Chapel Hill: University of Virginia Press.

Gillingham, J. (1991) *Coal, Steel and the Rebirth of Europe, 1945–55: The Germans and French from Ruhr Conflict to Economic Community*, Cambridge: Cambridge University Press.

Gillingham, J. (2003) *European Integration 1950–2003: Superstate or New Market Economy?* Cambridge: Cambridge University Press.

Ginsborg, P. (1990) *A History of Contemporary Italy 1943–1988*, London: Penguin.

Golub, J. (1999) 'In the shadow of the vote? Decision-making in the European Community', *International Organization*, 53:733–64.

Granieri, R. (2003) *The Ambivalent Alliance: Konrad Adenauer, the CDU/CSU, and the West, 1949–1969*, Oxford: Berghahn.

Gray, W. (2003) *Germany's Cold War: the Global Campaign to Isolate East Germany, 1949–1969*, Chapel Hill: University of North Carolina Press.

Griffiths, R. (1990) *The Netherlands and the Integration of Europe 1945–57*, Amsterdam: NEHA.

Griffiths, R. (1997) *Explorations in OEEC History*, Paris: OECD.

Griffiths, R. and Ward, S. (1996) *Courting the Common Market: The First Attempt to Enlarge the EC 1961–1963*, London: Lothian Foundation Press.

Grosser, A. (1963) 'General de Gaulle and the foreign policy of the V Republic', *International Affairs*, 39(2):198–213.

Guasconi, M.E. (2003) 'Italy and the Hague conference of 1969', *Journal of European Integration History*, 9(1):101–16.

Guasconi, M.E. (2004) *L'Europa tra continuità e cambiamento: Il vertice dell'Aja del 1969 e il rilancio della costruzione europea*, Florence: Edizioni Polistampa.

Guderzo, M. (2000) *Interesse nazionale e responsabilità globale: Gli Stati Uniti, l'Alleanza Atlantica e l'integrazione europea 1963–9*, Florence: AIDA.

Haas, E.B. (1958) *The Uniting of Europe: Political, Social and Economic Forces, 1950–1957*, Stanford: Stanford University Press.

Haftendorn, H. (1996) *NATO and the Nuclear Revolution: A Crisis of Credibility, 1966–1967*, Oxford: Clarendon Press.

Harryvan, A. and van der Harst, J. (2003) 'Swan song or cock crow? The Nether-lands and the Hague summit conference of December 1969', *Journal of Euro-pean Integration History*, 9(1):27–40.

van der Harst, J. (1986) 'The Netherlands and the EDC', European University Institute working paper 86/252.

Heathcote, N. (1966) 'The Crisis of European Supranationality', *Journal of Common Market Studies*, 5(2):140–71.

Hellmann, R. (1966) 'Schlussakt einer Krise? Die europäischen Institutionen nach Luxemburg', *Europa Archiv*, 7:259–68.

Hentschel, V. (1998) *Ludwig Erhard: Ein Politikerleben*, Berlin: Ullstein.

Herbst, L. (1989) *Option für den Westen: vom Marshallplan bis zum deutsch-französischen Vertrag*, Munich: Deutscher Taschenbuch Verlag.

Heuser, B. (1998) *NATO, Britain, France and the FRG: Nuclear Strategies and Forces for Europe, 1949–2000*, London: Macmillan.

Heyen, E.V. (1992) *Die Anfänge der Verwaltung der Europäischen Gemeinschaft*, Baden-Baden: Nomos.

Hiepel, C. (2003) 'In search of the greatest common denominator: Germany and the Hague summit conference 1969', *Journal of European Integration History*, 9(2):63–81.

Hoffman, S. (1963) 'Discord in the community: the North Atlantic area as a partial international system', *International Organization*, 17:521–49.

Hoffman, S. (1966) 'Obstinate or obsolete? The fate of the Nation-State and the case of western Europe', *Daedelus*, 95(3):862–915.

Hofmann, A. (2003) 'Kennedy, Brandt and the origins of Ostpolitik', unpublished Ph.D. thesis, University of London.

Horne, A. (1988) *Macmillan*, vols 1–2, London: Macmillan.

Houben, P. (1984) *Les conseils de ministres des Communautés européennes*, Leiden: A.W. Sijthoff.

Hrbek, R. (1998) *40 Jahre Römische Verträge: der deutsche Beitrag*, Baden-Baden: Nomos.

Institut Charles de Gaulle (1992) *De Gaulle en son siècle*, vols 4 and 5, Paris: Plon.

Ionescu, G. (1972) *The New Politics of European Integration*, London: Macmillan.

Istituto d'Affari Esteri (1966a) 'The EEC after Luxembourg', *Lo Spettatore Inter-nazionale*, 1(2):30–42.

Istituto d'Affari Esteri (1966b) 'Britain and the Common Market: narrowing the gap', *Lo Spettatore Internazionale*, 1(4):18–34.

Jaumin-Ponsar, A. (1970) *Essai d'interprétation d'une crise*, Brussels: Bruylant.

Jouve, E. (1967) *Le Général de Gaulle et la construction de l'Europe (1940–1966)*, Paris: R. Pichon et R. Durand-Auzias.

Keeler, J.T.S. (1987) *The Politics of Neocorporatism in France: Farmers, The State, and Agricultural Policy-making in the Fifth Republic*, Oxford: Oxford University Press.

Kirt, R. (2001) *Die Europäische Union und ihre Krisen*, Baden-Baden: Nomos.

Kitzinger, U. (1968) *The Second Try: Labour and the EEC*, Oxford: Pergamon.

Kitzinger, U. (1973) *Diplomacy and Persuasion: How Britain Joined the Common Market*, London: Thames & Hudson.

Kleiman, R. (1965) *Atlantic Crisis: American Diplomacy Confronts a Resurgent Europe*, London: Sidgewick & Jackson.

Knudsen, A.-C. (2001) 'Defining the policies of the Common Agricultural Policy. A historical study', unpublished Ph.D. thesis, European University Institute, Florence.

Kobbert, E. (1966) 'Eine stille "Revision" der EWG: Hat der Luxemburger Kompromiß die Gemeinschaft verwandelt?', *Europa-Archiv*, 4:119–22.

Koerfer, D. (1987) *Kampf ums Kanzleramt: Erhard und Adenauer*, Stuttgart: Deutsche Verlags-Anstalt.

Kolodziej, E. (1974) *French International Policy under de Gaulle and Pompidou*, New York: Cornell.

de La Serre, F. (1970) 'La Communauté économique européenne et la crise de 1965', *Revue française de sciences politiques*, 20:402–20.

Lacouture, J. (1985) *De Gaulle*, vols 2–3, Paris: Editions du Seuil.

Lahr, R. (1983) 'Die Legende vom "Luxemburger Kompromiß"', *Europa Archiv*, 38(8):223–32.

Lambert, J. (1966) 'The Constitutional Crisis of 1965–66', *Journal of Common Market Studies*, 4:195–228.

Lappenküper, U. (1991) '"Ich bin wirklich ein guter Europäer" Ludwig Erhards Europapolitik 1949–1966', *Francia*, 18(3):85–120.

Lappenküper, U. (2001) *Die deutsch-französischen Beziehungen 1945–1963*, vols 1 and 2, Munich: Oldenbourg Verlag.

Laschi, G. (2000) *L'agricoltura italiana e l'integrazione europea*, Berlin: Peter Lang.

Lassalle, C. (1968) 'Les comités et l'evolution institutionelle de la CEE', *Cahiers de Droit Européen*, 4:395–419.

Laursen, J. (2002) 'Towards a supranational history? Introduction', *Journal of European Integration History*, 8(1):5–10.

Leçerf, J. (1975) *Communauté en péril. Histoire de l'unité européenne 2*, Paris: Gallimard.

L'Ecotais, Y. (1976) *L'Europe sabotée*, Brussels: Rossel Edition.

Lee, D. (1999) *Middle Powers and Commercial Diplomacy: British Influence at the Kennedy Trade Round*, London: Macmillan.

Lee, D. (2001) 'Endgame at the Kennedy round: a case study of multilateral economic diplomacy', *Diplomacy and Statecraft*, 12(3):115–38.

Lemaitre, P. (1968a) 'La Communauté face à sa première crise économique', *Revue du Marché Commun*, 115:740–2.

Lemaitre, P. (1968b) 'Le problème anglais et la poursuite des travaux communautaires', *Revue du Marché Commun*, 116:895–8.

Lindberg, L. (1963) *The Political Dynamics of European Economic Integration*, Stanford: Stanford University Press.

Lindberg, L. (1965) 'Decision making and integration in the European Community', *International Organization*, 19(1):56–80.

Lindberg, L. (1966) 'Integration as a source of stress on the European Community system', *International Organization*, 20(2):233–65.

Loch, T. (1963) *Die Neun von Brüssel*, Cologne: Europa Union Verlag.

Loth, W. (2001) *Crises and Compromises: The European Project 1963–1969*, Baden-Baden: Nomos.

Loth, W. and Picht, R. (1991) *De Gaulle, Deutschland und Europa*, Opladen: Leske & Budrich.

Loth, W., Wallace, W. and Wessels, W. (1998) *Walter Hallstein: The Forgotten European?* London: Macmillan.

Louis, J.-V. (1966) 'La fusion des institutions des communautés européennes', *Revue du Marché Commun*, 97:843–56.

Lucas, H.-D. (1992) *Europa von Atlantik bis zum Ural? Europapolitik und Europadenken im Frankreich der Ära de Gaulle (1958–1969)*, Bonn: Bouvier Verlag.

Ludlow, N.P. (1997) *Dealing With Britain: The Six and the First UK Application to the EEC*, Cambridge: Cambridge University Press.

Ludlow, N.P. (1999) 'Challenging French leadership in Europe: Germany, Italy and the Netherlands and the outbreak of the Empty Chair Crisis of 1965–6', *Contemporary European History*, 18(2):231–48.

Ludlow, N.P. (2003) 'An opportunity or a threat? The European Commission and the Hague Council of December 1969', *Journal of European Integration History*, 9(1):11–25.

Lundestad, G. (1997) *Empire by Integration: The United States and European Integration, 1945–1997*, Oxford: Oxford University Press.

Mahant, E. (2004) *Birthmarks of Europe: The Origins of the European Community Reconsidered*, Aldershot: Ashgate.

Maillet, P. (1968) *L'économie de la communauté européenne*, Paris: Sirey.

Malgrain, Y. (1965) *L'intégration agricole de l'Europe des Six: tensions internes et défis extérieurs*, Paris: Editions Cujas.

Marcowitz, R. (1996) *Option für Paris? Unionsparteien, SPD und Charles de Gaulle 1958 bis 1969*, Munich: Oldenbourg.

Marjolin, R. (1967) 'Le Marché Commun – dix ans après sa signature', *Revue du Marché Commun*, 100:106–7.

Masala, C. (1997) *Italia und Germania: die deutsch-italienischen Beziehungen 1963–1969*, vol. 2, Cologne: SH-Verlag.

Massip, R. (1963) *De Gaulle et l'Europe*, Paris: Flammarion.

Mayer, H. (1996) 'Germany's role in the Fouchet negotiations', *Journal of European Integration History*, 2(2):39–59.

Milward, A. (1984) *The Reconstruction of Western Europe 1945–1951*, London: Methuen.

Milward, A. (1992) *The European Rescue of the Nation-State*, London: Routledge.

Milward, A. (1993) *The Frontier of National Sovereignty: History and Theory 1945–1992*, London: Routledge.

Milward, A. (2003) *The Rise and Fall of a National Strategy 1945–1963*, London: Frank Cass.

Ministero degli Affari Esteri. (1987) *Attilio Cattani*, Rome: Ministero degli Affari Esteri.

Moravcsik, A. (1998) *The Choice for Europe: Social Purpose and State Power from Messina to Maastricht*, London: UCL Press.

Moravcsik, A. (2000) 'De Gaulle between grain and grandeur: the political economy of French EC policy, 1958–1970', *Journal of Cold War Studies*, 2(2); 2(3):3–43 and 4–142.

Müller-Roschach, H. (1974) *Die Deutsche Europapolitik: Wege und Umwege zur politischen Union Europas*, Baden-Baden: Nomos.

Muth, H.P. (1970) *French Agriculture and the Political Integration of Western Europe: Toward 'An Ever Closer Union Among European Peoples'*, Leiden: A.W. Sijthoff.

Neville-Rolfe, E. (1984) *The Politics of Agriculture in the European Community*, London: Policy Studies Institute.

Newhouse, J. (1967) *Collision in Brussels: The Common Market Crisis of 30 June 1965*, London: Faber & Faber.

Newhouse, J. (1970) *De Gaulle and the Anglo-Saxons*, London: André Deutsch.

Nicoll, W. (1984) 'The Luxembourg Compromise', *Journal of Common Market Studies*, 23(1):35–43.

Noakes, J., Wende, P. and Wright, J. (2002) *Britain and Germany in Europe 1949–1990*, Oxford: Oxford University Press.

Noël, E. (1967) 'Quelques considérations sur la déconcentration et la délégation du pouvoir de décision dans la CEE', *Revue du Marché Commun*, 100:127–33.

Noël, G. (1988) *Du pool vert à la politique agricole commune: les tentatives de communauté européenne entre 1945 et 1955*, Paris: Economica.

di Nolfo, E. (1992) *Power in Europe? Great Britain, France, Germany and Italy and the Origins of the EEC, 1952–1957*, Berlin: Walter de Gruyter.

Nuti, L. (1999) *Gli Stati Uniti e l'apertura a sinistra. Importanza e limiti della presenza americana in Italia*, Rome: Editori Laterza.

Olivi, B. (1995) *L'Europa difficile: storia politica della comunità europea*, Bologna: Il Mulino.

Oppelland, T. (2002) *Gerhard Schröder (1910–1989): Politik zwischen Staat, Partei und Konfession*, Düsseldorf: Droste Verlag.

Ortoli, F.-X. (1967) 'Le développement économique français et le marché commun', *Revue du Marché Commun*, 100:108–10.

Parr, H. (2002) 'The Wilson government, Whitehall and policy towards the European community, 1964–1967', unpublished Ph.D. thesis, University of London.

Parr, H. (2005) *Harold Wilson and Britain's World Role: British Policy towards the European Community, 1964–1967*, London: Routledge.

Parsons, C. (2003) *A Certain Idea of Europe*, Ithaca: Cornell University Press.

Pine, M. (2004) 'Application on the table: the second British application to the EEC, 1967–1970', unpublished D.Phil. thesis, University of Oxford.

Pine, M. (2005) 'British private diplomacy and public policy: the Soames affair', *Journal of European Integration History*, 10(2):59–76.

Pirotte, O. (1988) *Trente ans d'expérience euratom: la naissance d'une Europe nucléaire*, Brussels: Bruylant.

Plisson, H. (2004) 'La Mésentente cordiale franco-britannique: la deuxième tentative d'adhésion britannique au marché commun à l'épreuve du veto français (octobre 1964 – avril 1969)', unpublished Ph.D. thesis, University of Paris IV.

Poidevin, R. (1986) *Histoire des débuts de la construction européenne*, Brussels: Bruylant.

Poidevin, R. and Spierenburg, D. (1993) *Histoire de la haute autorité de la communauté européenne du Charbon et de l'Acier: une expérience supranationale*, Brussels: Bruylant.

Preeg, E. (1970) *Traders and Diplomats: An analysis of the Kennedy Round of Negotiations Under the GATT*, Washington: Brookings.

Pryce, R. (1989) *The Dynamics of European Union*, London: Routledge.

Raniero, R. (1999) *Storia dell'integrazione europea*, Rome: Marzorati.

Rasmussen, M. (2004) 'Joining the European Communities: Denmark's Road to EC-membership, 1961–1973', unpublished Ph.D. thesis, European University Institute, Florence.

du Reau, E. (2001) *Europe en mutation: de la guerre froide à nos jours*, Paris: Hachette.

Rhenisch, T. (1994) *Europäische Integration und industrielles Interesse: Die deutsche Industrie und die Gründung der EWG*, Stuttgart: Franz Steiner Verlag.

Roussel, E. (1994) *Georges Pompidou 1911–1974*, Paris: Editions Jean-Claude Lattès.

Roussel, E. (2002) *Charles de Gaulle*, Paris: Gallimard.

Rueff, J. (1958) 'Le Marché institutionnel des communautés européennes', *Revue d'Economie Politique*, 68(1):1–10.

Salmon, A. (1967) 'L'évolution des échanges de produits agricoles entre les états membres de la CEE et entre ceux-ci et les pays tiers', *Revue du Marché Commun*, 104:403–14.

Schaad, M. (2000) *Bullying Bonn: Anglo-German Diplomacy on European Integration, 1955–1961*, London: Macmillan.

Scheingold, S. (1965) *The Rule of Law in European Integration: The Path of the Schuman Plan*, New Haven: Yale University Press.

Schrafstetter, S. and Twigge, S. (2002) 'Spinning into Europe: Britain, West Germany and the Netherlands – uranium enrichment and the development of the gas centrifuge 1964–1970', *Contemporary European History*, 11(2):253–72.

Schwabe, K. (1988) *Die Anfänge des Schumans-Plan 1950/1*, Baden-Baden: Nomos.

Schwabe, K. (2001) 'The cold war and European integration, 1947–63', *Diplomacy and Statecraft*, 12(4):18–34.

Schwartz, T. (2003) *Lyndon Johnson and Europe: In the Shadow of Vietnam*, Cambridge: Harvard University Press.

Schwarz, H.-P. (1991) *Adenauer. Der Staatsmann: 1952–1967*, Stuttgart: Deutsche Verlags-Anstalt.

Serra, E. (1989) *The Relaunching of Europe and the Treaties of Rome*, Baden-Baden: Nomos.

Smets, P.-F. (1980) *La pensée européenne et atlantique de Paul Henri Spaak (1942–1972)*, Brussels: J. Goemaere.

Soutou, G.-H. (1990) 'Le général de Gaulle, le plan Fouchet et l'Europe', *Commentaire*, 13(2):757–66.

Soutou, G.-H. (1996) *L'alliance incertaine: les rapports politico-stratégiques franco-allemands, 1954–1996*, Paris: Fayard.

Soutou, G.-H. (2001a) 'France and the cold war, 1944–63', *Diplomacy and Statecraft*, 12(4):35–52.

Soutou, G.-H. (2001b) *La guerre de cinquante ans: les relations est-ouest 1943–1990*, Paris: Fayard.

Steineger, R. (2001) *Der Mauerbau: die Westmächte und Adenauer in der Berlinkrise 1958–1963*, Munich: Olzog.

Streinz, R. (1984) *Die Luxemburger Vereinbarung: rechtliche und politische Aspekte der Abstimmungspraxis im Rat der Europäischen Gemeinschaften seit der Luxemburger Vereinbarung vom 29 Januar 1966*, Munich: Florentz.

Suri, J. (2003) *Power and Protest: Global Revolution and the Rise of Détente*, Cambridge: Harvard University Press.

Talbot, R. (1978) *The Chicken War: An International Trade Conflict Between the United States and the European Economic Community, 1961–1964*, Ames: Iowa State University Press.

Taylor, P. (1983) *The Limits of European Integration*, London: Croom Helm.

Teasedale, A. (1993) 'The Life and Death of the Luxembourg Compromise', *Journal of Common Market Studies*, 31(4):567–79.

Tichelen, J. (1981) 'Souvenirs de la négociation du traité de Rome', *Studia Diplomatica*, 34:327–43.

Tortora, F. (1968) *Origine ed evoluzione dei trattati communitari*, Milan: Giuffrè.

Tracey, M. (1989) *Government and Agriculture in Western Europe, 1880–1988*, London: Harvester Wheatsheaf.

Trachtenberg, M. (1999) *A Constructed Peace: The Making of a European Settlement 1945–1963*, Princeton: Princeton University Press.

Tsebelis, G. and Kreppel, A. (1998) 'The history of conditional agenda-setting in European institutions', *European Journal of Political Research*, 33:41–71.

Vaïsse, M. (1993) *L'Europe et la crise de Cuba*, Paris: Armand Colin.

Vaïsse, M. (1998) *La grandeur: politique étrangère du général de Gaulle 1958–1969*, Paris: Fayard.

Vanke, J. (2001) 'An Impossible Union: Dutch Objections to the Fouchet Plan, 1959–62', *Cold War History*, 2(1):95–112.

Varsori, A. (1988) *Il patto di Bruxelles (1948): tra integrazione europea e alleanza atlantica*, Rome: Bonacci.

Varsori, A. (1998) *L'Italia nelle relazioni internazionali dal 1943 al 1992*, Rome: Editori Laterza.

Varsori, A. (2001) 'La storiografia sull'integrazione europea', *Europa Europe*, 10(1):69–93.

Varsori, A. (2005) *Inside the European Community: Actors and Policies in European Integration (1957–1972)*, Baden-Baden: Nomos.

Viansson-Ponté, P. (1971) *Histoire de la république gaullienne*, vol. 2, Paris: Fayard.

Weiler, J. (1981) 'Supranationalism revisited – retrospective and perspective. The European Communities after 30 years', EUI working paper, 2.

Weiler, J. (1991) 'The transformation of Europe', *Yale Law Journal*, 100:2403–83.

Wenger, A. (2004) 'Crisis and opportunity: NATO's transformation and the multilaterlization of Détente, 1966–1968', *Journal of Cold War Studies*, 6(1):22–74.

White, J. (2003) 'Theory guiding practice: the neofunctionalists and the Hallstein EEC Commission', *Journal of European Integration History*, 9(1):111–31.

Wielenga, F. (1997) *Nachbarn: Niederländer und Deutsche und die Europäische Einigung*, Bonn: Niederländische Botschaft, Presse- und Kulturabteilung.

Wilkens, A. (1999) 'Westpolitik, Ostpolitik and the project of economic and monetary union: Germany's European policy in the Brandt era (1969–1974)', *Journal of European Integration History*, 5(1):73–102.

Wilkes, G. (1997) *Britain's failure to enter the European Community, 1961–1963: the enlargement negotiations and crises in European, Atlantic, and Commonwealth relations*, London: Frank Cass.

Willis, F.R. (1968) *France, Germany, and the New Europe 1945–1967*, Stanford: Stanford University Press.

Wilson, J. (2003) 'Négocier la relance européenne: les Belges et le sommet de La Haye', *Journal of European Integration History*, 9(2):41–61.

Winand, P. (1993) *Eisenhower, Kennedy, and the United States of Europe*, London: Macmillan.

Wurm, C. (1995) *Western Europe and Germany: the beginnings of European integration, 1945–1960*, Oxford: Berg Publishers.

Young, J. (2003) *The Labour governments 1964–1970: International policy*, Manchester: Manchester University Press.

Zeiler, T. (1992) *American Trade and Power in the 1960s*, New York: Columbia University Press.

Zimmerman, H. (2000) 'The sour fruits of victory: sterling and security in Anglo-German relations during the 1950s and 1960s', *Contemporary European History*, 9(2):225–43.

Zimmerman, H. (2001) *Money and Security: Troops, Monetary Policy, and West Germany's Relations with the United States and Britain, 1950–1971*, Cambridge: Cambridge University Press.

Index